Television and Public Policy

Change and Continuity in an Era of Global Liberalization

Television and Public Policy

Change and Continuity in an Era of Global Liberalization

Edited by

David Ward

LEA Lawrence Erlbaum Associates
Taylor & Francis Group

New York   London

Lawrence Erlbaum Associates
Taylor & Francis Group
270 Madison Avenue
New York, NY 10016

Lawrence Erlbaum Associates
Taylor & Francis Group
2 Park Square
Milton Park, Abingdon
Oxon OX14 4RN

Printed in the United States of America on acid-free paper
10 9 8 7 6 5 4 3 2 1

International Standard Book Number-13: 978-0-8058-5645-3 (Softcover) 978-0-8058-5644-6 (Hardcover)

Visit the Taylor & Francis Web site at
http://www.taylorandfrancis.com

Contents

Preface

This is a book about public policy and its approach to the television sector and how policy approaches to television have changed in the past 20 years with the rise of a policy paradigm of liberalization, so-called consumer choice and deregulation, which have come to dominate the manner in which governments today approach the broadcast media. In many ways, it provides a map of how the traditional television industries have changed and have also, in some cases, retained the features of the past. The contributors provide an analysis of the current state of the television systems in a selected group of countries by providing national chapters that explore the political, economic, and technological factors that have shaped the sector over the past two decades.

There are literally mountains of publications about changes in the television sector; changing consumption habits of the audience, evolving delivery systems, and altered economic models. One might be forgiven, reading all this literature about the developments in the television sector, for forgetting that these changes are underpinned not only by technological and market dynamics, but public policy and regulation.

The future of television today is probably more uncertain than any point in its history, which has been very much shaped by the politics of a large part of the 20th century. What is perhaps surprising is that the changes described in this book have happened in such a short space of time. The 1990s seem to be a point of rupture for the television sector (whether for positive or negative reasons) in all of the countries analyzed in the following chapters. The political shifts that brought about the radical economic reforms across the world, most notably in the United States and the United Kingdom in the late 1970s were only the starting point for a global shift in policy trajectories of governments and their approach to the television sector. With the promise of a cornucopia of information beamed into our living rooms, nation-states overhauled their regulatory frameworks in preparation for revolutionary transformations in the television industry. Some of these changes materialized and others have yet to develop and even more have fallen by the wayside. Most ideas put forward for the future of television have gravitated around the idea of technology, market mechanisms or the digital revolution. This book is intended as a counterweight to some of the more exaggerated claims made for technology and market mechanisms and their impact on television. One of the fundamental purposes of this book is therefore to put questions of media regulation back into the spotlight about the future of the media.

The chapters testify to the enduring influence of the nation-state on television and the profound impact that public policy and political structures have on the medium. They provide an analysis of the shifts in public policy and the subsequent transformations of the traditional structures of television. Liberalization of the television sector is a trend that has profound consequences on the traditional structures of the sector and in this context, this book attempts to outline and assess these trends across different countries.

ACKNOWLEDGMENTS

I would like to thank all of the authors for their invaluable contributions as well as Emily Wilkinson of Lawrence Erlbaum Associates, who has become a valued friend over the past years, for encouraging me to undertake the project in discussions over lunch in London. Thanks also to Nadine Simms, Senior Book Production Editor at Lawrence Erlbaum Associates, for the almost endless editorial support.

Introduction

This book assesses the current state of the television sector in the contemporary world after a turbulent 20 years of almost constant speculation about the future of the medium and its traditional institutions and structures. Each individual chapter maps out the transformations that have taken place over the last two decades in a number of national case studies by situating television broadcasting in a historical context that underpins an understanding of the consequences of the changing nature of television policy, as it moves increasingly away from traditional models of regulation. By positioning the television sector within issues of media policy and the regulatory framework, the volume asks what liberalization actually means for television and its historical, political, and cultural role in our societies in a comparative context.

A major premise of arguments about broadcasting over the past two decades is that it is undergoing revolutionary changes that fundamentally transform its structures. These changes, it has been argued, make historical and contemporary instruments and arguments for the need of media regulation partially redundant. The consequences of such arguments are profound. For good or for bad, public policy has played a crucial role in establishing the parameters of the television sector, its content and the structures that underpin the philosophical approach taken by broadcasters, as well as their perception of their role in individual societies. The changing nature of State regulation therefore has incredibly important consequences for the future of the medium at a time when it appears to be in a state of flux brought about by technological developments and innovation. Markets and technological developments do not act in a vacuum and neither does television policy. Both operate in political and historical conditions that affect the nature of the institutions and structures of television as well as the nature of policy-driven liberalization and its wider impact.

Television policy is based on choices and decisions made by governments and parliaments and one of the factors highlighted in the following chapters is that the nature of the television services that viewers receive is profoundly influenced by these forces: this is to say, by the State. However, despite the fundamental role of the State in establishing the nature of the television sector, the following chapters testify to the force and growth of the market economy over the last 20 years. In many States the market has been embraced as a panacea for all kinds of ills, from employment to public sector malaise. These trends have clearly tipped the scales in favor of markets and commercial forces in television in many countries in the world as the State partially retreats from regulating the sector. Markets have either been harnessed to further the interests of the State or have challenged the traditional structures that television has evolved within and today the television sector is in a profound age of uncertainty as to what the future will hold for its institutions.

The developments in the television sector over the period covered in this book are significant. The growth of multichannel television and new, digitalized forms of delivery have, to some extent, changed certain fundamental features of the sector that have been evident from the beginnings of radio. Crucially, spectrum scarcity has been reduced by compression techniques and more efficient use of spectrum together with new delivery platforms such as cable and satellite allows an unprecedented number of channels to be received in homes. However, spectrum scarcity has only ever been one of the arguments for State regulation of the sector and, indeed, perhaps not even the primary one. As Garnham has argued the nature of the broadcasting medium and the scarcity of terrestrial frequencies and the limited possibility of competition has acted as the *legitimizing* rationale, but not necessarily the *justification* for high levels of regulation (Garnham, 1992). Garnham suggests the real justification for public regulation in the television industry lies in the question of the social objectives set for broadcasters and, in this manner, the central rationale for public intervention is the selection of one method of allocation, and the supremacy of public regulation over the market as a mechanism for distributing on a universal and equal basis a set of high-quality and diverse programs.

This book sets out to place television in the context of these changes and identify not only changes in the industry, but also continuity and the features that persist and are likely to remain in the future. There is much written on audience fragmentation, although evidence would suggest the main historical actors in the television sector remain key players. There are also many claims made for the age of abundance and multichannel television, but the evidence set forth in this book would suggest this is overhyped, for the time being at least, as there is little novel or original programming on multichannel television. That is not to say that in the future the increased capacity provided by technological developments cannot be harnessed to the maximum benefit of society, but it will be public policy, not market mechanisms, that will provide such an environment for television broadcasters. The challenge therefore is to shift the arguments that have legitimized public regulation to a mode of justification and base these arguments on television's importance in our societies.

Talk about change often disguises continuity. As the forces that are acting to partially reshape the television industry redefine certain parameters, it is important to hold on to the historical factors that have acted to shape the industry. Markets have done little to solve problems of State interference in the television sector where there has been a history of negative State involvement in the sector. Likewise, and on a more positive note, there is a great deal of continuity of the actors involved in the television sector, the public service broadcasters in small pockets of the world being a case in point. The future of television has perhaps never been so questioned and debated as it is today, witnessed by the numerous parliamentary reports and inquiries referred to in the following pages. In this respect, the book hopes to contribute to this debate in order to further our understanding of liberalization of the television sector on a global scale in order to highlight the need for continuity, while at the same time embracing new technological developments in the television industry, but ensuring that the public interest is best served by the appropriation of these changes to the benefit of viewers and the public. Liberalization of the television sector is about markets and the growth of commercial drivers based around profit accumulation for private companies. It is also about the future of television regulation and public policy and whether the normative statements made by media policy in the past will be carried over into the future.

Given the changes over the last two decades in the television industry, the changing shape and nature of broadcasters and the growth of innovations such as subscription services the question is left as to what extent do the arguments for continued State regulation hold up? The following chapters all suggest that it will be even more important in an age of channel abundance and the Internet to ensure meaningful content is available to the viewer and regulation is a key factor in achieving this objective.

REFERENCE

Garnham, N. (1992). *Capitalism and communications*. London: Sage.

PART ONE

Americas

CHAPTER ONE

Television in Canada: Continuity or Change?*

David Skinner
York University, Toronto

Canadians are avid television watchers. On average they watch about 23 hours per week. However, producing television programs that represent Canadian perspectives on the world has been an ongoing challenge. Geographically, Canada is the second largest country in the world, but has a population of only 31 million. With two official languages, more than 60% of Canadians share English as their primary language with their U.S. neighbors, whereas almost 25% speak French. Eighty-five percent of the population lives within 200 miles of the border with the United States, Canada's main trading partner and the world's largest producer and exporter of television products. In this context, Canadian ownership and control of media properties has been viewed for decades as key to cultural sovereignty. Just as in the late 19th century, the railway was envisioned as binding the disparate colonies of the northern half of North America in the common political economic cause of Canadian nationhood, so too broadcasting, at first radio and later television, has been seen as a vehicle for developing and distributing a common culture across the country.

*The author would like to thank the York University faculty of Arts for a research grant that helped with this chapter, Isabel MacDonald for her help researching the project, and Mike Gasher for getting it started.

Framed by vast geography and scarce economic resources, broadcasting in Canada developed as a public service, comprised of both public and private elements. Historically, the public sector has been mandated to pursue a broad set of social and cultural goals whereas, driven by the profit motive, the private sector has been harnessed to a set of public responsibilities in exchange for the privilege of holding broadcast licenses. However, from the beginning, foreign—mainly American—broadcast products have provided the mainstay for many media outlets, particularly in English-speaking Canada. Simply put, these products recover their costs in their home market and are then licensed to Canadian broadcasters at a fraction of their cost of production. In the face of these constraints, a complex weave of regulations in the broadcasting, cable, and telecommunications industries has developed to try to create an economics of Canadian production and prevent Canadian media companies and markets from becoming mere extensions of their American cousins. Since their inception, these regulations have been the product of ongoing struggles between both federal and provincial governments, private corporations, and public interest groups, as a range of public interest objectives have clashed with the profit motive. However, across the last 15 to 20 years, market imperatives have increasingly gained hold of the system and the public interest has increasingly been defined in terms of consumer choice.

Set in three sections, this chapter explores the dimensions of this shift. Taking a broad historical sweep, the first section illustrates that although broadcasting policy in Canada has been driven by efforts to control the incursion of foreign programming and make new technologies responsible to the public purposes of the system, recent events have introduced a sea change in the system's management and development. The second section provides a snapshot of the structure and operation of the system today. Finally, opening with a discussion of the broad dimensions of regulation, the third section provides some assessment of these changes and their impact on the abilities of both policymakers and industry players to maintain the historical social and cultural objectives of broadcasting policy.

BACKGROUND AND CONTEXT OF THE DEVELOPMENT OF BROADCASTING

Although broadcasting began in Canada in 1919, through the 1920s signals from high-powered American transmitters flowed freely across the border, often blanking out or overpowering those of the smaller Canadian stations (Vipond, 1992). Set against this growing presence and influence of U.S. radio, the government legislated Canada's first broadcasting Act in 1932 and with it created the Canadian Radio Broadcasting Commission (CRBC). The CRBC was initially envisioned as taking over all aspects of broadcasting in Canada, including private stations, but the necessary funds were never forthcoming and private broadcasters remained in business. Consequently, today's *mixed system,* comprised of both public and private organizations, began to take form. A new broadcasting act was legislated in 1936 and the commission was remodeled into the Canadian Broadcasting Corporation (CBC)—a government-owned crown corporation set at "arm's length" from the government.

Financed through radio license fees and advertising revenue, the early CBC was charged with two sets of responsibilities: (a) to produce programming and extend services to parts of the country without Canadian radio; (b) to license and regulate the private sector. On the regulatory side, the CBC practiced a "light touch" approach and although there were rules governing such things as the number of commercial minutes per hour and some Canadian content regulations, transgressions generally went unpunished. Despite this restraint, however, as the private sector grew stronger, broadcasters complained that the structure of regulation was unfair because it subjected them to being "regulated by their competitor" and pressed for easing commercial constraints.

In the late 1940s, American television signals came creeping across the border where 60% of Canadians had access to them. Faced with this onslaught, the CBC began to make plans for the introduction of Canadian television in 1949. By this time, however, much of the direction for the growth of the system was set. Earlier that year, the government had decided to allow the private sector to hold television broadcasting licenses, as well as "take advantage of the advances" in television technology that had been made by the Americans (McCann, cited in Anderson, 1976, p. 44). Subsequently, Canada adopted the NTSC television standard. Moreover, before any Canadian stations were on air, thousands of Canadians had already purchased television sets and were tuning into U.S. stations, some of which were explicitly built to broadcast over the border and exploit Canadian advertising markets. Consequently, driven by the profit motive and enabled by the technology, the door was opened to rapid expansion of the Canadian system based on American broadcast techniques and products.

In the context of the post–World War II development of consumer society, it quickly became clear that commercial television was going to be quite lucrative and the private sector stepped up their campaign against regulation by the CBC. A newly installed Conservative government provided a sympathetic ear and, in 1958, a new Broadcasting Act was legislated. The 1958 Act recognized the system as being comprised of both public and private elements with both reporting to an independent regulatory board—the Board of Broadcast Governors (BBG). This legislation forced the CBC to appear before the regulator for both license renewals and to compete with the private sector for new television licenses.

Fueled by applicants' heady promises of big contributions to the production of Canadian programming, the BBG licensed a large number of private stations and a private television network—the Canadian Television Network (CTV). However, recognizing that private broadcasters would find it much more profitable to import U.S. programming than produce their own, the BBG introduced content regulations that specified criteria for defining Canadian content in programs, as well as provisions requiring that particular percentages of Canadian content be broadcast across different periods of the day. To avoid charges of censorship, these regulations focused on the nationality of the factors of production, such as the place where the work was produced and the nationality of the people employed in and/or financing production. These kinds of nationalist technical criteria continue to form the basis of content regulation today (Canadian Radio-Television and Telecommunications Commission [CRTC], 2004a).

Following trends in the United States, the television system grew sharply and by 1965, 92% of Canadian homes were considered television households (Canada: Committee on Broadcasting, 1965). Given the huge expense of television production, the CBC began receiving an annual appropriation from Parliament in the late 1950s. However, advertising remained an important source of income and American programs were key to providing it. Equipped with its not-for-profit mandate, the CBC worked to convert commercial revenue from such programs to the production of Canadian programs and the extension of broadcast services. For the private sector, however, producing domestic programs entailed a double jeopardy. Not only was Canadian programming more expensive to produce than foreign programs were to purchase, but if a Canadian program was scheduled to replace a foreign program—even if it drew as large an audience as it replaced—any return on investment would be severely reduced if not lost altogether unless the cost of the Canadian program was roughly equivalent to that of the imported program. Consequently, the BBG constantly struggled to get private broadcasters to meet with their content obligations (Babe, 1979).

Meanwhile, entrepreneurs began building coaxial cable television (CATV) systems in Canadian cities. With their ability to import large numbers of distant, mainly U.S., signals, these systems threatened to flood the broadcasting system with foreign content. Because cable did not utilize the radio spectrum, these systems were outside the jurisdiction of the BBG and the Board stood helplessly by as Canadian audiences and advertisers switched to American stations.

Partially in response to the cable problem, the federal government legislated a new Broadcasting Act in 1968. This legislation was the first to enunciate the social goals for the system. For instance, Section 3 (b) stated that "the Canadian broadcasting system should be effectively owned and controlled by Canadians so as to safeguard, enrich and strengthen the cultural, political, social, and economic fabric of Canada" (Canada: Statutes of Canada, 1991). The new act also brought cable companies under regulation and created a new, stronger regulator—the Canadian Radio-Television Commission (CRTC)—complete with powers to issue, amend, and suspend broadcast licenses.

The years 1968 through 1976 are generally seen as a period of close management by the CRTC as it worked to both protect the revenues of private broadcasters and make the different elements of the system more responsible to the cultural and nationalist goals of legislation. For instance, to help keep advertising revenues in Canada, the commission took aim at cross border broadcasters and asked the government to amend the Income Tax Act so that advertising expenditures with broadcasters not under Canadian ownership would not be eligible for tax deduction. To protect advertising markets for "local" broadcasters, the commission began to prescribe geographic boundaries within which stations might solicit advertising. Also, under a policy directive from government, foreign ownership restrictions on broadcast properties were established and the commission set out to repatriate a number of cable, television, and radio holdings. On another front, the CRTC moved to make cable systems more responsible to the larger purposes of the system. Carriage rules were imposed to limit the import of distant signals and foreground the availability of the CBC, local stations, and educational broadcasters. To ensure that private stations received the most from their licensing agreements for U.S. programs, in cases where a cable system carried Canadian and U.S. stations offering the same programming in the same time slot, "simulcast" rules were imposed whereby the cable operator was required to replace the commercials on the foreign station with those of the Canadian signal. And, in response to pressures to broaden representation within the system, cable operators were directed to provide a community access channel and provincial governments were issued licenses for educational stations (Raboy, 1996).

Although the CRTC's efforts to establish a firm economic foundation for private television were quite successful, harnessing the private sectors' profits to Canadian program production proved more difficult and, between 1968 and 1979, the amount of Canadian programming the CTV network scheduled from 8:00 P.M. to 10:30 P.M. fell from 22.8% to 5.7% (CRTC, 1979). Meanwhile, through the 1970s, the CBC's share of the system's revenue declined significantly and its parliamentary appropriations rode shifting political tides (Audley, 1983).

Other events also began to spell trouble for the regulator. In 1976 the CRTC's regulatory responsibilities were expanded to include telecommunications, but its budget was not increased to meet with these duties. And, on another front, footprints of American broadcast satellites began edging into Canada, attracting viewers outside of the reach of urban cable systems who were dissatisfied with their television choices. In the face of these incursions the government began to press the CRTC to introduce pay television as a way to develop new programming and keep audiences tuned to Canadian services. The CRTC, however, was loathe to introduce any new services for fear they might fragment audiences and undermine their recent work to rationalize the system. But the commission's efforts to hold back the tide of technological change would soon prove for naught.

The Seeds of Change

With economic tremors from the end of the postwar boom rocking the economy and U.S. satellite signals nibbling at the edges of the broadcast system, the federal government developed a new policy vision for the communications sector in the early 1980s. Within this plan, culture was clearly framed as an industry, and the development of both the cultural field and information technologies clearly linked with the de-industrialization of traditional manufacturing industries (Canada: Department of Communications, 1983a).

Broadcasting, and particularly cable, had a central role in this evolving policy field (Canada: Department of Communications, 1983b). Set against the impending threat of foreign satellite broadcasters, cable television was positioned as the "cornerstone" of a new system that would help "sweep Canada into the information age" (Babe, 1990, p. 212). Not only would expanded cable systems provide a much-increased range of Canadian and foreign programming services to pull Canadian viewers back into the system, but they would also be encouraged to provide "a range of non-programming services, such as videotext, databank services, intrusion alarms, meter reading, medic alert, etc." (Babe, 1990, p. 212). A new Broadcast Fund, later renamed Telefilm, was also set up to help seed independent program production. To boost this effort, the CBC's Canadian content targets were raised and it was charged with contracting 50% of its programming from private producers within 5 years.

In the face of rising deficits, a new government took power in 1984. The Prime Minister declared the country "open for business" and set about paving the way for market reforms and establishing a free trade agreement with the United States. During the next decade, privatization and restructuring resulted in the sale of 15 crown corporations and a major cut in public-sector employment (Winseck, 1995). One of the government's first directions in the broadcasting sector was to direct the CBC to pare about 10% off its budget (Raboy, 1996). In the midst of this shifting environment, a Task Force was appointed to review broadcasting policy and the ensuing investigation became the backdrop for legislation of a new Broadcasting Act in 1991. Running counter to government concerns for restraint, many of the Task Force's recommendations built on traditional cultural concerns for broadcast-ing and looked to strengthen and expand the place of the public sector within the system. Most of these recommendations were never taken up but, to a large part, the breadth of their concerns was reflected in the ensuing regulation.

The Shift Begins

The 1991 Broadcasting Act builds on the 1968 Act to set out a wide range of social and cultural goals for both the system in general and its different parts (Sec. 3.1b). It defines broadcasting as a "public service essential to the mainte-nance and enhancement of national identity and cultural sovereignty" and expands the definition of the components of the system to include not only pub-lic and private elements, but a community element as well (Sec. 3.1b). Building on the 1983 policy initiative to promote independent production, it also specifies that the system should include "a significant contribution from the Canadian independent production sector" (Sec. I [v]). As for the regulator, the act extended the commission's purview to regulate a wide range of broadcasting technologies that were unknown in 1968 and, rising out of the dispute around the institution of "pay TV," it also gave the federal government the power to issue policy directives to the CRTC. The act also recognizes the importance of aboriginal and educational broadcasting.

Under the sway of broad political forces developing around market liberalization and globalization, changes that had been gestating in the system since 1983 began to bloom in the 1990s. With the threat of a range of new technologies—particularly direct-to-home satellites (DTH), with their inexpensive, pizza-sized delivery dishes—looming on the horizon, the CRTC undertook a review of the system. The commission identified "three intersecting environmental forces" as forcing change on the system: "changing technology, increasing competition and what has been described as the 'new consumer'" (CRTC, 1993b, p. 4). The central technology driving this shift was characterized as the "digital revolution," which was seen as giving rise to a host of new "programming services and concepts" that might be delivered interchangeably through "cable, over-the-air broadcasting, satellite and MDS (multi-point distribution systems) transmission" (p. 4).

In turn, the greater choice and customization of services heralded by this new technology was framed as "serving to produce a new consumer environment and consciousness . . . (that would) transform the captive subscriber into the discriminating consumer" (p. 4). The commission concluded that in the swiftly changing technological environment protectionist measures to control foreign competition "would only prove counterproductive and impractical" and, instead, the focus should be on direct competition by "aggressive encouragement to the production and distribution of more and better Canadian programming" (p. 4). In this context, the CRTC called for the development of new Canadian services, pay TV and pay-per-view channels, as well as the creation of a new production fund with major contributions from the cable industry. In June of 1993 the Commission also took the first step to remove cable as the key distribution technology within the system and announced that it considered "DTH satellite services to be an important vehicle for delivering services in competition to cable" (CRTC, 1995b). With these changes the CRTC announced the arrival of a new era of "Consumer-Driven TV" (CRTC, 1993a). Meanwhile, deregulatory forces were also gripping the telecommunication sector and, as one commentator described it, starting to "reflect a 'power shift' towards the subordination of the public interest to private, commercial interests" (Winseck, 1995, p. 101).

While plans were being laid for the expansion of the system under the hand of private capital, the public sector met with setbacks. The main opposition party began to call for privatization of the CBC and in the face of rising government deficits the CBC's budget was cut by almost one third between 1993 and 1997, heavily impacting local programming services (Friends of Canadian Broadcasting, 2001). From 1992 through 1995 the CRTC's budget was sliced by approximately 25% (CRTC, 1995a), and in 1997 community broadcasting also suffered when, in return for increased contributions to program production, the CRTC ruled that cable companies would no longer be required to provide a community channel (Canada: Standing Committee on Canadian Heritage, 2003).

Meanwhile, in January 1994 the federal government announced its commitment to develop a Canadian strategy for the "Information Highway" (CRTC, 1995a; Information Highway Advisory Council [IHAC], 1997). Key among new policy directions was a convergence policy that broke a 60-year-old regulatory tradition of keeping telecommunication and broadcasting markets separate and allowed telephone and cable companies to offer competitive services (Winseck, 1998). Over the next several years the CRTC undertook a series of steps toward reregulating cable and telephone markets in preparation for competition (Industry Canada, 1996; IHAC, 1997). Further committing to liberalization, the CRTC announced in May 1999 that the Internet did not fall under the purview of the Broadcasting Act and thereby it would not be regulating Internet content under the terms of the Act (CRTC, 1998). The licensing process began to change too, as in December 2000, the commission noted that with the increased capacity heralded by digitization, they were moving from "traditional licensing mechanisms that provide significant regulatory support for emerging Canadian services . . . (toward) a more . . . competitive framework that encourages greater risk-taking and allows the success of services to be increasingly determined by customers" (CRTC, 2000).

The year 2000 also saw the first major step toward realizing the new media environment envisioned in the convergence policy as three major cross-media ownership deals radically altered the Canadian mediascape. CanWest, owner of the Global Television Network, purchased the Southam newspaper group and a 50% share in the *National Post*—one of Canada's two national newspapers—from Hollinger Corporation. Today, CanWest controls one of Canada's two private English-language television networks and close to 30% of the country's daily newspaper circulation (Canada: Senate of Canada, 2004). In another deal, Bell Canada Enterprises (BCE, Canada's largest telecommunications company) purchased the Canadian Television Network (CTV, the country's largest private television network), and then struck an alliance with Thomson Newspapers (publisher of the *Globe and Mail,* Canada's principal national daily newspaper) to form Bell Globemedia. And in Quebec, Quebecor, one of Canada's largest newspaper groups, purchased Videotron, the largest cable service provider in Quebec, and the private French-language television network TVA.

Although this spate of market consolidations gave Canada one of the most concentrated media markets in the world, it appears to be only a harbinger of changes to come as cable operators and telephone companies prepare to unleash a range of competitive telephone and broadcast services that might well lead to yet another reconfiguration of industry.

BROADCASTING TODAY

Today, cable systems, satellites, and other distribution systems all deliver a range of Canadian and foreign, mainly U.S., channels. Of the three different elements of the system—public, private, and community—the private sector is by far the largest component. Private broadcasters had revenues in excess of C$11.5 billion in 2001 including the production industry, or about C$7.7 billion without it (Canada: Standing Committee on Canadian Heritage, 2003). In 2002, subscription revenue totaled C$4.61 billion whereas advertising brought in C$2.6 billion (Canada: Standing Committee on Canadian Heritage, 2003). By comparison the CBC, by far the largest of the public and community broadcasters, had revenues of C$1.2 billion in the same period, and devoted less than C$1 billion to television (Canada: Standing Committee on Canadian Heritage, 2003). Each of these sectors is briefly discussed in the following section.

The Private Sector

Under the terms of broadcast regulation, all elements of the system have public responsibilities. With regard to private broadcasters, Section 3(s) of the

Broadcasting Act, states that "to an extent consistent with the financial and other resources available to them," they are charged to; "(i) contribute significantly to the creation and presentation of Canadian programming, and (ii) be responsive to the evolving demands of the public" (Canada: Statutes of Canada, 1991). In regulatory terms, the private, profit-driven television sector has several facets: (a) conventional broadcasters, (b) pay and specialty services, (c) distributors, and (d) independent producers. In practice, however, there is a large degree of cross-ownership between these divisions so, at that level, distinctions tend to blur.

Conventional Broadcasters

Conventional broadcasters' signals are available "over the air" through roof or set-top antennae as well as by cable and satellite. Although today very few viewers use traditional antennae, because these were the first kind of television licenses awarded, they remain a key regulatory category. As opposed to specialty and pay TV, which generally focus on specific television genres, conventional broadcasters carry a broad range of programming. In 2004 there were 73 conventional English-language television stations, 23 French-language, and four "third-language" outlets—that is, stations that sometimes broadcast in languages other than French, English, or Aboriginal languages (CRTC, 2004b). There are two private national English language networks (CTV with 26 stations, and CanWest Global Communications with 21 stations) and one private French-language operator, as well as a number of smaller regional networks. Ownership among these stations is quite concentrated and in 2003, four ownership groups took in 93% of the revenue reported by conventional English-language broadcasters, whereas in French television, two groups accounted for 92% (CRTC, 2004b).

In the face of growing competition from pay and specialty television services, the audience share of conventional broadcasters fell from 44.1% to 35.1% from 1993 to 2003. In the face of further fragmenting advertising markets, there is some pressure on regulators from conventional broadcasters to allow them to implement a subscription fee (Canada: Standing Committee on Canadian Heritage, 2003). However, with growing concentration of ownership, in 2003 the four largest ownership groups accounted for approximately 34.8% of audience share in English-language markets. In French markets, two groups accounted for almost 50% (CRTC, 2004b). Moreover, despite fragmentation, revenues for conventional broadcasters continue to grow and increased from C$1.601 billion in 1996 to C$2.105 billion in 2004. In English television, profits before interest and taxes (PBIT) averaged 13.6% between 1996 and 2003 (CRTC, 2004b). For French television, PBIT over the same period averaged 11.25%.

For conventional broadcasters the CRTC requires that "not less than 60% of the broadcast year and not less than 50% of the 6 p.m. to midnight evening broadcast period . . . be devoted to Canadian programs" (Canada: Standing Committee on Canadian Heritage, 2003, p. 131). And conventional broadcasters do contribute to the production of Canadian programming. Expenditures on English-language Canadian programming rose from C$389.1 million in 1999 to C$406.1 million in 2003 (CRTC, 2004b). However, because returns are generally better on news programming, spending during this period averaged C$298.52 million per year on news, whereas drama averaged only C$62.9 million (CRTC, 2004b). At the same time, investment in foreign drama far outstrips that in Canadian drama. For instance, in 2004 investment in Canadian drama was only C$81.9 million, whereas investment in foreign drama was C$372.8 million (Friends of Canadian Broadcasting, 2005). A 2005 study found that, measured in 2004 dollars, spending on Canadian programming held relatively steady from 1994 to 2004, whereas expenditure on foreign programming during the same period increased by 85% (Friends of Canadian Broadcasting, 2005). Viewing patterns reflect these spending patterns and in 2003 to 2004 over 90% of drama and comedy viewed in major English markets on conventional private networks was foreign. On the other hand, 41.9% of viewing time on the CBC was devoted to Canadian drama and comedy (CRTC, 2004b). In Quebec, the situation is quite different and audiences for French-language programs, other than news, draw two to three times the share they do in English markets (Canada: Standing Committee on Canadian Heritage, 2003). Moreover, in French markets a much higher percentage of the most popular programs are Canadian than in English television (Canada: Standing Committee on Canadian Heritage, 2003).

Private Pay and Specialty TV

Specialty and pay TV services have grown dramatically since the early 1980s and, in 2004, there were 115 of these channels. Unlike conventional channels, they carry only a specific genre or type of programming—such as sports, music and music videos, comedy, and so on—and are geared to specific audience groups. Specialty channels are licensed as either part of the basic cable package or as part of a discretionary service. Generally, they are financed by advertising and subscription fees, although they are generally allowed fewer advertising minutes per hour than conventional broadcasters. Pay TV services are offered on a discretionary basis by both cable and satellite distributors and pay-per-view (PPV) is a discretionary service offered via cable or satellite on a pay-per-program basis.

Revenues for these kinds of services have risen rapidly in both English and French markets and in 2004 they hit C$2.05 billion and topped those of conventional broadcasters for the first time. On average they are more profitable than conventional broadcasters as well with PBIT of 20.39% in 2004 (CRTC, 2005). Their audience share has also risen dramatically, from 11.7% of the viewing audience in 1993 to 34.7% in 2003 (CRTC, 2004b).

Although these licenses are subject to Canadian content regulations, regulations vary with the type of station and the length of time of operation. In 2003, specialty, pay and pay-per-view services spent C$553 million on Canadian programming. This compares with C$406 million spent by conventional broadcasters and C$484 million spent by the CBC (CRTC, 2004b). However, just as applicants for conventional broadcast licenses often made overly ambitious promises about the amount of Canadian programming they might produce, so too it appears some applicants for specialty licenses have made unrealistic projections about their contributions and a number of licensees have had to return to the CRTC in the middle of their licensing periods to ask for relief from their assigned Canadian content quotas (Killingsworth, 2005).

Broadcast Distribution Undertakings

Broadcast distribution undertakings (BDUs)—that is, cable, satellite, or microwave multipoint distributions systems (MDS)—are a key feature of Canada's broadcasting system. By 1975, 60% of Canadian households subscribed to cable, and in 2003 over 97% of Canadian households had access to cable and 9.3 million of Canada's 12.3 million households subscribed to some form of BDU (Canada: Standing Committee on Canadian Heritage, 2003).

Under the terms of the 1991 Broadcasting Act (Section 3.1t), BDUs have a number of responsibilities, including giving priority carriage to Canadian stations and programming and providing "efficient delivery of programming at affordable rates, using the most effective technologies available at reasonable cost." Regulations also require that broadcast distributors contribute a minimum of 5% of their annual revenues "derived from broadcasting activities to the creation and presentation of Canadian programming" (CRTC, 2004b). In 2003 distributors' contributions to production funds totaled C$129 million, with C$83 million coming from cable companies.

From offering a dozen or so channels at the beginning of the 1980s, cable systems have grown to include hundreds of conventional, specialty, and pay channels delivered in a series of program packages or "tiers." Signals are delivered in both digital and analog form, with digital providing a growing proportion of the offerings.

Given the industry's traditional monopoly status, cable rates have often been controversial and historically they have been regulated (Babe, 1979). However, since the mid-1990s, the CRTC has been working to develop market discipline through what they refer to as "effective competition" in broadcast distribution markets. Toward this end, the Commission licensed two DTH satellite services in 1997 (CRTC, 1997). Offering more than 400 channels each, these services have made strong inroads and between 1998 and 2003 their market share rose from 2.7% to 23.7%. Meanwhile cable's share fell from 97.2% in 1998 to 72% in 2003. With the advent of this competition, the CRTC has established conditions under which operators might apply for rate deregulation (CRTC, 2004b).

Overall, the distribution industry has enjoyed strong growth in revenues in recent years, with revenues rising from C$3.19 billion in 1999 to C$5.37 billion in 2003. Competition, high debt levels, and investment in plants have contributed to falling profits for cable companies; however, and in 2004, satellite penetration levels were still not high enough to generate profits. But, as cable companies have upgraded their technology, television programming is not the only service they offer and nonprogramming services, such as Internet access, have provided cable operators with growing revenue streams over the last few years. Cable subscribers to the Internet have grown from 480,000 in 1999 to 2.36 million in 2003 and revenue from nonprogramming services such as the Internet grew from 4% of total revenue in 1999 to 22% in 2003 (CRTC, 2004b).

Ownership in the cable industry is highly concentrated, with the top six companies accounting for 93% of the market in 2003 (CRTC, 2004).

Efforts to manage the distribution market have been complicated by illegal reception of both cable and satellite signals, although the latter appears to be the greater problem. To combat theft, there are ongoing efforts on the part of industry to tighten controls on access as well as calls to strengthen legislation (CRTC, 2004b).

Although the last few years have seen much change in the structure of the distribution industry, more changes are imminent. The four largest cable companies are in the process of rolling out an Internet-based phone service using "voice-over Internet protocol" (VoIP). One study estimates that there will be 1.5 million subscribers by the end of 2007 (Mclean, 2005). Telephone companies, however, are expected to fight back and begin distributing television signals and the same study estimates that they will have 500,000 television clients by the end of 2007.

Production

Primarily because there was no film production industry in Canada when television broadcasting first began, most programs were either purchased from outside the country or made in-house. There was very little independent production and, because there is much more money to be made importing programming than producing it, encouraging the production of Canadian programming has been difficult. As the CBC (2002) points out, to acquire Canadian programming, "Canadian broadcasters pay a license fee of between C$200–250K per hour for Canadian programming, which in turn is likely to generate only C$65–90K per hour in advertising revenues." On the other hand, broadcasters can acquire "the simulcast rights to popular U.S. sitcoms for between C$100–125K per hour . . . the most successful ones generate revenues of between C$350–450K per hour, which amounts to three to four times their cost, and five times the revenue that top Canadian programming can generate" (Canadian Broadcasting Corporation [CBC], 2002). The economics of dramatic programming are structured similarly and "even after subsidies and advertising revenues are taken into consideration, an English-language broadcaster averages a net loss of about C$125,000 for each hour of Canadian drama, and a net profit of about C$275,000 for each hour of American made drama" (Canada: Standing Committee on Canadian Heritage, 2003, p. 136). American programs also get the benefit of advertising that spills over to the Canadian market through print, television, radio, and the web. It should be noted, however, because of their lower cost and greater popularity, some profits can be made from Canadian drama in French markets.

Despite these difficulties, since 1983 a vibrant Canadian production industry has been built. The development of specialty channels, each with their own Canadian content requirements, coupled with regulations that require broadcasters to utilize independent producers, have spurred this sector's development (CRTC, 2001). Production is subsidized by a number of production funds, the largest being the Canadian Television Fund (CTF), which is a product of a partnership between cable and satellite distributors, the Department of Heritage and Telefilm Canada. The CTF had a budget of about C$250 million in 2003 and from 1997 to 2002 supported more than 2,228 projects or about 11,500 hours of Canadian programming (Canada: Standing Committee on Canadian Heritage, 2003). "Certified" Canadian television production—that is, programs that qualify as Canadian content under current rules—rose from C$2.53 billion in 1996–1997 to C$4.03 billion in 2001–2002 (Canada: Standing Committee on Canadian Heritage, 2003). But given the economics of production, it is a rule of thumb that for every hour of programming created at least 50% is funded by tax dollars through production funds (Canada: Standing Committee on Canadian Heritage, 2003). Coproductions are also an important source of revenue. Canada is the world's largest coproducer and in 2001 to 2002, C$432 million was spent in Canada on coproductions (Canada: Standing Committee on Canadian Heritage, 2003).

Despite the apparent success of the independent production industry, critics point to problems with the definitions of Canadian content that govern access to production funds and subsidies. Some argue that many productions, and particularly English language coproductions, are produced with an eye to sales in foreign markets and thereby tend to hide or wash over their specifically Canadian elements. Consequently, these productions make use of tax dollars but have little cultural relevance and do little to enhance national identity and cultural sovereignty (Canada: Department of Canadian Heritage, 2003). Others charge that the rules are too complicated and do not take into account the transnational dimensions of contemporary television production (Posner, 2005).

The Public and Community Sectors

Traditionally, the CBC has been seen as the public element of the system although, more recently, the category is sometimes taken to include a range of not-for-profit broadcasters, including what are defined under the terms of the 1991 Broadcasting Act as provincial educational broadcasters, aboriginal broadcasters, and cable-based community television (Raboy, 1996). Although the private sector has undergone rapid expansion across the last 15 years, the public and community sectors have met with significant deregulatory pressures resulting in cutbacks to the CBC, pressures to privatize provincial broadcasters, and changes in cable regulation that cut off mandatory funding of community television (Canada: Standing Committee on Canadian Heritage, 2003). Although these smaller broadcasters play important roles in the system, their presence is still quite small compared to other actors. Consequently only the CBC is dealt with in detail here.

The CBC/SRC[1]

The CBC is structured as an independent government-owned (or crown) corporation, complete with its own president and board of directors. In terms of

---

[1]The English-language operations of the government-owned broadcaster are called the Canadian Broadcasting Corporation (CBC), the French-language operations la Société Radio-Canada (SRC).

policy and day-to-day operations the CBC enjoys almost complete autonomy, although the president and board are appointed by government. Financially, however, the corporation is held on a rather short leash. Despite many recommendations that it be funded on a multiyear basis, Parliament continues to allocate the CBC's budget annually, making long-term planning difficult. The corporation's borrowing powers are also heavily circumscribed.

The CBC operates two national conventional television services. There are 23 CBC-owned stations, 15 English and 8 French. As well, there are 20 private affiliated stations and more than 850 rebroadcasting antennae that extend the corporation's reach across much of the country. The CBC also operates news and information specialty services in both English and French, a service in northern Canada that broadcasts in English, French, and eight aboriginal languages, an extensive web service, and it has partial ownership in two other specialty services. Under the terms of regulation, these services generally enjoy priority carriage by BDUs. Ninety-seven percent of English-speaking Canadians can receive the English service and 99% of French speakers have access to Radio-Canada (Canada: Standing Committee on Canadian Heritage, 2003).

In 2002 to 2003, the CBC had an operating budget of approximately C$1.5 billion, C$937 million of which came from government appropriations and C$294 million from advertising. Of this, approximately C$910 million was spent on television. The specialty services are funded separately through advertising and subscription revenues. The annual costs of the CBC average approximately C$29 for each Canadian (CBC, 2004). On a per-capita basis, funding is quite low and as a percentage of GDP, spending on public broadcasting in Canada, ranked 22nd out of 26 OECD countries in 1999 (Canada: Standing Committee on Canadian Heritage, 2003).

As laid out in the 1991 Broadcasting Act (Sections 3[l] and [m]), the CBC's mandate starts from the premise that the Corporation should provide "a wide range of programming that informs, enlightens and entertains." The Act specifies that this programming should have a range of specific characteristics including: being "predominantly and distinctively Canadian"; reflecting "Canada and its regions to national and regional audiences"; be "in English and in French"; and "reflect the multicultural and multiracial nature of Canada."

Building on these points, the CBC is the largest single source of Canadian television programming. On the English side, 90% of programming during peak viewing hours (7:00 p.m. to 11:00 pm) in 2000–2001 was Canadian content, whereas the private stations averaged less than 25%. On the French side, Canadian programming averaged 88%, whereas the private French networks averaged about 50% between them (Canada: Standing Committee on Canadian Heritage, 2003). Moreover, during peak viewing hours, 93% of viewing time on CBC's English television was devoted to Canadian content whereas on the private conventional networks, it accounted for less that 15%. On the private French networks, the percentage was considerably higher and averaged about 50% between them. However, SRC still led the way with 93% of viewing time devoted to Canadian programming (Canada: Standing Committee on Canadian Heritage, 2003).

Audience fragmentation resulting from new services has hit the corporation hard. The CBC's share of the national English audience fell from 16.4% in 1985–1986 to a low of 6.6% in 1999–2000 and then made a 12% recovery to 7.5% in 2001–2002. On the French side, the audience share fell from 31.7% in 1985–1986 to 14.5% in 2001–2002 (Canada: Standing Committee on Canadian Heritage, 2003). This loss of audience share has been the focal point of much criticism.

For the CBC, the 1990s were characterized by a litany of budget cuts. By 1998, the CBC's full-time staff was reduced to half its 1984 level and, calculated in real dollars, from 1990–1991 to 2000–2001, parliamentary appropriations fell by more than 20% (Canada: Standing Committee on Canadian Heritage, 2003). In the wake of these cuts, local news and public affairs programming have been heavily cut back (Canada: Standing Committee on Canadian Heritage, 2003).

REGULATION TODAY: SUMMARY AND ASSESSMENT

Saddled with both broadcasting and telecommunications regulation the CRTC has, as one analyst puts it, been "regulating on the run" since the early 1990s as it has worked to keep up with the avalanche of technological change overtaking the system (Doern, 1997, p. 516). The job was made even more difficult in 1993 when government restructuring set the CRTC under the responsibility of the Department of Canadian Heritage—a department devoted to promoting Canadian culture and citizenship—but gave Industry Canada—a department focused on economic development—jurisdiction over the telephone and telecom sector. In an era when convergence was blurring the distinctions between broadcasting and telecoms, this juxtaposition promised tension.

Under some pressure from government, key features of the commission's recent regulatory approach have been to simplify or "streamline" the regulatory process and to develop flexibility in terms of the ways in which licensees might meet their obligations in the face of changing circumstances within the system (Canada: Department of Canadian Heritage, 2005). In this regard, the commission has undertaken actions such as shifting the license period for broadcasters from 5 to 7 years, loosening rules around hearings for cable rate increases, relaxed rules around cable operators' provision of a community channel, and gave television broadcasters more flexibility in terms of the ways they meet their content obligations (CRTC, 1999; Doern, 1997). Similarly, as seen with BDUs, the commission has been working to develop what it calls "fair competition" across different markets for telephone and broadcast services, with an eye to giving market forces more play in determining rates and the provision of services (CRTC, 1999). This hands-off approach is also reflected in the commission's decision not to regulate the Internet, although access remains within its purview as do some Internet applications such as Web-based telephone services or VoIP. At the same time, the commission has also been working toward the smooth introduction of new technologies such as digitization, with its promises of high definition TV (HDTV), greatly increased channel capacity, and a host of new "value-added" interactive and transactional services (CRTC, 2002).

Across the last 15 years there has also been a growing international dimension to regulation. Although both the North American Free Trade Agreement (NAFTA), and its predecessor the Canadian American Free Trade Agreement (CAFTA), specifically exempted the culture industries, as Mosco (2003) points out, "liberalized trade in this sector was permitted by a not withstanding clause that allowed retaliation against cultural protectionism through measures in other industries, by general agreements restricting government activity, and by liberalizing trade in sectors converging with the cultural industries" (p. 297). Treaty provisions also require governments apply "national treatment" to each other's corporations that, as Mosco (2003) acknowledges, "means that the CRTC is required to treat American companies on the same terms as they do Canadian ones, within the limits of foreign ownership restrictions" (p. 298). To date several issues have raised the specter of trade retaliation—one involving the replacement of a U.S. specialty music channel with a Canadian version, the other around the licensing of DBS companies (Canada: Department of Industry, 1995; Jeffery, 1996). Both were resolved informally. Meanwhile, however, such restrictions limit "the ability of governments to establish new government or public institutions to provide services in competition with the private sector . . . such as a CBC for the age of computer communication, . . . (and) prohibit restrictions on the entry of foreign Internet service providers" (Mosco, 2003, p. 298).

Copyright has also been a growing issue. For instance, in 1999 iCrave TV began re-transmitting Canadian and American television signals over the Internet without copyright permission. Legal proceedings against the company were quickly launched in both Canada and the United States and these operations were shut down. However, the situation exposed the fact that Internet re-transmission is not covered under current copyright legislation, as well as a seeming shortcoming in the CRTC's Internet policy (Canada: Standing Committee on Canadian Heritage, 2003).

Ownership

In Canada, the economic forces underlying concentration of ownership have been complicated by a range of government regulations that, on one hand, have tried to keep the ownership of Canadian media in Canadian hands, while on the other hand, have wrestled with the drawbacks and supposed benefits of large, privately owned media companies. Consequently, within broadcasting policy, ownership regulations have been largely decided on a case-by-case basis and over the years, concentration of ownership has slowly escalated. On the heels of the 1996 convergence policy, concentration began to accelerate and today Canada's commercial media systems are a maze of cross ownership ties. Table 1.1 offers some illustration of the range of cross-media holdings of four of the largest companies with broadcast holdings.

The degree of cross-media ownership is particularly apparent at the local and regional levels. For instance, in Vancouver, Canada's third largest city, CanWest

TABLE 1.1

Holdings of Canada's Top Four Cross-Media Ownership Groups in 2005

	CanWest Global	*Bell Canada Enterprises (BCE)*	*Quebecor*	*Rogers*
Conventional TV	Yes	Yes	Yes	
Pay and/or Specialty TV	Yes	Yes	Yes	Yes
TV Production	Yes	Yes	Yes	Yes
Radio	Yes		Yes	Yes
Cable Distribution			Yes	Yes
Satellite Distribution		Yes		
Other Distribution		Yes	Yes	Yes
Daily Newspaper	Yes	Yes	Yes	
Weekly Newspaper	Yes		Yes	
Magazines		Yes	Yes	Yes
Telephony, Networking		Yes	Yes	Yes
Internet	Yes	Yes	Yes	Yes

Note. Format adapted from Canada (CRTC) (2003). Information retrieved June 14, 2005, from company Web sites: www.canwestglobal.com; www.bce.ca/en; www.quebecor.com; www.rogers.com.

Global controls 100% of the daily newspaper market and 70% of local television news (Canada: Senate of Canada, 2004, p. 37). And in Quebec, Quebecor is the dominant player in newspapers, television and cable (Raboy & Taras, 2004). Escalating concentration has raised serious concerns over a number issues such as deteriorating editorial diversity and direct editorial meddling by owners. At the time of writing this chapter, a public inquiry into the issue is under way (Canada: Senate of Canada, 2004).

With much of the broadcast, newspaper, and telecommunications markets now in the hands of a few large companies, there has been pressure for relaxing ownership regulations, particularly in the telecommunications and cable sectors. Both industry players and Industry Canada argue that such regulations stifle innovation and investment. On the other hand, the Department of Heritage, union officials, and a range of other interests argue that removing such restrictions would unleash a tide of transnational consolidations that would make maintaining the regulatory framework and cultural sovereignty across media outlets practically impossible (Tuck, 2005). As two well-established experts on Canadian broadcasting policy put it, "To imagine that Viacom or News Corporation or Sony would become major producers of Canadian programming is to live in a fantasy world" (Raboy & Taras, 2004, p. 64).

DEREGULATION AND MEDIA FREEDOM

If deregulation is defined as providing market forces greater play in the structure, operation, and development of the system then, in the Canadian context, the process has been ongoing since at least 1958 when the Broadcasting Act set the private sector in competition with the CBC. Policy shifts in the 1980s that emphasized the role of private broadcasters in expanding the system accelerated the process. But through the 1990s, the process mushroomed as the CRTC introduced a series of measures to expand the size of the system and create competition in both distribution and program services. At the same time, budget cuts to the CBC, the CRTC, and the Department of Canadian Heritage illustrated that deregulation was not confined to the private sector, nor the ideological preserve of any particular Canadian political party.

Despite these changes, Canadian sovereignty over control of the system remains a key concern as does the ongoing production and availability of Canadian programming (Canada: Standing Committee on Canadian Heritage, 2003). Further, although convergence and changes in technology are shifting the regulator toward more flexible regulation, managed competition rather than simple regulation by market forces appears to be the goal. But in Canada, the increased market freedom heralded by flexible regulation does not necessarily equate with media freedom, particularly if one defines such freedom in terms of encouraging a range of diverse services and perspectives in media. As market forces have been given increasing play within the system, the diversity of perspectives available therein have come under pressure from a number of directions.

For instance, critics contend that by giving conventional broadcasters more flexibility in how they meet their content obligations has made it "easier for broadcasters to exhibit Canadian programming in off peak hours, . . . to fill their schedules with reruns . . . (and) to sidestep the purchase or production of dramatic shows in favor of less expensive forms of programming, such as reality television series" (Canada: Standing Committee on Canadian Heritage, 2003, p. 171). In terms of distribution, there are concerns that new specialty and pay-channel services may not be able to gain access to distribution networks, particularly in instances where distributors also hold such licenses and there is a danger of anticompetitive behavior (CRTC, 2004c). Easing ownership regulations has encouraged concentration of ownership and unleashed a range of problems in terms of media diversity (Canada: Standing Committee on Canadian Heritage, 2003; Canada: Senate of Canada, 2004; Skinner, 2004). Also, although increasing flexibility in ownership regulations has helped private broadcasters maintain their profits and market share through market consolidation and the addition of new services, the CRTC has consistently denied requests from the CBC for expanding the range of services it offers (Raboy, 1996). Given that the CBC is a consistently better performer in terms of bringing Canadian programming to audiences, this would seem to run counter to the CRTC's goal of increasing Canadian content within the system. Moreover, increasing flexibility in the way cable companies deal with community stations has resulted in a wave of complaints over changes in access to these channels (Canada: Standing Committee on Canadian Heritage, 2003).

Relying almost exclusively on private capital and commercial forces to expand the system has also worked to limit the range of programming and services available. The ongoing struggle to induce private broadcasters to produce or purchase Canadian programming, rather than simply import it, illustrates one dimension of this problem. At another level, as profit-oriented broadcasters seek out audiences comprised of demographics that can be either sold to advertisers and/or are willing to pay directly for programming, services that do not generate profits (such as community access and educational broadcasters) and/or segments of the population who cannot afford to purchase programming are left out of the line-up. Local and regional perspectives suffer too as broadcasters seek to aggregate as large audiences as possible across national and even transnational dimensions. As the Report of the Standing Committee on Canadian Heritage points out, under the sway of these kinds of economics, "community, local, and regional broadcasting services have become endangered species in Canada" (Canada: Standing Committee on Canadian Heritage, 2003, p. 13).

Chasing the most lucrative demographics also contributes to foreclosing on the diversity of representation within broadcast programming (Fleras, 2001). Although Canada claims to be one of the most multicultural countries in the world, numerous studies illustrate that a range of institutional and organizational practices—such as commercial imperatives, "systemic stereotyping," and "systemic bias"—tend to distort the ways in which minorities are portrayed in Canadian broadcast media (Fleras, 2001, pp. 317–319). Through licensing a range of services focused on serving specific communities and requiring broadcasters to develop plans to help ensure cultural diversity, the CRTC has taken steps to try and address these problems (CRTC, 2004b, pp. 112–115). However, critics continue to raise a number of issues in this regard (Canada: Standing Committee on Canadian Heritage, 2003).

Applied as a market-driven regimen, digitization threatens to complicate and accelerate these problems. For instance, as digitization continues to erode distinctions between different media, "once divided sectors are rapidly collapsing into one large information and entertainment arena" (Mosco, 2003, p. 294). Such convergence invites further concentration of ownership as corporations seek to capitalize on greater economies of scale and scope. At the same time, the increased interactivity of digital systems promises to further attenuate the transactional broadcast model announced in the early 1990s. "Audience preferences," indicated by the program choices people make, can be coupled with demographic information to allow programmers and advertisers to target and develop audiences with specific age, income, gender characteristics, and so on (Mosco, 2003, p. 292). Similarly, under the guise of "consumer choice," audiences will be offered an increasing range of value added services that will further commodify the relationship between broadcaster and viewer. From being able to choose between camera angles at sports events, to building one's own program schedules, to purchasing products seen on the sets of sitcoms, interactivity offers myriad market opportunities. These practices will put further pressure on expanding the commercial elements of the system.

Digitization also threatens a number of key regulatory mechanisms. For instance, the increased flexibility in program scheduling offered by hard disk recorders, web downloads of programs, and multiple start times for programs undermines regulations that specify the exhibition of Canadian content in peak viewing times. As this kind of flexibility allows consumers to build their own program schedules from a range of content providers, such regulations will become meaningless. Similarly, increased scheduling flexibility also threatens the simultaneous substitution rules that bolster Canadian advertising revenue from foreign programs. Perhaps most important, increased flexibility in program delivery threatens to unhinge the historic system by which the production of Canadian programming is cross-subsidized by the advertising and subscription revenues generated by the consumption of American programs. As Internet-based methods of program delivery offer an increasing number of ways to access programming—some directly from producers or distributors outside of the country—it will become increasingly difficult to capture portions of the revenue generated from those transactions to devote to Canadian program production.

Meanwhile, it is still not clear how the development of new media will impact television audiences. A 2004 study by Cyber Trends found that, in some cases, Internet use spurred an increase in television viewing but overall there was "a net decrease in the use of broadcast media, particularly television, commensurate with an increase in Internet use" (CRTC, 2004b, p. 128). As television and computer screens continue to merge the long-term impact on television remains unknown.

CONCLUSION

Although broadcast regulation in Canada has been framed by social and cultural goals from its inception, commercial imperatives have gained increasing play within the system, particularly since the early 1990s (as technological developments combined with an ideological shift toward market liberalization to accelerate this shift). This expanding market-driven system claims to enhance consumer choice but, at the same time, it is also undermines the broader social and cultural goals of the system and impacting the range of programming available. Restoring balance between the public and private dimensions of the system will require both reframing the current objectives of regulation and restructuring the role of public and community broadcasters.

As noted by the 2003 Standing Committee on Canadian Heritage, an important step toward reform is to better focus to the "mandate and responsibilities of the agencies involved in the broadcasting system," such as the CBC, Telefilm, the CTF, and the CRTC (Canada: Standing Committee on Canadian Heritage, 2003, p. 586). Perhaps key among these recommendations is a proposal to "overhaul the CRTC and provide it with a new mandate focused on cultural objectives" (Canada: Standing Committee on Canadian Heritage, 2003, p. 592). As the committee observed, the breadth of the commission's current mandate has allowed it too much latitude in restructuring areas such as community broadcasting, definitions of priority programming and ownership regulations.

Although finding an operational definition of "culture" that is broad enough to include a comprehensive range of community and social interests would require some adept political negotiating, putting greater emphasis on the cultural dimensions of broadcasting in regulation would provide a counterbalance to the commercial imperatives that are increasingly framing the system (Murray, 2001). It would provide a central rationale for coordinating the different elements of the system and would create ground for increasing diversity at all levels, including strengthening controls over concentration of ownership, encouraging the production of local and regional programming, and developing better cultural representation in programming itself.

Similarly a greater emphasis on culture might provide impetus to the expansion of the public and community elements of the system—another necessary step to restoring and building diversity. Unlike the private sector, public and community broadcasters are driven by mandates, not profit. Consequently, revenues are focused on program production and distribution, not generating returns for shareholders. In a system characterized by scarce resources these not-for-profit broadcasters represent one of the best ways to generate a diverse range of distinctive Canadian programming. Yet, they have not been well supported. There are many ways to fund these broadcasters other than government subsidy. With a little regulatory imagination, mechanisms that have been used to fund private, profit-driven broadcasters such as subscription revenues gleaned from mandatory cable carriage, commercial revenue, cross-subsidies from revenue earned from the broadcast of foreign programs, and tax incentives that support investment in production, might also be applied to building the not-for-profit sector.

Nested in the folds of the American empire, both the Canadian State and the Canadian broadcasting system are the product of social struggle and imagination. As the technological and ideological pressures of the new millennium continue to press on the historic rationales for broadcasting policy, to keep and nurture both will continue to require such efforts.

REFERENCES

Anderson, P. S. (1976). *The CBC and its mandate.* Unpublished thesis. Simon Fraser University.

Audley, P. (1983). *Canada's cultural industries: Broadcasting, publishing, recording and films.* Toronto: James Lorimer.

Babe, R. E. (1979). *Canadian television broadcasting structure, performance and regulation.* Ottawa: Economic Council of Canada.

Babe, R. E. (1990). *Telecommunications in Canada: Technology, industry, and government.* Toronto: University of Toronto Press.

Canada: Committee on Broadcasting. (1965). *Report.* Ottawa: Queen's Printer.

Canada: Department of Canadian Heritage. (2003). *Canadian content in the 21st century.* Retrieved June 2005, from www.culturescope.ca/ev_en.php?ID=2095_201&ID2= DO_TOPIC

Canada: Department of Canadian Heritage. (2005). *Reinforcing our cultural sovereignty—Setting priorities for the Canadian Broadcasting System.* Retrieved April 20, 2005, from www.pch.gc.ca/progs/ac-ca/progs/ri-bpi/pubs/lincoln2005/cont_e.cfm

Canada: Department of Communications. (1983a). *Culture and communications: Key elements of Canada's economic future.* Ottawa: Department of Supply and Services.

Canada: Department of Communications. (1983b). *Toward a new broadcasting environment.* Ottawa: Ministry of Supply and Services.

Canada: Department of Industry. (1995). *Direct to home satellite broadcasting: Report of the Policy Review Panel.* Ottawa: Industry Canada.

Canada: Senate of Canada. (2004). *Interim report on the Canadian News Media.* Ottawa, Canada.

Canada: Standing Committee on Canadian Heritage. (2003). *Our cultural sovereignty: The second century of Canadian broadcasting.* Ottawa: Communication Canada.

Canada: Statutes of Canada. (1991). Broadcasting Act.

Canadian Broadcasting Corporation. (2002). *CBC fact sheet: The economics of Canadian television.* Retrieved April 19, 2005, from http://cbc.radio-canada.ca/submissions/index. shtml#cancon

Canadian Broadcasting Corporation. (2004). *CBC/Radio-Canada fact sheet.* Retrieved April 20, 2005, from www.cbc.radio-canada.ca/about/pdf/CBCFacts.pdf

Canadian Radio-Television and Telecommunications Commission. (1979). *Special report on broadcasting in Canada: 1968–1978.* Ottawa: CRTC.

Canadian Radio-Television and Telecommunications Commission. (1993a). *CRTC News Release: Consumer-driven TV: A Canadian bridge to the future.* Ottawa: CRTC.

Canadian Radio-Television and Telecommunications Commission. (1993b). *Public Notice CRTC 1993–74: Structural hearing.* Ottawa: CRTC.

Canadian Radio-Television and Telecommunications Commission. (1995a). *Remarks by Keith Spicer, Chairman, Canadian Radio-Television and Telecommunications Commission before the Standing Committee on Canadian Heritage.* Retrieved April 17, 2005, from www.crtc.gc.ca/eng/NEWS/SPEECHES/1995/s950516.htm

Canadian Radio-Television and Telecommunications Commission. (1995b). CRTC competition and culture on Canada's information highway: Managing the realities of transition. Retrieved May 17, 2005, from www.crtc.gc.ca/ENG/HIGHWAY/HWY9505.htm

Canadian Radio-Television and Telecommunications Commission. (1997). *Public Notice CRTC 1997–25: New regulatory framework for broadcasting distribution undertakings.* Retrieved May 16, 2005, from www.crtc.gc.ca/archive/eng/Notices/1997/PB97-25.htm

Canadian Radio-Television and Telecommunications Commission. (1998). *Telecom Decision 1998–9: Regulation under the Telecommunications Act of certain telecommunications services offered by broadcast carriers.* Retrieved May 2, 2005, from www.crtc.gc.ca/archive/eng/Decisions/1998/DT98-9.htm

Canadian Radio-Television and Telecommunications Commission. (1999). *Public Notice CRTC 1999–97:* Building on success—A policy framework for Canadian television. Retrieved April 23, 2005, from www.crtc.gc.ca/archive/eng/Notices/1999/PB99-97.htm

Canadian Radio-Television and Telecommunications Commission. (2000). *Public Notice CRTC 2000–171-1: Introductory statement—Licensing of new digital pay and specialty services.* Retrieved April 24, 2005, from www.crtc.gc.ca/archive/ENG/Notices/2000/PB2000-171-1.htm

Canadian Radio-Television and Telecommunications Commission. (2001). *Decision CRTC 2001–457: Licence renewals for the television stations controlled by CTV.* Retrieved April 23, 2005, from www.crtc.gc.ca/archive/ENG/Decisions/2001/DB2001-457.htm

Canadian Radio-Television and Telecommunications Commission. (2002). *CRTC fact sheet: TV distribution and the evolution to digital transmission.* Retrieved April 24, 2005, from www.crtc.gc.ca/eng/INFO_SHT/Bdt14.htm

Canadian Radio-Television and Telecommunications Commission. (2004a). *Canadian content.* Retrieved April 17, 2005 from www.crtc.gc.ca/eng/INFO_SHT/b306.htm

Canadian Radio-Television and Telecommunications Commission. (2004b). *Broadcasting policy monitoring report.* Retrieved April 18, 2005, from www.crtc.gc.ca/eng/publications/reports/PolicyMonitoring/2004/bpmr2004.htm

Canadian Radio-Television and Telecommunications Commission. (2004c). *Broadcasting Public Notice CRTC 2004–24: Revised procedures for processing applications for new digital Category 2 pay and specialty television service.* Retrieved April 24, 2005 from www.crtc.gc.ca/eng/public/2004/8045/noticebr.htm

Canadian Radio-Television and Telecommunications Commission. (2005) *News release: Revenues for Canadian specialty, pay, and pay-per-view television services exceed the $2 billion mark.* Retrieved April 17, 2005, from www.crtc.gc.ca/ENG/whatsnew/2005/mar3.htm

Doern, B. (1997). Regulating on the run: The transformation of the CRTC as a regulatory institution. *Canadian Public Administration, 40*(3), 516–538.

Fleras, A. (2001). Couched in compromise: Media-minority relations in a multicultural society. In C. McKie. & B. D. Singer (Eds.), *Communication in Canadian society,* (5th ed.; pp. 308–322). Toronto: Thompson Educational Publishing.

Friends of Canadian Broadcasting. (2001). *Follow the money who paid for Canadian television, 1990–2000.* Retrieved May 16, 2005, from www.friends.ca/files/PDF/publications/followthemoney.pdf

Friends of Canadian Broadcasting. (2005). *Investment in Canadian and foreign drama programming by private conventional broadcasters.* Retrieved April 17, 2005, from www.friends.ca/files/PDF/privinvest2004.pdf

Industry Canada. (1996). *Convergence policy statement.* Retrieved May 12, 2005, from strategis.ic.gc.ca/epic/internet/insmt-gst.nsf/en/sf05265e.html

Information Highway Advisory Council. (1997). *Preparing Canada for a digital world.* Ottawa: Industry Canada.

Jeffrey, L. (1996). Private television and cable. In M. Dorland (Ed.), *The culture industries in Canada* (pp. 203–256). Toronto: James Lorimer & Company.

Killingsworth, J. (2005). Licence and poetic licence: A critical examination of the complicated relationship between the CRTC and Specialty channels. *Canadian Journal of Communication, 30,* 211–232.

Mclean, C. (2005, April 14). Picture brighter for cable companies in 2005, report says. *Globe and Mail,* p. B3.

Mosco, V. (2003). The transformation of communication in Canada. In W. Clement & L. F. Vosko (Eds.), *Changing Canada: Political economy as transformation* (pp. 287–308). Montreal: McGill-Queen's University Press.

Murray, C. (2001). Wellsprings of knowledge beyond the CBC policy trap. *Canadian Journal of Communication, 26*(1). Retrieved April 24, 2005, from www.cjc-online.ca

Posner, M. (2005, February 14). TV producers blast fund's "parochial" Canadian content rules. *Globe and Mail,* p. R1.

Raboy, M. (1996). Public television. In M. Dorland (Ed.), *The culture industries in Canada* (pp. 178–202). Toronto: James Lorimer & Company.

Raboy, M., & Taras, D. (2004). The politics of neglect of Canadian broadcasting policy. *Policy Options,* 63–68.

Skinner, D. (2004). Reform or alternatives? Limits and pressures on changing the Canadian mediascape. *Democratic Communiqué, 19,* 13–36.

Tuck, S. (2005, April 4). Feds butt heads on telecom regulation. *Globe and Mail,* p. B3.

Vipond, M. (1992). *Listening in: The first decade of Canadian broadcasting 1922–1932.* Buffalo: McGill-Queen's University Press.

Winseck, D. (1995). Power shift?: Towards a political economy of Canadian telecommunications and regulation. *Canadian Journal of Communication, 20* (1), 81–106.

Winseck, D. (1998). *Reconvergence: A political economy of telecommunications in Canada.* Cresskill, NJ: Hampton Press.

CHAPTER TWO

Television in Brazil

Carlos Eduardo Lins da Silva
Consultant

This chapter intends to describe the state of the Brazilian television industry in the beginning of the 21st century, focusing particularly on the prospects of increasing regulation by government fueled by two main factors: 1) demands from civil society impressed by the assumed great power of television in setting the national agenda and influencing public attitudes and behavior and 2) the rise to power of an originally left-wing political party that, despite great ideological transformation in several public policy agendas, tends to remain faithful to its original doctrine in a few issues, among them social communication policies.

Brazil under the rule of President Lula cannot be compared to other recent leftist experiments in Latin America, notably the one in Venezuela under President Chávez. In all fields, from macroeconomic policies to due respect to the Constitutional order, Lula's government has been much more conventional than Chávez's or even Kirchner's in Argentina.

Even on the issue of the relationship between the State and the mass media, despite some tension, there has not been in Brazil anything similar to the open conflict between media owners and government officials that can be witnessed in Venezuela. However, the government's will for exerting more control over the media, specially television, is undeniable, and often receives support from broad sectors of the population, including some that historically have opposed Lula and

27

his party. This trend raises concerns among those who believe in freedom of expression and in the benefits of a media system that is fully independent from the State.

Initiatives taken by Lula's government may never materialize in the form of laws or codes, but they will surely become an essential item of the debate about media and society in Brazil.

BACKGROUND

Television in Brazil is not only the most pervasive of all mass media, but also one of the most important agents of cultural cohesion and diffusion of innovations in the fifth largest country in the world (the Brazilian territory is larger than mainland U.S.).

On average, according to a national poll released in January 2005 and carried out by Ibope, one of the most prestigious public opinion poll institutes in the country, every Brazilian spends almost five hours a day watching television (Castro, 2005a). An international survey made by NOP World shows a different result: on average, Brazilians spend 18.4 hours per week watching television, eighth in the ranking of all countries polled, below Thailand, Philippines, Egypt, Turkey, Indonesia, U.S. and Taiwan (Mattos, 2005).

Around 90% of the approximately 51 million households in the country are equipped with a television set, according to the official national census figures (IBGE, 2002). For the first time ever, in 2001 the number of households with a TV was larger than the ones equipped with radio. According to the most respected annual study on media demographics in Brazil, 98% of the population watched TV at least once a week in 2004 (Grupo de Mídia, 2005, p. 36). This is more than the percentage of people who listened to the radio at least once a week (91%) and much more than that of those who read newspaper (54%) or a magazine (47%).

It was on September 18, 1950, that the first television station in Latin America, PRF-3 TV Tupi-Difusora, started broadcasting in São Paulo. Since the beginning, the model adopted was very similar to the American one, that already prevailed in Brazil for radio: of private companies that operate under licenses granted by the Federal State—that holds the monopoly over the airwaves—for a determined and renewable period of time, since some technical, economic and ethical requirements are met by the applicants in the licensing process.

One year later, in 1951, there were three channels broadcasting from São Paulo, and several others in cities, such as Rio de Janeiro, Belo Horizonte and Recife. The spread of television sets, whose manufacture within the country began in 1951 was limited to higher middle-class households during most of the 1950s as it was simply too expensive for the vast majority of Brazilians.

Television experienced extraordinary growth after the 1964 military coup and served as a fundamental resource for the consolidation of the authoritarian rule that lasted for 20 years afterward. The military regime invested heavily in the construction of a very efficient network of microwave towers that allowed universal reception of programs throughout the country. It also made it easier for the general public to buy TV sets in monthly installments at low interest rates.

As commonly occurs in countries such as Brazil, the expansion of television and other new communication technologies took place before the consumption of the more traditional media (newspapers, magazines) became universal. Therefore, television grew among a population with a high illiteracy rate and that remained very close to oral traditions of communication. It was quite common until the 1980s (and this continues to happen nowadays) that traditional forms of communication and the structures shaping them coexist alongside modern forms.

An example of this is that a city-based local newspaper (and sometimes there are two or three titles in a single city) is produced with state-of-the-art technology although its advertising revenues and circulation are very low. This is made possible by the political arrangements that provide the newspapers with different kinds of income in exchange for support for political parties or leaders. The same thing happens with television: households are equipped with modern color television sets that receive sophisticated programming despite the fact that the local market does not provide the conditions for the finance of such programming.

The military regime's policy of industrialization reached its peak in the 1970s with GDP growing at an average rate above 7% a year (Lins da Silva 1985, p. 26), in what was then called the "Brazilian miracle." One of the consequences of the industrialization policy was the growth of the middle class and the amount of disposable income this group had to spend on consumer goods. Sales of television sets boomed during this period and the advertising industry was stimulated by the increasing demand for a range of goods.

Although during this period control over programming content became stricter the technical and artistic quality of both news bulletins and television dramas reached higher standards. Brazil became a distinct case among developing nations: its prime time programming consisted of almost all national productions with relatively very few imported programming shown on Brazilian television. Today, 85% of the content broadcast by the major networks is produced in Brazil (Guerra, 2005). Globo by itself produced 2,546 hours of programming in 2004, which makes of it one of the largest media producers in the world (Narloch, 2005, p. 55).

The fact that the major networks themselves produce most of the shows they broadcast is not the only distinctive feature of the television system in Brazil. In contrast to most countries, there has been little synergy between television and movie production in Brazil and independent productions rarely find room to be broadcast on the major networks.

Early in the 1970s, Brazilian programming, particularly the lengthy soap operas that were characterized by high artistic and production quality constituted a new genre in itself, began selling well and became audience hits in dozens of countries, from Latin American to Asian. Presently, Brazil exports television shows to the value of US$7.7 million a year to more than 40 countries, from

France to Kuwait, from Japan to Sweden; almost all of them produced by Globo network. Globo International also broadcasts live programs transmitted from Brazil and has more than 372,000 subscribers in the U.S., Europe, South America, Africa and Japan. Its programming is an important source of content for a chain of cable companies in Latin American countries who combined have a total of 1.4 million subscribers across the continent.

In 1970, only 24.1% of all households were equipped with television sets. Ten years later, that figure had already reached 54.9% (73.1% in metropolitan areas). At that time, it was usual in small towns whose poorer citizens could not afford their own television sets for local authorities to provide community sets installed in the main squares. Today, virtually every person has access to a television either in the home or in the home of a relative

Another feature of television development in Brazil is the concentration of audience and revenue shares dominated by the Globo television network. Globo is owned by a family involved in journalism since the early 20th century and has achieved an extraordinary leverage on political and economic power since its first television station was inaugurated in 1965. There was also a very close association between Globo and the military regime that opened the way for its unusually powerful influence over the national agenda.

Although its power has been grossly and unduly exaggerated by its critics, Globo television network has been able to exercise a considerable deal of control over some issues and was an excellent platform that benefited the military regime and some of the most conservative leaders within it.

However, such tacit agreement between Globo and the establishment was never without its own contradictions. The pursuit of excellence by the television network inevitably led to it employing some of the best journalists, performers, authors and dramatists; a large number of which were opposed to the military government. Despite censorship and its owner's ideological support of the prevailing regime, there were instances between 1965 and 1985 in which Globo programs performed a fundamental role in disseminating attitudes and values in opposition to the military, mostly on moral and social issues.

In 1984, when civil society almost entirely withdrew its support for the authoritarian cycle of governments, Globo was forced to retreat to the opposition. The popular movement for direct and free elections for the Presidency of Brazil began in late 1983 and was ignored by Globo for some months, but was finally publicized on a large scale by the network as it broadcast live some of the most important street demonstrations that took place in 1984 and it openly released its artists to perform at such public events.

THE CONTEMPORARY MEDIA SECTOR

Since the end of the military regime, Globo has been able to maintain strong leadership in the television market, both in audience and advertisement revenue; though far from the extremely impressive figures it had in the 1970s and early 1980s. In the last 20 years, while the country built up democratic institutions that have proved themselves very vigorous, Globo has also changed substantially its political and ideological behavior, distancing itself from openly supporting particular parties or candidates as it had done many times in the past. However, Globo has been facing serious economic challenges since 1999 due to the general crisis that has plagued the media market in Brazil, mostly because of macroeconomic problems. In many respects these trends have dominated media issues for the past decade and will continue to be at the forefront of the political agenda.

In this respect *the* most important issue regarding the relationship between the state and the mass media in recent years in Brazil has been the profound financial crisis that has plagued most of the important media conglomerates in the country since 1999. During the 1990s, Brazil's economy was stable due to the control of inflation and the creation of a new national currency, the Real, whose rate was kept in parity with the US$ for several years.

The successive international financial crises of 1998 (Mexico, Russia, Asian countries, Argentina) had consequences for a range of emerging countries, Brazil among them. The flow of foreign investment decreased dramatically and the many structural deficiencies of the Brazilian economy resurfaced.

In February 1999, the government was forced to devalue the real, putting an end to its parity with the U.S. dollar. In the following months and years, the value of the U.S. dollar climbed to be the equivalent of four Real. It is estimated that around 85% of the media groups' debt were in dollars and therefore with the collapse of the Real their debts more than tripled over a very short period of time precipitating a financial crisis across the sector. The collapse of the domestic consumer market also had an impact on the investments these companies had made in the new media sector as consumers cut their spending on non essential goods and a range of new media services such as pay TV collapsed leaving financial losses for the companies. The total debt of the media conglomerates has been estimated to be around US$3 billion; 60% of this debt belonging to Globo, an amount that is a little less than the annual total advertising revenues in Brazil (in 2002, the total debt of the media sector was 86% of its total revenues). The media group's accumulated debts roughly equivalent to two thirds of this amount on the top of their debt every year from 2000 to 2002 (Lobato, 2004).

Such financial crisis inevitably led to austerity measures in the industry and during this period some 17,000 members of the workforce were made unemployed in the media industry (Lobato, 2004). In October 2002, when its debt corresponded to 121% of its annual revenues, Globo defaulted on the payment of interest on its foreign currency loans. An agreement between Globo and its creditors was only reached in April 2005. The Abril Group also reached an agreement with its own creditors in April 2005, after having sold part of the company to foreign investors.

Free-to-air television is by far the most consumed of all mass media in Brazil. Pay TV is present in more or less 7% of households in the country. In 2004 Globo had an average share of audience of 57% (Grupo de Mídia, 2005).

The second largest group (with a share of 20%) is SBT, owned by a talk show host, Silvio Santos, who became famous in the 1960s and 1970s with his show (then broadcast by Globo) that lasted several hours in the afternoon and early evening on Sundays. Mr. Santos obtained a license to operate his own network in the aftermath of the bankruptcy of Tupi, the first TV station in the country. Mr. Santos used to praise the military regime's achievements in his shows and that was one of the main reasons for the government granting him the license in the early 1980s.

SBT programming follows a pattern of popular shows that appeal to the lowest ranks of the audience in terms of both cultural and economic standards. These social groups achieved greater consumption powers in the mid 1990s, due to the end of inflation and stabilization of the national currency. Subsequently Globo was forced to lower its programming quality to compete with SBT for this section of the audience. Globo to lower the quality of its own programming.

The third largest share of audience belongs to Record network (around 7%), which is owned by an Evangelical denomination, very popular among the working classes in Brazil and some countries in Africa (Universal Church of God's Kingdom). The programming of Record also appeals to what is considered by most critics as low taste consumption. Besides religious shows, it broadcasts newscasts mostly devoted to crime and police repression of criminal activities, reality shows that exploit family problems.

The other two national TV networks, Bandeirantes and RedeTV!, have together a 7% audience share and follow a pattern of low cost/low taste programming. The public television network, which shows better quality programming, has an average audience share of less than 1%.

An impressive and distinctive feature of the Brazilian mass media system is the extremely high percentage of advertising revenues. In 2004, the total advertisement investment in the mass media system totaled 15 billion Real (equivalent to US$6.3 billion at the average exchange rate of June 2005). That is three times more than the advertising expenditure of Argentina, Chile, Colombia and Venezuela, the largest markets of South America after the Brazilian one, but it is half the value of the Mexican one. Open television received a share of 61% of that total; newspapers 17.1%, magazines 8.6%, Internet five%, radio 4.4%, pay TV 2.2% (Grupo de Mídia, 2005).

These figures reflect the ubiquity of television in Brazilian society and produce decisions by the advertising industry that may look dysfunctional. For instance, television advertising for luxury items that are only affordable by a small percentage of the population has a prominent position on television.

Indeed, other media, such as newspapers, have seen declining advertising revenues and the number of copy sales. The best-selling serious daily newspaper in the country, *Folha de S. Paulo*, had an average daily circulation of 924,000 copies in 1996 that declined to 379,000 in 2004 (Graça, 2004). All of its competitors have experienced similar decreases in the same period of time.

Free-to-air television in Brazil is a "no cost" medium in that the viewers do not have to pay a license fee or tax contribution to fund the channels and in this respect television was less affected in terms of audience habits by the economic hardships of the turn of the century. The economic slump may even have been favorable to television companies as their audience grew as consumers abandoned the newspaper and magazine sectors. The free-to-air broadcasters may also have benefited by the fact that pay TV was introduced at this time and the financial woes of the country meant that there was little significant take up of the technology leaving traditional economic models favoring free-to-air television. The total of pay television subscribers remained more or less the same 3.5 million of 2000 until 2003, the year when it had been anticipated (at the moment when the debts were contracted) that it would reach 10 million—in December 2004, this number was around 3.8 million (Castro, 2005b).

This is also probably one of the reasons that the traditional Brazilian television sector has not suffered as much as in other countries with the advent of new technologies such as the Internet. Where audiences have migrated to new media from the traditional sectors this has largely been at the expense of the print industry, further cementing the financial difficulties of the sector.

Significantly, newspapers in Brazil have been able to sustain a higher degree of credibility among the public. The latest polls show that the newspaper industry is the second most trusted institution in the country, with the support of 63% of the people, surpassed only by the Post Office and above the Church and the Armed Forces, among others. Television, on the other hand, is in eighth place, with the trust of 45% of the people (Ipsos-Novaction, 2005). At times these figures may seem contradictory, but they illustrate how pervasive, time-consuming and advertising attractive television in Brazil is and the influence of the medium as a whole is probably larger now than 20 years ago in the country.

TELEVISION AND POLITICS

Political campaigning is considered more and more decisive in the electoral process. In Brazil, all political parties and candidates have the right to free time for their party political broadcasts on radio and television. The parties spend huge amounts of money to produce their advertisements and such programs are seen to be a key influence on patterns of voting behavior. Moreover, at every new election the number of candidates who owe their popularity to their appearances on television programs appears to rise. The endorsement of television idols is keenly sought by all major candidates.

Another example of the relationship between politics and the media is the extraordinary growth of several religious groups, mostly Evangelical, that exploit the charismatic and presentational styles of their leaders on television. The third most popular television network in Brazil, Record, is owned by one of these groups and has large audience shares in other Portuguese speaking countries, such as Mozambique and Angola. It is also the case that the most popular religious leaders of these groups become politicians. The so called Evangelical caucus in Congress is very influential and is constituted by several religious broadcasters. One of the political parties that is part of the coalition presently in power, the Liberal Party, is mostly composed of Evangelical leaders. The former governor of Rio de Janeiro and aspiring presidential candidate (who was the third most voted candidate in the 2002 election), Anthony Garotinho, made his fame as a religious broadcaster.

One more symptom of the increasing influence of television over society in Brazil is the predominant role that has been achieved by some talk show hosts in shaping segments of public opinion on issues that range from the need for the death penalty as a tool to combat urban violence to the moral and ethically issues of allowing stem cell research. These talk show hosts earn a great deal of money to publicize not only consumer goods but ideas and political manifestos and issues.

There are several other cases and situations to demonstrate how relevant television has become in Brazilian society. Such power, aggravated by high degrees of concentration of property has understandably fueled arguments in favor of mechanisms for more public regulation over the media.

STATE AND MEDIA

With the end of the military regime, in 1985, there was an intense public desire for less intervention of the State in the communications industry. The years of censorship should never emerge again and that was made very clear by the new Constitution, passed by Congress and adopted by the country in 1988.

Since the 1980s freedom of expression has been in the ascendancy in Brazil in respect of the State. Even subtler forms of pressure from the State toward the media have been reduced in these years. For instance, State-owned companies and the State itself have traditionally been responsible for a large share of advertising revenues for the media industry in general and this share remains one of the largest in the world—7.1%, compared to 1.8% in the U.K. and 1.6% in the U.S. (Rodrigues, 2003). It is, however, much smaller today than it was before the privatization process that took place in the 1990s. A large portion of this budget is spent on public awareness campaigns such as the need for vaccines and other public health issues, but a good share is still advertising that promotes and supports the administration.

In some regions of Brazil, mostly the least developed ones, local officials still exert improper influence over the media through the allocation of advertising budgets controlled by them. But such intrusion has become less and less relevant over the last few years.

There are of course other areas where the State still plays a key role and it has retained its influence on the licensing of new television and radio stations. The executive branch of government (ad referendum of the legislature) is responsible for such processes and has constantly used it as a political instrument.

At least 25% of the television stations operating in Brazil are owned by politicians or their relatives—36% of the members of Senate own at least one television or radio station (Lobato, 2003). In the case of Globo, this relationship with political leaders is even more impressive: at least 40 of its affiliated stations belong to regional political leaders (Narloch, 2005, p. 53).

The religious groups who also own stations and have representatives in parliament also are an important political influence on television and some analysts believe that this fact conflicts with the constitutional principles of separation between State and Church, since these stations, licensed by the State (that has the monopoly of the airwaves), are being used for the proselytism of specific denominations. Although there has been no judicial review proving that these concessions or at least some of these licenses were subject to political deals, the indications that they were is clearly the case.

While the State no longer represents a threat to the freedom of privately owned stations, various branches of the State have created their own television stations. The Senate, the House of Representatives, the Executive branch, the Supreme Court, several state governments as well as several state legislatures have their own television channels. Cable and DTH networks carry these channels and provide thousands of jobs given out probably with political and electoral objectives in mind. These television channels, however, also perform a role that may be considered supportive of the democratic process, since they broadcast live sessions of the legislature and its committees and Courts and give the population the opportunity to engage in the discussion of public policies. Another State-owned television station is scheduled to be in operation in 2005 and this is the most ambitious of all them. It is TV Brasil, aimed at international audiences, starting with the South American ones. It is an initiative of the three branches of the federal government and seems to be part of a recently adopted strategy of asserting, in a more emphatic fashion than ever before, the aspirations of Brazil as a regional power.

THE DEVELOPMENT OF PUBLIC SERVICE TELEVISION

The concept of public television has only been discussed recently in Brazil. As other state governments, the São Paulo administration owns a television station, TV Cultura. But Cultura is not controlled directly by the state government, but through a foundation, Padre Anchieta, and it is almost entirely funded by the State of São Paulo. Budget problems have impoverished the foundation and the channel in recent years and this led to a proposal by TV Cultura to transform the channel into a public, rather than State-owned channel.

In some respects, TV Cultura (and the network that it leads, mostly composed of television stations owned by federal universities or state governments throughout the country) has already been operating in conditions somewhat similar to those of CPB/PBS in the U.S., and under some influence of the principles that rule the BBC and ITV in the U.K.. The original purpose of TV Cultura and other "educational" stations in Brazil was to offer public distant learning courses that would provide students with formal education qualifications.

From 1986 onward TV Cultura's programming has changed and has become more focused on journalism, high quality entertainment, and programming aimed at children and the youth audience with educational but not instructional content. At this point in time TV Cultura also initiated its policy of attracting forms of commercial sponsorship, despite the fact that the law licensing "educational" television stations (dated of 1967, during the military regime) prohibited them to air commercial advertising of any kind. With the approval of São Paulo's state government (led by the social democrat party) TV Cultura has become more aggressive in raising commercial sponsorship for its programs. The central objective of such a policy is to make the channel less dependent on the state government and, therefore, more responsive to the public.

In March 2005, a Bill was passed to formally allow "educational" television channels to air commercial advertising to supplement the insufficient funds provided by the State, although there is still dispute if this legal issue is solved as the Bill only referred to one "educational" channel in Rio de Janeiro.

Some observers in Brazil disagree with these premises and condemn the direction taken by TV Cultura. Members of center left parties led by the Workers Party criticize the move as incongruent with the ideals of public television and the changes will leave TV Cultura to be guided by the same principles that guide Globo and other commercial networks, a move that would put an end to the only alternative currently available to the audience (Castro, 2005c).

Those who support the commercial sponsorship of "educational" stations claim that it will allow the channels to achieve independence from political purposes of state governments and will provide the country with real public service television and an alternative to commercial television. Other models put forward include funding the "educational channels" through public subsidies and taxes levied on the commercial broadcasters or television sets.

With or without commercial advertising and sponsorship revenues the fact remains that the audience share of TV Cultura and other similar channels is extremely low, and it is never higher than 2% and around 1% on average across the country. On the other hand, TV Cultura has been able to control its debts and in 2004, it showed an impressive profit for the first time in many years. Its advertising revenues increased five times from January to December 2004, reaching a yearly income of almost US$8 million (Altman, 2005). In terms of the quality of its programming there is no consensus among analysts. Although it is clearly superior to the average of what is broadcast by the commercial networks, it remains well below the levels of quality of its schedules in the 1990s, when some of its programs won international awards.

Among the measures taken by TV Cultura to improve its concept of public service television was the establishment of an ombudsman to act as a representative of the viewers and express concerns and criticism of the schedule and programming. This is the first ombudsman ever in the Brazilian television system (the position was created in September 2004). There are today a dozen ombudsmen in the Brazilian press and several in private and public companies.

It is interesting to note that in May 2005, the association of news ombudsman (ONO) in its annual meeting in London rejected an attempt by two ombudsmen from the American Corporation for Public Broadcasting (CPB) to join their organization questioning its independence. The reason given was that the CPB is a quasi-governmental organization that provides funds for NPR (National Public Radio) and PBS (Public Broadcasting System) but does not itself gather or produce news.

MEDIA OWNERSHIP AND DIVERSITY

The Brazilian television sector is dominated by Globo. Its income in 2004 was around US$1.5 billion (almost one third of the total advertisement expenditures in the country) and its average national audience share was 65% (in the 1970s it reached to around 80%). All of the ten most popular television programs in Brazil in January 2005 were produced and broadcast by Globo. In the first quarter of 2005 Globo's net profit was equal to the total income of the second largest television network in the country, SBT (Castro, 2005d).

The dominance of Globo and the economic slump in Brazil have led policy makers to look for policy solutions to support the television industry. On one hand it has looked at options to provide more inward investment for the sector and secondly, and more recently, at proposals to make television in Brazil more plural.

An important policy change in the Brazilian mass media system occurred in 2002. The 1988 Constitution, as the previous ones, provided (Article 222) that the ownership of all audiovisual media should be restricted to Brazilian citizens who were either born in the country or naturalized for at least ten years. However, a constitutional amendment passed in Congress in 2002 allowed foreigners to possess up to 30% of the shares of a media company. This amendment was supported by Globo and other companies after the problems they had experienced in the aftermath of the 1999 economic crisis. The companies had previously objected to such amendments in order to protect their own domestic markets.

Despite this amendment and the opening up of the market to inward investment only a couple of investors have moved into the market and these largely related to the print media. The Abril Group, which includes a magazine publishing house in its holdings, sold 13.8% of its shares to Capital International. The Folha Group, whose activities include activities in the print media merged with its Internet branch that was partly owned by Portugal Telecom, which now has 20% of the whole group. Besides these minor transactions, Net, the cable division of the Globo Group, was partly sold in 2004 to the Mexican company Telmex, which will control up to 60% of the assets of the company that owns 51% of Net (36.5% of the voting shares). Because Net is a cable company the restrictions on foreign capital are not applicable.

The television business has to-date failed to attract significant foreign investment, although the Venezuelan media tycoon Gustavo Cisneros has repeatedly declared his intention to enter the Brazilian market. Even if there was a greater interest from foreign investors it is unlikely that such a move would significantly alter the prevailing conditions in Brazilian television. A couple of final provisions of the constitutional amendments have opened the possibility of a media company in Brazil being owned by another company rather than an individual legal person. As part of this process media companies are now allowed to be listed on the stock exchange and become public limited companies. Neither of these options have been taken up by the media companies although the Folha Group has announced it will offer shares on the stock market at some future point in time.

There are 31 bills dealing with forms of media control in Congress at the present time, most of them proposed by parties that support the government. One of them would prohibit national television networks. Furthermore, no company would be allowed to own more than ten stations and no more than two in a single state (Brazil has 27 federal states). Furthermore, the bill would not allow any network to reach more than 50% of all households in the country. Another bill would establish quotas for programs produced by independent companies rather than by the television station itself (Globo, for instance, produces all its own programs).

THE REGULATION OF THE MEDIA AND REGULATORY INSTITUTIONS

As part of the political bargaining process that allowed the passing of the amendment on foreign ownership in 2002, 15 years after its legal establishment by the Brazilian Congress, the Social Communication Council was finally made operational. The establishment of the Council was unsuccessfully and perennially argued for by the left-wing parties for more than a decade, due largely to the pressures against such a body by Globo and its contemporaries. However, in order to obtain the qualified majority required to pass the constitutional amendment, an agreement was reached and the Council was at last put in motion.

The Council is formed by representatives of the companies that own broadcast and print media, journalists and workers in these media, members of civil society and academics who specialize in media. The total number of members of the Council is 13. Among its responsibilities the Council advises Congress about all legislative decisions concerning the media sector.

The Council has become an important forum for discussion of controversial issues such as the introduction of digital television in Brazil, the quality of television programming and media concentration, it does not, however, have any enforcement or legislative powers. Moreover, although it was an initiative supported by the left-wing parties, the Council, as of the beginning of 2005 largely consists of representatives of media companies and has been a much more conservative entity than anyone could have forecast a couple of years ago.

In contrast, a very successful self-regulatory institution is Conar, formed by the advertising agencies. Its remit covers the whole media sector; though it's most public decisions have been concerned with television. Conar receives complaints against advertisements that may be considered insulting, inappropriate, unfair, irresponsible or harmful to individuals or society. It assesses each case and issues recommendations that may include suspending an advertisement indefinitely. Conar has gained respect from the industry and has shown itself to be an effective body.

Since 1992, a committee at the Ministry of Justice of Brazil has determined the suitable time slots for programming within the television schedules. The committee analyses scripts and summaries of soap operas and other programs. It considers the times when minors are watching television and decides the most suitable time for a program within the schedule. If channels fail to follow the recommendations they may be sued by the government. In reality this kind of action has rarely materialized. In 2003, due to a large number of complaints from viewers the government reviewed the work of the committee and imposed stricter criteria to improve the committee's work, as it was perceived to be too lenient in its decisions.

There are also pressures from civil society groups for broadcasters to improve the quality of their programming. In this respect a group of NGOs launched a campaign "Those Who Sponsor Trash TV Shows Work against Citizenship," which releases a ranking of the worst programs on television. The idea behind the campaign is it to encourage sponsors not to support such programming. The initiative has had some interesting results with some television channels shortening or even cutting programs that have been present in these rankings, fearful of losing sponsors or in response to the actual withdrawal of some advertisements.

COMPETITION AND MARKET ISSUES

Government agencies that are charged with ensuring free competition are another forum where media issues, notably those that have to do with concentration issues, might be debated and eventually resolved. One of them, the Secretariat for Economic Follow Up, is subjected to the Ministry of Finance. It recommends actions against presumable cartels that are to be taken by the other agency, named Cade (Administrative Council for the Defense of Economy). However, special provisions conceived to secure freedom of expression exclude newspapers, magazines, and television and radio ownership issues from their remit and therefore the body does not usually deal with the media sector.

However, a couple of cases involving the television sector have come before Cade. One has to do with the fact that Globo has denied access to other stations to football matches in Brazil including almost all of the important tournaments since it acquired the exclusive rights to the games. This case has been under examination since 2001 and has not been resolved. The other case examines the proposed merger of Sky and DirecTV in the DTH technology sector. There has not been a decision on this case either.

Globo and other television networks are concerned by the competition they will face from telecommunications companies that are preparing to distribute a range of content via mobile telephones. The television networks argue that they depend solely on advertising revenues while the telecommunications companies are able to charge tariffs as a significant complementary revenue source. As a result of these differences they claim that there must be separate and differing regulatory approaches to the two kinds of companies in order to guarantee fair competition.

On the other hand, distribution of television content through telecommunications systems and the growth of the Internet may be a factor in the roll out of pay-TV. Some cable television operators, such as TVA (Abril Group) are already planning to offer "triple play" packages that include television, the Internet and telephony. It has already been launched successfully in Chile and many believe it could be a successful model for the Brazilian market. Even

Globo has demonstrated an interest in this strategy with the tie in it has with Telmex, the Mexican telecommunications company, in Net, Globo's cable operator.

Another outstanding issue surrounding new technologies is the choice of standards for digital television. The current federal administration favors the development of a national technology standard instead of opting for one of the three that already exists: the ATSC (U.S.), DVB (European) and ISDB (Japan). Globo, Abril and other networks demand a selection based on one of the three existing systems and criticize the decision to pursue a national alternative, comparing it to the one taken in the 1970s by the military regime that also chose to develop a national system for color television. A decision that was later to prove shortsighted as Brazil is the only country that uses such a system and the industry has spent considerable resources in adapting the formats of programs for both export and imported programs in order to make them compatible with international standards. Since 2004 a huge amount of resources have been invested in research and development in the area of digital television, which are estimated to be in the region of US$16 million.

CALLS FOR MEDIA REFORM

Arguments for a larger degree of public control over the television industry and its activities have been growing since the end of the military regime. However, it was not until 2003 that concrete legislative action was recommended by government. On January 2003 the coalition government led by the Workers Party took office and put forward a number of reform proposals. These proposals met stiff opposition from the business community and conservative party members.

Subsequently two of these proposals were retracted. One of them would have created a National Journalists Council to "orient, discipline and monitor" journalists across the media sector. The second would have established an agency to regulate the audiovisual sector.

Although these two initiatives were abandoned the current government is still sponsoring a Bill that would force quotas for the production of programming to support regional culture. As well as a constitutional amendment to impose a limit of 30% on foreign ownership of all forms of telecommunication, cable television, DTH and Internet service providers to bring it into line with the legislation governing foreign ownership of other areas of the media industry.

Although in confrontation with the President Luiz Inacio Lula da Silva's government on some issues, Globo has supported several policy initiatives of the administration and is especially supportive of the government's economic and fiscal policies. At the current time there seems to be room for a coalition between Globo and the government for legal reforms to support national production quotas and protect the market from foreign investment and once its financial troubles are overcome, Globo will most certainly return to its previous stand of defending national television as a way to improve and sustain its own position as a big producer of national content to across the media sector. In this context the quotas would favor Globo as any foreign investors entering the market would have to meet these obligations and also by extending the ownership provisions to the carriage and new media sectors Globo is to some extent protecting its own position with the growth of new forms of content carriage and packaging (such as mobile phones and pay TV services) where there are a number of significant foreign investors such as Telefonica, who are developing new media and niche services.

CONCLUSION

Though the party has its roots in the left-wing movements the conservative economic policies introduced by the Lula government were fiercely contested by many voters. This led to a volte-face by the administration who decided to be loyal to its former ideals in areas less sensitive to the conservative forces than economic policies. One of these areas in which government decided to remain consistent with the previous Workers Party proposals of 20 years was its media policy. But, of course, it has faced strong opposition to the proposals for reform it has tabled.

It is unlikely that any of the bills discussed about will pass before another legislative initiative proposed by the Executive branch comes to life. The government has created a committee directly subordinated to the Presidency to draft a new General Law of Communication. This committee will have the task to encompass all bills presently running in Congress and consolidate them all in one single and coherent text.

Nobody questions the need for such a law. The regulations presently followed date from 1962 and do not address many of the new regulatory challenges brought about by the growth of new technologies and the social and economic changes that have happened in the country in the last 40 years. Many of the provisions of the 1962 Code of Telecommunications have been surpassed by reality and some became unconstitutional after 1988. The previous administration had promised to present a bill to Congress since 1997, but it never materialized. The amount of separate bills presently running in Congress and the intense public debate on the content of television programming (particularly of reality shows) demonstrate that there is a social demand for new forms of regulating the medium.

Arguably, every government in the world would like to exert as much control over television and other media as possible. Lula's administration is not different from others in this sense. However, he and some of his ministers have been particularly outspoken about this subject and breaking with their predecessors. On several occasions, the president himself or close aides have subsequently offered advice to those responsible for television decisions, such as that they should have a "positive agenda" and show more good things about Brazil instead of focusing on its problems. The insistence and frequency of this kind of discourse raises concerns among media executives and those who defend the principles of freedom of expression.

The macro- and microeconomic developments discussed about will be one of the two key factors that will determine the shape of the Brazilian television system in the future. The other one will be the content of the new General Law of Communication that is presently being drafted.

If any future proposals for change are considered too left, there will be fierce resistance in Congress. It is highly improbable that most of the new control mechanisms defended by the Workers Party will succeed in promulgation. This obviously does little to solve the growing number of issues that the government are faced by the current shape and growth of the television sector and leave the lacunae in the law left by the wide disparities in the 1962 Law and the contemporary television industry.

REFERENCES

Altman, F. (2005). A roda viva da TV Cultura. *Dinheiro*, 06/04/2005, 72–74.

Ávila, C. R. (1982). *A Teleinvasão*. São Paulo: Cortez, 1982.

Catro, D. (2005a). TV paga cresce 7% e chega a 3,8 milhões. In *Folha de S. Paulo*, 28/03/2005, E6.

Castro, D. (2005b). Brasileiro consome quase cinco horas de TV por dia. In *Folha de S. Paulo*, 11/01/2005, E10.

Castro, D. (2005c). Cultura estagnada. In *Folha de S. Paulo*, 08/05/2005, E1.

Castro, D. (2005d). Caixa Um. In *Folha de S. Paulo*, 11/06/2005, E14.

Costa, A. H., et al. (1988). *Um País no Ar*. São Paulo: Brasiliense, 1988.

Costa, C. T. (2004). *Modernidade líiquida, comunicação concentrada*, paper presented to the seminar "Quem Manda em Nós. São Paulo.

Graça, M. C. (2004). Os números são de assustar. In *Comunique-se*, 12/09/2004.

Grupo de Mídia. (2005). *Mídia Dados*. São Paulo: Grupo de Mídia, 2005.

Guerra, F. (2005). TV ainda resiste a se aliar ao cinema. *O Estado de S. Paulo*, 03/06/2005, D7.

IBGE. (2002). *Pesquisa Nacional por Amostra de Domicílios*, vol. 23.

Ipsos Novaction. (2004). Correios têm o maior índice de confiança. In *Exame* 28/09/2004, 16.

Junior, G. (2001). *O País da TV. São Paulo*. Conrad, 2001.

Lins da Silva, C. E. (1985). *Muito Além do Jardim Botânico*. São Paulo: Summus.

Lins da Silva, C. E. (1986). Transnational Communication and Brazilian Culture. In R. Atwood & E. McAnany (Eds.), *Communication and Latin American Society*. Madison: The University of Wisconsin Press.

Lins da Silva, C. E. (1993). The Brazilian Case, Manipulation by the Media? In T. Skidmore (Ed.), *Television, Politics and the Transition to Democracy in Latin America*. Baltimore: the Johns Hopkins University Press.

Lins da Silva, C. E. (2004). Televisão e Política na Virada do Século. *Revista* USP 61 (março/abril/maio 2004), 78–85.

Lobato, E. (2003). Governo divulga nomes de acionistas de rádio e TV. *Folha de S. Paulo*, 29/11/2003, A10.

Lobato, E. (2004). Mídia nacional acumula dívida de Rr$10 bi. In *Folha de S. Paulo*, 15/02/2004, B6–B7.

Macedo, C. et al. (2001). *TV ao Vivo*. São Paulo: Brasiliense.

Mattos, L. (2005). Brasileiro gasta 18,4 h com TV. In *Folha de S. Paulo*, 29/06/2005, E10

Melo, J. M. (1988). *As Telenovelas da Globo.* São paulo: Summus.

Narloch, L. (2005). A Voz do Brasil. *Superinteressante,* junho 48–57.

Oliveira Sobrinho, J. B. (org) (2000). *50 Anos de TV no Brasil.* São Paulo: Editora Globo.

Rede Globo. (1984). *15 Anos de História.* Rio: Riográfica.

Ribeiro, R. J. (2005). *O Afeto Autoritário.* São Paulo: Ateliê Editorial.

Rodrigues, F. (2003). Gasto oficial responde por 7% do mercado publicitário. *Folha de S. Paulo,* 10/11/2003, A4

Sodré, M. (1977). *O Monopólio da Fala.* Petrópolis: Vozes.

CHAPTER THREE

United States of America: Continuity and Change

Christopher H. Sterling
George Washington University

American television has long served as either a model for emulation or a target of derision for other countries. Surely the largest system in terms of number of stations (1,750 in 2005) or revenue (nearly US$55 billion in 2004), commercial broadcast and cable television remains the primary U.S. entertainment medium, a role it has served for nearly six decades. Based on advertiser support, supplemented by a weaker educational/public television sector, and very limited regulatory oversight, American television nonetheless faces substantial change in coming years, a transition that is already evident.

This chapter summarizes the development and current status of American television; reviews the primary regulatory players and policies, including ownership concerns; and assesses the growing impact of changing technology on the legacy systems of broadcasting and cable.

DEVELOPMENT AND BACKGROUND

The business and regulatory structures of American broadcasting date to the late 1920s when advertising became generally accepted as the means of supporting radio stations; the first national radio networks were established, and the Radio

Act of 1927 created the Federal Radio Commission (FRC) to license and regulate stations. Listeners could finally purchase plug-in receivers that had loudspeakers, eliminating the need for cumbersome batteries and headphones. The first audience research results began to appear. And program types still familiar—especially drama, comedy, and various music formats—were largely established by that time. The Communications Act of 1934 replaced the FRC with the current Federal Communications Commission (FCC), but largely continued the same regulatory approach couched in terms of stations being required to operate in the public interest. Spectrum frequencies were defined as belonging to the people rather than users who were to be licensed for set terms (3 years until the early 1980s), which could be (and usually were) renewed (Sterling & Kittross, 2002).

After more than a decade of research into, and development of, an all-electronic television system by several manufacturers, chiefly the Radio Corporation of America, commercial television broadcasting was authorized by the FCC to begin in the United States on July 1, 1941, utilizing a dozen VHF channels each with 6 MHZ. CBS and NBC placed New York stations on the air and a handful of others began service in the weeks that followed. Wartime operations to 1945, however, were very limited to about a dozen stations and very few hours per week, catering to a few thousand receivers.

As more stations began service in the late 1940s, interference concerns and the lack of sufficient channels to effectively cover such a large country become evident. From 1948 to 1952, the FCC instituted a "Freeze" on authorizing new stations while it worked out problems of allocation and interference. In April 1952, the Freeze ended with the commission's landmark "Sixth Report and Order," which added 70 UHF channels to the dozen VHF channels already in service and decided (against engineering advice) to intermix the two in individual markets in order to increase the number of channels per city, as well as setting aside some channels in both bands for noncommercial stations (Sterling & Kittross, 2002). As many had predicted, however, UHF struggled for years, unable to compete equally with VHF channels that served larger areas and thus more viewers, and enjoyed network affiliations and advertising revenue usually lacking for UHF. The FCC spent much of its time in the 1950s trying to resolve this issue. In 1962, Congress mandated that all television receivers had to receive both VHF and UHF bands, and that helped somewhat, but only expansion of cable television after 1975 really eliminated the UHF limitation for most viewers.

Three national networks (CBS, NBC, and a weaker ABC) dominated the television business (most local stations were affiliates, meaning they had contracts to carry network programs, though they were not network-owned). Several attempts to create a fourth network failed for lack of sufficient stations in most markets, making it impossible to reach as large an audience as the existing three. Each network owned five VHF major-market local television stations, which provided much of their income. After FCC rule changes in the early 1970s, an extensive program syndication market also developed, encouraging the formation of independent (nonaffiliate) stations in the largest cities.

PUBLIC SERVICE TELEVISION

American public service broadcasting, on the other hand, has always been a distinctly secondary service in terms of the number of stations, funding, and audience. Noncommercial radio stations had operated from the dawn of regulator broadcasting in 1920, and with the authorization of FM radio services in 1941, the FCC, for the first time, reserved channels for noncommercial operations. Although the commission also reserved hundreds of channels for exclusive noncommercial television use in 1952, the stations were dubbed "educational," a label that surely did not help to build an audience, and they suffered from very limited funding. Some programs were shared in a so-called "bicycle" network of mailed film and later videotape recordings, but there was no national network. Most stations programmed and raised funds on their own (the Ford Foundation was a substantial financial supporter). Despite these drawbacks, the number of noncommercial stations slowly grew into the 1960s (see Table 3.1).

One of the last of the Johnson administration (1963–1969) "Great Society" programs sought to improve the lot of educational television with more structure, increased funding, and a national network. The idea fitted well within the expansive domestic policy initiatives of the administration. Many people long concerned with the plight of limited educational television had worked closely with

TABLE 3.1
U.S. Television Growth Indicators: 1950–2003

	1950	*1960*	*1970*	*1980*	*1990*	*2000*	*2003*
Number of Stations							
Commercial	98	515	677	734	1112	1243	1366
Educational	0	44	185	277	353	373	382
Employment							
Television	14,000	40,000	58,400	78,300	114,700	138,800	NA
Cable	NA	NA	NA	33,700	125,800	215,800	NA
FCC	1,285	1,396	1,553	2,094	1,705	1,933	NA
Homes with:							
Television	9%	87%	95%	98%	98%	98%	98%
Cable	0	1%	8%	20%	59%	69%	70%
DBS	0	0	0	0	NA	NA	15%
Pay Cable	0	0	NA	51%	77%	73%**	NA
VCRs	0	0	0	1%	69%	85%	92%

Notes. Adapted from *Stay Tuned: A History of American Broadcasting* by C. H. Sterling and J. M. Kittross, pp. 827–828, 864–865, 870–871, and 875. Recent employment data from Media Information Center Web site: www.mediainfocenter.org/ (accessed April 2006). Data for stations in 2004 from FCC Web site www.fcc.gov (accessed April 2006).
*Indicates data for 1995. **Is actually data for 1999. NA indicates no data available.

administration officials and the resulting landmark Public Broadcasting Act of October 1967 provided a better label and boosted federal funding to help program and operate more stations (Public Broadcasting Act, 1967). The law created a Corporation for Public Broadcasting (CPB) to channel government and privately donated funds into new national "public" networks. CPB created the Public Broadcasting Service (PBS) in 1969 to link local television outlets and promote the production of programs.

Well into the 1970s, however, CPB and PBS both became arenas of often bitter infighting as a new cadre of Washington-based public TV officials faced an old guard of educational television pioneers who had survived (though few had thrived) with little help from Washington. This battle was made worse by a conflict over so-called long-range funding. Rather than seeking government appropriations annually (as with federal agencies), CPB sought 5-year funding cycles to (hopefully) minimize the role of politics in program funding decisions. The Nixon administration (1969–1974), unhappy with PBS's perceived liberal program bias, vetoed several funding bills and only in 1975, under President Ford (1974–1977), did Congress finally set up a 3-year funding cycle for CPB. That was not the end of the issue, of course, for less than a decade later; Congress would *rescind* some of the money appropriated due to a budget crisis, something that happened several times.

SATELLITE TELEVISION

That same year (1975) also witnessed the first use of satellites to distribute a national cable signal (Ted Turner's Atlanta UHF station was first, followed by pay-cable service, HBO) and the number of satellite-delivered cable networks expanded rapidly after 1980 (Sterling & Kittross, 2002).

The first home VCR was sold in America in 1975 and they were ubiquitous within a dozen years, allowing viewers for the first time to time-shift and archive programs. The first video rental shop opened in Los Angeles in 1979. By the mid-1980s, broadcast networks also used satellites for national program distribution. Since 1980, viewing of legacy broadcast stations, both network affiliates (including Fox, which first aired in the late 1980s, backed by Rupert Murdoch's millions) and others, has declined by half in prime-time viewing hours, as viewers increasingly spend time with cable services, alternate video sources, or even the Internet (see Table 3.2). Indeed, just a few years into the new millennium, cable audiences exceeded those for broadcast television. Direct-to-home satellite television served about 22% of American households by late 2004. The main competitors, DirecTV and Dish Network, have more customers combined than the 21.5 million subscribers to Comcast, the nation's largest cable provider. But the cable industry as a whole, some 74 million subscribers, still dwarfs satellite.

MODERN MARKET FOR TELEVISION

Table 3.1 makes clear the essential pattern of American television development—commercial and more briefly educational broadcast station—centered to about 1980,

TABLE 3.2

National Prime Time Audience Shares: 1985–2004

	Broadcast Television				Cable Channels		
	Channels Received (Average)	Network Affiliates	Independent Stations	Public Television	Total	Basic Channels	Pay Channels
1985	19	74%	16%	4%	94%	6%	7%
1990	33	67%	14%	4%	85%	20%	6%
1995	NA	62%	11%	4%	77%	31%	6%
1999	62	54%	11%	3%	68%	41%	7%
2004					47%	49%	

Notes. Data through 1999 adapted from 2000 Report on Television by A. C. Nielsen, p. 17: 2004 summary data adapted from Cable Industry Overview 2004 by the National Cable and Telecommunications Assn., p. 13.

and cable-television centered in the ensuing 25 years. The number of broadcast outlets continues to grow, but at a slower pace, especially in the noncommercial service where funding is an increasing problem and most likely markets are already served. By the 21st century, cable had become the primary means of program distribution and reception for most Americans, though satellite-delivered services to the home were rising rapidly. The major result of this pattern is a sharp increase in the number of channels received in the average home (see Table 3.2).

American television has been characterized almost from the start by national network and syndicated program distribution through local stations and (increasingly during the past 30 years) cable systems. Economics of expensive television program production make this sharing of costs almost imperative. Until the expansion of cable after 1975, most markets had no more than three to five television stations; only the very largest were served by more. Cable began as a means of improving reception, then to import so-called distant signals (usually nonnetwork stations with movie and sports packages), and after 1980, to deliver cable network programs, some original local material, and multiple pay-cable services such as HBO.

American television is characterized by a multichannel delivery process. By the turn of the 21st century, nearly 70% of American households subscribed to a cable service (about 15% use direct-to-home satellite service) providing upwards of 200 channels, and 85% own a VCR. Home computer ownership and Internet connectivity is rising annually. Movies and old television programs, once restricted to broadcasting, can also be viewed on videotape or DVDs available from rental or sales outlets or by mail services such as Netflix. All of these many options siphon viewers from traditional broadcast television. Digital video recorders (such as the

TABLE 3.3
Top Communications Companies, Ranked by Revenue: 2003

Rank	Company	Revenue (Million US$)	Sample of Electronic Media Holdings
1	Time Warner	45,545.0	CNN, Turner
2	The Walt Disney Company	23,828.0	ABC, ESPN
3	Viacom	21,353.7	CBS, MTV. VH1
4	Comcast	17,492.0	Largest cable MSO
5	Sony	13,436.7	Motion pictures, electronics
6	DirecTV Group	8,291.9	Direct-to-home satellite service
7	Vivendi International	7,585.9	MCA/Universal
8	General Electric	6,871.0	NBC, MSNBC, Bravo, USA Network
9	Fox Entertainment Group	6,742.0	Fox, Fox News
10	Gannett	6,711.1	USA Today TV

Notes. Omits firms with few or no electronic media holdings. Adapted from Media Information Center (www.mediainfocenter.org/), citing 2004 Veronis Suhler Stevenson Communications Industry Report and PQ Media.

pioneering TiVo device) go a step further in allowing viewers to screen broadcast or cable programs without having to watch advertisements.

Ranking companies by revenue is always a precarious business, given varied ways of counting and reporting data. But Table 3.3 offers an indication of the major players in electronic media, and especially television and cable. Virtually all of these companies are conglomerates, some of them with extensive international operations. But television (including cable and satellite) plays a large revenue role for each them. Indeed, network television made US$22.5 billion in advertising revenue in 2004, a rise of more than 10% from the year before. To that must be added US$17.3 billion from "spot" (regional and local) television advertising, and another US$14.2 billion in advertising on cable television (up nearly 14%)—totaling nearly US$55 billion in television advertising revenues (TNS Media in IT Facts, n.d.).

PUBLIC TELEVISION

Although the majority of the American television-viewing audience (95%) watches commercial stations, networks, or cable channels, public television stations—most of them networked by the Public Broadcasting Service—provide a public service alternative that is especially strong in children's programs (e.g., *Sesame Street*), documentaries, and imported drama. Although their audiences are comparatively tiny, they are also very loyal and made up disproportionately of better educated political and social activists. On this level, then, the public television system works well. The PBS network allows the system to achieve a level of national prominence and provides the best window into foreign (chiefly English language) productions.

Of the 356 public television stations, ownership is spread across four types of licensees: nonprofit community organization with 138 stations; state governments holding 126 stations; universities and colleges with 85 stations; and local governments with only seven stations (CPB).

The system operates, however, on a financial pittance—far less money per capita than other industrial nations. Part of the problem is a multiplicity of sometimes overlapping entities that work on this issue—the system looks a bit like the plumbing diagram for a submarine. Table 3.4 shows the revenue sources for all of public broadcasting (including radio), making clear that just over 43% comes from tax revenues, primarily on the local and state level. Although the dollar amounts vary from year to year, the percentages change very slowly. But fundamental here is the degree to which the system is *always* seeking more funding. On a per capita basis, for example, American public service broadcasting is nowhere nearly as well supported as parallel systems in Britain (BBC) and Japan (NHK). Also, the annual federal appropriation is always under fire from conservatives in Congress, some of whom (unhappy with the system's perceived liberal bias) have tried for a decade to "zero" it out, arguing that the system should stand on its own, not on an annual "federal handout."

Although individual "membership" donations account for a quarter of all public system funding, business is a vital source of program funds. Most business income comes from underwriting the production costs of individual programs or program series. Such underwriting, once acknowledged with a terse announcement at the opening and close of a program, is now touted in near-commercials

TABLE 3.4
Public Broadcasting Revenue Sources: 2002

Source	Amount (000s US$)	Percentage
Individual "Membership" Donations	594	26
Business Underwriting, Donations	376	16
Federal Appropriation	350	15*
State Government Appropriations	322	14*
Public Colleges and Universities	209	9
Foundation Grants	147	6
Miscellaneous	125	6
Federal Grants and Contracts	59	3*
Local Governments	58	3*
Private Colleges and Universities	33	2
On-Air Auctions	12	1
Total	2,287	100

Note. Adapted from the Corporation for Public Broadcasting (www.cpb.org).
*Sources are tax revenue-based.

that can go on for a half minute or more, very much as on commercial networks. This is due largely to a loosening of FCC rules restricting such announcements, part of the deregulatory sweep of the 1980s, designed in this case to prompt more business donations, and thus reliance on taxes.

To a considerable degree, American public television acts as a "steam valve" for commercial broadcasters—if it did not exist, they might well have to invent it. The very existence of the public system takes some regulatory pressure off commercial stations to produce public affairs, documentaries, and cultural programming. Indeed, many commercial broadcasters, well aware of this role, help support the public system in kind or with funding.

AIMS AND LIMITS OF REGULATION

Government regulation of television in the United States relies on two provisions of the 18th-century Constitution. Article I, Section 8 (1789), the so-called "commerce clause," gives Congress the right (but not the requirement) to regulate commerce among two or more states. And the First Amendment (1791) makes clear that Congress (the courts have held this to mean any part of government) shall make no law "abridging freedom of speech or of the press" (Carter, Franklin, & Wright, 2003). Both remain regulatory benchmarks today and underpin the unique nature of American television policy. There has long been strong agreement among all political parties to limit government's overall role in the media, especially concerning content. However, there are strong differences in details. The newspaper press is virtually uncontrolled due, in part, to the First Amendment, and the lack of any technical factor (such as spectrum use) requiring government oversight.

Electronic media, on the other hand, require spectrum and, as in every other country, the United States grants the allocation and licensing right to that limited resource to a national regulatory agency. The first laws controlling wireless telegraphy (in 1910 and 1912) established government control and licensing of transmitters. The Radio Act of 1927, the first legislation tailored to broadcasting, set up the "public interest, convenience, or necessity" as the prime rationale for licensing and regulating stations. The broader Communications Act of 1934 (which superceded the 1927 law and has often been amended since), continued that standard. Not defined in either law, those "public interest" words have been subject to varied readings by both commissioners and the courts over the past 70 years. But they continue to define the basic purposes of television regulation, being cited for whatever regulatory (or deregulatory) initiative is being suggested (Carter et al., 2003).

American broadcast regulation has traditionally been of two types—structural and behavioral. Structural policies are designed to indirectly maintain (or increase) multiple points of view and program diversity by such actions as limiting ownership concentration or encouraging ethnic minority station ownership or employment. Many of these policies have been substantially deregulated over the past decade. Behavioral regulation is more direct and controversial, for it is more subject to challenge on First Amendment grounds. A behavioral rule may require (or ban) a specific action concerning programming—such as mandating a service to a specific audience segment (e.g., children), or banning a specific program practice (e.g., airing information on commercial lotteries).

DEREGULATION

Beginning about 1975, a fundamental shift in regulatory thinking about government's role in communications and transport (among other sectors) became apparent, and grew increasingly important after 1980 under the general term *deregulation*. Evidence from several fields including transportation and banking made it increasingly clear that the federal government could no longer regulate so many aspects of the country's economic and cultural life—the nation was too complex and government personnel and revenue too limited. Additionally, cost–benefit analyses and paperwork reduction mandated by Congress added impetus to refocusing regulation only on those factors felt to be essential to station operation in the public interest. Newer technologies on the horizon suggested more competition was coming if it was not throttled by policy restrictions at birth. All of this was further underpinned by a fundamental ideological shift, to a considerable degree bipartisan, that held government should not continue President Franklin Roosevelt's "New Deal" (1933–1941) approach of trying to be all things to all people. The marketplace (variously defined, depending on who was talking) was now presumed to act in the best interest of most people, most of the time, with regulatory intervention needed only to correct market failure.

Concerning television specifically, deregulation began with the removal of some minor regulatory "underbrush" (such as various rules requiring reports from licensees, and some minor technical regulations) in the early 1980s, and then expanded to loosen station ownership and other structural and economic restrictions. Most behavioral regulations disappeared in the rising tide of deregulation (e.g., the Fairness Doctrine was abandoned in 1987), which had, for decades, encouraged equal access to broadcast stations or networks by spokespersons for conflicting views on issues of public importance. So did various rules concerning carriage of programs on cable and colocated television stations, although some returned later. No longer was government regulation presumed—rather the opposite was now true. The result is that American broadcast television is among the least-regulated electronic media systems in the world. There is virtually no specific program censorship or dictation by government. News editorial and entertainment program decisions are made by networks or stations with no government oversight. Only a few behavioral requirements remain.

Political Campaigns

There are some fairly complex rules concerning broadcast political campaign advertising (as television is the single most important political medium). These include a series of requirements often confusingly termed *equal time,* covering such things as conditional rights of access by competing candidates for the same office, limits on how much stations may charge for political advertising time, and additional rules mandating like treatment of competing candidates (FCC Media Bureau, n.d.). But none speak to the vast differences in available political funding which often control how much a candidate or party is heard over the air. Republican candidates, for example, usually have far more money for the purchase of broadcast time than the Democrats. In 1960 (when they helped tip the election to John F, Kennedy), then not again until 1976 (and in virtually every election since), presidential candidates have faced off in national debates that are now controlled by the major television networks. These were once tightly controlled by FCC rules that have virtually all but disappeared.

Children and Minors

For decades, television was lauded for its cultural potential—and just as strongly criticized for largely ignoring the "under-12" viewer. Networks provided cartoon programs and little more—only public television's *Sesame Street* and related programs seemed to serve young children. Public interest groups pressed for years to redress this problem, but were rebuffed by an FCC loathe to mandate any programming. Change finally came with the Children's Television Act of 1990, which required prosocial programming and limited advertising in such programs. The FCC has thus mandated a minimum 3 hours per week of prosocial programming for young children on all television stations. The number of advertising minutes per children's program hour is limited (10 or 12 minutes per hour, depending on the day)—the only formal regulation of U.S. television advertising time or content (FCC Media Bureau, n.d.).

Indecency

Children were also the primary concern with another type of program content. There has long been an FCC-mandated rule limiting the hours when *indecent* program material may be aired by broadcast stations (only from 10 p.m. to 6 a.m., when, presumably, fewer children are in the audience). *Obscene* content (generally meaning hardcore pornography) is not protected by the First Amendment, and may not be aired at any time. The legal difference between the two has been defined in two landmark Supreme Court cases, *Miller v. California* (1973) set overall media obscenity guidelines, and *FCC v. Pacifica Foundation* (1978), which more specifically defined what is acceptable in broadcasting.

Indecency again became hugely controversial in the mid-2000s as a strongly conservative religious movement, upset by what many observed on the air, pressured Congress and the FCC to more closely control television depictions of sex or violence—and heavily fine transgressors. The number of complaint letters (and, increasingly, e-mails) sent to the FCC—strongly prompted by organized campaigns—rapidly increased to more than a million a year (it had been mere hundreds as recently as 2000). By 2005, members of both Congress and the FCC were arguing to expand indecency restrictions to cable and satellite video services. As made clear in more than a generation of court decisions concerning the First Amendment, however, such subscription services have not been as tightly controlled, the legal reasoning being that one must seek out and pay for them, as opposed to free, over-the-air broadcasting which is more easily accessibly by children (FCC Media Bureau, n.d.). As this was written, pressure for greater content control was rising.

Copyright Issues

Also controversial and subject to considerable recent change is copyright or intellectual property regulation. All popular music in the United States, for example, is licensed for use by one of the performance societies (ASCAP, BMI, or SESAC) under provisions of the Copyright Act of 1976 (Carter et al., 2003). Film studios and broadcast networks were behind the recent extension of the "normal" copyright period to 70 years—and even longer in some cases. Cable television systems must pay quarterly for the right to use some distant broadcast signals (www.copy right.gov). Developing digital means of recording have struck considerable fear into copyright holders who are supporting strong limits on consumer access to, or use of, such devices in order to protect their control of programs and motion pictures. Thus far, court decisions in this area have offered mixed results.

OWNERSHIP OF THE AMERICAN MEDIA

Although American television is licensed at the local station level, decades of takeover and merger and acquisition activity have created a national oligopoly to serve (and, in many ways, to control) those local outlets. The system is increasingly characterized by both vertical integration and horizontal control.

Although the FCC has long espoused a theory of "one (station) to a customer," it has never enforced such a policy in radio or television on a national basis. On the other hand, from about 1940, it allowed an owner to control only one station of each type (AM, FM, television) in any one market. In the early 1950s, it settled on allowing up to seven television stations (of which two had to be UHF) under one owner nationally. An entity could control a radio and television station in the same market, but not a cable system and television station. That policy held for three decades. In the growing deregulation of the early 1980s, the number of television stations was extended to 12 anywhere in the country (see Table 3.4). Group ownership focused on the more valuable VHF stations—even in 1995; whereas 92% of VHF stations in the largest 100 markets were group-owned, only 62% of UHF stations were group-owned (Howard, 2003).

The Telecommunications Act of 1996 mandated that the FCC reconsider its television ownership limits (Telecommunications Act, 1996). Working under that mandate, the FCC decided to determine an ownership limit based on the proportion of the country's television households reached, and settled on 35% as the right line (FCC Media Bureau, n.d.). The FCC's attempts to expand that number up to 40% (or more) of the nation's viewers proved highly controversial in the early 2000s, and Congress finally intervened with a "compromise" at 39%. Congress therefore finally legislated at the 39% limit. From the old limit of seven stations, many group owners by the early 2000s owned 30 and more stations (fewer, of course, if they were concentrated in larger markets). Indeed, one owned 60 outlets, and another 53 by 2002, and newspapers owned just over a quarter of the stations in the top 100 markets (Howard, 2003).

Group ownership concentration soon extended into newer media, especially cable system ownership (see Table 3.5). Vertical integration characterizes the video entertainment market (broadcasting and cable) by 2000 with five firms— Fox News Corporation, Viacom, Disney, General Electric, and Time Warner controlling all of the broadcast networks, many of the most popular cable networks, dozens of television stations and often hundreds of cable systems (Compaine & Gomery, 2000). The "new" network world integrates Hollywood program production with a variety of distribution modes (cable, satellite, broadcast). The new world is also largely one of multiple channels in which the single-channel broadcast television station is at a competitive disadvantage. That is one factor behind the post-1995 consolidation among group owners evident in Table 3.5—groups are getting larger and now control a substantial majority of all commercial stations.

TABLE 3.5
U.S. Television Station/Cable System Ownership: 1950–2002

Year	Number of Groups	Number of Group Owned Stations	% of Commercial Stations That Are Group-Owned	% Cable Households Served by Top Five MSOs
1950	17	52	53	—
1955	62	165	40	—
1960	84	252	49	NA
1965	109	301	55	NA
1970	NA	NA	NA	20
1975	115	405	57	31
1980	144	506	69	33 (1981)
1985	180	660	73	35
1990	207	843	77	38
1995	210	898	78	53
2002	142	1150	86	60 (1999)

Notes. Adapted from *Electronic Media: A Guide to Trends in Broadcasting and Newer Technologies, 1920–1983* by C. H. Sterling, p. 60 (for data through 1980); and "Television Station Ownership in the U.S.: A Comprehensive Study (1950–2003)" by H. Howard, p. 45 for 1985–2002 data.
NA = not available.

CHANGING TECHNOLOGY

The biggest challenge to American broadcast television is not regulation, but growing competition from an expanding menu of digital options. Generally speaking, newer technologies have been less regulated than older systems. For three decades, the FCC has pursued a policy of authorizing new services with as little regulatory oversight and limitation as possible. Regulation of newer services is often limited to spectrum interference or other technical concerns. This leads, of course, to an asymmetric system of regulation about which legacy broadcasters constantly complain, arguing that the competitive marketplace is being played out on anything but the proverbial "level playing field."

The first competition came from cable television in the 1960s and broadcasters fought at the FCC to severely restrict cable services, not realizing how valuable it would be to UHF stations. The second wave was the arrival of the VCR and the scheduling and archiving power it delivered to viewers. But these were analog, not digital, and it is the latter that will dramatically change television.

DIGITAL TELEVISION

Although the conversion to broadcast high-definition television (HDTV) has been under way since the first regular HD broadcasts in the largest 10 markets in November 1998, the process has taken far longer than expected. Many smaller television stations are behind the FCC-mandated schedule in converting to HD capability. Audience penetration (households owning HD-equipped receivers) is less that 2% as this is written (early 2005), though projections suggest falling receiver prices will greatly increase the HD audience within 5 years. Not many programs are yet telecast in HD. As part of the conversion, all existing television stations, commercial and public alike, were given a second broadcast channel in the 1990s to encourage conversion. The plan is that the original channel will be turned back to the FCC for auction to other services. But the broadcast lobby has assured this will not happen until 85% of households can receive HD broadcasts either with a converter box or new television receiver. In the meantime, some stations are planning not HD, but existing quality television standards so that, using digital compression, they can transmit up to four signals on each of those two channels—and thus better compete in a multichannel world. To be fair, broad-casters face a difficult situation—an expensive conversion (a million or more dol-lars per station), yet they will not see increased revenue after the conversion (FCC Media Bureau, n.d.).

But convert they will, for television broadcasters face growing competition from digital cable and satellite services and an expanding list of portable video options, not to speak of the call of the Internet and reception of video on portable digital devices. The once mass audience for television has become increasingly splintered among a host of digital video devices and services com-peting for leisure time.

CONCLUSION

The American television business claims to be the best in the world as it consistently appeals to the interest of millions—both here and abroad. Although total audiences for legacy network prime-time programs are down by nearly half over the past 15 years, they are still larger than for any other medium, or other television program channel. Television program technical quality is unsurpassed, though there is far less agreement on program content.

Indeed, domestic criticism of American television programs, both news and entertainment, continues as strongly as ever. Many public interest groups complain that they have little voice in decisions about programming. Critics bemoan the dearth of public service and documentary programs on broadcast stations, though defenders note the availability of such material over cable networks, including Discovery, the History Channel, and CSPAN, let alone news channels.

In one sense, Americans have more viewing choices then most other countries' offer—it is not at all out of the ordinary to be able to tune 150 or 200 channels. The technical quality is unexcelled and a growing number of digital signals are becoming available. Yet Americans are offered and watch far less international news, for example, than is seen in most European nations. Successful political campaigns are increasingly defined by extensive and expensive television advertising, and thus poorer candidates or parties rarely do well.

Relatively little of this debate rises to regulatory levels anymore. In an era of conglomerate corporation control of networks and content there seems little likelihood of reinstating past rules (such as the fairness doctrine) and the general trend to deregulation will likely continue—save, perhaps for such culturally emotional content areas as indecency on the air. Whether this hands-off stance has worked and will continue to work in the public's interest, however, will only become clear with the passage of time.

It has often been said that technology is driving the American media train. Viewers can choose from off-air reception (by far the smallest choice now), cable television, direct-to-home satellite services (the fastest-growing option), as well as expanding networks by mail DVD subscription services. Further digital options will change how television looks to its viewers, though programming will remain much the same. Most Americans are perfectly happy with the television choices they have.

REFERENCES

Carter, T. B., Franklin, M. A., & Wright, J. B. (2003). *The First Amendment and the Fifth Estate: Regulation of electronic mass media* (6th ed.). New York: Foundation Press.

Communications Act of 1934. (1934). (48 Stat. 1064 as amended; 47 U.S.C.). Retrieved from www.fcc.gov/Reports/1934new.pdf

Corporation for Public Broadcasting. Retrieved from www.cpb.org

Compaine, B. M., & Gomery, D. (2000). The television industries: Broadcast, cable, and satellite. In B. M. Compaine & D. Gomery (Eds.), *Who owns the media? Competition and concentration in the mass media industry* (3rd ed.). Mahwah, NJ: Lawrence Erlbaum Associates.

Copyright Office. Retrieved from www.copyright.gov

FCC v. Pacifica Foundation. (1978). 438 U.S. 726.

FCC Media Bureau. Children's programming website: www.fcc.gov/mb/policy/kidstv.html

FCC Media Bureau. *Digital television.* Retrieved from www.fcc.gov/dtv/

FCC Media Bureau. *Obscene, profane and indecent program information.* Retrieved from www.fcc.gov/eb/broadcast/obscind.html

FCC Media Bureau. *Media ownership policy reexamination.* Retrieved from www.fcc.gov/telecom.html

FCC Media Bureau. *Political rules.* Retrieved from www.fcc.gov/mb/policy/political/

Howard, H. (2003). *Television station ownership in the U.S.: A comprehensive study (1950–2003).* Knoxville, TN: University of Tennessee, College of Communication and Information.

IT Facts. Retrieved from www.itfacts.biz/index.php?id=C0_22_1

Media Information Center. (2004). *Veronis Suhler Stevens on Communications Industry Report and PQ Media.* Retrieved March 2004, from www.mediainfocenter.org/compare/revenuews/+50_revenue-size.asp

Miller v. California. (1973). 413 U.S. 15.

Nielsen, A. C. (2000). 2000 report on television.

Public Broadcasting Act of 1967 (47 U.S.C.). Retrieved from www.cpb.org/about/history/uscode.html

Radio Act of 1927. (1927).

Sterling, C. H. (1984). *Electronic media: A guide to trends in broadcasting and newer technologies, 1920–1983.* New York: Praeger.

Sterling, C. H., & Kittross, J. M. (2002). *Stay tuned: A history of American broadcasting* (3rd ed.). Mahwah, NJ: Lawrence Erlbaum Associates.

Telecommunications Act of 1996. (1996). (110 Stat. 56, 47 U.S.C.). Retrieved from www.fcc.gov/telecom.html

PART TWO

Asia and the Pacific Rim

CHAPTER FOUR

Australia: Concentration, Competition and Revaluing the Public Interest

Nick Herd
University of Technology, Sydney

At the start of the 1990s, the Australian television system was in a state of shock. Commercial television had just gone through the largest and most disruptive round of ownership change and speculative investment in Australia's history. Caused by a major change in ownership policy, it had left the sector mired in debt. At the same time, the final phase of introducing television to this large continent was being played out with the extension of the full range of terrestrial channels to those living in regional Australia. The country was being bound together as never before by networks of time and space.

Reform was in the air. The half-century-old broadcasting law was abolished. New law intended to be technologically neutral and to facilitate the introduction of new services would be administered by a new lighter touch regulator. The prospect of new services was on the horizon as the government finally decided, after two decades of delay, to introduce subscription television. Reform of broadcasting paralleled reform of telecommunications. The staid old government telecommunications monopoly was introduced to competition. Talk of convergence was commonplace as broadcasters, telecommunications, and information technology companies began to mark their dance cards.

Some 15 years later, terrestrial television is still here. It went digital in 2001, but slow growth in take-up is a policy quandary for a government banking on

HDTV as a driver, rather than terrestrial multichanneling. The commercial television sector has recovered and is possibly more profitable than it has ever been, based on its traditional business of aggregating mass audiences and selling them to advertisers. But, its audience is fragmenting with increased competition for attention from other media, even though it has resisted the introduction of new terrestrial television services. Subscription television has arrived, but it has taken a decade and much cash to reach a quarter of the Australian population. More people have DVD players and are connected to the Internet than are connected to subscription television. The partly privatized telecommunications monopolist, Telstra, has a finger in many of these pies. The public broadcasters still live in a precarious position seeking to define their role in a multichannel universe.

BACKGROUND

The Context of Television Development

The contemporary television market in Australia consists of the publicly funded national broadcasters, the advertiser-supported commercial television broadcasters, and the subscription broadcasters. A measure of the size of the market is the amount of revenue generated, which in 2002–2003 was estimated to be nearly $A5 billion (Australian Film Commission, 2006), of which about 65% came from advertising, the rest coming from subscriptions and government allocations. Thus, the entire Australian television market is less than the annual budget of the BBC.

Almost all of Australia's 20 million people have access to five free-to-air broadcasters. Two of these are public broadcasters—the Australian Broadcasting Corporation (ABC) and the Special Broadcasting Service (SBS). The main service of each of the public broadcasters consists of one analog channel, although more recently each has been providing an additional channel in digital mode. Funding for both broadcasters comes predominantly from the government, although the SBS is allowed a limited amount of advertising. In 2002–2003 combined revenue of the public broadcasters was $A652 million (Ibid.).

Television was introduced into Australia in 1956, when the ABC and two privately owned broadcasters started in both Sydney and Melbourne. This followed a Royal Commission in 1954 that looked extensively at the role television would play in Australian society, particularly to ensure that the perceived negative influences were ameliorated and the positive influences accentuated.

The structure of the television system was decided by the government in 1953. Just as had been the case in radio, there was to be a dual commercial and national system. The initial conception was that the ABC would provide a unified national service funded by listener license fees, whereas the commercial stations would be much more closely tied to serving the needs of the communities they were licensed to serve and be funded by advertising.

Three aspects of this decision on structure are worth noting for the impact they had on subsequent policy development. First is that only superficially does the Australian system resemble an amalgam of the United States and United Kingdom approach. In the United States, the predominance of the philosophy of corporate liberalism in the way the relationship between the State and private enterprise was thought of led to a licensing system that favored the constitution of a station as a privately owned tradable commodity (Streeter, 1996). In contrast the "licensing" of the BBC through a royal charter and then the creation of the commercial service as subcontractors to the Independent Television Authority constituted stations whose primary purpose was service in pursuit of a greater public good (Jones 1999, 2000).

The ABC may have aspired to be like the BBC and have prized its independence, but its public service role was less clearly articulated and its independence contested by successive governments. What is more the functioning of the Independent Television Authority in the United Kingdom demonstrates, as Kerley (1992) argues:

> In Britain, it had been more politically acceptable to place greater bureaucratic constraints on commercial television because of the existence of a broader dominant consensus about the values to be propagated, a consensus which extended beyond political party lines. (p.72)

In comparison to the United States, it is true that commercial television stations in Australia were constituted as privately owned entities and were at least potentially tradable commodities. But, they were also subject, again potentially, to a level of political control and supervision that would have been unacceptable to the broad consensus in the United States on the role of the State in broadcasting. I say *potentially* in relation to this control, because it was not necessarily exercised and there was often a contradiction between the black letter law of regulation and the laissez-faire manner in which it was administered.

Second, although the public and the commercial sector were not competing with each other for revenue, it was assumed from the start that, as was the case in radio, there would be limited competition between commercial licensees in each market. That is, unlike the United States, the number of entrants would not be determined by the market, but by the government. This was a political decision to meet the interests of the newspaper and radio companies that wanted to enter the television market. However, this competition had later implications for the ability of the commercial sector to support the social and cultural obligations that were seen as important, and was unlike the regional monopolies being granted to the ITV companies in the U.K. (Jones, 1999, 2000).

Third, the government rejected a proposal that the transmitters of the commercial broadcasters remain in public hands, as had been the case in the United Kingdom with the introduction of ITV. The decision reflected the desire of the government to have the private sector bear a substantial amount of the cost of establishing the television system, but the investment in equipment thus gave the commercial licensees a claim on incumbency not initially intended to be a feature of the television system.

The first commercial licenses went to groups that were already well established in newspapers and radio, helping to confirm a trend toward concentration of media ownership between three groups: *The Herald* and *Weekly Times* (whose growth had been driven by Sir Keith Murdoch), Australian Consolidated Press (the Packer family), and John Fairfax Ltd. (owners of *The Sydney Morning Herald*). In the second round of commercial licenses, much the same groups were favored, except that Rupert Murdoch's News Ltd. acquired a license in Adelaide.

As was the case with radio, the administration of television was undertaken by the Minister, the Postmaster General, with the assistance of a nominally independent regulator, the Australian Broadcasting Control Board (ABCB). The function of the ABCB was to advise the Minister on the award of licenses, determine and enforce program standards for the commercial sector, and determine the technical standards of the television system. The ABCB was regulated by a board of directors appointed by the government.

The commercial and national service was extended to the other state capital cities from the end of 1959, and between 1960 and 1969 extended to provincial and rural Australia. By the late 1960s there was nearly 100% television ownership in the capital cities. A third capital city commercial service was introduced to eastern Australia in the mid-1960s.

In the roll out of television in this period a struggle occurred between the first licensees and the government over localism and networking. The licensees' vision was that television would extend out from Sydney and Melbourne that would act as hubs for the distribution of programming to the rest of the nation. If this programming network could be supported by networks of ownership, then that was all the better. However, the government insisted that each station, particularly in rural Australia, should be owned by local interests and that no station should lose control over its programming. This was a settlement that lasted until the mid-1980s.

Color television was introduced in 1975 and quickly replaced black and white. In 1980, the government established SBS TV as the second national broadcaster.

By the mid-1980s the Australian television system was relatively stable. The commercial sector was divided between Kerry Packer's Australian Consolidated Press, which controlled the Nine Network; Rupert Murdoch's News Ltd., which controlled Network Ten; and the Fairfax and HWT groups that jointly controlled the Seven Network. These networks were based in the capital cities the key to which was ownership of stations in the largest markets of Sydney and Melbourne. Outside the capital cities, regional Australia continued to be served by only one national and one commercial service.

In 1983, a Labor government led by Robert Hawke with Paul Keating as Treasurer came to power. This was a reformist government characterized by an embrace of neoliberal economic policies and progressive social policies. The long postwar boom was in decline and although Australia remained relatively prosperous, it seemed clear to Hawke and Keating the Australian economy needed to be restructured. The Australian economy was internationalized as the dollar was floated in 1983 and tariffs began to fall. This was followed over the next decade and more by microeconomic reform designed to reduce regulation, reform the labor market, make the economy more efficient, and develop a comprehensive competition policy. Many government services (e.g., transport, banking, and telecommunications) were corporatized to make them more efficient and many of these were also privatized, thus turning them over to the control of the market. The approach to government became more technocratic and economic rationalist while the size of the public service relative to GDP was reduced (Fairbrother, Svensen, & Teicher, 1997; Schwartz, 2003).

The reformist approach extended to broadcasting and to telecommunications, with dramatic changes to the structure of television from the mid-1980s. The government decided to launch the first domestic satellite, something that, among other things, greatly facilitated the networking of programming across the nation and allowed for the establishment of DBS services to remote areas of the country not previously served by television.

The government also proposed to increase the number of television services in regional Australia so that most Australians would have access to two national and three commercial channels. This policy of *equalization,* as it was called, was facilitated by aggregating smaller markets into larger ones in the eastern states so that three commercial stations served the newly enlarged market. A practical effect of this was to force the regional stations to align themselves with one of the capital city networks in order to receive a continuous stream of programming.

Next the government changed the media ownership laws. Prior to that date, no bar existed on companies owning interests across radio, television, and newspapers, which is what the major media companies did. In television, control of licenses was limited to no more than two on a national basis. In 1986–1987 the government changed the two station limit to a population reach test. A person could control licenses reaching up to 75% of the Australian population. It also introduced a ban on cross-media ownership whereby no one could control more than one radio license, television license or a daily newspaper in any one market. As Paul Keating put it companies had to choose between being "princes of print, queens of the screen or rajahs of radio" (Martin, 2001).[1]

The combined effect of the satellite, equalization, and the audience reach rule was to entrench networking in commercial television and make control of such a network more attractive, whereas the effect of the cross-media prohibition was to benefit the Murdoch and Packer interests at the expense of Fairfax and the *Herald* and *Weekly Times.* This was because Packer had no newspaper interests and Murdoch needed to sell his television interests in Australia as he had just become a U.S. citizen to pursue his media interests in that country. On the other hand, Fairfax and the *Herald* and *Weekly Times* were active in all three media and faced the prospect of seeing their respective groups broken up. What followed was a round of ownership changes that was both turbulent and economically damaging against the background of the stock market crash of 1987. (For a fuller account of these changes, see Chadwick, 1989.)

---

[1]This is a version of a remark widely attributed to Keating, the exact source of which is obscure. For another version, see Carew (1988, p. 171).

It should also be said that the satellite, equalization, and the extension of net-working led to the effective end of localism as a workable policy in television broadcasting, although its still remains a policy objective. In a country as large in area, but as sparse in population as Australia, television networking in the last two decades has been the most effective means of binding people together in both space and time and allowing for participation in what could be regarded as a truly national community (ABT, 1978–1992).

At the same time, the government began the process of introducing competition to the telecommunications market. The national government telephone monopoly was corporatized. A new carrier, Optus Communications, was licensed in 1992 to provide competition to the government-owned monopoly Telstra Corporation and both were given mobile telephone-carrier licenses. From 1997, the telecommunications sector became open to further competition (Barr, 2000).

Reform of the media sector continued with the introduction of the Broadcasting Services Act of 1992 (the Act), which now forms the basis of broadcasting law and regulation. The Act replaced the 50-year-old Broadcasting and Television Act of 1942, set up a new regulator—the Australian Broadcasting Authority (ABA)—and moved toward deregulation or coregulation in a number of areas. This is dealt with in more detail in the following section.

PRINCIPAL MEDIA POLICY OBJECTIVES

In 1976 in an earlier attempt at reform, F. J. Green, the Secretary of the Postal and Telecommunications Department, reported to his minister on the structure of the Australian broadcasting system. In the report, he recommended changes to the administration of broadcasting regulation and that the legislation giving effect to these changes should contain the following objective:

> The Australian broadcasting system should offer varied and comprehensive programs catering for diverse tastes within mass, special interest and minority audiences on a national, regional and local basis. An Australian national identity should be fostered, and programs should enrich the social, cultural and moral values of the Australian people. News and other information services should be presented in an objective and balanced manner. There should be regular pursuit of high standards, innovation and experimentation, and wherever possible, programs should be produced in Australia using Australian creative and performing talent. (Postal and Telecommunications Department, 1976, p. 42)

Green was motivated to recommend this because after more than 50 years of Australian broadcasting, no statement of objectives existed by which the performance of the broadcasting system could be assessed. Although at various times Ministers had stood in Parliament to make statements of general philosophy they were not, by and large, given any certain legal foundation, and when they were, often compromised by political expediency.

The government chose not to implement Green's recommendation, but in many ways it is a characteristic expression of the implicit values that lay behind media regulation and policy, at least since the Royal Commission on Television and would continue until the move to market-based reforms in the early 1990s.

It was notable in that it focused exclusively on programming and the role of broadcasting output in fostering prosocial outcomes, rather than on structural/economic or technological aspects of the system. These were not unimportant and featured explicitly in the contemporary broadcasting legislation (e.g., rules on ownership and control, requirements for financial viability and detailed management of technical planning), but were more tools that would allow social and cultural values to be achieved. The values espoused were diversity of program output, the importance of local interests, the promotion of Australian identity and expression, fairness, and objectivity in the presentation of news and a desire to see broadcasting leading rather than following the formation of public taste.

This is not the place to make an assessment of the strengths and weaknesses of the television system before the reforms of the 1980s and 1990s (see, e.g., Armstrong, 1980; Australian Broadcasting Tribunal, 1984, Vol. 1, chap. 10). My point is to provide a reference for the following discussion of change and continuity in media policy objectives. However, before doing that let me briefly outline the current legal status of television broadcasters and with some comments on how that came about.

The Legal Status of Television Broadcasters

Australia has a federal system of government, but the Constitution vests with the Commonwealth government the sole power to legislate and to regulate broadcasting, which it does through the *Broadcasting Services Act of 1992* (BSA) and the *Radiocommunications Act of 1992* (Radcoms Act). The BSA sets out the regulatory policy determined by the Parliament, a set of objectives for the broadcasting system and the regulatory framework for broadcasting. The Radcoms Act sets out the framework for the management of the radio spectrum.

Commercial television services operate by licenses under the BSA, which are fixed to a particular geographic area and to the use of a particular band of the spectrum. They are for a period of 5 years, but there is a presumption of renewal unless the regulator is satisfied that renewal would result in breaches of the Act. In reality, no license has failed to be renewed since the commencement of television.

The number of commercial television licenses has been strictly limited for decades and the decision to issue new ones remains one that the government will make when the current legislated moratorium runs out at the end of 2006. A super tax is also applied to the revenue of all commercial licenses and is paid into the consolidated revenue of the government.

Commercial television licenses are also subject to meeting minimum levels of Australian content and children's television that do not apply to other sectors. But, as with other broadcasting sectors, a coregulatory scheme of codes of practice applies to other areas of content regulation, such as standards of taste and decency.

Subscription television broadcasting licenses are issued under the BSA, but they are not geographically, time, or delivery mechanism specific. There is no regulated limit on the number that may be issued and they may be acquired for a small fee from the regulator. However, the utility of the license is dependent on access to a delivery mechanism, which means a relatively small proportion of the licenses issued since 1992 are actually providing services. That is, those that are controlled by the three subscription platforms—Foxtel, Optus, and Austar.

The drafters of the BSA had a less-than-perfect understanding of the subscription television business and, as a result, no license is needed to aggregate programming into a channel and supply it to one of the delivery platforms. The national broadcasters stand outside of this structure and are dealt with separately in the following section.

Regulatory Policy

Regulatory control is applied according to the perceived degree of influence a broadcasting sector is able to exert over community views (BSA S.4). This leads to the specification of a hierarchy of broadcasting service categories with commercial television subject to the most regulation, and subscription narrowcasting subject to the least regulation. This was intended to be technologically neutral because regulatory control is no longer based around the use of spectrum or the method used to deliver the service, but around the long-standing concept of influence (both positive and negative). The protection from competition that was still to be accorded to the most influential broadcasters is now to be based on their ability to shape community views, not just about political matters but also about citizens/consumers and their place in the nation (Armstrong & Lindsay, 1991).

The attempt to be technologically neutral has not lasted as we will see in the following section with the conversion to digital television, as well as the fact that since 1999, the BSA has been used as the means for what some would see as a futile attempt to regulate Internet services (see Lidgerwood, 2002, for a discussion of the divergence from the original regulatory scheme).

The BSA gives to the regulator, now the Australian Communications and Media Authority, a series of regulatory tools, but the regulatory policy requires these tools be used in a manner that in the opinion of the regulator "enables public interest considerations to be addressed in a way that does not impose unnecessary financial and administrative burdens on providers of broadcasting services *and will readily accommodate technological change"* (BSAs. 4[2]). There is in this an explicit acceptance that any regulation must impose an economic burden. Those who would argue for social and cultural goals to be achieved must demonstrate they have public interest attributes that justify this intervention in the market. Although the regulator has a degree of discretion in many areas, it is expected to exercise a form of regulatory forbearance where the public interest does not justify regulatory intervention or where such intervention may inhibit technological change.

The desire not to inhibit technological change and to see the encouragement of that as the mark of a government facilitating economic development through technological advancement was a substantial change from the caution and gradualism of previous decades (Armstrong & Lindsay, 1991, p. 15). It represented a substantial pendulum swing from the view that new technologies had to be carefully managed to avoid unwanted economic and social outcomes. This gradualism delayed the introduction of FM radio, color television, and then subscription television. This technologically conservative view was often encouraged by incumbent service providers fearful of the competition that change may bring.

The encouragement of technological change also reflected the acknowledgment Australia was quickly transforming into a service economy and that knowledge and creative industries utilizing new technologies were central to these developments. The mood of the 1990s was that government must not only avoid hindering technological development but, in many areas, seek to drive it. This can be seen in some of the Keating government's initiatives in their Creative Nation policy statement of 1994, the Howard government's incorporation of information technology policy with communications, and the decisions surrounding the conversion to digital terrestrial television.

Elements of Broadcasting Policy Objectives

The objectives for the broadcasting system as expressed in the BSA may be thought of as encompassing three broad categories—economic, cultural, and social (Armstrong & Lindsay, 1991; Flew, 1999; Screen Producers Association of Australia, 1999). Each of them is quoted from Section 3(1) of the BSA and discussed in the following paragraph.

Economic

Diversity of services: *"to promote the availability to audiences throughout Australia of a diverse range of radio and television services offering entertainment, education and information."* Diversity, especially in the context of broadcasting policy can have a number of meanings. It can refer to diversity of programs made available, to the diversity of programs chosen by viewers, to diversity of views expressed or as it does here to the diversity of services made available to audiences. It is an economic objective because it assumes the construction of a marketplace in which many different kinds of services will be offered to audiences viewed as consumers. It implies the end of the diversity dilemma by leaving it to an imagined fully competitive market to meet audience needs.

Regulatory environment: *"to provide a regulatory environment that will facilitate the development of a broadcasting industry in Australia that is efficient, competitive and responsive to audience needs."* There are two ways that this is an economic objective. First, it conceptualizes broadcasting as an industry that is intended to be efficient and competitive, rather than as a system that may have attributes that cannot be measured by economic values. The needs of the audience to which the industry is to be responsive are those needs of a consumer of entertainment, education, and information. Second, it gives to the market place a primacy in delineating the regulatory environment that echoes the admonition to the regulator not to impose unnecessary financial and administrative burdens.

Diversity of control: *"to encourage diversity in control of the more influential broadcasting services."* This is not a new objective, in that rules to mitigate concentration of ownership have been part of broadcasting legislation for some decades. What is notable is that the diversity of control is linked to influence, so that the ownership and control rules laid out elsewhere in the BSA relate to commercial television and radio only. So there is the national audience reach rule and limitation of one station to a market for commercial television, but no such restriction on subscription television. Nor do the cross media rules apply to subscription television, which allows PBL and News Ltd. to exercise control over Foxtel and a potentially unlimited number of licences.

Australian ownership: *"to ensure that Australians have effective control of the more influential broadcasting services."* Again this is not a new objective. Regulation of foreign ownership dates from the early 1950s when Parliament became concerned about British investment in Australian newspapers and radio. There is now a prohibition on foreign persons controlling a commercial television license by having company interests of more than 15% or 20% in the aggregate. (Note: CanWest meets this requirement in the TEN network stations, even though its economic interest is significantly higher.)

The foreign ownership limit for subscription television broadcasting licenses is 20% in the individual and 35% in aggregate. However it is not a control test, which is why Optus and Austar are foreign-controlled.

Program quality: *"to promote the provision of high quality and innovative programming by providers of broadcasting services."* This is also to some extent a cultural objective, but it is an economic objective because it presupposes that there will be a level of expenditure necessary to fund quality and innovation. But quality and innovation are ambiguous concepts that are difficult to define and even harder to measure.

Quality and innovation are relative to the values of the observer and tend to be loaded with class bound ideas of taste. For example, it is possible to argue that Australian commercial television produces some of the highest quality coverage of sport in the world and has been highly innovative in the techniques it has developed to bring to the viewer a heightened sense of immediacy and participation in the events being covered. This has made it highly popular and attracted substantial revenues from advertisers. Yet, in terms of cultural policy, sports programming is not valued as much as drama. Instead, subsidy is directed to underwriting the production of drama, which is more prone to market failure than is sport.

Social

Taste and decency: *"to encourage providers of broadcasting services to respect community standards in the provision of program material."* Concern about the potential of broadcasting to not only cause offense, but to also be a danger to public morality is a long-standing issue reflecting the belief that the media have the power to adversely affect social behaviors. However, the long-term trend in policy on this issue has been to move away from a process of censorship to one of providing consumer advice through a system of program classification. Also, to move away from the idea of standards imposed on broadcasters to standards developed by the broadcasters in consultation with the community. The BSA was an important step in this process. Consequently program codes that deal with the depiction of sex, violence, and offensive language and the times of day when they may be broadcast stem from the broadcasters and are registered with the regulator.

Complaints: *"to encourage the provision of means for addressing complaints about broadcasting services."* The BSA introduced a new complaints-handling mechanism whereby the broadcasters were given primary responsibility for dealing with and resolving complaints under the various codes of practice. Again it was a coregulatory approach, with the regulator becoming the forum for dealing with unresolved complaints and assessing the effectiveness of complaints handling in general.

Children: *"to ensure that providers of broadcasting services place a high priority on the protection of children from exposure to program material which may be harmful to them."* This objective may seem to be implicit in the taste and decency objective but its inclusion reflects the real politic of getting legislation through the Parliament. It was one of the amendments insisted on by Senator Brian Harradine, an independent Senator with conservative Christian values and a prominent advocate of stronger censorship, who held the balance of power in the upper house when the BSA was passed.

Balance and localism: *"to encourage providers of commercial and community broadcasting services to be responsive to the need for a fair and accurate coverage of matters of public interest and for an appropriate coverage of matters of local significance."* The pursuit of fairness and accuracy in the presentation of news has been another long-standing principle of media policy in Australia, as in many countries. Australia does not have a bill of rights and there is no explicit acknowledgment of free speech within the constitution; however, in the last decade, the High Court, in a series of decisions, has found there to be an implied right of free speech. Currently, the requirement for fairness and accuracy is operationalized through the codes of practice of the broadcasters, but it is not often tested, except through the examination of complaints.

Localism in the television system is much less than it was two decades ago and is chiefly achieved by local news and current affairs programs of both the commercial and national broadcasters. Otherwise, national networking of programs predominates with the only likely variations being to meet the differential interest in some sporting coverage.

Cultural

Australian identity: *"to promote the role of broadcasting services in developing and reflecting a sense of Australian identity, character and cultural diversity."* A high priority is placed on the use of the television system to ensure that Australians see themselves and their lives on the nation's screens and that creative expression in film and television is supported. This is a long-standing objective, but one that at times has not been easy to deliver. The start of television in Australia coincided with the availability of filmed drama programs from the United States, which very quickly came to dominate because they were popular and because it was more profitable to import these cheaper programs than it was to produce Australian equivalents. The policy response to this has been the imposition of mandatory minimum quotas for Australian content, and drama in particular, on commercial television, requiring subscription television to spend minimum amounts on Australian drama and making support for Australian production a key part of the national broadcasters charters. Direct support is also provided through subsidies for television miniseries, telemovies, and documentaries by the Commonwealth's film bank, the Film Finance Corporation.

The previous section sets out a reasonably coherent set of objectives for the broadcasting system and could be used as the indicators to measure the performance of the system as a whole and television, in particular. In reality, they are not. The regulator is under no obligation to assess the performance of commercial licensees, the national broadcasters, or subscription broadcasters against these objectives either individually or as a whole. Although the regulator may inform itself on service trends and report to the Minister on the broadcasting industry, in practice it does not do so. This reflects the move to a regulatory style characterized by a reliance on either industry coregulation or the market to meet these regulatory objectives.

THE PUBLIC BROADCASTING SYSTEM

The ABCB and the SBS as public broadcasters each have differing remits. The ABCB was founded in 1932 after the government nationalized the so-called A-class radio stations that had been licensed to provide a less populist and more uplifting programming mix that proved not to be commercially viable. Domestically the ABCB is intended to be a comprehensive broadcaster providing information and entertainment that contributes to a sense of national identity and cultural diversity. It also has specific obligations to provide educational programming and to promote the arts in Australia. Internationally, it broadcasts into the Asia-Pacific region to promote knowledge about Australia and meet the needs of expatriate Australians.

The SBS was founded in 1980 out of the developing policy of multiculturalism, which was a response to the demographic changes wrought by postwar migration to Australia, first from Southern Europe and then from Southeast Asia. Multiculturalism seeks to achieve a balance between the expectation that immigrants will assimilate the political, social, and economic values of Anglo-Celtic Australia and the contribution the cultural and language diversity of immigrants can make to the newly developing society. It is idealistic and imperfect and, to some extent, acts as a screen for persistent strains of racism in Australian society. The role of the SBS is to provide programming that meets the needs of differing language and cultural communities in Australia while exposing the wider society to that diversity.

Both broadcasters provide a single national analog television channel, which more recently has been supplemented by a digital channel. In the case of the ABCB, each state has its own daily news service.

The charter and operations of the public broadcasters are defined by legislation. They are each governed by a board of directors appointed by the Governor-General on the recommendation of the government. However, they are not subject to direction by the government in the performance of their functions on the principle that they maintain strict editorial independence from the government. This principle is adhered to but, in practice, the government can exercise a degree of control through its appointment of the Board and in its allocation of funding to the broadcasters.

Historically, the ABCB has been subjected to continuing criticism from whatever party holds power over what they perceive as political bias. In the current political climate of a conservative Commonwealth government, that bias is generally suggested to be leftist. However it is hard to demonstrate where this so-called bias exists, at least in the provision of news, and if bias does exist it is certainly countered by a strong neoconservative worldview in the News Ltd. newspapers.

Part of the reason for this level of antagonism lies in one of the strengths of the ABCB as a public broadcaster: the provision of comprehensive news and current affairs. The ABCB devotes considerable resources to its own news gathering and reportage, independent of commercial sources and government information, and with a tendency not to treat news as entertainment. This means that there are times when what it reports is unfavorable to the government. In other words, it is doing what a responsible news organization in a democratic society should be doing, treating its viewers and listeners as citizens, not consumers.

Nevertheless the current government has been at times highly critical, to the extent that in 2003, Senator Richard Alston, the Minister for Communications, lodged 68 complaints about alleged bias in the ABCB's coverage of the Iraq war. A few of them were found to be justified but the attack represented a continuation of pressure that has been applied to the ABCB since the Howard government came to power in 1996 and cut the funding to the ABCB.

Both broadcasters are funded by an annual appropriation from the Parliament, revenue generated from program sales, music and book publishing and in the case of the SBS a limited amount of advertising and sponsorship. There are no listener/viewer license fees and funding from the Parliament is not tied to movements in inflation.

Funding for the public broadcasters is contentious and the ABCB in particular argues, with some justification, that it is underfunded to perform the role with which it is charged. In actual dollars the level of appropriation to the public broadcasters has increased over recent years, but there is a real question as to whether that has been adequate, as well as whether the application of that funding has been appropriate.

In 2002–2003 of the total revenue of $A3,586 million generated by the free-to-air television system, 18% was the revenue generated by the public broadcasters. Yet the public broadcasters provide 40% of free-to-air programming annually (Australian Film Commission [AFC], 2006).

This is having an effect on programming. The commercial broadcasters are required to devote a minimum of 55% of transmission time to Australian programming. In 2000–2001, just over 59% of programming on the ABCB was Australian. Four years later, in 2003–2004, that level had declined to 49.3%, with the proportion of new Australian drama standing at 15% of total drama broadcast (AFC, 2005, p. 12).

This is an indication of the struggle the ABCB has in fulfilling its role as a comprehensive broadcaster meeting the additional objectives of education and arts programming. Historically, the ABCB has been unwilling to retreat from the obligation to be comprehensive for fear that this would lead to marginalization and justify further restrictions on funding. Yet, as the Mansfield Inquiry in to the ABCB pointed out in 1997, the ABCB is neither fully comprehensive (it has lost most sporting rights to commercial and subscription television) nor fully complementary (it competes for audiences in the same program genres as commercial television; Mansfield, 1997).

The Mansfield Inquiry recommended the ABCB remain committed to being a distinctive and comprehensive broadcaster, but that its structure should be refocused to make better use of its resources. This has happened in some areas such as devolving the management of symphony orchestras to the states. But the main recommendation that the ABCB be restructured as a program publisher, with production largely outsourced has never been implemented.

Conversely the dilemma for the SBS is that it has to meet the special needs of language and cultural communities while providing programming that attracts a more general audience. Strategically it attempts to do this by providing a mix of non-English language material subtitled in English combined with original English language programming. This mix means that, in rating terms, it rarely competes successfully with any other broadcaster, but that because of the specialist programming, its reach into the community is significant and this is what attracts the advertisers to the channel.

SBS is smaller than the ABCB and is structured more like the publisher model advocated for the ABCB. It produces original programming, including news and current affairs in-house, but outsources its drama and documentary production from the independent production sector. In its news and current affairs coverage, it tends to have a greater focus on international news, particularly relevant to the ethnic background of its audience.

TECHNOLOGICAL DEVELOPMENTS AND PUBLIC POLICY

The most significant technological developments in the television sector since the 1980s have been the introduction of multichannel television or subscription television and the start of the transition to digital television. As indicated in the previous section, the avowed aim of media policy has been to be technologically neutral and to allow the marketplace, not the government, to determine the rollout and development of new technologies; however, this has not always been the case.

Subscription Television

Australia came late to the introduction of subscription television, although its introduction had been under consideration for at least two decades prior to its start in 1995. In 1982, after an extensive inquiry, the Australian Broadcasting Tribunal recommended its introduction "as soon as practicable." The Hawke government did not act on this, and instead instated a moratorium until 1992 with the enactment of the BSA.

The original scheme in the BSA was that subscription television would be a direct-to-home satellite service utilizing the transponders of the satellite controlled by the newly established Optus. This was not only to ensure that the sale of the government's satellite assets would be more attractive, but because cable television was believed too expensive and would take too long to roll out to a significant portion of the population. Microwave was seen as technically unsuitable to be used for television in most areas of Australia. Satellite was seen as the best means of launching services that would become immediately available to the entire population. The ABCB and the SBS were to be given licenses but the other satellite licenses were to be auctioned and it was widely accepted they would go to established companies like PBL and News Ltd. The government also mandated the transmission standard for the satellite be digital, potentially putting Australia in the forefront of technological change.

The BSA envisaged cable and microwave-delivered services would come later after the satellite services were established. As a result, the BSA also provided for licenses utilizing these technologies to be allocated after payment of a small fee. What is more, the government proceeded to also auction microwave spectrum, believing that it would be used for other communication services.

This plan for the introduction of subscription television came quickly and spectacularly undone. The auction process was bungled administratively to the embarrassment of the government. The company that emerged from this Australis Media was associated with none of the already-established media players who found themselves frozen out of subscription television in the short term. The government had to ban subscription television, utilizing microwave in the short term because the purchasers of the microwave spectrum had also acquired subscription licenses and intended to start broadcasting before Australis Media could commence.

Australis eventually bought out the microwave licensees and was also saddled with the cost implications of starting a subscription service with a digital transmission standard that applied nowhere else in the world. It also paid very large sums of money for Hollywood movie rights, but was prevented from getting access to significant sporting rights because of the antisiphoning regime that was designed to keep major sporting events on free-to-air television.

Despite this, Australis might have succeeded if the two telephone carriers had not also started their own subscription television services in competition. In policy terms, the introduction of a successful subscription television service was ultimately sacrificed to pursuit of competition policy, even if that competition turned out to be ruinous.

Optus started Optus Vision and Telstra formed a joint venture with News Corp and Kerry Packer's Publishing and Broadcasting Ltd. called Foxtel. The carriers saw subscription television as the vehicle that would entice homes to connect to their networks and drive demand for other communications services. They also needed to get a head start on establishing their market position before open competition in telecommunications was introduced in 1997. To implement this plan, each carrier spent billions of dollars laying hybrid fiber-optic cable past just over 2 million urban homes, often in the same streets, before the massive losses incurred in doing this duplication of infrastructure stopped the construction in 1997.

Both Foxtel and Optus Vision launched their services in 1995 in competition with Australis. All three services lost substantial amounts of money—$A105,8 million in 1996–1997. Australis was the first to succumb collapsing in 1998, after an attempt to merge with Foxtel was vetoed by the competition regulator. The assets of Australis were divided between Foxtel and Austar, which took over the satellite service of Australis (Westfield, 2000).

The ABCB's plan to launch a subscription news channel was defeated by the economics of subscription television and by competition from Sky News, a joint venture between B-Sky-B, PBL, and the Seven Network. SBS more successfully launched a foreign language movie channel as a joint venture.

In June 2005, there were a total of 1,694,450 subscribers across all three platforms out of just over 7 million television households; a penetration rate of 24% after 10 years (AFC, 2006). The platforms are reluctant to publish their "churn" rates, but it is assumed that a significant number of households have tried subscription television and rejected it. It is not that Australians are reluctant to pay for content, as the spectacular success of DVD players demonstrates; metropolitan households with DVD players have grown from 12% in 2001 to 62% in 2004 (AFC, 2006). It may be a timing issue and the rise of the DVD has cut into the growth of subscription television, presenting many households with a better value proposition to extend the range of their television viewing.

The platforms as a whole have yet to see a profit, although it is understood that Austar is closest to doing so. This does not mean that certain sections of the industry are not profitable; it is understood that many of the channels are quite profitable as more than 60% of subscription revenue goes to the channels.

In November 2002, the Australian Competition and Consumer Commission approved a channel sharing arrangement between Foxtel and Optus that allowed both platforms to show the same channels and to bundle subscription television and telephony. In effect, Optus has been withdrawing from the subscription business and is becoming a reseller of Foxtel services, which now claims two thirds of all subscribers. In March 2004, Foxtel commenced a transition to digital, including offering subscribers new video-on-demand, higher levels of interactivity, additional radio channels, and a PVR. It is not known how many customers have converted to digital.

Digital Television

In January 2001, Australia introduced digital terrestrial television broadcasting and began what is supposed to be a period of transition in which the free-to-air television system is converted from analog to digital. The initial period of transition is to be 8 years but that is being reviewed in 2006.

During this time of transition, the free-to-air broadcasters are required to simulcast their services in both digital and analog modes. From July 2003, they have been required to provide, in addition to standard definition digital television, at least 1,040 hours per year of HDTV.

Shortly after the passage of the BSA, the future of the terrestrial television system began to be considered when the Australian Broadcasting Authority in 1993 established the Specialist Group on Digital Terrestrial Television Broadcasting. As the name suggests, it was made up predominantly of broadcast engineers and planners and it went about its work in a relatively low-key manner with no public input and virtually no public discussion. The Group viewed its work as purely technical and saw no need to consult with other potential stakeholders such as telecommunications providers and subscription television.

The Group provided its first report to the ABA in 1995 and its second report in 1997. The Specialist Group's recommendations were taken up by the ABA and provided in advice to the Minister, which put a heavy emphasis on HDTV, recommended against the introduction of new services, such as terrestrial subscription services or new commercial television services.

The recommendations of the Group were supported by both the national and commercial broadcasters. They argued the transition to digital television was a natural evolution of television technology similar to the migration from black and white to color. It was a quality issue, they said, designed to give the consumers compelling reasons to upgrade their television sets and provide a service equal to that being offered by the digital subscription services and the DVD.

They argued that they be given a 7Mhz channel on loan, probably from 2000 until the digital transition was complete, then they would hand the channel back. Initially they also argued for a 15-year moratorium on the licensing of new commercial television services. They offered to pay for the digital conversion themselves, at least in the capital cities, for the regional operators wanted some assistance in the form of rebates on their license fees.

However, by 1997, it was increasingly evident that digital terrestrial conversion was not simply a technical issue and that it had serious implications for the future development of communications in Australia. Outside the television sector, there was significant opposition to what was proposed. Opponents argued that this was not an extension of the existing analog service, but potentially created a substantially new service. The allocation of 7 MHz was more than was needed to provide a digital SDTV service and would allow enough spectrum for multichannel television and data casting.

Existing and potential telecommunications providers argued that the spare spectrum should be made available for new communications services and the subscription sector opposed free-to-air multichannel television while they were still in the development phase of their business. Others were skeptical of the attractiveness of HDTV as a consumer technology, that it was not different enough to attract audiences to make the switchover. In March 1998, the government announced its decision:

- Broadcasters would be loaned the second 7Mhz channel;
- They would have to simulcast until the end of 2008;
- They would have to commence digital broadcasting by January 1, 2001, or no later than 2004, in regional areas;
- The commercial broadcasters could not multichannel, but the ABCB and SBS might be able to do so;
- Spare capacity not needed for HDTV could be used for enhanced services or data casting, but there would have to be a license fee paid for data casting.

By the middle of 1998, the Parliament had approved this framework, but the Minister was required to undertake a series of reviews to flesh out some of the detail. These reviews were conducted by the Minister's Department throughout most of 1999. Coincidentally, the Treasurer also asked the Productivity Commission to look at the Broadcasting Services Act, as part of the series of regular reviews stemming from the competition policy agreement between the Commonwealth and the States. This review was not intended to be about digital television, but it quickly became so as it became another venue for argument between the parties and the Commission itself took a keen interest in the digital television policy of the government (Productivity Commission, 2000; for an extensive account of the transition to digital see Given, 2003).

By the time that the transition to digital commenced, it seemed only the terrestrial broadcasters and the government were convinced the policy outcome made sense and was going to work. Along the way to commencement, a number of compromises were made. Instead of using the whole 7Mhz to broadcast a 1080 line HD signal, the spectrum could be used to broadcast a 720 line HD signal and a 576 line SD signal. This was done to ensure that consumer equipment at a reasonable price was available from the start, in recognition of the fact that no other country was proposing to use as advanced a HDTV system as Australia.

Also, a lot work went into defining what was meant by data casting, multi-channeling by the national broadcasters, and enhanced programming. This work had two principle objectives. The government perceived a need to ensure that the commercial broadcasters were, in fact, not being given permission to start new services and there was the need to ensure that the new services that were proposed would not provide competition to the terrestrial broadcasters. The consequences of this were data casting was so narrowly defined so as to exclude television programs in any of the genres commonly provided by free-to-air television. As a result, interest from new players in providing data casting services evaporated when the government made the spectrum available for allocation. Only the established broadcasters have so far taken up data-casting licenses.

For the national broadcasters, although they could multichannel national news, sport and drama programs were excluded from what could be in the multichannels. The ABCB attempted to provide a children's channel and a youth channel, but with restricted financial resources, they did not last.

Nearly 5 years after the start of digital television, it is clear the first target date for analog switch off at the end of 2008 will not be met. About 15% of television households have converted by the end of 2005 to digital and an unknown number of subscription television households (DCITA, 2006). Many households have more than one television so that the total set population is likely to be between 14 and 20 million sets.

It is also hard to know what to make of digital subscription television because this has not so far formed a part of the government's digital transition strategy, but arose from the sectors desire to improve their offering to attract more subscribers. In fact, many households with subscription television may also still have sets connected to the analog terrestrial system.

In March 2006, the government announced it was in the process of developing what it called "a road map to digital conversion" by calling for more public input. It acknowledged analog switch-off will not take place as planned and is hoping for 2010–2012 as the new goal. The restrictions on multichanneling by the national broadcasters will be lifted, but the commercial networks will not be able to multichannel until after analog switch-off. However, it remains uncertain about what other measures might be needed to drive digital.

MEDIA CONCENTRATION AND PLURALISM

The commercial sector is constituted by 48 stations that form nine ownership groups but are organized into three program networks led by the ownership groups based on the mainland state capital city stations. Seven Network Ltd. is controlled by the company interests of Kerry Stokes, and is also the second largest magazine publisher in Australia. Publishing and Broadcasting Ltd., which is controlled by James Packer, owns the Nine Network, as well as having investments in subscription television, magazine publishing, gaming, and the largest Australian Internet portal Ninemsn. Kerry Packer, James's father, was one of the most influential people in Australian media but died in December 2005. There is speculation James Packer wants to exit the television business. TEN Network Holdings owns Network Ten and although CanWest does not control the licenses within the meaning of the relevant broadcasting law, the largest financial interest is held by this Canadian company.

There are six regional television groups. Southern Cross Broadcasting (Australia) Ltd. also controls a significant network of radio stations and the largest independent television producer and distributor, Southern Star. WIN Television is controlled by the Gordon family and also owns the independent production company, Crawford Productions. Prime Television Ltd. is controlled by Paul Ramsay, whose other substantial interest is pharmaceutical retailing. The other groupings are NBN Television, Sunraysia Television, and Imparja Television.

There are three cable/satellite subscription television platforms. In addition there is a small community television broadcast sector.

In subscription television, two of the three platforms are foreign-controlled; Optus TV, which is a subsidiary of the second largest telecommunications company, is owned by Singapore Telecom; and Austar, the regional platform is controlled by a partnership between United Global Communications and Castle Harlan Mezzanine Partners.

The largest platform, Foxtel, is 50% owned by the dominant telecommunications provider Telstra Corporation with PBL and News Ltd., each having a 25% stake. Telstra Corporation is still majority-owned by the Commonwealth government. At the level of the three platforms, ownership concentration is high and competition between them has arguably reduced with the advent in 2003 of arrangements whereby they share most of the same programming. On the platforms there are more than 60 channels, the majority of which are not owned by the platforms themselves, consisting of a mix of locally constructed channels and international brands like CNN, BBC World, and Discovery.

In terms of viewers, the commercial broadcasters between them share about 62% of viewing, the public broadcasters about 19%, and subscription television about 17%. Traditionally, the Nine Network takes the largest share of viewers. The Seven Network is the perennial second place network, with Network Ten in third place which, by targeting the 16- to 39-year-olds desired by advertisers, is the most profitable. Overall, commercial television in Australia is arguably the most profitable in the world regularly returning margins more than 20% of turnover before taxes.

The ABCB's share fluctuates around 12% with strong news, current affairs, and factual programming and a heavy reliance on imported drama from the United Kingdom. SBS-TV market share is small, which reflects its brief to provide a substantial amount of programming in languages other than English in order to meet the cultural and linguistic diversity in the Australian community.

This sets out briefly the contours of the contemporary television market and shows the main company interests. Ownership is relatively concentrated, but also a number of the companies are run by proprietors who are used to shaping the voice and direction of the asset they control. The most important of these are the late Kerry Packer, Rupert Murdoch, and Kerry Stokes. Rupert Murdoch is important because although it might seem News Ltd. is a relatively minor player in the Australian television landscape, the combined media interests of News Ltd. in

Australia give the company and Rupert Murdoch enormous clout when it comes to the determination of television policy.

As just indicated, the introduction of the cross-media rules in 1986–1987 combined with the audience reach rule and television aggregation produced two main effects. First, it introduced a greater degree of competition between radio, television, and newspapers by breaking up two of the companies that had been prominent in all three—the *Herald* and *Weekly Times* and John Fairfax. Rupert Murdoch sold his interests in the TEN Network so as to concentrate on making what was eventually a successful bid for the *Herald* and *Weekly Times* group in 1987. This move gave Murdoch dominance in the Australian newspaper market controlling more than 60% of capital city newspaper circulation. John Fairfax moved out of television and radio entirely to concentrate on newspapers.

Second, it exacerbated a tendency for concentration of ownership and control within the sectors as a result of which the Australian television sector is relatively highly concentrated across its three elements—public, commercial, and subscription television. The introduction of subscription television produced the potential for a greater diffusion of control, but as we have seen the relatively weaker rules on ownership have allowed for subscription television to be largely controlled by telecommunications, newspaper, and television interests.

It has been a long-standing objective of the Howard government to change the media ownership laws in Australia. In particular they propose to remove the foreign ownership rules entirely and to reinstate some of the ability of companies to own businesses across radio, television, and newspapers. What has stopped this in the past has been the opposition of the Senate to changes, which blocked the legislation in 2002 (see Given, 2002, and Thomas, 2002, for a critique of the proposal). During the 2004 election the government gained control of the Senate, and in 2006 foreign ownership and cross media ownership were allowed, prompting the Seven and Nine Networks to enter into substantial partnerships with foreign private-equity firms.

A number of reasons have been advanced for change. The first is technologically determinist pointing to the rise of the Internet and other communications services since 1987. This, it is argued, has changed the way people access news and information and created a plurality of voices that were not present in 1987. Although this effect of the Internet is no doubt true the argument tends to overplay the extent of the change in consumer behavior. Most people still access news and information from the mainstream media, with television regularly nominated as the major source of news. The behavior of politicians also shows mainstream media still play a dominating role in determining the news agenda.

It is also argued that technological change is creating opportunities that the existing media ownership framework may be constraining. How this is so is not quite clear. For example, despite being restricted to television, PBL has established a series of successful online businesses, such as the Ninemsn joint venture with Microsoft, which is one the most accessed Internet portals in Australia. The new media opportunity for PBL the current rules prevent is the takeover of John Fairfax, with its large classified advertising business that could be combined with PBL's online directory business.

Another argument is that the rules put a drag on the growth of internationally competitive Australian media companies—the foreign ownership rules deter offshore capital raising and cross-media rules prevent synergies. This argument has been most consistently advanced by John Fairfax. However, the ownership rules do not seem to have prevented News Ltd. from its international expansion over the last two decades.

Then there is the argument that consistent with the National Competition Policy Agreement between the State and Commonwealth governments: Industry specific rules should be lifted in favor of the application of general competition policy. This argument tends to downplay the idea that the media are not like other industries and that they have social and cultural benefits—positive externalities—that are not produced by the market alone.

Most of these arguments are economic in nature and reflect the growing tendency to see issues of media policy largely in terms of managing the market, making it more efficient and promoting competition. Given the desire of the government and its legislative control, it is likely that there will be changes in media ownership law and the structure of the media. The expectation being that the number of media companies in Australia will decline in number.

What is not clear is whether the ownership law changes will be combined with the introduction of new services. Nor is it clear that there is any serious analysis of the effect that changes in market structure will have on pluralism and diversity. For as Richard Van der Wurff (2004) has argued:

> . . . the relationship between broadcasting market structure, broadcaster conduct, and diversity are complex and multidimensional. Both competition and concentration can have positive and negative consequences for diversity. Policymakers and regulators, therefore, should systematically investigate the specific consequences of intended or unintended changes in market structure for broadcaster conduct in their particular market, rather than rely on general political–economic guidelines. (p. 148)

What is also not being addressed is the role the public broadcasters might have in a more highly concentrated media market, particularly given the trend to maintain public service expectations while restricting funding.

CONCLUSIONS

The major shift in public policy objectives in the last 15 years has been the rise and implementation of a neoliberal economic agenda that began under the Labor party government in 1983–1996 and has been continued since by the Liberal-National party government. This has led to a wave of microeconomic reform that has strengthened the economy and stimulated growth in productivity, investment, and consumption. These trends have benefited advertiser-funded media such as commercial television which arrested and reversed a decline in profitability in the late 1980s and helped underwrite the cost of introducing new consumer media, such as subscription television.

Microeconomic reform led to changes in the role of government in the economy. In particular, reform has led to the privatization of government services that could be supported by the market, and to the foregrounding of competition policy in the machinery of government. Market values and competition have grown in importance in media regulation since 1992 with fostering of deregulatory or coregulatory approaches. Paradoxically, this apparent retreat from industry-specific regulation has been more than matched by a strengthening of competition, fiduciary, and corporate governance regulation of business.

The major breaks with past television policy approaches came first in 1986–1987 with the changes in media ownership rules and in 1992 with the BSA. The former, in combination with the domestic satellite and aggregation facilitated greater networking and the consolidation of commercial television into a unified national system. The ownership changes led to a lessening of ownership concentration across media sectors but to an increase in concentration within television and newspapers.

The BSA formulated a more coherent expression of media policy, helped introduce new services and marked a more enthusiastic embrace of technological change. However, the transition to a multichannel television universe and a fully digital world has been slower than would have been predicted in 1992. Digital competitors to broadcast television such as the Internet and DVD have arisen and affected the growth of both subscription and digital terrestrial television. However, commercial television has also been particularly successful in being able to influence policy so as to preserve its oligopoly and central role in the Australian television landscape. In large measure this represents a continuation of the "media mogul" orientation of media policy/politics in Australia.

What has also characterized the period, fostered in part by the centering of the market in policy deliberations and the resulting tendency to recast citizens as consumers, has been a shift in the notion of public interest. Public interest in broadcasting now encompasses economic values in a way that was not the case two decades ago and has led to a lessening in the idea of public interest in broadcasting being primarily about social and cultural values. These have not gone away and remain as stated goals, but in the last decade the idea that commercial television is there to perform a public service or to meet the public interest in the old sense has withered considerably in public debate. This puts the public broadcasters in an increasingly difficult position when they face increased competition for audiences and challenges to their relevance.

REFERENCES

Armstrong, M. (1980). The Broadcasting and Television Act, 1948–1976: A case study of the Australian Broadcasting Control Board. In R. Tomasic (Ed.), *Legislation and society in Australia* (pp. 124–145). Sydney: Law Foundation of NSW and Allen and Unwin.

Armstrong, M. (1982). *Broadcasting law and policy in Australia.* Sydney: Butterworths.

Armstrong, M., & Lindsay, D. (1991). *The fifty year revision of broadcasting law: The Exposure draft Broadcasting Services Bill.* South Melbourne: Centre for International Research on Communications and Information Technologies.

Australian Broadcasting Tribunal. (1978–1992). *Annual report.* Canberra: Australian Government Publishing Service.

Australian Broadcasting Tribunal. (1984). *Satellite program services: Report of the inquiry into the regulation of the use of satellite program services by broadcasters.* Canberra: Australian Government Publishing Service.

Australian Broadcasting Authority. (1992–2005). *Annual reports.* Canberra: Australian Government Publishing Service.

Australian Film Commission. (2005). *Submission to the Department of Communications Information Technology and the Arts ABCB Funding Adequacy and Efficiency Review.* Retrieved June 13, 2006, from www.afc.gov/au/downloads/policies/abcreview_afcsub_final.pdf

Australian Film Commission. (2006). *Get the picture online.* Retrieved June 13, 2006, from www.afc.gov.au/gtp/http://www.afc.gov.au/gtp/wftvfast.html

Barr, T. (2000). *Newmedia.com: The changing face of Australia's media and communications.* Sydney: Allen and Unwin.

Bonney, B., & Wilson, H. (1983). *Australia's Commercial Media.* South Melbourne: Macmillan.

Carew, E. (1988). *Keating: A biography.* Sydney: Allen & Unwin.

Chadwick, P. (1989). *Media mates: Carving up Australia's media.* Melbourne: Macmillan.

Cook, J. R. (1992). *The development of Broadcasting policy in Australia with particular reference to the period of the Hawke Labor Government.* Unpublished doctoral dissertation, University of Washington.

Department of Communications Information Technology and the Arts (DCITA). (2006). *Meeting the digital challenge: Reforming Australia's media in the digital age, Canberra.* Retrieved from www.dcita.gov.au/broad/media_reform_options

Fairbrother, P., Svensen, S., & Teicher, J. (1997). The ascendancy of neo-liberalism in Australia. *Capital and Class, 63,* 1–12.

Flew, T. (1999). *Submission to the Productivity Commission Inquiry into broadcasting. Submission #64, Productivity Commission.* Retrieved May 14, 2005, from www.pc.gov.au/inquiry/broadcst/subs/sub064.pdf

Given, J. (2002). *Submission 31 to the Senate Environment, Communications, Information Technology and Arts Legislation Committee, Broadcasting Services Amendment (Media Ownership) Bill 2002 Inquiry, Parliament of Australia.* Retrieved from www.aph.gov.au/senate/committee/ecita_ctte/completed_inquiries/2002-04/media_ownership/submissions/sublist.htm

Given, J. (2003). *Turning off the television: Broadcasting's uncertain future.* Sydney: UNSW Press.

Jones, P. (1999). *Submission to the Productivity Commission Inquiry into Broadcasting, Submission #143, Productivity Commission.* Retrieved June 13, 2006, from www.pc.gov.au/inquiry/broadcst/subs/sub143.pdf

Jones, P. (2000). Democratic norms and means of communication: Public sphere, fourth estate, freedom of communication. *Critical Horizons, 1*(2), 307–339.

Kerley, M. (1992). *Commercial television in Australia: Government policy and regulation 1953–1963.* M.A. Unpublished doctoral dissertation, Australian National University, Canberra.

Lidgerwood, C. (2002). Reactive, not proactive: Recent trends in Australian broadcasting regulation. *Agenda, 9*(1), 22–32.

Mansfield, B. (1997). *The challenge of a better ABCB.* Canberra: Australian Government Publishing Service.

Martin, P. (2001). Alston steps up campaign for media ownership review, PM, 30 August, ABCB Radio. Retrieved June 13, 2006, from www.abc.net.au/pm/stories/S355297

Postal and Telecommunications Department. (1976). *Australian broadcasting: A report on the structure of the Australian broadcasting system and associated matters.* Canberra: Australian Government Printer.

Productivity Commission. (2000). *Broadcasting: Inquiry report, Report No. 11.* Canberra: Ausinfo.

Schwartz, H. (2003). Economic rationalisms in Canberra and Canada: Public sector reorganisation, politics and power. *Australian Economic History Review, 43*(1), 45–65.

Streeter, T. (1996). *Selling the air: A critique of the policy of commercial broadcasting in the United States.* Chicago: University of Chicago Press.

Screen Producers Association of Australia. (1999). *Submission to the Productivity Commission Inquiry into Broadcasting, Submission #47, Productivity Commission.* Retrieved June 13, 2006, from www.pc.gov.au/inquiry/broadcst/subs/sub047.pdf

Senate Environment, Communications, Information Technology and Arts Legislation Committee. (2002). *Report on the Broadcasting Services Amendment (Media Ownership) Bill 2002, Parliament of Australia.* Retrieved June 13, 2006, from www.aph.gov.au/senate/committee/ecita_ctte/completed_inquiries/2002-04/media_ownership/report/report.pdf

Thomas, J. (2002). *Submission 34 to the Senate Environment, Communications, Information Technology and Arts Legislation Committee, Broadcasting Services Amendment (Media Ownership) Bill 2002 Inquiry, Parliament of Australia.* Retrieved June 13, 2006, from www.aph.gov.au/senate/committee/ecita_ctte/completed_inquiries/2002-04/media_ownership/submissions/sublist.htm

Van der Wurff, R. (2004). Program choices of multi-channel broadcasters and diversity of program supply in the Netherlands. *Journal of Broadcasting and Electronic Media, 48*(1), 134–150.

Westfield, M. (2000). *The gatekeepers: The global media battle to control Australia's pay TV.* Sydney: Pluto Press.

CHAPTER FIVE

China's Television in Transition

Hu Zhengrong
Hong Li
Communication University of China

Like many other countries, China has witnessed breathtaking changes in the media industry during the past half-century. Its difference lies in the miraculous reforms undertaken that resulted in creating dynamism in many fields, including the media industry.

This chapter intends to examine, from a multidimensional perspective and with a historical and critical approach, the changes that have occurred in China's media industry, the roots and drivers of these changes, and the future trend toward media commercialization and democratization. It will then attempt to investigate how media policymaking affects the regulation and deregulation of media practice, and its consequent influence on the developing pace and scale. The challenging part centers on the contradiction between the uncompromising view about reform movements adopted by the Chinese government, and the rather unsteady actions of the media industry due to the fact that no existing models can be imitated in a Chinese context. From an academic perspective intended to pin down the hidden rules of the game, we can assume that the controversy, to some extent, will dissolve when we find the correct relationship between the market economy and political influence.

This chapter consists of eight parts, each of which explores different aspects regarding the development of the media industry. For instance, Part I examines chronologically the history of China's television and the underpinning principles of China's media policy before the 1990s. Part II focuses on the chief objectives of media policy separated into three distinct divisions. Parts III and IV touch on both the public sphere of broadcast media and the freedom of press. This is a sensitive topic for China, as it is extremely hard to determine whether to be more politics-led or more market-oriented. Part V discusses the notion that the attributes of market economy are only accepted partially by the media organs—"partially" refers to the concepts of market economy being introduced gradually with regard to the consolidation of political or ideological intentions. Part VI concentrates chiefly on the rapid changes in technology, which have played crucial roles in the advancement of China's media. Part VII investigates media concentration and pluralism, though with strong Chinese characteristics, and predicts the trends in the regulatory framework to protect media pluralism. Finally, Part VIII assesses the media industry by discussing the major shifts in public policy objectives over the past 15 years, the television sector's increasingly popular concept of providing a service, and the balance between public interest and the market. The final conclusion will highlight crucial problems faced by the media, such as the major threats to media freedom, and the health of the sector in terms of quality, diversity and serving the public interest.

BACKGROUND

China's television industry has undertaken an incredible increase both in scale and capacity since its foundation on May 1, 1958, when China's first television station was launched at its experimental stage (Guo, 1997). By the end of 2003, the total number of China's television stations reached 363 with channels rocketing up at 2,094, covering 94.82% of the population of 1.3 billion. Meanwhile, the number of cable subscribers increased to 100 million (China's Radio & TV, 2005). China's television system can be investigated further by looking at the sequence of the growth of the country's socialist construction as a whole. The entire picture can be divided chronologically into four sections: (1) the early years; (2) the cultural revolution; (3) the reform and opening up; and (4) the WTO and globalization.

Early Years

On May 1, 1958, China's first television station was first tested in a trial stage, and then officially put into operation on September 2. China was in the period of the domestic movement known as the "Great Leap Forward," motivated by the Communist Party of China (CPC), with international, technical, and political assistance from the former Soviet Union. The introduction of Shanghai Television on October 1 and Harbin Television (which later became a provincial television station) on December 20 marked the birth of China's television sector.

However, this political inspiration led to a rapid increase in the number of television stations with little consideration of the economic and social situation at that time. In accordance with the policy known as the "Great Leap Forward in Broadcasting" proposed in the Fifth National Broadcasting Working Conference in April 1958, television stations and relay stations grew to 36 in early 1963 (Guo, 1997, p. 8) which resulted in a contradiction between economic development and spiritual demands. As a result, the unprecedented economic hardships of 1960–1963 brought to a halt the importing of television sets, and possessing domestic sets was seen as excessive consumption. Toward the end of 1960, a policy was implemented at Beijing Television known as "Slimming Administration & Reducing Programs," which led to the readjustment of national broadcasting to only eight stations from the original 36, until August 1965 when two more were added. Although the established alliance with the former Soviet Union had broken up due to both national interests and ideological differences, markets in other parts of the world were there to embrace China's self-made programs. To meet the requirements of State foreign policy in 1963, the Central Broadcasting Bureau formulated a brand-new guiding principle emphasizing a policy of "setting foot in Beijing while keeping the whole world in view" (Guo, 1997, p. 8).

The media, without any relative autonomy, can only rise and fall with the Party (Zhao, 1998, p. 33). It is obvious that the policies made only considered the media to be nothing more than propaganda for the Party's policies and ideologies. Accordingly, the Central Bureau for Administration of Broadcasting was set up to handle this task, and was responsible for the News Department of the State Council. In its 1958 report submitted to the Central Committee of the CPC and the State Council, the task of the television sector was defined as "1) to propagate the policy of the Party and the State; 2) to report the achievement of the socialist cause; 3) to proliferate technological and social education; 4) to enrich the cultural life of people and 5) to promote international exchange" (Chinese Academy of Social Science, 1987, p. 10). So, the television sector of this period was heavily politicized, and used principally as the mouthpiece of the Party and the State. The needs of the mass population were largely ignored. The Cultural Revolution can be viewed as such an example.

The Cultural Revolution

The Cultural Revolution (1966–1976) presented an inhumane picture that reflected China's political, economic, and cultural undertakings at that time. The undemocratic tendencies in the Party's concept of the media became unquestioned tools of Mao's movement (Zhao, 1998, p. 32). It has been suggested that the Cultural Revolution was a period when the "glorious traditions" of "the Party and people's journalism" were violated, and that the press was not under the leadership of the Party but in the hands of a few individuals in their pursuit of power. During this 10-year period, the television sector was a political instrument of the Gang of Four (Si Ren Bang) whose sole intention was to impose their will on the nation. They labeled television as "a full-scale instrument for the proletariat dictatorship," hence it was subjected to the delivery of the message from above and turned a blind eye to the requests of the masses from below.

Once out of harmony with the Party's intentions, programs were discontinued with no consideration of public opinion. As a result, the Beijing Television was ordered to stop broadcasting on January 6, 1967, and this was followed by similar actions by most of the television stations in China. It was not until April 1969 when the Ninth National Conference of the CPC was held, announcing the end of this chaotic operation (Guo, 1997). Then in early 1970, a policy was devised at the National Television Seminar initiated by the Central Broadcasting Bureau, which introduced the experimental testing of color television while maintaining the dominance of black-and-white television sets. In 1973, color was introduced to stations in Beijing, Shanghai, and Tianjin (Chang, 2002). In the early 1980s, all television stations were equipped to broadcast in color on the phase alternation line (PAL) system, which was formally approved by the State Council (Chang, 2002). By the end of 1976, the total number of television stations amounted to 39, reaching 300 million people (Xu, 2003). The 10-year Cultural Revolution produced an abnormal media system overshadowed by the power of ultra-leftists, which eventually fueled the movement toward media reform in the post-Mao era.

Reform and Opening Up

There seems to be no question that the Cultural Revolution was not only a gross policy error in the name of ideological purity but was also a dark page in CCP's history (Wang, 2002, p. 29). It was not until the late 1970s and early 1980s when Deng Xiaoping returned to power (after being purged three times) and gained complete control over the party's Central Committee and its Politburo, and intelligently generated pragmatic reform called "opening up to the world." In December 1978, the Third Plenary Session of the 11th Central Party Committee convened to discuss the fate and future of China. Finally, a strategic decision was made to shift the focus of the Party from the ideological "class struggle" to practical economic development.

The development of Chinese television witnessed peaks and troughs with China's political and social changes for almost two decades until the 1980s when, as a result of an ever-increasing awareness of development and rapid technological advances, Chinese television evolved into what has now become an essential part of people's everyday life. In January 1979, the Shanghai Television broadcast an advertisement for wine, the first of its kind in China, and was an indication that the television sector was seeking some degree of economic independence.

In 1983, the 11th National Working Conference on Radio and Television issued the "Program of Radio and Television" decree, which allowed television stations to be established at the county, city, provincial, and national levels (also known as the Four Tier Operation of Radio & TV and Overlapping Coverage). This can be seen to have strengthened the television infrastructure (Chang, 2002). By partially decentralizing regulatory powers to a lower level, this guideline was intended not only to speed up infrastructural developments, but also to increase the population's exposure to television programs. Consequently, radio and television stations sprung up all over the country and by the end of 1987, the total number of television stations reached 586 and covered 81.3% of the entire population, showing that decentralization obviously breeds competition in the media industry (Chang, 2002, p. 14). It is equally noteworthy that cable television stations increased to 429 and had 200 million subscribers since the introduction of cable in 1976 (Ai, 2002).

In 1982, the Ministry of Radio and Television was formed to oversee the accelerating radio and television industries. From then on, numerous decrees, regulations, and laws have been issued to govern every aspect of television and cable production, dissemination, and consumption, as well as foreign imports and services. The policies before 1992 were created fundamentally for the purpose of serving the dual functions the media is supposed to play, as a part of the propaganda machine of both the party and the state institutions. It was not until 1992 when Deng Xiaoping wound up his trip to southern China, that all facets of industry embraced the concept of a market economy.

The introduction of market mechanisms indicates a lower dependence on state subsidies and more competition at different levels. Although once blessed with a monopoly on broadcasting, CCTV's (China Central Television) dominance in transmitting news and other programs was evidently shaken. In 1993, regional television stations were allowed to transmit signals and by the end of 1998, 28 provincial stations were transmitting their programs via satellite. The shape and size of the world's largest television network made it necessary for CCTV to turn to the wants and needs of the people. To some extent, the market is the message, even in a Communist society (Ai, 2002). By the end of 2000, the total number of television stations totaled 354, and covered 93.65% of the entire population. Cable television subscribers increased to more than 800 million (China Radio & TV, 2002).

However, in a market-oriented system, media policymaking was being made with a changing market capacity. The four-tier administrations of television stations eventually turned out to be a chaotic and irrational maneuver, which hindered the healthy development of the television industry. Accordingly, a decree was issued by the Ministry of Radio, Film and TV in 1997 which demanded that the radio, television and cable stations at the municipal and country level should be merged to form TV and radio stations, and then integrated with the local radio and RV Bureaus. In 1999, another decree strove to reduce the "four-tier" to "two-tier" (focusing on facilitating the merger of local cable and television stations at the level of city or provinces). However, these measures were still based on administrative regions, and the actual execution was far from satisfactory. A peculiar phenomenon prevailed; policy was promulgated and countermeasures ensued, which was a typical indication of aiding local vested interests. The following are the flaws of the regulatory system: (1) nearly all the regulations are administrative orders rather than laws passed by the legislative body; and (2) there was no independent supervisory body to secure policy instruments.

Further exploration reveals that several factors contributed to the rapid development of the television sector in China after 1992. First, the market-driven reform within the television sector realized its possibilities and more audience-favored programs were produced. Second, the potential rural market was allowed to promote infrastructure development. In 1999, the second session of the 9th National People's Congress approved the plan of "radio and television in every village," which substantially increased television coverage in rural areas. Third, the technological advances enabled the television sector to promote programs. Since the initial launch of a communication satellite in 1984, CCTV (formerly Beijing Television) has adopted Digital Satellite News Gathering (DSNG). In 1999, China was successful with the relay-test for Digital High Definition TV, and in 2004, CCTV and the National Geographical channel joined forces in creating four digital subscription television channels in China. Finally, the diffusion and popularity of the Internet brought about a novel broadcasting concept—online cast.

WTO and Globalization

In December 2001, after a 13-year period of negotiations, China entered the WTO. Its media, seen as the market with most potential, again became the focus of international conglomerates. Though China's television sector is not mentioned specifically in the "open-up list" with reference to international competition, other media-related sectors started looking outward. Under such a radical situation, commercialization, conglomeration and capitalization became hot issues. In early 1998, the first radio and television group—Wuxi Radio and TV Group—was founded and was soon followed by the establishment of the largest media group in China, the Radio, Film and TV Group of China in Beijing, in 2001. By the time of China's entry into the WTO, there were 26 newspaper groups, eight radio, film and television groups, six print groups and four publishing groups (Jiang & Jiang, 2003).

Although aware of the possible double-edged effects of a liberal economy, Chinese policymakers took careful note of world economic and political trends. In the media, this led to a peculiar phenomenon of "single system, dual operations." Single system is the state ownership of the television sector, and dual operations concerns fulfilling its political mission with the money earned from market competition. In 2003, the State Administration of Radio, Film & Television (SARFT) and the State Administration of the Press and Publication separated further the television, radio, Party press and magazine divisions from other "profit-making" sectors—the ideological and news programs were kept in the hands of the Party, but the social service, entertainment, and professional newspapers and magazines were to be outsourced to be relatively independent enterprises.

PRINCIPAL MEDIA POLICY OBJECTIVES

China's media policy is formulated alongside the reform and opening-up policies adopted by this country since the late 1970s. Similar to what is happening in other areas of industry, the development of China's media is closely associated with advances in the political economy. Scholars have conducted investigations into the relationship between the development of the industry and the institution of policymaking. For example, after having analyzed the different aspects of the telecommunications industry, some institutional economists concluded that intelligent regulatory policies must take into account the institutional foundations and endowments of a nation, and how they can be extended and applied (Karamanis, 2003). So it is vital to locate policy objectives while taking into account those mechanisms which create transformation.

For more than five decades, China's media sector has been under a strict supervision and control system with regard to the consolidation of the Party's politics and ideology. However with the exception of the market economy, accompanied by global deregulation, Chinese media policymakers have broken free with their creation of numerous decrees, regulations, and laws in favor of the commercialization of the media industry.

In China, laws and regulations are generally fashioned and implemented by four distinct government offices: the Standing Committee of the National People's Congress, the State Council, the Ministries and the State Administrations under the State Council, regional and local regulatory and administrative organizations. It is stipulated that the laws and regulations of a lower level should not go against the principles of those at higher levels.

The Chinese Constitution gives power to the National People's Congress to make laws in areas of national concern, including matters pertaining to media policy. Though China has not yet made its first law relating to mass media, or television specifically, there are currently three regulations issued by the State Council for the radio, film, and television sectors. There are also dozens of administrative rules put forward by SARFT, the primary regulatory body for electronic media under the State Council, as well as other related administrative rules from various government departments. These rules are all in accordance with the Chinese Constitution and the national interest.

SARFT is responsible for the regulation of the development of radio, film, and television sectors nationwide and acts as a professional supervisor that examines television and film production, approves the content of radio and television programs and films, and controls foreign film imports and their subsequent broadcast in China. It is also the supervisor and director of the country's satellite and cable networks. Divisions of SARFT provide guidance and restrictions of China's radio, film, and televisions sectors.

Some standard regulatory provisions function as basic principles of the radio and television sector, and are as follows:

1. The television broadcasting industry is developed by the State.
2. Broadcasters are set up by their respective administrations at county-level government or city government without districts. No other units or individuals can establish broadcasting stations. Various forms of foreign enterprises are prohibited from setting up radio and television broadcasting stations.
3. Radio and television administrations of county-level government or above should build and manage broadcast transmission coverage networks.

4. Radio and television stations and administrations of county-level government or above can approve broadcasting production units. They should also produce broadcast programs.
5. Censorship must be taken before broadcasting foreign movies and television series. (State Council, 1997)

These provisions ensure control of the radio and television sector by the State, with national interests being highlighted. The radio and television sector is seen as a supporting factor for maintaining social stability and a sound environment for China's economic development.

With economic restructuring and the gradual market reform of the media sector, China's media no longer serves as just a mouthpiece for the Party or State, but now also must produce programs to meet the audience's demands and to attract advertisers. Evidence of this is with the consistently increasing array of entertainment and educational programs which are believed to represent the wants and needs of the masses.

To provide better services to the audience, China has adjusted its media policy in the areas of market operation, technological innovation and public interests protection. The following parts will illustrate these adjustments respectively. After the 14th National Congress of the CPC, the media sector was recognized as a tertiary industry engaged in the country's reform of its enterprises. Furthermore, the 16th CPC National Congress in 2003 stated that the media industry was an important component of the cultural industry in China.

GENERAL MARKET SITUATION

Consolidation, restructuring, and alliance have been the keywords of media reform during the past several years. A number of multimedia and regional groups have been established to challenge fierce market competition. The State encourages various types of capital, State-owned and private, domestic and overseas, to invest in the media sector and support its rapid development.

Contemporary Television Market and Major Players Involved

The television sector is under relatively tight control compared with other media sectors. This control focuses on licensing television stations and channels, and on censoring broadcasting programs. However, gaining permission to enter the market has become easier for those interested.

Pursuant to a recent policy initiative adopted by SARFT, the radio and television sector has been divided into two parts, the public and the business sectors. The business sector refers to service and entertainment programs and television dramas, but not news related programs. It can be separated from the current structure and allowed to be run as individual companies, still owned by the State (SARFT, 2003a). Currently, State-owned institutions are given priority although all kinds of business are encouraged in the market.

In recent years, television related services have generated huge profits. When a television program obtains high popularity among its audience, the intangible assets of its fame, sometimes being regarded as its brand, can be turned into profit. Television-related products, such as audio and video productions, costumes, and other such royalties, exist in a market which at present has not yet been fully exploited, but demonstrates potential as a supporting industry in the future.

The Concept of Public Broadcasting in the West and China

Television systems around the world can be divided into three categories: State owned, commercial, and public. However in China, the concept of "public broadcasting" has a different meaning, due to the somewhat hazy analysis of the word "public."

In Western meaning, public broadcasting normatively refers to radio and television systems established for the public interest. They are neither State nor commercially owned, relying mainly on license fees or taxes paid for by the audience. The aim of public broadcasters is to protect public interests and to meet the demands of the audience at different levels. Generalist services, diverse and quality content, independent editorial policies and public finance and noncommercial activities are the main features of the philosophy in the European-based model of public service broadcasting. As McChesney (2003) explains, "what we mean by public broadcasting historically or globally is full-service broadcasting, with education, entertainment, and public affairs aimed at the entire population of a country. Its attributes are being nonprofit and noncommercial; dealing directly with the public instead of using ratings; have a relationship with the entire population to develop programming, not just the boring educational stuff, not just journalism and public affairs, but entertainment, the whole works" (McChesney, 2003, p. 11).

In China, the concept of "public broadcasting" is quite different. The State ownership of China's media has largely determined its characteristics, and because the Party is apparently the embodiment of the people, it justifies this control on ideological grounds. So in this context, the word "public" refers to public use and ownership by the State.

China's public policy focuses mainly on services in rural areas, where television is the most easily accessible medium. China is currently making efforts to construct the rural television public service system and 2005 has been designated by SARFT as the "Year of Rural Service." SARFT also decided to provide eight free television channels for rural audiences across the country and to extend the coverage of television networks in rural areas.

The public broadcasting channel in China plays the role of a multichannel platform that airs programs at various levels. At present, broadcasting outlets at the county level have been brought into the public broadcasting network in an attempt to serve the interests of rural areas. Additionally, in some areas in the country the concept of public service has also been stressed in the promotion of existing public broadcasting channels, such as those of Zhejiang Television and Jiangxi Television.

MEDIA FREEDOM

Media freedom in China has long been a controversial issue due to its unique political structure and ideologies. For a long time China's media was seen as a tool to help the class struggle, but under strict Party control with "unified propaganda lines." It was not until the 1980s, when calls for freedom of the press became more intense, that the media was redefined as an "information communication industry." In July 1992, a lawsuit concerning press freedom caught the nation's attention. Shanghai's Liberation Daily published an opinion piece in which Qian Bocheng, a publisher and National People's Congress deputy, wrote, "If we really want to become an open China in the eyes of the world, we must first have an open press or must open up the press. Journalists have the right to interview, the media has the right to report, and the public has the right to know" (Zhao, 1998, p. 165).

The Third Plenary Session of the 11th Central Party Committee initiated China's economic reform, and the subsequent media reform. However, economic reform inevitably caused some social evils such as corruption, crime, drug abuse, unemployment, and most striking, conspiracy, all of which have resulted in bitter complaints from ordinary people. As a result, some investigative programming surfaced for the first time in China's media history. In 1994, a brand-new program known as "Focus Interview" was aired, which concentrated on critical coverage of social problems. The reason behind its success as a form of public expression is that almost every problem it investigated raised greater concerns from the government. By imitating "Focus Interview," provincial and local television stations have produced their own watchdog programs with the intention of supervising their local social problems.

However, the calls for substantial media reforms concerning the freedom of press have never ceased, as the Party continues to attach great political and ideological importance to the media. On September 26, 1996, Chinese President Jiang Zemin's visit to CCTV, the only national television network, was a clear sign indicating that as part of the life of the Communist Party, journalism is intertwined with the destiny of the nation and the party; authority still lying in the hands of the party and the people. There are still some deciding factors which prevent complete freedom of press. Firstly, the shifting balance of public equality in the media has become the best evidence the party could find to reiterate the importance of regulation and centralization. Some supporting views state that Western commercialization of the media industry has developed an elite system of ownership with an absence of the public interest. Second, the regulations imposed on media organizations mostly concern the obligations the media should fulfill, but never their legal status, editorial autonomy and free access to factual information. Freedom of the press can only be guaranteed by the validity of a legitimate legal system that is produced under the supervision of the public, and which above all, serves the purpose of the public interest. Third, the progress of media law is closely related to the reform of China's entire legal system. So the biggest obstacle impeding press freedom is the existing control of the media by the Party.

However, the gradual maturity of the market system occurring in China has provided fertile ground for establishing credible media growth. The audience, no longer just at the receiving end of programs, has begun to take the initiative to form a social force that can supervise the government. In this manner the media has become a bridge between the Party and public. But some experts firmly believe that the interplay of political and commercial forces will not necessarily lead to the increase in public voice, but rather to the expanding prosperity of privation and commercialization. This, in turn, may bring about uneven political, market and civil rights and upset the current developments. As Wei Qian analyzed, the transformation of television's role from the sole political conduit to a public server is neither attributed to the power imposed by the middle classes nor the result of top-down political reform. Instead, it is an unexpected result and consequence of the commercialization of China's media undertaken by the Chinese government (Qian, 2002, p. 209).

MICROECONOMIC CHANGES AND FINANCE
FOR THE TELEVISION SECTOR

Never before has the media market been so diverse and dynamic, with an even more competitive market estimated to grow in the next few years. Technically speaking, the presence of specialty channels and digital television is the best evidence to indicate the rapid improvements undertaken in China's television industry, but a newcomer now looks to set the standards. Online media use has grown exponentially because of the remarkable increase in mainstream audiences using the Internet. There are two distinct ways to analyze this—first, in its domestic context. Reforms on China's political system and culture industry have created a favorable environment for structural changes in the media market. The most recent policy known as No. 44 Document, for example, refers to a profound and comprehensive media reform of the culture industry's institutions. Second, in its international context. Globalization has enabled transnational capital to move from developed countries to developing ones, which is expected to vitalize the domestic media market so long as deregulation continues to promote investment.

Financial Characteristics of the Television Sector

As a result of the remarkable transformation during the past two decades, China's pursuit of economic modernization has progressed steadily. The television industry, like all other business sectors, was cut off from State financial support and has scrambled on for its survival. In 1998, the First Session of the 9th National People's Congress produced a timetable to make the media industry completely self-sufficient in just three years, acting as a strong reason to commercialize the television sector. Advertising has subsequently increased by 20% yearly so that by 2003, the revenue generated reached 25.504 billion Yuan, more than the combined total of newspapers, magazines and radio. For most television stations, advertising revenue covers more than 90% of the total earnings, as it does with CCTV that calculated its advertising revenue as 5.74 billion Yuan by 2000, standing at more than 93%. CCTV's dominant position has not been threatened even though China's media policy encourages the competitive development of diverse television stations and channels.

However, the prime position of television advertising has been shaken in the past few years due to the changing economic structure. For example, the growth of the real estate sector has enabled the print media to regain some of its market. As shown in Table 5.1, it is only since 2000, that television advertising has slowed to an annual 10% increase.

Having realized the danger of the dominance of television advertising revenue, China's media began to seek multilevel business solutions. The growth of program marketing for cable and pay TV are among the list of ideas to change from the current monolithic model. Estimating how big China's media market will be, the CEO of Tom.com said recently at the "E-Talking New Economy Forum" that in the coming several years, the value of China's advertisement market will exceed 100 billion Yuan and gross media volume will be divided into three or four portions, which means the advertisement market will be worth about 40 billion Yuan.

TABLE 5.1
Advertising Revenues of Different Media (1993–2003)

Year	Newspaper	Magazine	Radio	TV Advertising (by 100 Rate million, RMB Yuan)	Increase	Total	TV %
2003	243.01	23.38	25.57	255.04	10.4%	1078.68	23.64%
2002	188	15.21	22	231	28.76%	903.15	25.58%
2001	157.70	11.86	18.28	179.4	6.22%	794.89	22.57%
2000	130.33	11.34	14.62	168.91	8.17%	712.66	23.7%
1999	112.33	8.92	12.52	156.15	15.1%	622.05	25.1%
1998	104.36	7.13	13.30	135.66	18.57%	537.84	25.22%
1997	96.83	5.27	10.58	114.41	26.02%	461.96	24.77%
1996	77.69	5.61	8.73	90.79	39.72%	366.64	24.77%
1995	64.68	3.83	7.38	64.98	45.17%	273.27	23.78%
1994	50.54	3.95	4.96	44.76	52.04%	200.26	22.35%
1993	37.71	1.84	3.49	29.44	43.28%	134.09	21.96%

Note. All figures in the table courtesy of Liu (2004).

Audience and Content Distribution

Due to technological developments and media policies initiated by the government, the Chinese audience has changed from a passive participant to an active one. Moreover, the segmentation of the audience has shown that the media is becoming more market-oriented and less a tool of the government.

Despite the booming media market, a shortage of content still remains a serious problem. This comes as a result of China's media policy and the tight control of editorial content by the government. China's media has therefore developed a considerable network, which although affluent in knowledge, has an absence of intelligent creators and producers.

Content production and distribution have become so diverse that besides State-owned institutions, the sector includes private and foreign investment. SARFT and the Ministry of Commerce (MOFCOM) jointly issued "The Provisional Regulations on the Administration of China-Foreign Joint Venture and Cooperation Radio and Television Production and Distribution Enterprises," in October 2004. Under the rules, effective from November 28, 2004, foreign television enterprises were permitted to establish Sino-foreign film and television production joint ventures in China, with the Chinese partner holding no less than 51% of its ownership. The operation of a joint venture is subject to certain restrictions, including that it may not produce news programs and that at least two thirds of its total annual production must relate to Chinese issues (SARFT, 2004a). The regulations also prohibit wholly foreign-owned media companies from entering China, and financial investors from investing in China's radio and television stations. In addition, foreign companies approved to set up production joint ventures are not allowed to apply for a second company.

Despite these restrictions, the rules were seen as China's attempt to further open the radio and television sectors to foreign investment. The latest regulations permit cooperation between foreign and domestic private companies. The change in regulations was seen as widening the access for internationally renowned media companies.

During 2004, China approved several joint venture companies engaged in film and television production. News Corp, Time Warner and Sony Pictures Entertainment have obtained SARFT approval to form partnerships with CCTV and China Film Group. Viacom, the third largest media group in the United States, has also obtained the approval of SARFT to establish a content production joint venture between its popular children's network, Nickelodeon, and the Shanghai Media Group (SMG).

Meanwhile, the amount of foreign programs imported into China has increased, despite the restrictions regarding censorship and broadcast times imposed on them. For private program companies, there are also great opportunities. They have successfully initiated and highlighted entertainment and information programs, which have become their trademark during the past decade. Famous domestic private program companies in China include Enlight Media Co. Ltd, Joyful Media Group, Pegasus and Taihe Entertainment International (P&T),

Tanglong International Media. To aid the distribution and exchange of programs and television series, the annually run international television festival, held alternately in Shanghai and Chengdu, functions as the main channel for imported programs.

DEVELOPMENTS AND THE IMPACT OF TECHNOLOGICAL CHANGES IN THE SECTOR

Technological development has been the catalyst for the rapid expansion of China's television sector. With recent innovations, greater numbers of people now have access to a television, and have encountered an increasing degree of choice and improved quality of programs.

Cable Television: A Milestone of China's Television Development

In the past decade, cable television has played a key role in China's television development. With on average 40 to 60 channels available Chinese audiences have established ever-closer ties with the cable system. Prior to the introduction of satellite television, cable television was the most significant new form of technology, introduced into the Chinese broadcasting industry. The number of subscribers increased annually by 5 million households in the 1990s, and by 2004 the total length of cable exceeded 3 million kilometers with optical cable standing at 0.4 million kilometers. Almost 2,000 cities and counties have set up cable networks. By the end of 2004, numbers of subscribers had reached 114.7 million, and more than 30 cities with a total 1.22 million subscribers had initiated digital services (National Statistics Bureau of People's Republic of China, 2004). The impetus behind the rapid diffusion of cable television lies in two factors: (1) support from the "four-tier administration and overlapping coverage of Radio & TV" in 1983 generated the rapid expansion of cable television; and (2) the low cost of access to cable has generated a belief among the audience of "free television watching," that, in turn, contributes to the difficulties in promoting pay TV in China.

China's cable television research and construction began in the 1960s, but it did not experience rapid development until the 1990s. It was launched on a huge scale across the country as hundreds of cable television stations were established in the period from 1992 to 1996. Its main purpose was to improve the signal quality of free-to-air television stations in cities, since the "television boom" was spreading across the country. Cable television was seen as an extension and supplement of terrestrial television. The normal subscription fee per cable household is 18 RMB per month, less than one U.S. dollar, and the money is used entirely for the maintenance of cable system facilities. In China, satellite television programs are received through the cable system. Because China is so large and the signal of each terrestrial television station so limited in area, SARFT encouraged some provincial television stations to put their programs on satellite, as it is the cheapest and quickest way to cover remote areas in these provinces. By the end of 1999, all the provincial television stations had gone on air and were available to a nationwide cable television audience. Provisional Measures of Cable TV Management, issued in 1990 by the Ministry of Radio, Film and Television (MRFT), the predecessor of SARFT, was the first regulation on cable television development in China. Since then, a series of rules and measures were published to regulate cable television activities. Within an administrative region, only one cable network was allowed. Foreign enterprises and corporations were prohibited from operating cable stations (State Council, 1997).

In 1997, the MRFT reorganized local radio and television institutions by integrating all radio, television, and cable television at a county level, including education stations and relay stations, into a single station. It also combined all cable systems into a regional cable network. By the end of 2000, it had begun to incorporate cable television stations into terrestrial television stations of the same region. Provincial cable television stations ceased to exist from the second half of 2001. So far, China has the world's largest number of cable television subscribers, with more than 114 million by the end of 2004, and is expected to have 150 million by 2010.

Digital Television

Digitalization is an industrial innovation in the development of broadcasting technology. Using digitalization, the current cable network will become a universal platform for delivering new products and services, to provide its customers with greater value in the face of growing competition.

Since 2003, digital television has been a key mission in developing the television industry in China. The plan is to enable the cable system to become a broadband, digital, and truly interactive medium. China has made breakthroughs in digitalizing the production and transmission of television, but most television sets are still only configured to receive analog signals. To upgrade the current cable systems, households do not need to replace their existing television sets to access interactive and digital services, but they do require a set-top box. Several cities in the country have become trial areas of digital television. Qingdao, Hangzhou, and Foshan have experienced a transformation from analog signals to digital television and households were provided with free set-top boxes for receiving digital signals.

SARFT plans to complete the transition from analog television to digital television in four stages, in 2005, 2008, 2010, and 2015, respectively. The plan anticipates that all cable television stations at provincial level will introduce digital systems, and the number of digital television subscribers will reach 30 million by the end of 2005. By 2008, 100 million urban households are to have digital television and digital transmission will begin on a national level. Full implementation of terrestrial digital television is expected to be realized nationwide by 2010, and the country will end analog broadcast by 2015 (SARFT, 2003b). According to the plan, by the time digitalization is realized, Chinese audiences will be able to receive television programs with a picture quality as clear as DVD and audio effects as good as those in the cinema. Their choice of channels will be multi-plied from the tens to the hundreds. They should also have access to personal-ized information services through television such as home shopping, weather forecasts, traffic reports, and the stock market.

SARFT has tried to attract different institutions and enterprises who deal with digital television. State-owned media groups, social organizations, as well as pri-vate capital are permitted to invest in digital television. By the end of 2004, SARFT had licensed 112 digital television channels, and another 95 were under consideration (Zhang, 2005).

Satellite Television

Alongside digital television, China is constructing a detailed satellite television sys-tem. In the long run, satellite and digital technology are to be integrated, as satel-lite digital transmission is another key aim of China's television development.

China started satellite television transmissions in the 1980s and made improve-ments in the following decade. With its vast territory, the cable network cannot reach some regions, especially in rural areas. However, with Direct Broadcast Satellite (DBS) channels can be transmitted straight to a viewer's home dish.

The high demand for these services has resulted in a growing market, although China's satellite television market is a heavily regulated one. Except for satellite television programs passing via the cable systems, which are mostly domestic and provincial television programs, the Chinese audience has little access to overseas satellite channels. According to regulations set by the State Council, only approved institutions may receive limited overseas satellite pro-grams and a license system will be applied to the production, import, sale, instal-lation, and use of reception hardware. Individuals are not allowed to install satellite reception equipment (State Council, 1993). Since 1990, SARFT has also issued a series of regulations to control the reception of overseas satellite pro-grams. However, on approval, registered overseas satellite television channels are allowed to be broadcast in three-star quality (and above) hotels, which receive foreign guests. These channels are also allowed in certain specific areas, such as offices and apartments exclusively for overseas people (SARFT, 2004b). By 2004, 31 overseas satellite television channels had been granted the right to be transmitted in limited areas. Meanwhile, since 2001, China has also approved six overseas satellite channels, including China Entertainment TV, Star TV, Phoenix TV, and MTV, to broadcast programs through cable networks in south China's Guangdong Province (Sun & Liu, 2001; Xinhua News Agency, 2004). China's first DBS was launched in 2006, with coverage of 260 million households.

Other Technological Developments: IPTV, Mobile, and Cell Phone Television

The spectacular growth of the Internet and mobile communications has created high expectations for every new technology that springs up. These technological breakthroughs include the emergence of Internet Protocol Television (IPTV), mobile television, and cell phone television.

IPTV merges traditional television, the video rental store, and the Internet. Viewers can enjoy high quality, live streaming broadcasts from hundreds of television stations, as well as video-on-demand from enormous online film databases. IPTV symbolizes the convergence of the television and telecommunications networks, previously separated in terms of laws and regulations. So far, China's fixed-line telecom operators, China Telecom and China Netcom, have led the way with IPTV services. In March 2004, China Netcom's Tiantian Online, was awarded a television-quality broadcast license by SARFT to transmit television content over telecom networks to personal computers (PCs). China Telecom has already begun offering a form of IPTV in top-tier cities and regions, including Shanghai, Guangzhou, and Hangzhou. China's State-run media conglomerates, including CCTV and the Shanghai Media Group, have already made deals with a number of different IPTV providers. Major foreign media companies are also actively seeking entry because IPTV appears as a possible loophole circumventing SARFT's control on sensitive content and non-Chinese programs.

Another new means of receiving television is mobile television, or mobile digital television, which can be found in transport systems. In 2004, thousands of buses in Beijing and Shanghai were equipped with mobile television. Passengers on board have been able to watch television programs, a service which soon should also be available in the metro, trains, and taxis. At present, State-owned media groups have dominated the market for mobile television, although the content providers are beginning to diversify into this area.

For cell phone users, cell phone television, also sometimes called mobile television, is available due to technological improvement in third-generation mobile technology (3G). In 2004, China Unicom, a Chinese mobile service provider, launched such a service. Shortly after, its main rival China Mobile started a mobile phone television service through the GPRS network. However, mobile phones with television capacity are still at an early stage of development in China due to the limited broadband capacity, small range of handsets, sky-high prices, and lack of standards and policies.

MEDIA CONCENTRATION AND PLURALISM

It is always a complex and, at times, controversial issue to define media concentration and pluralism, and even more so to pin down their specific relationship. Whereas media concentration is generally interpreted as media ownership concentration, the clarification about pluralism has long been disputed. According to the Committee of Experts on Media Concentrations and Pluralism (MM-CM) attached to the Council of Europe, the term of pluralism can be defined as follows:

> Media pluralism should be understood as diversity of media supply, reflected, for example, in the existence of a plurality of independent and autonomous media and a diversity of media contents available to the public. (Doyle, 2002, p. 12)

This means that pluralism, which embraces both diversity of ownership and diversity of output, refers mainly to public access of a range of voices and content, irrespective of the patterns of demand. More generally, the concept of pluralism is comprised of two aspects: political pluralism, that is about the need in the interests of democracy for a range of political opinions and viewpoints to be represented in the media; and cultural pluralism, that is about the need for a variety of cultures, reflecting the diversity of society to find expression in the media (Doyle, 2002).

When trying to analyze the tangled connections of concentration of media ownership and pluralism, the commonly perceived danger lies in the fact that "excessive concentration of media ownership can lead to overrepresentation of certain political viewpoints or values or certain forms of cultural output at the expense of others" (Doyle, 2002, p. 13). The rising of media moguls such as Rupert Murdoch is the best evidence to demonstrate this threat. However, others argue that concentrated ownership actually increases pluralism on the grounds that large organizations are more likely to generate cost efficiencies, and may be better placed than their smaller rivals to innovate in products and to add to the range of media output and "because of the tendency to consolidate editorial resources, different owners cannot be fully equated with different voices" (Doyle, 2002, pp. 21–22). It sounds even more convincing when arguing "since economies of scale and scope are available to large media firms, it is possible that a more monopolistic industry structure would yield a greater diversity of media output (content) than would be economically feasible in a more fragmented and competitive industry structure" (Doyle, 2002, p. 17).

This era of consolidation, ownership, and mega-mergers presents regulators and policymakers with difficult and complex challenges. China's media is, by many, considered to be a promising market, but it is also widely perceived to be exacerbating those difficulties faced by its policymakers. This seems rather strange when examining China's media concentration and pluralism against a global background, because it has a completely different media system, stemming from its unique social and economic system.

Despite the global trend toward the involvement of transnational capital, China's media policymakers still manage to exert a professional approach in this dynamic field, making sure they continue to uphold the core spirit of Party control and State ownership. Nevertheless, when investigating media concentration and pluralism with Chinese characteristics, we find that China's media is now experiencing transformation not only from bottom up market driven practices. But also from top down politics-led legal attempts, the latter of which advocates the reform of long held beliefs cherished by Chinese people. So with reference to media concentration, it refers to, in a Chinese context, more political and ideological cohesion rather than ownership concentration as monopolistic State ownership prevails. When speaking of pluralism, it means the diversity of content and format rather than real cultural pluralism. However, certain media groups have gradually regained the awareness of their function as a public channel to voice different opinions, such as coverage about the life of disadvantaged groups in China.

With the proceeding reformation of China's media, pluralism, reflected in content and format diversity, can be seen most easily with the rising prosperity of programming and diversity of customer choice. Entertainment programming and television dramas are two distinct genres outweighing traditional news programs. These types of programs, ranked as top in the ratings, tend to get rid of political influence in an attempt to be compliant with the nature of the program. Recently, pluralism in China is also demonstrated in the diversity of its operating patterns. The incorporation of private and international capital in certain legitimate media sectors are welcomed and predicted to be a dominant trend in the near future. The inclination toward the nature of capital-based operations for the business sector of China's media can be traced back to a series of regulatory initiatives.

In July 2003, the No. 21 Document proposed a trial reform indicating that the restructuring of China's media industry had entered a new era. The separation of the public sector and the business sector was the principal act of this reform. Accordingly, the system of State ownership was to apply to key media outlets such as the party-run newspapers, magazines, radio, and television stations, as well as key publishers. Then, as to "nonpropaganda" resources such as advertising, printing and distribution, they were to be controlled by enterprises. The focus of this was institutional innovation, transformation of mechanisms, opening up of the market, and the stimulation of economic activities (Hu, 2004).

From this point on, a variety of other innovative reforms on media institutions and policies, have been undertaken in order to provide a favorable environment for media development. In 2004, reforms on ownership and the stock market mainly concerned the separation of the government administration from the public sector (a substitute for Party ideological leadership) and the business sector. In 2005 the predicted merging trends of various government organizations will occur, to allow greater efficiency in the implementation of regulatory aims to protect media pluralism, even if it is no longer total. However, as the culture industry in China tries to attach equal weight to its components, it makes it difficult to implement a comprehensive media policy. Different categories have justified their right to self-administration. A bigger problem is that China's current interpretation of pluralism is no more than the presence of several different products or several separate suppliers, which does not yet represent the true essence of pluralism. "The need for pluralism is, ultimately, about sustaining representation within a given society for different political viewpoints and forms of cultural expression" (Doyle, 2002, p. 14).

However, a promising feature lies in the wider access to different sources of investment, both private and foreign. Some big movements concerning ownership reforms have taken place, such as music radio networks, whose ownership is no longer monopolized by the Chinese government. To sum up, the developing trends in the reforms of media policy and regulation should present a blank canvas where interplaying forces can paint their own futures.

ASSESSMENT

China's media has gone through three distinct stages of transition, known as marketization, conglomeration, and capitalization. Marketization started in the early 1980s, and was characterized as "single system, dual operations" (the single system refers to the State ownership and the dual operations are seen as a unique approach to commercialize China's media while fulfilling the political tasks). However, it developed into a bottleneck in the 1990s when, as the size of the media market was in a state of expansion, the increasing awareness of ideological control became so serious that economic infiltration was deepened. In January 1996, the first newspaper group "Guangzhou Daily Newspaper Group" was established, suggesting that China's media had entered a new era of economic scope. However, the conglomeration of China's media raised suspicions regarding its purpose and effect. In contradistinction to Western countries, political purposes rather than economic intentions drove the conglomeration of China's media. All that remained intact was the root of the reforms, and on a profound level, the institutional arrangement. Unable to break through the long-established structure of political and economic power, the conglomeration was not an entirely complete one. The largest broadcasting group, China Radio, Film, and TV Media Group, was disbanded in May 2005. Some other broadcasting groups have been asked to change to be pure business companies, without affiliated radio and television stations. Nevertheless, capitalization was carried out and it became known as a process of re-institutionalization, during which intermingled forces strengthened their control of the media and maximized their profits (Hu, 2005).

The bumpy process of China's media reforms throughout the nation implies that media policymaking is more of an administrative governance rather than systematic public management. In other words policymakers have not been emancipated from the concept of a State-planned economy, which has resulted in an inability to set an institutional agenda under the system of a market economy. This rapid change in policy has negatively affected the birth of the legal system, and consequently has prevented any effective implementation of the rules and regulations. Therefore, the insufficiency in planning strategic media policies has resulted in inappropriate public policies and improper institutional arrangements.

Other noteworthy issues need to be emphasized here. First, the relationship between the media and cultural institutions, or more simply how the reform of social institutions will affect the reformation of cultural institutions. Second, regulatory systems need to be reexamined, to make sure that the purpose of regulation is to perfect the media industry as a means to serve the public interest. The third issue that needs to be highlighted is the increase in social stratification and the change in audience consumption. Rapid economic development has accelerated the separation of social classes, profoundly affecting the audience's consumption of new media. For instance, the expense of digital television or satellite and cable services can be a barrier to the less wealthy members of society. Last, but not least, is the ideological issue, which is still too sensitive to be mentioned. Nonetheless, it should explain whether or not the party's will is an appropriate illustration of the public interest. Given that the media is meant to voice public opinion, and that the party represents the masses, the party must justify its control of the media when propagating its ideology. The issue of concern is the absence of a new ideological direction on behalf of the political sphere that will leave a space for capital and its value system to erode the public interest and the rather vulnerable value system that currently exists. Even worse, through the process of seeking opportunities to curb the implementation of policies and by intending to bend policies to their own advantage, some vested interest groups will employ painstaking efforts to force politics into a conspiracy by obtaining profits beyond policy constraints. So the alliance between political and capital forces becomes more likely to undermine the public interest. The question is how the Chinese government would maintain its role as a representative of the public. In this case, it must consider the conservation of the public interest whilst struggling with its transformation from a chief market player to a satisfactory policy provider or macro-institution designer. Generally, in Western countries, it is through law that the equilibrium is located among capital, the government and the public. So, in China, the question of how to seek the balance among these three forces remains.

The most dynamic sector to be thrown into the real market, television media, has been directly affected by these changing policies. Several regulatory documents are considered to be significant landmarks in China's broadcasting history since the 1980s. In the pre-WTO era, Decree No. 37 in 1983 focused on the acceleration of capacity development, and highlighted a proposal known as the "operation of radio and television by four-tier authorities, and its mingled coverage over four-tier regions." Having created the developing structures of regional administration for radio and television, this regulation has doubtlessly resulted in sector and regional protectionism when implementing central policy. On the other hand, the embracing commercial distribution of television, emphasized in other regulations in the mid-1990s, has since witnessed an incredible rise in advertising revenues for television stations. Decree No. 82 in 1999 concentrated on improving quality as is emphasized in the reform of the four-tier to two-tier systems (as mentioned earlier). In response to this television stations both at the national and provincial levels began to attach more weighting to the quality of their programs. Apparently, policies before the WTO were characterized by a planned economy directly managed by the government rather than optimally integrated by a competitive market.

In the post-WTO era, Decree No. 17 in 2001 was seen as an important document to deepen media reform and also as a government resolution in response to the WTO. The distinct features reflected in this regulation are: (a) the function of the government has shifted from a market player to a policymaker and supervisor; (b) media outlets have shifted their status from affiliated organizations to market players, enjoying relative autonomy of economic activities; and (c) more emphasis is placed on the integration of capital and business, and lowering market entry. Decree No. 21 in 2003 intended to deepen the institutional reform of the culture industry and remarked that the reform of China's media policy had entered a revolutionary stage. The separation of the public and business sectors, and also the capitalization of operational resources in all respects, became the main focus. More noticeably, it allowed businesses access to all forms of ownership to participate in a range of media activities with the exception of news coverage.

These policy changes have affected the television sector in all areas, by generating the dynamics of television programming and its distribution. Program ratings have never before drawn so much attention among television producers, advertisers and distributors. A more market-led television system is being put together after the incorporation of foreign and private capital into the existing traditional structure. This recent policy intends to promote the joint operation of program production and distribution. In 2004, SARFT issued a directive on the cooperative production of television programs, dictating that Sino-foreign joint productions could be produced by establishing joint ventures, but with strict regulations restricting investors. For example, the registered capital of a joint venture should be no less than 50 million RMB (about US$6 million), and the proportion of foreign capital should be no more than 49%.

However, in the pursuit of marketing television programs, how many public elements have been taken into account? The public sphere perspective suggests that society's needs cannot be met entirely through the market system, and profitability should not be viewed as the sole indicator of a healthy media industry. It should be the government that plays the decisive role in ensuring that other public interest criteria, such as diversity and substance, are used to assess the performance of the media and above all, to ensure that the media meets the needs of the citizens and not just the consumers (Croteau, 2001). As previously mentioned, it is more likely that the public interest will be sacrificed when political and capital forces join hands to exploit these rapidly changing policies. As to China's current television environment, although the top-down initiative to promote digitalization prevails over the suspicion about the new media, commercial driving forces are the real stimuli behind the question as to whether the public interest has even been considered. The existence of public television channels such as Beijing public television channels are not sufficient evidence to demonstrate the importance attached to the public sense, because no substantial content other than television dramas can be seen in these channels. Public representatives urge the launch of a "real" public broadcasting system, which would carry out its original obligation to serve public interest.

CONCLUSION

In the process of China's media transformation, the tremendous changes that occurred in China's television industry have aroused high levels of attention among domestic and international market players. To sum up, these changes are reflected in three areas: (1) structural changes, (2) policy changes, and (3) predictable changes in the process of globalization.

The structural changes include the size and scale of the television market, and the diversity of its viewers and developing technology. Since its foundation in 1958, China's television stations have numbered 363, with channels rocketing up to 2094, covering 94.82% of its population of 1.3 billion by the end of 2003. China's profits from advertising in 2003 might make it the world's second largest television commercial market according to AC Nielsen's Asia and Pacific branch. Statistics from AC Nielsen show advertising revenue generated US$14.5 billion in China in 2003, a 28% increase from the previous year, of which television commercials accounted for 75%.

New technology has broken up the old scenario of spectrum scarcity that had long been exploited by the main player, the State television network, and has left more alternatives for Chinese viewers. These new technologies include examples such as satellite television, IP TV, cell phone TV, and so on, with cable TV being the most distinct of all. With an audience of almost 115 million cable subscribers by the end of 2004, China's television has turned into the most attractive market place for both domestic and foreign capitals. Additionally, the resolution made by SARFT to accelerate the popularity of digital television will be another factor in stimulating the television industry. The latest information suggests that China will provide low-interest loans to cable companies to convert 100 million urban households to digital television by 2008. It is also predicted that there will be more than 30 million digital television users in China in 2008. The goal is to have all 380 million households in China using digital technology just ten years later. Currently, the number of households with digital television stands at 280,000 (People's Daily Online, 2005). The diversity of current technology has contributed to the rising trend in consumer choice, indicating an escalating demand for quality programs, with niche content in various programming genres. As a result, specialty channels have sprouted up in the past few years. However, as mentioned before, advanced technology does not necessarily equate with the changing need for free expression of public opinion. For one thing, the ensuing subscription fee would probably bar some viewers from accessing the new technology. For another, powerful media groups are more likely to exploit new technology to initiate a new run of acquisitions and concentrated ownership, which may bring about even more threats to pluralism.

As to the reasons behind China's changes in media policy, the impetus came from central government, other political interest groups, economic interest groups and transnational media conglomerates. It is clear that the crucial problem facing policymakers at the moment is how to defend the status of the Central Party while facilitating market-led mechanisms. So, some degree of equilibrium needs to be found between political and economic values. Nevertheless, political forces have embraced economic ones, and unprecedented importance has been attached to the role of capital, which will eventually propel the revolutionary transition of media institutions. On the other hand, no matter how urgent the reform, the Party will never lessen its ideological control of the media, indicating that it has never ceased to adjust its strategies and approaches in exerting complete and total political control.

In the past few years, the deregulation of China's media sector, accompanied by the rapid growth of domestic private capital, has allowed private investment into different sections of media practice such as program production and distribution. But the question is the extent to which private investment is allowed to be involved in the media industry. A rising concern how private capital manages to survive when squeezed between the State-owned conventional media outlets and transnational media moguls. Worse still is the fact that lobbying by international conglomerates is more likely to overshadow minor business entities, and become strong enough to talk the State media into a promising future—the conspiracy between political forces and foreign capital. In response to this, how should policymakers formulate regulations for the purpose of protecting minor economic forces, as well as the public interest? On the whole, it is urgent that policymakers find equilibrium among politics, economy, and society.

Nevertheless, although influenced by the wave of globalization, China's television industry will develop into a mature market place where the import and export of television programs and the cooperation in distribution sectors will become common practice. The components of capital will no longer remain monolithic, and will indicate a possible diversity in operating profitability. The current statistics suggests a capacity of 150 billion RMB (about US$18 billion) in the media market needs to be cultivated, whereas only 80 billion (about US$10 billion) has been developed (Yu & Zhang, 2005, p. 7). The reason behind this is the low efficiency of research and development in the media industry. The more critical reason for it is that the regulation set by policymakers has barred foreign capital from full-scale involvement.

After all, despite numerous difficulties with the processes of media policy-making and regulation, the trends reflected in the television industry are towards more market liberalism and deregulation. The dilemma where the Chinese government remains the key player in the market is an incomparable situation urging Chinese elites to find their own solutions to key problems.

REFERENCES

Ai, H. (2002). *Historical analysis of China's Radio & TV.* Jinan: Shandong University Press.
Chang, T. K. (2002). *China's window on the world TV news.* Cresskill, NJ: Hampton Press.
China Radio & TV. (2002). *China's radio & TV yearbook of 2001.* Beijing: China Radio & TV Publishing House.
China Radio & TV. (2005). *China's radio & TV yearbook of 2004.* Beijing: China Radio & TV Publishing House.
Chinese Academy of Social Science. (1987). *Contemporary China's radio & TV.* Beijing: China Social Science Press.
Croteau, D. (2001). *The business of media.* Thousand Oaks, CA: Pine Forge Press.
Doyle, G. (2002). *Media ownership.* London: Sage.
Guo, Z. (1997). *TV history of China.* Beijing: Beijing Broadcasting Institute Press.
Hu, Z. (2004, December). *The equilibrium between the government and the market: An analysis of China's media policy in post-WTO era.* Paper presented at the conference Media Cultures and Globalization in China. Stockholm: Stockholm University.
Hu, Z. (2005). Institutional dilemma and its ideological origin in the transition of China's media regulation. *Journalism University, 1,* 1–7.
Jiang, L., & Jiang, S. (2003). *China Culture Industry Development Report 2003.* Beijing: China Social Science Press.
Karamanis, T. (2003). *The role of culture and political institutions in media policy.* Cresskill, NJ: Hampton Press.
Liu, L. (2004). *Accelerated growth of China's advertising industry, 1979–2003.* Beijing: Huaxia Publishing House.
McChesney, R. W. (2003). Public broadcasting: Past, present, and future. In M. P. McCauley & E. E. Peterson (Eds.), *Public broadcasting and the public interest* (p. 11). Armonk, NY: M. E. Sharpe.

National Statistics Bureau of People's Republic of China. (2004). National economic and social development statistics of People's Republic of China. China: Author. Retrieved February 28, 2005, from www.stats.gov.cn

Office of the State Administration of Radio, Film & TV. (2003a). Proposal on promoting the development of radio, film and television industry. *Review of Important Documents of Radio, Film & TV*, pp. 7–18.

Office of the State Administration of Radio, Film & TV. (2003b). Transitional timetable from cable to digital TV in China. *Review of Important Documents of Radio, Film & TV*, pp. 33–37.

Office of the State Administration of Radio, Film & TV. (2004a). Provisional regulations on the administration of China's foreign joint venture and cooperation radio and television production and distribution enterprises. *Review of Important Documents of Radio, Film & TV.*

Office of the State Administration of Radio, Film & TV. (2004b). Measures for the administration of the landing of overseas satellite television channels. *Review of Important Documents of Radio, Film & TV*, pp. 82–85.

Qian, W. (2002). *Politics market and media.* Henan: Henan People's Publishing House.

People's Daily Online. (2005). *China to fully promote digital TV this year.* Retrieved March 21, 2005, from www.english.people.com.cn.

State Council. (1993). *Regulations for the administration of satellite television broadcast terrestrial receiving facilities.* Author.

State Council. (1997). *Regulations for the administration of radio and television.* Author.

Sun, Z., & Liu, T. (2001). *Review of Chinese media in 2001.* Retrieved April 14, 2006, from www.shszx.eastday.com/epublish/gb/paper759/200207/class015900002/hwz563307.html

Wang, J. C. F. (2002). *Contemporary Chinese politics.* Upper Saddle River, NJ: Prentice Hall.

Xinhua News Agency. (2004). *China's deregulation on foreign investment in the film/TV industry.* Xinhua News Agency, 11.

Xu, G. (2003). *Brief history of China's radio & TV.* Beijing: China Radio & TV Publishing House.

Yu, G., & Zhang, X. (Eds). (2005). *Media competitiveness: Case study of media value chain and its model.* Beijing: Huaxia Publishing House.

Zhao, Y. (1998). *Media, market, and democracy in China.* Urbana, IL: University of Illinois Press.

Zhang, H. (2005). Speech at the 3rd session of 7th Committee of Science and Technology of SARFT. Retrieved April 14, 2006, from www.sarft.gov.cn/manage/publishfile/12/3443.html

CHAPTER SIX

Television in India: Growth Amid a Regulatory Vacuum

Prasun Sonwalkar

University of the West of England

TV rules our lives. We arrange our time around it. Families sit to dinner in front of it. It is an electronic grandma whose tales and songs send the family to sleep. Our perception of the entire world is governed by this little presence. (Deepak Shourie, publisher, *TVWorld*, defunct Indian TV guide)

INTRODUCTION

India is well suited for the television medium—or rather, India and television are made for each other. Teeming with a population of over 1 billion, its kaleidoscope of cultural diversity and social, political and economic energies provides a rich repertoire for television serials and 24-hour rolling news. Perhaps no other audio-visual medium can capture a snapshot of the shifting sands of contemporary Indian life the way television does. India, currently being hailed as a future economic giant along with China, likes to see itself as a cultural superpower. Its cultural industries—Bollywood and television being prime examples—have reach and appeal beyond its political borders. Within South Asia, other countries perceive Indian cultural content in imperialistic terms (Sonwalkar, 2001) even as the growing numbers of transnational satellite channels beaming into the region "Indianise" their programming to cater to the vast Indian market.

115

There are several major themes in the discourse of Indian television. But the real story is that most of the phenomenal growth in the television sector in the last 15 years has taken place in a regulatory vacuum. Unlike China, Iran or Malaysia, India did not try to ban foreign television networks beaming into India or operating from India, nor did it provide an adequate legislative framework to deal with the new broadcast sector. It has been slow to acknowledge that the situation requires a comprehensive review of the broadcasting sector at a time when the idea of public service broadcasting also needs re-definition to take note of contemporary realities.

From a scenario in which the government initially refrained from investing in television because it was considered a luxury in a developing country, the situation prevailing today could not be more different. The viewer today is literally spoiled for choice as hundreds of Indian and transnational channels vie for viewers. This change has mainly taken place in the context of further liberalization of India's economy since 1991 that has seen the size of the Indian middle class grow to over 350 million. Sporadic attempts to fashion an adequate broadcasting law coincided with this period of economic liberalization. As in the case of India's much-acclaimed information technology industry, the television sector grew to its current strength primarily because of entrepreneurs who seized upon the potential of new communication technologies (e.g., cable). Also crucial to the growth was the lack of regulatory intervention by the government in the initial stages. If today market imperatives have come to dominate the television sector in terms of content and distribution it is mainly because the Indian government allowed it to do so—willingly or unwillingly—by not putting in place a regulatory framework. As of late 2005, such a framework remains a chimera.

India has always been a media-rich poor country—but now television has become the most important mass medium in the country. India's engagement with television differs significantly from that of western countries—while elsewhere, broadcast regulation evolved along with the evolution of the sector, in India the medium has grown exponentially since the early 1990s without any regulation of consequence accompanying its development. It was only after 1997 that some steps were initiated to put in place a framework but these steps too have been mired in differences of opinion among policy makers about how best to proceed. Major private television companies—Indian or transnational—who are by now well entrenched in the sector are generally happy with the current volatile situation, and are not too keen on regulation.

As in other areas of Indian public life, regulation—if and when it is established—is also likely to encounter the fate of poor implementation. So far, the Indian government has found it difficult to distinguish between its role as a regulator and its role as a broadcaster. The government has been reluctant to give up control of the State broadcasting media—Doordarshan (DD), its television wing, and All India Radio (AIR), its radio wing—and this has held up progress on regulatory issues. Limited autonomy was granted to the two organizations in 1997, but being funded mostly from State coffers means they continue to be tied to the government of the day, which is always keen to retain control over a powerful propaganda vehicle. Moreover, due to the proliferation of satellite and cable television, Doordarshan has been reduced to being one among many channels and its reputation as a boring mouthpiece of the government does nothing to enhance its standing among brighter and more competitive channels.

The reality is that sections of society with cable connections hardly watch Doordarshan channels, while those without cable are forced to watch Doordarshan's terrestrial broadcasts. Doordarshan claims that despite the growth in audience reach of satellite channels, its channels continue to be watched by most Indians. Faced with superior content from private channels, the Indian State has presided over a massive commercialization of Doordarshan's own output to retain audiences; in the process, it has neglected other kinds of programs. Doordarshan, being the only television service that is allowed to broadcast using terrestrial frequencies, claims to reach 89% of India's population through its 1314 transmitters.

Today, India has one of the largest television networks in the world—it is said to be the third largest television markets in the world, with 109 million television homes and 61 million cable television homes. The television network is largely similar to the European model, representing a major network dedicated to public service (Doordarshan) and a number of private satellite channels primarily offering entertainment. However, given the sheer size of the sector and the numbers of players involved, this "mixed" model poses some challenge to regulators.

ORIGINS OF INDIAN TELEVISION

The story of Indian television is linked to the development of radio during British rule. Radio was established to strengthen the role of the empire in India and began as a private enterprise in the 1920s by Indian businessmen who saw potential in developing it into a major entertainment business. The colonial government took over the fledgling network of transmitters and radio clubs when the business potential could not be realized. The government-owned radio was first called the Indian State Broadcasting Service and later, All India Radio. During the World Wars, its mandate was to engage in colonial propaganda and, like the BBC, was transformed into a vehicle for anti-Nazi propaganda.

After independence in 1947, the Jawaharlal Nehru government saw the radio network as a means by which an indigenous Indian culture could be forged and disseminated. The government gave priority to the expansion of the radio network, but the efforts to create a national narrative through government policies failed. The emergence of popular cinema and Hindi film songs forced the government to introduce Vividh Bharati, a commercial radio channel, in 1957. By the late 1950s, the technology of television had reached India, but unlike other developing countries such as Brazil or Kenya, television took a long time to develop in India. The first telecast is officially dated September 15, 1959, from the capital New Delhi, but it was not until 1976 when Doordarshan was formed that television reached a small section of the population.

The first television broadcast in India was made possible by aid from a variety of external sources: equipment from electronics manufacturer Phillips, UNESCO grants of US$20,000 and 180 free sets, technical and other help from Germany, and financial support for 10 years from the Ford Foundation. That policy makers of the day were not too keen on television—believing that it was a luxury for a country with serious problems such as poverty reduction, health, education and so forth—was evident from the fact that it was All India Radio that was given the task of producing and broadcasting the first television programs. Some officials of the radio network were hastily trained and deployed in the television wing.

The first telecasts had a range of only 40 km and mainly comprised educational programs for 20 minutes, twice a week. There were only 41 television sets in New Delhi in 1962, but these grew to 4,170 by 1966. Procuring a license from the government was mandatory to own a television set. Most of the television sets were imported. For several years, the government continued to accord low priority to television by annually allocating much less funds to it compared to radio; moreover, much of the funds for television would remain underutilized. Due to a lack of institutional focus, the quality of programming on television suffered. As Gupta (1998, p. 21) notes,

> The roots of this problem, which continues to haunt Doordarshan even today, lie partly in the fact that these programs were produced by teams from AIR whose only experience was in the audio medium . . . Thus, television programs were often little more than radio programs with static, unimaginative visuals.

They did not sustain interest, and after the novelty of the new technology wore off, few bothered to switch the television set on. However, interest began to pick up when a one-hour daily service comprising news and entertainment programs in Hindi and English was started on August 15, 1965. By 1970, the duration of service was increased to three hours; in that year, the number of television sets had risen to 22,000. In the mid-1970s, television stations were set up in the other three metros of Mumbai, Kolkata, and Chennai, and in Lucknow, Srinagar, and Amritsar. Indian manufactured television sets entered the market, and soon the number of sets had risen to 100,000. Manufacturers, advertisers and television owners demanded further expansion of the sector, and in January 1976, commercials were allowed on television. Three months later, Doordarshan, the television wing of AIR, was set up as a separate organization. As part of its public service mandate, educational programs for farmers and others were produced and distributed.

Such objectives were taken further under a project called the Satellite Instructional Television Experiment (SITE), which ran for 1 year from August 1, 1975. Several departments were involved in the project to use television for education and developmental objectives. The National Aeronautic and Space Agency (NASA) of the United States allowed the free use of one of its satellites for 1 year for the project, but the results were none too encouraging. Frequent depiction of the then Prime Minister Indira Gandhi and official announcements put off many viewers, including farmers to whom the broadcasts were specifically targeted. It marked the beginning of what later came to be seen as official propaganda through television, and Doordarshan as the official mouthpiece. Doordarshan continues to be seen in such negative terms in popular perception.

In 1977, when Indira Gandhi's Congress party lost elections and the Janata Party came to power, there were demands to make AIR and Doordarshan autonomous of the government. According to the Verghese Committee Report, the broadcast media were "necessarily part and parcel of the larger process of national planning and development." The committee envisaged a "national broadcasting service predominantly Indian in content and character," and recommended several changes to its programming. It also recommended that there should be a shift towards genuine autonomy: "We are of the opinion that all the national broadcasting services should be vested exclusively in an independent, impartial and autonomous organization established by law to act as a trustee in the national interest."

These recommendations were the first to set in motion a series of bills in India's parliament; the first such was the Prasar Bharti Bill introduced in 1979. It involved the setting up of an autonomous organization called Prasar Bharti that would be tasked with running Doordarshan and AIR, ostensibly independent of government control. However, in the Bill, the government reserved the right to issue directives to the organization as and when necessary, which would have to be followed. But the Bill was never carried through when the Janata government fell and Indira Gandhi returned to power. Since 1979, providing autonomy for AIR and Doordarshan has been one of the promises made in election manifestos by major political parties, but no government ensured its realization until 1990. The Bill was passed in parliament in 1990 but it was not until 1997 before the Act was implemented by officially notifying the setting up of Prasar Bharati (Broadcasting Corporation of India).

POST-1982: TOWARD GROWTH AND FEEBLE REGULATION

As the tortuous path of granting autonomy to Doordarshan and AIR progressed, India's television sector continued to be regulated by the two colonial laws—the Indian Telegraph Act, 1885, and the Indian Wireless Act, 1933. From the mid-1970s, realizing the propaganda potential of television, successive Indian governments made huge investments to establish a nationwide television infrastructure. This was aided by India putting in space a series of satellites (imported and indigenously produced) and setting up regional television centers across the country. The idea was to cover the entire population, and propagate the activities of the ruling party in power. In 1984, one new transmitter was commissioned every day for four months in different parts of the country. The indigenous television manufacturing industry also expanded its capacity and the government pitched in by cutting excise duty.

The expansion of Doordarshan's television network got a major boost when India hosted the Asian Games in 1982. Color television was introduced while duty free import of television sets and picture tubes was allowed during the period of the games. Later, Doordarshan launched new entertainment channels; first in New Delhi and Mumbai, and then in other towns. Doordarshan began earning huge revenue by telecasting popular serials such as "Hum Log," "Buniyaad," and later "Ramayana" and "Mahabharata." In 1987–1988, Doordarshan's revenue had risen to Rs 136 million and by 1990 it had reached Rs 256 million. By the end of 1990, there were more than 28 million television sets in the country.

Until 1991, Doordarshan enjoyed a monopoly over India's airwaves, but this was soon challenged by cross-border satellite television—or what has been called an "invasion from the skies" (Manchanda, 1998). It was CNN's coverage of the Gulf War that unleashed new forces that revolutionized the nature of Indian television. The changes began with a few five-star hotels hooking up to CNN through a dish and relaying it to their guests. The live coverage of the war aroused much interest and there was growing demand for more such channels by the elites and the fast growing middle class. Soon, entrepreneurs were slinging wires or cables across telephone and electricity poles in residential areas, offering channels such as the bouquet of Star TV and BBC World Service for a small fee of Rs 100 per month. From two Doordarshan channels prior to 1991, Indian viewers could suddenly receive 50 channels by 1996, providing a range of entertainment and choice.

Cable television had arrived in India, and millions of miles of cables were soon slung over electricity poles, trees and buildings across residential areas across the country. Since most of Doordarshan's programming was seen to be unimaginative and dull, large audiences switched to satellite television channels made available through cable. The developments coincided with the Indian government accelerating its process of economic liberalization. In keeping with the new thinking, did not try to restrict or ban the reception of foreign channels. But it was also true that it took the government some time to realize the implications of satellite television and the cable networks changing the rules of the game. According to Kumar (1998):

> The government's initial response to the illegal transmission and distribution of cross-border television channels was one of tolerance rather than of resistance . . . (The) Congress party, which had ushered in a new economic policy of liberalization, did not wish to give the impression that it wanted in any way to restrict or block the transnational television channels. (p. 34)

As per the two colonial laws, the government held the monopoly of transmission of all forms of wireless signals over Indian Territory, but legally there was no prohibition on receiving a television signal in India. Thus, private television channels, owned by Indians or foreigners, have been able to beam into India without violating any law. Their telecasts are then received by cable operators and distributed to homes through the millions of miles of cables that have been laid. But if there were no legal problems in receiving signals, there was some uncertainty over the distribution of the signals by cable operators. The Indian Telegraph Act, 1885, could not have envisaged the technological developments in the 20th century—only a generous interpretation of the idea of "telegraph" can make the law applicable to the realities of cable and satellite transmission.

Manchanda (1998, p. 144) has argued, "the success of cable operations was due to a number of reasons: the urban middle class had spare time and resources to see more entertainment; 'the government channel' remained slow in satisfying that demand. Being hooked up to a cable network became fashionable among the hotels that catered to tourists' needs." The cable revolution was engineered not by large companies or corporations but by largely unorganized small-time entrepreneurs who recognized the demand for television and laid the largely illegal proliferation of cable networks across India. They first began by installing two dishes: one pointed at Palapa for CNN and the other at AsiaSat for Star TV and BBC. As Viswanath and Karan (2000, p. 101) note, "cable television in India has been the result of sheer entrepreneurial genius in the absence of a cohesive communication policy. It is an exemplar of entrepreneurial initiative leading and outrunning government policy."

In 1992, entrepreneur Subhash Chandra was the first to start a private Indian satellite channel, Zee TV, which immediately captured the imagination of viewers and generated large revenues. As a Channel 4 (1995) publication puts it, Zee has been a phenomenal success story: "from a less than shoestring operation . . . to without a doubt probably the most successful story in broadcasting history." Several other Indian owned or India-specific channels followed, focusing on a variety of genres—news, entertainment, sport, business, religion and films. A significant aspect of the Indian situation is the proliferation of channels in each of the major languages, particularly in languages in south India, such as Telugu, Kannada, Malayama and Tamil.

CONTEMPORARY POLICY ISSUES

Satellite television and the burgeoning cable industry complicated the rules of the game. The Prasar Bharati Bill was drawn up with the assumption that the government was the only agency that was authorized to transmit, or use the airwaves. However, the situation was further complicated in 1995 by a ruling of the Supreme Court of India, which declared that airwaves were the property of the people. The judgment proffered:

(Airwaves) or frequencies are public property and their use has to be controlled and regulated by a public authority in the interests of the public to prevent the invasion of their rights of freedom of speech and expression. The central government shall make immediate steps to establish an independent autonomous public authority representative of all sections and interests in the society to control and regulate the use of airwaves.

The ruling prompted more demands to set up an independent regulatory authority on the lines of Britain's Ofcom. Around the time the Supreme Court pronounced its judgment, the government sought to regulate the cable industry, which had become the fastest growing segment of the television sector. In the initial stages, the cable industry was highly fragmented as it comprised mainly a large number of small operators catering to specific residential localities. As business grew, these small operators entered franchise arrangements or merged with large operators and introduced value-added services such as Internet over cable, pay-per-view, etc. In recent years, broadcasters have integrated their businesses with the large cable operators to have greater and assured access to subscribers and revenue.

The government enacted the Cable Television Networks (Regulation) Act, 1995, which sought to regulate the cable industry to ensure uniformity in its operations throughout the country. The Act requires cable networks to be operated only after registration and to show programs that are in conformity with the program code drawn up by the Ministry of Information and Broadcasting. As per the Act, only an individual who is a citizen of India, or an association of individuals whose members are citizens of India, can be a cable operator and provide cable television networks or can be responsible for the management and operation of a cable television network.

The Act was opposed by the large number of small operators, who were expected to register themselves at the Post Office for a fee of Rs 50. Such registration—official recognition—made the operators liable for different taxes and accountability. Most of the transactions between the small operators and subscribers were cash-based and there were no records of large sums of money that would change hands during the monthly collection of the subscription fee. The Act caused a lot of resentment among cable operators as it also tried to prescribe a code into the kind of programming and advertising that could be distributed though cable. It stipulated that cable operators must carry at least two Doordarshan channels. As Crawley (1996) suggests,

> The moves to regulate the cable industry represent not just the filling of a legislative gap, but also a more recent recognition that this is by far the most promising way of bringing under control something which until now has been seen as beyond control. (p. 291)

A shake-up ensued in the cable industry as the number of small operators fell when many either merged with large operators or shut shop as it became unviable to continue under the regulated environment. Meanwhile, the government was faced with demands to do more to regulate content on private satellite channels when programs of a sexual nature offended Indian sensibilities and the subject became a matter of much debate inside and outside parliament. In 2000, the government drew up the Cable Television Networks (Amendment) Bill, which stipulated that all foreign and domestic channels, distributed through cable must abide by the country's program and advertising code. Under the earlier Act, only Doordarshan had to abide by the code. The Bill also imposed a "must carry" clause that bound cable operators to carry three Doordarshan channels (two national and one regional) on the prime band. The Bill was passed in parliament in August 2000. As per the new law, advertisements related to alcohol and tobacco products are not permitted on channels distributed through cable networks. Channels are also prohibited from showing advertisements that offend the morality, decency and the religious susceptibilities of people, degrades women, adversely affects India's friendly relations, etc.

Private and foreign broadcasters believe that it is difficult to monitor the content delivered through the cable network since there is no system of licensing of cable operators. Many cable operators under-report the number of subscribers, resulting in broadcasters losing subscription revenue. In the absence of licensing, large cable operators do not have security of investment. The solution, according to broadcasters, is to put in place a system of addressability through the introduction of a Conditional Access System (CAS). This system, which is implemented globally, would increase transparency in the subscriber base and pay channels would get their rightful share of subscription revenue.

To introduce addressability in the sector, the government brought another amendment to the cable legislation, now called Cable Television Networks (Amendment) Bill, 2002, which was finally passed in December 2002. Large operators welcomed CAS as they believed it would change their fortunes as they were squeezed in between broadcasters asking for more payout and last-mile small operators who were under-reporting their subscriber base. Independent cable operators also saw it as an opportunity, but soon several problems arose with CAS implementation. A set-top box costs between US$32 and US$106 and it is yet to be determined who will pay for it. Elsewhere, broadcasters and cable operators share the cost but in India, small operators do not have the finances to invest in the set-top boxes. Broadcasters are also reluctant to bear the cost. There is also uncertainty about the technical aspects of the box—should it be analog or digital? This bill is the latest example of a familiar story in Indian public life: well-intentioned initiatives failing at the stage of implementation.

THE CONTEMPORARY TELEVISION LANDSCAPE

Due to the ways in which the Indian television sector evolved, the contemporary landscape is haphazard. It has unique features, unlike any other television market. Unlike, for example the U.S. market, television software is still a separate industry— in the U.S., broadcasters buy out software companies or set up their own production wings. According to Kohli (2003, p. 79), the Indian television sector can be regarded as "a chain with three links—broadcasters, the cable industry and the software industry." However, broadcasters such as Zee TV, Star and Sony have begun moves to set up their own production units.

In late 2005, according to industry estimates, India has become the third largest television market in the world, with 109 million television homes and 61 million cable television homes. Its cable industry is the fastest growing in Asia with turnover growing at an annual rate of 18% to approach US$3 billion in 2004. There is much room for expansion with the television industry currently representing only 0.46 of the national GDP, while advertising spends amount to only 0.17 of the GDP. The 2005 market capitalization of media companies is estimated to be between US$3 and US$3.5 billion and is expected to scale unto US$20 billion by 2010. Profits in the television industry, as high as US$350 million are also expected to rise exponentially as the market expands. Addressing a gathering of Indian and transnational television representatives, S. K. Arora, the top official in India's Ministry of Information and Broadcasting, said:

> In relation to many major regional markets such as China or Taiwan or even Korea, India is lightly regulated. We are not in favour of micro regulation . . . we will only look at macro aspects. In most aspects, the TV industry has to self-regulate. We will look to continue to provide a framework that supports competition and development. We certainly envisage greater consumer choice and competition from rollout of and investment in free-to-air and pay direct-to-home satellite services along with the gradual introduction of mobile telephony and broadband TV . . . For the market to grow, there must be greater business unity—a common ground that unites the industry and pushes it to adopt new technology, invest in new content and distribute higher quality services to consumer. Today, the market remains characterized by adversarial politics with squabbles breaking out amongst all parties in the most important industry decisions. (Wanvari & Couto, 2005)

Thus, the overall television scenario is marked by "squabbles" at various levels within the television sector—between cable operators and broadcasters, between large cable operators (called Multi-System Operators, or MSOs) and small cable operators ("last mile" cable operators), the government and broadcasters over content quality, and so forth. In the prevailing situation, early-entry television channels dominate the market by cornering a majority of the advertising spends and ratings. The last decade has also seen the rise of television channels in various languages, each catering to niche audiences not only within India but also to the large linguistic diasporas settled outside India, mainly in the U.S. and the U.K.

India's television sector is dominated by the "Big Three"—Zee, Star, and Sony. Latest annualized fiscals show that these three channels have an aggregated turnover in excess of US$380 million, with Zee leading with US$309 million, and narrowly followed by Star with US$302 million. The scope for expansion in the south Asian region for the three channels is evident from the comparative turnover of China's CCTV of over US$970 million.

Until the early 1990s, India's press cornered the lion's share of advertising spends. Within television, Doordarshan cornered most of the advertising revenue, but satellite channels had overtaken Doordarshan by 1998–99 (Sonwalkar, 2001, p. 510). The share of the Indian press dwindled as television emerged on the scene in the early 1990s.

There are several Indian and transnational channels operating in the market. Due to the fluid nature of the market, there are instances of some channels being launched and closed down after some time. So it is difficult to arrive at a definite list of the number of channels operating at a particular point in time. But there are some major players in the market, such as Zee, Sony, Star and so forth. According to Arora, of the 350-odd channels operating in India, only 164 are being uplinked from the country (uplinking from India is allowed based on majority shareholding vesting in Indian hands). The major channels can be divided into four categories: the Doordarshan family (Table 6.1). Hindi satellite channels, regional language channels and 24-hour news channels.

There are also a range of Hindi language satellite channels including Zee TV, Star niche channels and regional channels as well as 14 news channels. Apart from these channels, transnational channels beam general entertainment and news programs into India—most of them tailored to suit Indian audiences. Some content on such transnational channels has proved controversial as it is perceived as offensive to Indian sensibilities. This is mainly in relation to content of a sexual nature. The government is keen to ensure that content on such channels does not offend Indian culture. However, since most of them do not uplink from Indian Territory, there is little control that the Indian government can exert, apart from making cable operators responsible for ensuring the quality of content on the channels that they provide to subscribers.

Doordarshan does not figure among the most-watched channels. Murdoch-owned Star Plus leads with the highest ratings because it has unabashedly tailored

TABLE 6.1

Doordarshan (DD) Channels (Regional and Satellite) (RLSC = Regional Languages Satellite Channel: SN = State Network

DD 1	National Channel
DD 2	News Channel
DD	RLSC-Malayalam
DD 5	RLSC Tamil: Podigai
DD 6	RLSC-Oriya
DD 7	RLSC Bengali
DD 8	RLSC Telugu
DD 9	RLSC Kanada: Chandana
DD 10	RLSC Marathi: Sahyadri
DD 11	RLSC Gujarati
DD 12	RLSC Kashir
DD 13	RLSC Assamese and Languages of North East
DD 14	SN-Rajasthan
DD 15	SN-Madhya Pradesh
DD 16	SN-Uttar Pradesh
DD 17	SN-Bihar
DD 18	RLSC-Punjabi
DD 19	SN-Himachal Pradesh
DD 20	SN-Jharkhand
DD 21	SN-Chhatisgarh
DD 22	SN-Haryana
DD-India	International Service
DD-Sports	Sports Channel
DD Bharati	Enrichment/Cultural Channel
DD-Gyandarshan	Educational TV Channel

its Hindi programming to suit Indian audiences. Three news channels also figure in the list (Aaj Tak, Zee News, Star News).

ATTEMPTS TO REGULATE THE TELEVISION SECTOR

The government ensured the passage of some bills to part-regulate the sector, but such attempts have invariably failed at the stage of implementation. Moreover, it had sought to regulate large areas of the sector through legislation that was primarily aimed at the cable industry. As India's television sector grows by the day, the demand to set up an independent regulatory authority is growing. As a paper based on the deliberation of the Entertainment Committee of the Federation of Indian Chambers of Commerce and Industry (FICCI) observed in 2003, "Specially appointed independent regulatory authorities, with expert knowledge in the broadcasting sector, have an important role to play in the development of the sector. The more the sector expands, and the more complex and dynamic it becomes, the more it would need well-considered and proportionate regulation to ensure efficient functioning."

The most important problem, according to FICCI, was not the absence of regulations but implementation and enforcement. It was concerned that moves towards regulation of the sector did not lead to over-regulation. It cited the example of Australia, where industry groups determine the code of practice applicable to their sector in consultation with the Australian Broadcasting Authority, and called for a similar framework in India.

The government led by the United Front first sought to begin the process of setting up a Broadcasting Authority of India by drawing up the Broadcasting Bill, 1997. The authority was to be given wide ranging powers—such as regulating content, making direct-to-home (DTH) broadcasters carry Doordarshan, differentiating between Indian companies and foreign companies in the granting of licenses, cross-media holdings, non-granting of licenses to broadcasters owning cable companies and so forth. The bill also envisaged allowing the setting up of private broadcasting stations by institutions that provide education, community services, environment protection or health awareness. But the implications of the Bill were so widespread that it was not even taken up for discussion in parliament. A committee of senior parliamentarians set up to study the bill had consultations with the industry and consumers, but before its report could be discussed in parliament, the United Front government of the day fell. The next Bharatiya Janata Party government did not share the previous government's enthusiasm for the Bill and allowed it to lapse.

The latest attempt to regulate the television sector is the introduction of the Communication Convergence Bill, 2001. It seeks to recognize and anticipate the convergence of communication technologies, including telecommunications, broadcasting and information technology. It seeks to establish an independent body called the Communications Commission of India (CCI) that would have a wide range of regulatory powers including the power to license and enforce license conditions in these sectors. The CCI will also be expected to oversee the development of communication services, establishment of new infrastructure, introduction of new technologies and formulate codes for television content and regulate content on the Internet and other broadcasting services. If passed the bill would replace laws such as the two colonial laws as well as the cable television network laws.

Critics of the Bill feel that the Communications Convergence bill is an attempt to reintroduce the Broadcast Bill of 1997 with much wider implications under a different name. They say the bill is silent on important issues such as cross-media holdings while various terms were left open and undefined. Given the differences of opinion among the various stake-holders in the television sector, the Bill is unlikely to be passed in parliament in the near future. According to Ram, the Communications Convergence bill:

> Is restrictive, undemocratic and authoritative piece of work. The Communications convergence Bill in its present form should not be rushed into . . . technology-related reforms should not be pushed through without taking into account the ground realities. (quoted in Jagannathan, 2001)

But why now does an industry that has shown much dynamism need to seek regulation? There are three reasons for this: because major investment in India's television sector is holding off, unwilling to invest in a scenario in which rules of the game are not in place; because until the cable industry knows what kind of licensing the government will put in place, it is not investing to upgrade infrastructure; and thirdly, because regulation is needed if the industry is to be organized in a professional manner.

Without a regulatory authority in place, the government is clearly caught in the vortex of being a regulator as well as broadcaster. On paper, Doordarshan and AIR have become autonomous after Prasar Bharti (Broadcasting Corporation of India) was set up, but Doordarshan remains partly funded through an annual grant voted by parliament. Even though it generates resources through commercial operations, it continues to be tied to the government of the day. The ruling parties in power continue to use Doordarshan for propaganda purposes. The government also tries to ensure protection to Doordarshan in the marketplace by making it obligatory for cable operators to carry its channels under the "must carry" rules in cable legislation. By not granting licenses for terrestrial telecast, the government also ensures that Doordarshan enjoys monopoly in the more easily accessible terrestrial transmission market.

As the Communications Convergence Bill, 2001, makes the rounds through committees and consultations, the government issued new directives on the nature of foreign participation in the television sector (to ensure that control remains in Indian hands), uplinking from Indian soil and on the rules granting DTH licences. The government has allowed uplinking from India to companies that have 80% management control in Indian hands. DTH licenses are now available for Indian companies whose foreign equity is not more than 49%. In the absence of a regulatory authority, the situation is marked by ad hoc measures and fluidity, leading to the further dominance of commercial interests in Indian television sector.

CONCLUSIONS: COMMERCE OR CULTURE?

For transnational media corporations, India represents a large market and an audience that is keen to join a global audience. It is true that the television sector in India has grown exponentially since the early 1990s, offering possibilities of extending civil society and reinvigorating the public sphere. But the dominating trend has been towards privatization of the media space, also witnessed in the extent to which news is sought to be presented in the form of infotainment on 24-hour news channels. The focus on commercial considerations is likely to be a mistake in India where despite the growth of the middle class, serious problems such as health, education rural development persist and need commensurate attention from the media. Since the early 1990s, when "Murdochization" of the Indian media began (Sonwalkar, 2003), news of events and issues related to such "downmarket" beats has fallen by the wayside. Given the size of India's population of over 1 billion, there remain vast sections that are media-poor, whose life situations are increasingly priced out of the market.

Doordarshan is likely to continue as an important player in India's television sector, even though it needs State protection in a market-driven scenario. By joining the market forces to generate revenues, Doordarshan has already lost the battle—its public service role will continue to remain in question. Unless Doordarshan is allowed to redefine itself as a counterpoise to the market driven media, it is unlikely to amount to anything of consequence. Its terrestrial broadcasts will continue to generate some revenue from a shrinking mass audience that is beyond the reach of cable networks. As Crawley and Page (2000) suggest:

Failure to take stock and to legislate for the new situation will leave more time for the commercialization of State broadcasting and the longer the trend continues the greater will be the difficulty in establishing a viable public interest role or the media in the future. Recent experience has demonstrated clearly the value of the Markey in widening choice in particular areas of broadcasting. But the states' responses have betrayed a lack of clear thinking, both about the future role of the state sector and about what can legitimately be required of commercial broadcasters in serving wider public needs.

The Indian television sector has been lightly regulated even though efforts are underway to set up a regulatory authority under the Convergence Commission of India. But given the history of such legislation, it is unlikely to be passed in Indian parliament in the near future. Both the government and parts of the industry have recognized the importance of regulation but given the fractious nature of the stakeholders, a consensus on key regulatory issues is unlikely in the near future.

REFERENCES

Channel 4 Television. (1995). Bazaar Television, Part 2, Satellite Wars series, April.

Crawley, W. (1996). Air wars: competition and control in India's electronic media, *Contemporary South Asia, 5*(3), 289–302.

Crawley, W., & Page, D. (2000). Satellites and South Asia, *Himal*, August.

Gupta, N. (1998). *Switching Channels: Ideologies of Television in India*. Delhi: Oxford University Press.

Jagannathan, V. (2001). Media industry demands redrafting the Communication Convergence Bill, www.domain-b.com. Accessed October 5, 2005 from www.domain-b.com/marketing/media/20010314_media_redrafting.htm

Kohli, V. (2003). *The Indian Media* Busines. London: Sage.

Kumar, K. J. (1998). History of Television in India: A Political Economy Perspective. In S. R, Melkote, P. Shields., & B. C. Agrawal (Eds.), *International Satellite Broadcasting in South Asia: Political, Economic and Cultural Implications*, pp. 19–46. New York: University Press of America.

Manchanda, U. (1998). Invasion from the skies: the impact of foreign television on India, *Australian Studies in Journalism, 7,* 136–163.

Sonwalkar, P. (2001). India: Makings of Little Cultural Imperialism? *Gazette, 63*(6): 505–519.

Sonwalkar, P. (2003). *Murdochisation of the Indian press: From by-line to bottom-line*. Media, Culture & Society, 821–834.

Viswanath, K., & Karan, K. (2000). India. In Gunaratne, S. A. (Ed.), *Handbook of the media in Asia* (pp. 84–117). London: Sage.

Wanvari, A. & Couto, V. (2005). The Indian Television Summit 2005. Accessed October 2005 from www.Indiantelevision.com

The Dilemmas of Reforming Japan's Broadcasting System: Ambivalent Implications of Its Liberalization

Kaori Hayashi*
Interfaculty Initiative in Information Studies
University of Tokyo

In the past six decades, Japan has developed into a highly media-dependent nation. Especially, television has become the most popular national medium. In 2005, the Japanese viewers watched television for more than four hours daily on average (Nippon Hoso Kyokai [NHK], 2005). It is thus fair to say that television has become an integral part of people's life in Japan.

While the broadcasting industry appears to enjoy its pervasive power on people's everyday life, the broadcasting system in Japan, as in other advanced industrial countries, is now at a major turning point. This arises in the context of globalization and the social transformation associated with the development and widening use of information technology which has precipitated an urgent need for the reappraisal of the institutional design developed in each country. However, what is particularly striking in the case of Japan is the way that change arising from deregulatory trends in the overall economy together with developments in the technological sphere have highlighted once again specific problems that already existed in the broadcasting system. This has made clearer than ever before the potentially catastrophic nature of the current crisis in the sector. On a number of

---

*The author thanks David Buist for his translation work.

occasions in the past, the Japanese broadcasting industry has given rise to various social problems, and on each such occasion the Japanese people have felt a mixture of anger and resignation.[1] Especially in recent years, amid the current climate of change, the already declining nature of the Japanese broadcasting system has become increasingly visible. In this context the situation in Japan is somewhat different to more liberal countries in the West. The three global media trends of commercialization, deregulation, and liberalization have thus to be interpreted differently because they have different effects depending on the cultural and social context in which they have been applied.

Notwithstanding the almost universal cry of "crisis" in Japanese broadcasting, Japan finds itself for some reason unable to offer a panacea to solve the current problems, and policy makers and broadcasters find themselves in a dilemma that makes it impossible to select any one measure as the correct one for the future.

Against this background, the aim of this chapter is to analyze the entangled problems of broadcasting in Japan from a number of different angles. Among other things, I examine the state of this crisis from three distinct perspectives: (1) the historical, (2) the institutional and policy, and (3) the cultural.

JAPAN'S POSTWAR BROADCASTING POLITICS

The Aftermath of Occupation Policy: From Radical Democratization to Red Purge

In 1945, Japan accepted the Potsdam Declaration, surrendered to the Allied Powers, and was placed under occupation. The whole direction of postwar Japanese mass media history was largely determined by the broadcasting policy adopted at that time by the occupation forces under the command of the American General D. MacArthur. Japan adopted a new constitution in 1947 with the support of General Headquarters (GHQ), the name of the occupying American military overseeing the government of Japan in the postwar period. Article 21 of this constitution guarantees freedom of speech, publishing, and expression. In theory, therefore, absolute freedom of speech was guaranteed as a fundamental human right of the Japanese people for the first time in their history. However, this constitution has been criticized by many as having been "imposed" on Japan under occupation. Therefore, the various rights granted to citizens under this constitution are not generally seen as having been actively won from the State by the people as the result of a democratic revolution. This so-called "positive democracy" continues to influence the general atmosphere of public expression in Japan today.

---

[1]Examples of recent scandals include manipulation of viewer ratings by a producer at Nihon TV (one of the five major commercial broadcasting networks), embezzlement of license-fee funds by an NHK producer, and plagiarizing of an Internet Web page by a manager at TBS (another of the big five commercial broadcasters).

A second feature of GHQ's media policy was that it allowed the continued existence and functioning of the prewar mass media organizations in contrast to the situation in postwar Germany. Therefore Nippon Hoso Kyokai (NHK) was allowed to continue broadcasting even after the radical overhaul of the media system after the war. This organization had originally been set up in 1926 as a nominally independent body, although in reality it had become little more than a State-run broadcasting agency. To this day, NHK has been the axis of Japan's broadcasting.

A third feature of postwar media policy under occupation was the beginning of a radical process of democratization within the media organizations bequeathed from the prewar period. This was especially so in the newspaper industry, where the process of questioning and redressing the wartime lapses of management took place in one company after another. The democratic ideas imported from the United States were especially well greeted by the Japanese Left, and were implemented in a radical manner. The tide of democratization under occupation seemed unstoppable and numerous cases of "revolution from below" were accomplished. For example, 44 out of 56 then existing newspaper companies experienced a change of management immediately after the end of the war (Tsukamoto, 1995). There were movements for worker control in many companies, and most of these succeeded for a while. Among leading Japanese newspapers, the *Yomiuri Shimbun* and *Hokkaido Shimbun* stood at the forefront of the Labor movement. Meanwhile, Japanese company managers and the political Right found themselves placed in a very difficult position.

In broadcasting, however, the process of democratization from the inside was less spontaneous. It therefore fell to GHQ to exert pressure for democratization from outside. NHK had, before the war, been a virtual colony of the government's Ministry of Posts and Telecommunications (which means, its management was made up largely of former bureaucrats from that ministry) and provided a very poor environment for the growth of journalistic ethics. Liberal programs were aired for the first time under the direction of GHQ.

At that time, NHK was the only broadcasting agency in Japan. Under the direction of the occupying forces, a thorough program of reform was pursued. In 1946, an independent advisory body called the "Broadcasting Committee" (*Hoso Iinkai*) was set up. This committee was independent from both the Japanese government and the American occupation army. It was a decision-making authority over the management of NHK, and NHK was obliged to follow its directives. One of the first acts of the committee was to appoint Takano Iwasaburo as the director of NHK. Takano was a well-known Marxist economist and director of the Ohara Institute for Social Research (a think-tank specializing in labor issues).

The fourth feature of postwar occupation media policy in Japan is that it underwent a massive reversal of direction in favor of conservative forces after the first years of radical democratization. This was largely in response to changing international circumstances and most notably the beginning of the Cold War, the communist victory in mainland China, and the situation on the Korean Peninsula. This led GHQ to adopt anti-communist policies in Japan. In order to build Japan up into an "anti-communist bulwark" in Asia, the United States put the brakes on the democratization process and began suppressing the spontaneous democratic forces it had earlier unleashed. Even as early as 1946, the occupation forces had intervened in a strike at *Yomiuri Shimbun.* Industrial regulations limiting the influence of the labor movement were enacted.

There was also a "red purge" in which large numbers of people with communist sympathies were dismissed from both public and private employment throughout the country. The occupation forces were particularly concerned to eradicate communists from the media. This had a particularly severe effect on NHK, where an especially large number of employees were considered to be communists and were ousted. The purge injured the morale of NHK journalists and succeeded in weakening union organizations among its employees. This incident has left its mark on NHK to the present day (Kawasaki, 1997) and the purge was a major relief for media management who had been placed under severe pressures by the democratization movement. The Japanese Left lost the United States as its moral custodian and in parallel employers and the Japanese Right forged close ties with the United States. In short, Japan's mass media experienced a shift from one ideological extreme to another within as few as 2 years directly after the war.

The Cold War Legacy: Editorial Rights

The key instrument of managerial reaction in the media industry was the concept of "editorial rights." First established during the occupation, the legacy of the concept today is almost taken for granted among press and broadcasting managers. The concept of "editorial rights," as it has come to be understood in postwar Japan, was established by a declaration issued on March 16, 1948, by the Japan Newspaper Publishers and Editors Association. However, this was in fact no mere declaration. It has been said that it:

> defined not only the manner in which newspapers are produced, but also established a distinctive regulatory concept underlying and legalizing the absolute authority of media owners and management over a wide range of matters relating to newspapers production . . . it came to function as if it possessed absolute and sacrosanct regulatory power itself. (Tsukamoto, 1995, p. 138)

Furthermore, the concept of "editorial rights" came to be applied not only to newspapers, but also to broadcasting, including NHK and the commercial stations, which were members of the Japan Newspaper Publishers and Editors Association. Thus, it can be said that it defined the very core of the postwar Japanese mass media.

> Newspaper financial and editorial management is charged with the responsibility of protecting its editorial rights against all challenges, whether these

be from individuals or groups, or from outside the organization or from within. External interference will be resisted no matter what. Furthermore, any person within the organization who deliberately interferes with the truth or fairness of reporting or commentary, or with the due process of publication, or who fails to follow editorial directives, will be excluded on the grounds that they have violated editorial rights. (Japan Newspaper Publishers and Editors Association, 1948, www.japaninc.net/contents. php?articleID=983)

As this quotation from the declaration indicates, the notion of "editorial rights" was conceived in such a way as to exclude all outsiders and oppositional elements from the world of the media. This exclusion applies not only to the editorial process but also to all aspects of media content and labor conditions within media organizations.

Some journalists and scholars are of the opinion that the concept is nothing more than an aspect of the history of the red purge and has since become only a dead letter. Nevertheless, recent events have not necessarily supported this view.

A case in point is a statement made last year by the then President of NHK, Ebisawa Katsuji. After NHK offended viewers in September by failing to broadcast live a Diet session (Diet is the formal name of the Japanese Parliament) in which Ebisawa had been summoned as an unsworn witness to explain a chain of scandals including bogus business trips and the embezzlement of license fees, he rebuffed this criticism by saying: "We have the editorial right to decide what to air." Although he later apologized for his "slip of the tongue" after having to confront even more complaints by angry viewers, this case reveals that the phrase "editorial rights" has always been retained at the back of media management's mind and is brought out as a trump card in order to exclude the public from the world of the media.

NHK has used the concept of "editorial rights" to justify its actions on a number of other occasions. In January 2005, the *Asahi* newspaper published an accusation that NHK had been the subject of political interference by members of the governing party. This accusation referred specifically to a documentary program on "Military Comfort Women" that had been broadcast four years earlier on NHK's educational channel. It is alleged that NHK executives met with certain leading politicians before the broadcast, and that this led directly to a revision of the program's content. The original source for this story was an NHK producer, who confessed at a media conference that political interference had led to key footage being removed from the documentary on the orders of his superior without anyone else's agreement. At the time when this story was made public, NHK rebutted the criticism by saying that the decision to remove the footage was in accordance with the management's special "editorial rights."

Time and again, scholars and intellectuals have demanded the abolition of this antiliberal concept on grounds that it seriously impedes the basic democratic right of freedom of speech. Media management, however, is still reluctant to discard the concept altogether, arguing that this right has never been used with any malicious intent. Therefore, even to the present day, the declaration of "editorial rights" is emblazoned on the official Japanese-language Web site of the Japan Newspaper Publishers and Editors Association. It is a historical irony that the United States, the self-proclaimed vanguard of free journalism and free speech in the world, invented this concept and left it behind in the country they occupied, leaving a legacy from the Cold War.

Government as an Active Regulator

Toward the end of the occupation in 1950, a series of three laws were enacted to lay the foundations for the postwar broadcasting system in Japan. These were: (1) the Radio Law, (2) the Broadcasting Law, and (3) the Law for the Establishment of a Broadcasting Supervisory Committee. Their enactment seemed to provide a secure foundation for the postwar broadcasting system. However, soon after the end of the occupation, the Law for the Establishment of a Broadcasting Supervisory Committee was abolished. It would have provided for the establishment of an independent body guaranteeing the democratic nature of broadcasting at arms length from government authorities. This committee was supposed to have been the cornerstone of the postwar broadcasting system.

But in the current system, without any such independent supervisory body, the granting of broadcasting licenses, the assignment of broadcasting frequencies as well as other areas pertaining to the administration of broadcasting, are overseen by the Ministry of Internal Affairs and Communications. Therefore, when new broadcasting licenses are granted, the ministry also tries to intervene in the process of determining who owns and manages the newly established channel. In addition, more often than not, retired officials of the ministry parachute to higher positions of the station (Sakamoto, 2000).

Although some scholars and intellectuals have expressed concern about the threat to Japanese democracy posed by this overall control of broadcasting by the government, there is no widespread perception of this threat among the general public. Therefore, no major popular movement has arisen to challenge the current system so far and it is unlikely that a national consensus for revival of the Broadcasting Supervisory Committee could be achieved in the foreseeable future. The organizational form of Japan's public broadcasting is also regulated in the Broadcasting Law and at the time the law was enacted in 1950, the broadcasting system was criticized for its "overemphasis on NHK." The original purpose behind the granting of special privileges to NHK was to make it more amenable to political manipulation (Matsuda, 1980). NHK was also placed under the close institutional supervision of the government. For instance, the amount of the license fee and NHK's annual budget are subject to parliamentary approval. Even now, NHK is often said to be "held hostage" by the government over its budget. Government discontent with the content of NHK's programs could easily lead to obstruction of its budget in the Diet.

Furthermore, the power to nominate members to the NHK Board of Executives is in the hands of the prime minister and in turn this board appoints the NHK

President. This makes it very unlikely that anyone out of favor with the government would ever be appointed as NHK President.

Meanwhile, the government also has considerable authority over commercial channels by means of issuing and extending their broadcasting licenses which the Radio Law stipulates. The broadcasting system as a whole is therefore under heavy government influence. A recent illustrative case is the government's response to the criticism it received in 1993 from the chief journalist at TV Asahi (a commercial broadcaster) Tsubaki Sadayoshi. Tsubaki's open criticism of the governing Liberal Democratic Party was met by the following statement by the Minister of Posts and Telecommunications (the present Ministry of Internal Affairs and Communications):

> Should any contravention of the Broadcasting Law occur, certain measures can be taken under Article 76 of the Radio Law. For example, broadcasting may be halted for a set period of time. This amounts to a suspension of operations. . . . If large numbers of people find [Mr. Tsubaki's remarks] inappropriate, we must conclude that political neutrality has been lost. (1993, p. 1)

In this case, the government's resort to the principle of political neutrality simply demonstrates the extent of its power to decide the future of one particular channel, and by implication its power to determine the general composition of the players in the broadcasting market.

INDUSTRIAL COMPETITION BETWEEN NHK AND COMMERCIAL BROADCASTERS

Postwar Broadcasting: The Dual System of NHK and Commercial Broadcasting

Commercial broadcasting began in Japan in 1951, almost at the same time as the legal institutionalization of the broadcasting system. Therefore, duality has been a fundamental feature of the postwar broadcasting system all along. Japanese broadcasting policy has been based on the principle of the dual system between NHK with its unitary nationwide organization funded by license fees, and private stations operating under regional licenses funded by advertising revenue.

As early as the 1920s Japanese newspaper companies had begun investigating the possibility of setting up their own radio stations. However, this movement was suspended as a result of the war. With the postwar democratization process under occupation, some journalists came to see commercial broadcasting as a necessary "antithesis to the prewar NHK" (Matsuda, 1980, p. 77). This is perhaps why commercial broadcasting is generally known in Japan by a term which translates more literally as "popular broadcasting" (*minpō*). Even today, this term implies the quality of being close to the people or close to citizens. In Europe and America, the phrase "commercial broadcasting" carries the primary implication of being driven by market forces. In contrast, the Japanese term *minôp* has a much more positive connotation. It suggests a form of broadcasting created by the people, and close to the lives of citizens. In many ways this is precisely a mirror image of the way NHK has been viewed throughout its history. Japanese public broadcasting by NHK has the image of being bureaucratic, elitist and intellectually aloof from ordinary citizens.

This perception toward NHK cannot be understood without reference to history. When considering the structure of Japanese broadcasting, we need to bear in mind that the postwar dual system was created against the backdrop of criticism of NHK for its wartime propaganda role and its history of self-righteous bureaucratism. In addition, in the early days of commercial broadcasting, many of those dismissed from NHK during the "red purge" were able to find employment in the newly established commercial stations (Matsuda, 1980).

However, neither the dual system nor red purge has been sufficient to prevent NHK from growing into a behemoth as a result of its exemption from antimonopoly regulations. It currently operates two terrestrial television channels, three satellite channels, an FM-radio station, and two AM-radio stations. These are all funded by license fees paid directly to NHK by the public. The license fee for viewing color television per household costs 1,395 yen (about US$13) per month. To subscribe to NHK's satellite services (there are two channels), the fee rises to 2340 yen (approximately US$22), with the residents of the island of Okinawa-ken paying a reduced fee. NHK also benefits from tax privileges on account of its special legal status. In addition, there are more than 20 commercial companies operating under the NHK umbrella (in publishing, for example), and other related public interest bodies such as the NHK Symphony Orchestra. The overall influence of NHK on Japan's media and cultural industries is clearly profound.

In order to survive in this NHK-centered system, commercial broadcasting has been organized into a small number of large networks in association with major national newspaper companies. These networks are hierarchical in structure and are headed by the so-called "Key Stations" based in Tokyo. These Key Stations have a relation of dominance over the smaller regional stations. This means in effect that the mass media in Japan are highly centralized. Long before the recent wave of deregulative trends and global concentration process in the media industry began, the principle of preventing concentration in the media industry in Japan had already become redundant.

Ownership of the Mass Media

In Japan, as in other countries, there is a principle of preventing market domination by a small number of companies in the media industry with the aim of securing a diversity of opinion and expression. However, in the present day, this principle has been thoroughly emptied of any real content. The current condition of the media market in Japan is the product of a postwar broadcasting policy which has encouraged media companies to make concessions to the government in return for protection of their interests.

At the time commercial broadcasting was first introduced in Japan, broadcasting licenses were issued to 16 companies, all but one of which were newspaper companies. A few years later the number of licensed commercial broadcasters increased dramatically and in 1957, 34 new licenses were issued by the then Minister of Posts and Telecommunications, Tanaka Kakuei. As a means of counteracting NHK's monopoly and establishing greater diversity in broadcasting the size of the initiative to introduce new licenses had some justification. However, Tanaka had other motives. He was playing to the interests of the national newspaper companies and Tokyo Key Stations by issuing new licenses to them. National economic interests were also involved, because television had been identified as one of Japan's "most important industries." Increasing the number of broadcasting licenses was partly motivated by the desire to stimulate economic growth in the media and electronics industries. Yet the most important factor behind the expansion of commercial broadcasting was a deliberate attempt at government control through the creation of large consolidated broadcasting networks linked to the national newspaper companies.

Currently, Japan has five national daily newspapers, all of which could be classified as "serious papers" with a significant influence on public opinion. The largest title in terms of sales is the *Yomiuri Shinbun*, which has a nominal daily circulation of more than 10 million copies. This is followed by the *Asahi Shinbun* with a circulation of more than 8 million, and the *Mainichi Shinbun*, with 4 million copies sold each day. On top of their huge circulation, each of these companies has its own commercial broadcasting network. This means in effect that each of the Key Stations in Tokyo is linked by capital and management with one or another of the national newspaper companies and this is the result of deliberate government policy. In the 1970s, Tanaka Kakuei used his influence to secure the segregation of commercial broadcasters into corporate groups with shared capital interests and management (such groups are known as *keiretsu* in Japanese). Each group is effectively headed by one of the national newspaper companies. The majority of commercial stations in the country is thus linked to one of the five groups. Having served as Minister of Posts and Telecommunications, Tanaka Kakuei went on to become Prime Minister from 1972 to 1974 and he continued to exert a major influence on Japanese politics until his death in 1993. One element of his very successful political life is said to be that he exerted a degree of control over the newspapers by granting them a major stake in commercial broadcasting.

In the formation of these media conglomerates, legal restrictions on the concentration of ownership were circumvented, hence:

> Legal restrictions on ownership of broadcast companies prevented the complete integration of these two types of media. Until recently, newspapers were limited to holding no more than ten percent of the shares of any single station. But the national newspapers have regularly circumvented this rule by getting other companies in their group to invest in stations as well. They have further extended their influence by sending key management

people to the station to work in top-level executive positions and by helping direct working capital to the stations by arranging for loans from their own banks. (Freeman, 2000, p. 155)

The resulting *de facto* concentration of media ownership has gained little national attention as a problem. On the contrary, recent trends are in the direction of even greater concentration. Since the 1990s, there has been a policy of encouraging the establishment of at least four commercial broadcasting stations in each region. This has resulted in an even greater tendency for regional stations to become virtual subsidiaries of the Tokyo Key Stations.

Such regional stations produce very little original program content of their own and simply relay material from the Key Station to which they are affiliated to the area of which they are in charge. This hierarchical arrangement is now becoming thoroughly institutionalized. In the words of one regional station manager, "Otemachi [the district of Tokyo where Yomiuri Shimbun has its corporate head quarters] is the white man, Kojimachi [the district where Nihon Television— Yomiuri's TV network—is based] is the aborigine, and the regional television stations are like slaves or cattle" (Suzuki, 2004, p. 18).

Due to NHK's behemoth-like presence in the Japanese media sector since the prewar period, the only way commercial broadcasting could ever challenge NHK was to develop its own form of monolithic concentration (see Freeman, 2000; Fujitake, 2000). The ideal of preventing concentration of media ownership has been further eroded by the recent wave of deregulation.

Signs of Market Restructuring Through Digitalization

Broadcasting in Japan was developed in line with the government's policy of pursuing economic growth through technological advancement. Under this policy, no clear distinction was made between the interests of the nation and the interests of the broadcasting industry. This is well illustrated by the cases of HDTV (high-definition television) and satellite broadcasting, as has been documented by Krauss (2000). The important point to emphasize here is that NHK has a legal obligation to fulfill the role of a technological pioneer in the broadcasting industry. It has therefore been quick to adopt to new technologies such as HDTV and satellite. As Krauss (2000) notes:

This rapid response to the new technology derived in part from NHK's obligations under its charter, the Broadcast Law. Article 7's statement of the "purpose" of the corporation obligates NHK's signals to be received all over Japan, and Article 9 empowers NHK to "conduct research and investigations necessary for the improvement and development of broadcasting and the reception thereof." (p. 178)

Overcoming reception difficulties in a country with many islands and mountainous areas was certainly a major task facing NHK in the postwar era and improving the reception of broadcasts was cited as a pretext for the introduction of satellite broadcasting in the early days. In reality, though, satellite broadcasting was used by NHK as a means of increasing its revenue, and by the government as a means of stimulating growth in the aerospace industry as part of its economic development plan. Now the technological focus of the Japanese broadcasting industry has shifted to digitalization. The digitalization of television broadcasting is being pursued as a major national project. According to the government's plan, every television program in Japan will be digitalized by 2011. To this end, since December 2003, terrestrial digital broadcasting launched in three major cities; Tokyo, Osaka, and Nagoya and digital satellite broadcasting began even earlier, in December 2000.

For the government, the development of a new industry based on broadcasting digitalization technology is a potential new source of revenues, especially for the Ministry of Internal Affairs and Communications. By promoting the digitalization of television, the Ministry can forge lucrative tie-ups with digital equipment manufacturers, and claim a larger share of the government's overall budget as a consequence.

For NHK, on the other hand, digitalization provides an opportunity to confirm its role as the technological leader in the media industry. The use of technological leverage as a means of self-expansion is already an established practice of NHK, as can be seen in the launch of digital satellite broadcasting in 2000. Digitalization is now being promoted in the name of its benefits to citizens, including increased visual quality, and the potential for real-time interactive broadcasting. At the time of writing, however, the diffusion of digital television sets remains low at 8.5%, according to a survey conducted in March 2005 by the Ministry of Internal Affairs and Communications. Along with such low diffusion of digital television, to the dismay of the government, more than 70% of the respondents in this survey did not know the time table regarding the digitalization of terrestrial television programs. Digitalization is, so we can conclude, not presently on people's mind in Japan yet, and is not likely to be imposed by the industry and the government without a popular consensus.

In terms of the future of digitalization, commercial broadcasters, especially small regional/local stations, face a rather bleak future because they have little prospect of obtaining sufficient funds for the introduction of the new technology. According to the Ministry of Internal Affairs and Communications, the crowded frequency spectrum will cost Japan 180 billion yen to convert to digitalization, two and a half times higher than the original estimate. There has been talk about increased charges for broadcasters to use spectrum, though this question remains open. Digital experts say the frequency spectrum is far more crowded in Japan than in other countries and analog terrestrial broadcasting has already used up much of the frequency spectrum available and some of it needs to be moved elsewhere before broadcasters start digitalizing. Combined Japanese broadcasters are destined to spend large sums of capital for the digitalization project and it is estimated that a total of at least 1.2 trillion yen will have to be invested for the purchase of necessary facilities for digitalization. This would mean an expenditure of about 6.3 billion yen per broadcaster, according to the estimates of the National

Association of Commercial Broadcasters in Japan. "The average sales of a local commercial broadcaster amounts to around 5 billion yen, with profits hovering around 300 million yen. Extraordinary effort would therefore be required if local broadcasters are to keep airing regular analog programs while simultaneously investing in digital facilities" (Suzuki, 2004, p. 5).

Given these conditions it is financially impossible for Japan's small local stations to achieve digitalization unless they undergo merger and consolidation. They have therefore adopted a more positive stance toward deregulation, despite their earlier opposition on the grounds that deregulation only favors Tokyo Key Stations. Digitalization is therefore likely to spur further concentration in the media industry.

The acceptance of further market deregulation as a necessary corollary of digitalization is a *fait accompli*. In the area of satellite broadcasting there is already a movement to relax the percentage of stock ownership allowed to existing terrestrial stations, such as the Key Stations. This is being pursued as a means of achieving financial stability in the satellite industry. However, if this trend toward the domination of satellite broadcasting by Key Stations continues, local commercial stations (most of whose programming is provided by the Key Stations) will lose their *raison d'être*. In Japan, therefore, digitalization presents very little prospect for the diversification of public expression. Instead, it will simply reinforce the already established trend towards concentration of media ownership. There is a very real danger that the structure of the industry will develop in such a way that any return to a free and open arena of public expression will become next to impossible.

New Players Enter the Market

As just described, the Japanese broadcasting market is now in a period of considerable upheaval. Not only have existing patterns of change intensified, but there are also signs of completely new developments. These new developments arise from the presence of newcomers in the broadcasting market.

Trading companies and electrical goods manufacturers with no previous involvement in broadcasting have started entering the field of satellite broadcasting by a revision of the Radio Law and Broadcasting Law in 1989. Until then, only companies with their own transmission facilities were licensed to provide programming. However, the revision made it possible for the production and editing of content to be contracted out to a newly formed category of "Contract Broadcasting Businesses" (*Itaku Hôsô Jigyôsha*). This provision was made for both communication satellites and broadcasting satellites. Businesses from outside the existing field of broadcasting are thus allowed to operate in the broadcasting industry. Such deregulation invited criticism that it would increase the commercial logic that dominates the world of broadcasting and weaken the spirit of journalism. On the other hand, it is also doubtful whether the media environment even prior to deregulation had formed an ideal space for public expression. Japanese television viewers are already suspicious of the vested interests and insincere attitudes shown by the established broadcasters that have so far been protected by government regulations. In this kind of environment, the entry of new players into the media market is not surprisingly welcomed by many people, especially by younger generations.

The most recent incident involving a newcomer into the field of broadcasting occurred in the earlier half of 2005. The newly formed and high-profile Internet company Livedoor succeeded in buying a large portion of the shares in Nippon Broadcasting System (NBS), an old and well-established commercial radio station. This sparked off much speculation about a possible shakeup in the broadcasting industry. A month long battle for NBS shares unfolded between Livedoor and Fuji TV (Japan's largest commercial broadcasting company) because NBS is a sister company of Fuji TV, and like Fuji TV is part of Fujisankei, Japan's largest media group. This incident stimulated much debate about the appropriateness or otherwise of new players with no prior connection to broadcasting or newspaper publishing entering the media market. It also raised questions about the possibility of future tie-ups or even outright convergence between the Internet and mass media. Eventually the two sides reached a compromise and Livedoor and Fuji TV declared their intention to work together in the future. In the end, it may have been no more than a speculative money game on the part of Horie Takafumi the owner of Livedoor.[2] Nevertheless, Livedoor's hostile takeover bid for NBS has forced the Japanese media industry to think seriously about its own future. Horie is known for his often stated opinion that the Internet will eventually eclipse the mass media, and that the mass media's social function will disappear. In an interview in December 2004, just before embarking on his bid for NBS, Horie Takafumi claimed "Although we will eventually kill off the newspapers and television stations, it would be more efficient if we killed them while owning them" (an interview by journalist S. Egawa; retrieved July 21, 2005, from www.egawashoko.com/menu4/contents/ 02_/_data_40.html).

Since the end of the Second World War, the Japanese broadcasting market has effectively been monopolized by NHK as well as the small number of Key Stations in Tokyo. For the first time we now see the possibility of new very different players entering the market. Some media scholars and commentators see this trend toward "liberalization" and "deregulation" as a threat to the fundamental journalistic values of public fairness, trust, and independence. There is some merit to this argument. Nevertheless, it becomes obvious that these fundamental values have not necessarily played a very central role in the actual workings of the Japanese mass media to date. The broadcasting institutions of the postwar period have functioned in such a way as to protect their own interests even while claiming superficially to embody the idealism of journalistic values and publicness. A liberalized system operating according to the market principles of viewer ratings and popularity rankings would surely be preferable to one in which journalism is manipulated for self-interest of the few and this is probably a widely shared

---

[2]Horie was, however, arrested on January 23, 2006, on suspicion of violating securities laws. Horie stepped down and Livedoor named a new president a day after his arrest.

view among the Japanese public. A number of reports and interviews confirm this sentiment in that many young Japanese people said they would welcome Livedoor's takeover bid for NBS, believing that it would bring a breath of fresh air into the media world.

The real threat to the Japanese broadcasting industry may not therefore be deregulation or liberalization, but rather dissatisfaction of the long-ignored Japanese public. Such public feeling is already being expressed in various forms, one of which is the increasing refusal of households to pay the license fee. Unlike many other countries, there are no fines for nonpayment of this fee. Collection of this fee by NHK depends entirely on the goodwill of citizens. It is still idealistically believed that fining nonpayers would make the television license fee "equivalent to a government tax, therefore amounting to effective government management of NHK, which would consequently lose its public and neutral character" (Nihon Hôsô Rôdô Kumiai, 2005, p. 41). However, such extreme idealism is maintained even while NHK has clearly failed in its attempt to maintain a real distance from the world of *real politique*. Following the most recent political interference scandal, the number of households refusing to pay the license fee increased sharply. It now seems very unlikely that there will be any return to the former near universal support for NHK. NHK chairman Genichi Hashimoto estimates that 970,000 households had so far refused to pay the license fee by the end of May 2005. This means an estimated loss of more than 14 billion yen (US$135 million) to NHK. Nonpayment of the license fee is therefore beginning to have a serious impact on NHK's finances.

The refusal by some television viewers to pay the license fee also occurs against the background of the existence of pay-for-view television. The introduction of pay TV television is another product of the recent deregulation of the media market. However, its impact is greater than simply the addition of one more aspect of choice for viewers. It has introduced a whole new way of thinking about the relationship between viewer and broadcaster. When a specific price is attached to each program and viewers pay individually only for what they watch, television content comes to be seen more and more as a commodity. People then start asking themselves why they should keep paying for a public television service, whose programs they find uninteresting and whose internal accountancy is obscure. Although this could be seen as a healthy awakening of consumer consciousness, it also indicates a decline in people's awareness of themselves as citizens in public life. Under present conditions in Japan, it is the newcomers to the media market, not NHK, nor even the established commercial stations, that are felt to be closer to the public.

LIMITS OF THE CONCEPT OF "PUBLIC" IN JAPANESE SOCIETY

The Japanese broadcasting system, as it has developed to the present day, hardly could be said to embody the ideal of a sphere of public expression devoted to the public interest as the notion of the public has been dwarfed by the twin forces of government authority and market forces. This is due to a number of factors—one of which is the meaning of the concept of "public" in Japanese society, which creates limits of the social system on a number of ways.

In European history, the concept of publicness has been understood as an idealized attribute of the public that emerged as the subject challenging political power in the citizens' revolution. In this sense, to be public means such things as being independent, rational, and critical of authority. Such publicness also implies something open to all, not restricted to the interest of a particular social class. It is a concept crucial to the ideal of the public sphere. However, in Japan, the word public, which is translated as *kô* or *kôkyô* in Japanese, is often interpreted differently, and it is this usage that give rise to part of the problem. *Kô*, which is also read as *ôyake* derives etymologically from a word meaning "great residence" and then took on the meaning of "the master" or "the authority" at a later date in premodern Japan. The antonym of *ôyake* is the word *watakushi*. Besides meaning "private," *wataskushi* is also used as a first person singular pronoun "I." It can also mean the subordinate of an *ôyake* master.

Thus, in Japanese, the word "public" interest designated (and still does, more or less) something like "the master's interest." In accordance with this etymological origin, the word for "public" in the Japanese language retains the connotation of fairness and justice on the part of the master, or of heaven (and thus it is above criticism). Meanwhile, the term "private" contains negative, redundant, and private connotations that must not be sustained in the public realm. It is only after the modernization of the Meiji era in the late 19th century that the European sense of public was introduced into Japanese academic circles. However its use in this European sense in common conversation was (and still is) rare. Overall, the conventional understanding of the "public" as a domain belonging to "them" (the masters) is still dominant. The western notion of the public as "us" (ordinary people) is not yet widely accepted.

The Japanese concept of "public" therefore combines the sense of a public independent of the State with the sense of public as official. And the latter sense of official is clearly dominant. Therefore, the idea that the government should not intervene in public broadcasting is not well established. This is confirmed by surveys of public opinion that indicate that many people do not clearly appreciate the difference between public broadcasting and State-run broadcasting. In a survey conducted by NHK in 1997, only 35% of those surveyed correctly identified NHK as a special public enterprise body, while 23% thought it was a semigovernmental corporation and 29% thought it was a State-run organization (Matsuda, 2005). NHK is one of the very few public broadcasters in the world that are virtually 100% financed by license fees. Nevertheless, even after 60 years of postwar history, it is still not widely perceived as either belonging to civil society or rightfully being under the management of civil society.

Sherman (1994), who worked for NHK as a foreign journalist, describes his experiences there as follows. "Most important conflicts between journalists from East and West are not shallow misunderstandings about terms of art, but reflect deep differences in the way they see their role in society" (p. 36). He describes Japanese journalists as living in "a culture of censorship" (Sherman, ibid.), where constant concern about their role in society leads them to hide shocking or unpleasant news, particularly about powerful institutions and corporations. The notion of the liberal public sphere developed in Western culture seems to find little space in Japanese newsrooms, not to mention among the management of media companies.

CONCLUSION: IS THERE A WAY OUT OF THE DILEMMA?

Does the process of "deregulation" and "liberalization" really have entirely negative implications for Japanese broadcasting? As a result of digitalization and the introduction of satellite broadcasting, it is highly likely that many local television channels will be forced out of business in the next 20 years or so, leading to a major restructuring of the television market. Meanwhile, the large newspaper companies together with Tokyo Key Stations and NHK will pursue their own interests even further, and there is grave danger of even greater monopolization of public expression.

Does this mean then that the situation would be any better if there were less deregulation and liberalization? From the outset, the possibility that Japanese journalism would develop into a free arena of public expression was severely limited by the "reverse course" in American occupation policy. GHQ set the precedent for a climate in which labor organizations were not allowed to flourish and management were given free reign to determine the direction of public expression. The still frequently invoked concept of "editorial rights" is a product of the political situation under occupation. In addition, as soon as the occupation ended, the committee composed of the representatives of social groups and private citizens that was supposed to supervise the administration of broadcasting (the Broadcasting Supervisory Committee) was abolished. This measure greatly increased the scope for government intervention in the broadcasting system. The present institutional arrangement provides legitimacy for such things as the parliamentary supervision of NHK's budget, the government's appointment of NHK governors, and the official granting of commercial broadcasting licenses. In addition, the introduction of new technology such as HDTV and satellites has been pursued under the direction of the government and industrial interests within the framework of national interest.

Government broadcasting policy is not challenged from the broadcasting organizations themselves either. The latter have been almost completely tied up in the web of government influence and simply pursue their own self-interests within the existing system. Commercial broadcasting was originally introduced as a counterpower to the national broadcasting organization inherited from the prewar period, NHK. However, the means by which commercial broadcasting was introduced, and the way it has been organized has simply further constricted the sphere of public expression in Japan. Commercial broadcasters are organized into hierarchical groups under the ultimate domination of the five big national newspaper companies. Regulations designed to prevent the concentration of media ownership and control had already been rendered ineffective as much as 50 years ago. Furthermore, "outsiders," whether they be from outside the existing industry or outside the country, have long been systematically excluded from the Japanese broadcasting market and they still have little chance to enter the market as major players. Now that Japan has developed into a major economic player in the globalization process, the closed world of its mass media has increasingly been exposed to international criticism.

Consequently, in light of such a closed system in the broadcasting market, some people have suggested that NHK, as the core institution of Japanese broadcasting, should be placed entirely in the hands of the private sector, including such organizations as NGOs, as a means of enlivening the old self-interest-oriented, bureaucratic broadcasting sector. At the moment, in the face of this changing information environment, new players, especially the commercial entertainment industry, are keen to enter the broadcasting market and are paving the way toward a new model of convergence between the Internet and broadcasting. Experts fear, however, that their programs are almost solely dictated by ratings that strengthen the tendency toward sensationalism and the tabloidization of content without any focus on quality.

Despite these profound problems, there remains those that recognize the high quality of the programs, especially documentaries, news reporting, current affairs and dramas produced by NHK. A case in point is that more than half of respondents to a questionnaire conducted by the Japan Newspaper Publishers and Editors Association in 2003 answered that they believed NHK's content was accurate and trustworthy. Although recognizing the existence of much criticism against current broadcasting, we should also not underestimate the extent of people's trust in journalistic professionalism. In particular, the relation of trust between NHK and its viewers has been built largely on the excellence and commitment of the individual journalists and producers in the organization, and on the outstanding record of their work up to now. There are very few other organizations in Japan other than NHK that are theoretically independent of both economic and political power while also possessing a degree of financial stability. In its strategy of resistance to the political elite and capital, civil society could hardly agree to the dissolution by its own hand of an institution that has been established, in theory at least, precisely for civil society.

Therefore, if we accept the reality there is an almost irresolvable dilemma emerging precisely at the point where opinions meet. If we decide not to abandon the ideal of the public nature of broadcasting and preserve it, we tend to end up perpetuating the existing system with all its faults. This would mean tacit acceptance for the continued existence of the highly concentrated TV network system and the conservative NHK.

Japanese society will at some point have to draw some conclusions regarding the reform of the broadcasting sector, including the possible dissolution of NHK. So far, the development of broadcasting has largely been determined by the interests of the government and existing broadcasters in the absence of any national debate about what kinds of organization are most suitable as broadcasters reflecting the public welfare. It is clear, however, that any liberalization of the Japanese broadcasting system in the true sense of the term cannot be achieved through an external imposition of a new model. To change the system in a truly democratic way will require the active will and efforts of Japanese citizens themselves.

REFERENCES

Freeman, L. A. (2000). *Closing the shop. Information cartels and Japan's mass media.* Princeton, NJ: Princeton University Press.

Fujitake, A. (Ed.). (2000). *Zusetsu Nihon no* masu media (*Japan's mass media*). Tokyo: NHK Books.

Japan Newspaper Publishers and Editors Association. (1948). *Henshûken seimei.* [Declaration of the Editorial Rights]. Retrieved July 21, 2005, from www.pressnet.or.jp/info/seimei/shuzai/1201henshuken.htm

Kawakami, S. (2003). Japan's TV broadcasters trail in race to go digital. *Japan Inc.* 1/1/2003. Retrieved April 18, 2006, from www.japaninc.net/contents.php?articleID=983

Kawasaki, Y. (1997). *NHK to Seiji* [NHK and Politics]. Tokyo: Asahi Shimbunsha.

Krauss, E. S. (2000). *Broadcasting politics in Japan. NHK and television news.* Ithaca and London: Cornell University Press.

Matsuda, H. (2005). *NHK—Towareru kôkyô hôsô* [NHK. Public broadcasting in question]. Tokyo: Iwanami Shinsho.

Matsuda, H. (1980). *Dokumento hôsô sengoshi IúShirarezaru sono kiseki* [A Document: Postwar broadcasting I. Its unknown trajectory]. Sôshisha.

Matsuda, H. (1981). *Dokumento hôsô sengoshi IIúSôsa to jânarizumu* [A document: Postwar broadcasting II. Manipulation and journalism]. Sôshisha.

Ministry of Internal Affairs and Communications. (2005). *Chijo Dejitaru Terebijon Hôsô ni kansuru Shintôdo Chôsa, Heisei 17-nen 6Gatsu. Sômusho Joho Tsushin Seisaku Kyoku* [Survey on the Permeation of the Terrestrial Digital TV, June 2005, by the Division of Telecommunication of the Ministry of Internal Affairs and Communications]. Retrieved July 21, 2005, from www.soumu.go.jp/s-news/2005/pdf/050614_2_1.pdf

Ministry of Posts and Telecommunications to start investigation on TV Asahi. (1993, October 14). Sankei Shimbun, p. 1.

NHK Hôsô Bunka Kenkyûjo. [NHK Broadcasting Culture Research Institute]. (2005). *Nippon-jin to Terebi 2005.* [Japanese and Television 2005]. Retrieved July 21, 2005, from www.nhk.or.jp/bunken/research/housou/housou_05062401.pdf

Nihon Hôsô Rôdô Kumiai. [Japanese Conference of Mass Media's Workers' Union]. (2004). *Kôkyô hôsô tte nandesuka? 2004 Aki Shokuba Sôtougi Houkokushû Nihon Hôsô Rôdô Kumiai* [What in the world is Public Broadcasting? 2004 Autumn Report on Discussions within NHK].

Sakamoto, M. (2000). *21 Seiki ni yûsei amakudari nado tûyo shinai!!—Hôsôkyoku no minasan iikagen ni yamemasen?* [No more appointments of retired government officials for positions at TV Stations in the 21st Century. It's high time to stop it]. GALAC, pp. 12–17.

Sherman, S. (1994, March/April). NHK TV: Japan (a Westerner's experience of working in Japan's biggest network, Nippon Hoso Kyokai). Columbia Journalism Review, pp. 32–36.

Suzuki, K. (2004). *Chihô terebi wa ikinokoreruka. Chijôha dejitaru de yuragu "Shûchû Haijo Gensoku"* [Can Local TV Stations survive? Terrestrial digitalization shaking media's decentralization principles]. Tokyo: Nihon Hy–ronsha.

Tsukamoto, M. (1995). Henshuken [editorial rights]. In I. Michio & N. Arai (Eds.), *Shimbungaku, Dai 3 Han* [Journalism studies, 3rd edition] (pp. 136–147). Tokyo: Nihon Hyôronsha.

CHAPTER EIGHT

Broadcasting and Public Policy: Television in New Zealand

Geoff Lealand
University of Waikato

In respect of the central theme of this collection television in New Zealand provides an ideal case study, and salutary lessons for television systems across the globe. Ever since its beginnings, in the early 1960s, television in this South Pacific nation has been subjected to continuous structural and policy change, strands of continuity in programming and cultural significance and, most significantly, has experienced an extraordinary level of economic liberalization and deregulation. Most recently, policy directives from the Labour government have initiated another wave of change; what might be characterized as "Back to the Future."

Television in New Zealand, over the past three decades, has experienced the waves of profound change that are the focus of this collection (withdrawal of public regulation, deregulation and the ascendance of free competition, and consumer choice, more foreign ownership). Having passed through such changes, it is now attempting, in respect of State-owned television, to reverse the years of deregulation and free market ideology, as Horrocks (2004a) notes:

> The so-called "New Zealand experiment" is now seen by its architect, the Labour Party, as having gone too far, and since returning to government in 1999 the party has struggled to reintroduce public service ideals. (p. 9)

In a Radio New Zealand interview, in early 2005, Michael Stedman, Managing Director of Natural History New Zealand, spoke of the consequences of the sale of this unique Television New Zealand asset to Twentieth Century Fox in 1998, saying "the selling of the Natural History Unit of Television New Zealand was a financial tragedy . . . and a cultural tragedy."

The quick, undisputed sale of a profitable subsidiary of State-owned Television New Zealand was one among many similar actions of the National government, which spent much of the 1980s and 1990s (until it was defeated in the November 1998 General Election) selling off State assets. Indeed, it is generally that much of New Zealand's "family silver" was sold off during these years; a consequence of a dominant discourse of deregulation and free market flows. Nevertheless, the National-led administration was following in a long tradition where "there have been more changes in New Zealand television than I've had hot dinners" (Stedman, 2005). One Australian academic has described recent broadcasting policy in New Zealand as a history characterized by a "recurring motif" of "extreme makeover." (DeBrett, 2005, p. 76). Indeed, the recent history of television in New Zealand clearly illustrates the processes of regulation and deregulation, policy intervention, and policy neglect, which currently obsesses television systems across the world. New Zealand offers a number of lessons for those seeking change in other parts of the world: some salutary lessons, as well as evidence of what can be done to improve the lot of television and viewer choice.

TELEVISION POLICY IN THE 1990s

Since its beginnings in 1962, television in New Zealand has experienced waves of change and restructuring. The State was also involved from the earliest days, transferring a model of firm control of radio onto television.

From it beginnings, television in New Zealand was characterized by mixed social objectives, and a mixed economy. Initially, it was inspired and shaped by a Reithian concept of public service broadcasting, tempered with early expectations of commercial considerations. The funding of television was founded on a mix of license income (a broadcasting fee levied on television sets), and advertising revenue. In the closing decades of the 20th century, a strong bias developed toward advertising income and other commercial imperatives, with revenue from the broadcasting fee being shifted from State-owned channels of Television New Zealand (TVNZ), to the funding body New Zealand On Air (NZOA). Nevertheless, TVNZ continued to be the primary beneficiary of the Broadcasting Fee (and, more latterly, direct government grants), receiving the bulk of programming underwritten by NZOA—in addition to recent top-up payments from the government, to fulfill certain Charter commitments.

Likewise, tensions between the mixed objectives of public service versus commercial imperatives, information versus entertainment, and regulation versus deregulation quickly developed in the early decades of New Zealand television, and persist until today. Debates about the purpose of television have frequently centered around the high proportion of imported programming in the schedule (New Zealand has always been a bulk importer of programming and formats, most especially from the United States and Britain), as well as desires to increase the amount and range of local programming (the agenda behind the setting up of NZOA).

Over the years, successive governments have sought to accommodate or reconcile such differences. On occasion, this has resulted in carefully considered policy directions or restructuring; on other occasions, radical transformations of television have been prompted by political whim, or an ideological swerve. In 1999, as a last-minute gesture before it was swept out of office, the National government abolished the Public Broadcasting Fee (PBF). This fee (a tax on television sets) had a very long history and had long ensured a reliable income for State-owned television (through various governing bodies, such as the Broadcasting Corporation of New Zealand between 1977 and 1989) and, more recently, a substantial funding pool (administered by NZOA) for important categories of local television production (drama, children's programs, documentaries).

The PBF was replaced by a direct, annual grant from general tax revenue and even though this meant that funding potentially came under more direct government control, instances of visible political intervention in programming or funding decisions do not seem to have increased. Nevertheless, there is evidence that the tensions between opposing imperatives have not completely dissipated. There is continuing debate (and inconsistent behavior) around the need for TVNZ to continue to operate as a financially profitable company, returning healthy annual dividends to the government, and its new (or revived) need to meet social and cultural objectives, under the Charter. Television New Zealand has also transgressed on numerous occasions in recent years (as in 2000, when it was required to pay out $NZ6 million to a wrongfully dismissed newsreader), but although the company maintains its audience domination and very healthy advertising income, rebukes from the State, as major shareholder, have not been severe nor permanent. Television New Zealand been pretty much left to "get on with it," in terms of generating income and working towards the directives of its charter.

Horrocks (2004a, p. 26) describes the 1990s in New Zealand as being characterized by three distinct trends, whereby TVNZ as a commercial broadcaster was counterbalanced by the cultural objectives of NZOA in the 7 years following the almost-total deregulation of the New Zealand television market in 1989, followed by 5 years (1995–1999) when a "dominant commercialism" prevailed against over all other considerations (the only effective opposition coming from Maori challenges, under the rubric of the Treaty of Waitangi). During this period, the National government was working toward further asset sales of State-owned television. However, the dramatic shift in 1999 brought in the third period, when Labour came to power, meant that sales were off and public service television was back on the agenda, with TVNZ being led in new directions, through legislation, targeted financing, and friendly persuasion.

THE TELEVISION MARKET IN 2005

Television in New Zealand in 2005 continues to be dominated by the State-owned (or "Crown-Owned Company") Television New Zealand, with its two channels TV One and TV2 gathering the greatest share of advertising revenue, and hogging the weekly ratings lists. In the period of July 2003 to June 2004, these two channels reported a combined peak audience share of 65.4%, a share which has been in decline in recent years, but still remains substantial.

The net surplus profit for July 2003 to June 2004 was $NZ28.2 million, but in a gesture of generosity which attracted little public attention, TVNZ also paid a dividend of $NZ38 million to the government. The amount and timing of this dividend was unprecedented, as Norris (2004) notes, "we found TVNZ paying the government the astonishing sum of $NZ38 million, historically one of the highest dividends ever" (p. A9). He raises a number of important questions about this "astonishing" payment: (a) Should not TVNZ be using this money to make more and better New Zealand programs? (b) Why is the dividend some NZ$10 million more than TVNZ's profit for the year? (c) Why is the figure twice the NZ$19 million projected in the statement of intent for this year (effectively TVNZ's contract with the government)?, and (d) Why is a dividend being paid at all by a company whose status has been changed from SOE [State-owned enterprise] to a crown-owned company and whose objectives are no longer mainly to make money? (Norris, 2004).

Norris (2004) provides one likely answer to these questions, in that TVCNZ may well have been a victim of its own success, in that "commercially, TVNZ has over-performed. It is awash with cash," and basking in the "golden weather of advertising revenue." The recent years of a vigorous advertising market and over-subscription of television slots has produced substantial cash reserves for TVNZ but this "bulging piggy-bank [has been] whisked away to the Treasury storehouse" (Norris, 2004).

As a result of objections from TVNZ, a healthy portion ($NZ11.4 million) of the dividend was returned to the company in November 2004—but with the stipulation that it be allocated to the social objectives of the TVNZ Charter. This payback was in addition to the direct payments to TVNZ from the Ministry of Culture and Heritage, to meet Charter objectives. In 2004, $NZ16 million was provided; in 2005, $NZ17 million.

By 2005, the dividend payment from net surplus profits was to be set "at a level to cover the cost of capital" (Norris, 2005). According to Norris, "no figure has been officially given" but he suspects the dividend level might be 7%. Another commentator suggests 9% (Thompson, 2005a). Given that the television advertising market shows no sign of faltering, with TVNZ announcing interim profits of $NZ30 million in the period from July to December 2004, the government seems assured of future healthy dividends from the company, irrespective of the payment level.

This pattern of "taking away with one hand and giving it back with the other" has become the norm in the funding relationships between the government and TVNZ. It makes reading the Annual Report of TVNZ a tactical nightmare, and greatly confuses (some commentators say "distorts") the television environment in New Zealand. Confusion reigns over considerations of financial autonomy and corporate responsibility, as it does over the objectives and outcomes of the TVNZ Charter.

There is much less confusion in the other sectors of the free-to-air New Zealand television environment, where objectives are less bifurcated and in conflict.

The other major television networks need to provide satisfactory financial outcomes for their parent companies: CanWest Global Communications (the parent company of CanWest MediaWorks NZ Ltd.) in respect of TV3 and C4, and Prime Television Ltd. Australia (the parent company of Prime Television New Zealand) in respect of Prime. (In February 2006, Sky purchased Prime.) In early 2005, CanWest reported that the combined earnings of its substantial radio interests and 70%-owned channels in New Zealand returned consolidated earnings (EBITDA) of $NZ37.9 million in the period September 2004 to February 2005 (CanWest, 2005).

Prime was claiming, in early 2005, that it was "the only free-to-air broadcaster currently recording audience growth" in New Zealand, despite only gaining a 5% to 6% audience share in 2004, and sustaining significant losses as a result of luring highly paid television personalities from TVNZ (see the following section).

The largely government-funded Maori Television Service (launched in June 2004), after 1 year in service, has judged its performance against its objectives (as set out in the Maori Television Service Act of 2003) of providing

- a high-quality, cost-effective television provider that informs, educates and entertains;
- broadcast mainly in te reo Maori;
- have regard to the needs of children participating in immersion education and all people learning Maori.

To this end, it needs only satisfy its two primary stakeholders: The Crown (the Minister of Maori Affairs and the Minister of Finance), and Te Putahi Paoho (The Maori Electoral College) and, to a lesser extent, the source of funding for much of its commissioned programming, Te Mangai Paho.

A number of city-based or regional low-power television services survive (such as Triangle TV in Auckland and campus-based Big TV in Hamilton) on a mixture of private or community funding. In an unprecedented move, in May 2005 the Labour government provided funding ($NZ3.5 million, over 4 years), through NZOA, to provide some support for these services.

The major pay TV service Sky Network Television, supplying packages of up to 40 subscription channels of either terrestrial or satellite digital television to more than 41% of New Zealand households (more than 600,000 subscribers in May 2005), reports to its parent company Independent News Limited. In 2004, INL took a majority shareholding (78%) in Sky, divesting its considerable New Zealand print media interests (which included leading dailies, and the leading weekend title *Sunday Star-Times*) to the major Australian media company, Fairfax (publisher of *The Age* and *The Australian Financial Review*). Rupert Murdoch's global media empire News Corporation maintains its interest in Sky Network Television (New Zealand), through a 43% shareholding.

Such major restructurings of New Zealand media ownership are commonplace, in a media environment where there are no legislative barriers to the entry of foreign capital, and the buying and selling of assets. In 2007, this means that television in New Zealand comprises a mix of free-to-air services (the dominant State-owned Television New Zealand and two overseas-owned networks) competing with each other, and Sky pay-services, for a television audience of close to 3 million viewers.

FREEDOMS AND CONSTRAINTS IN THE NEW ZEALAND TELEVISION MARKET

In the long tradition of prolonged conflict among rival agendas, television in New Zealand works to the benefit or detriment of a wide range of stakeholders. The primary stakeholders, and their declared (and undeclared) set of interests, include the following:

The Labour Government

With an inheritance of past legislation, which enabled free and unfettered entry of foreign interests into New Zealand broadcasting, there is little the current Labour government can do about directing or regulating privately owned FTA or pay TV. In fact, government policy can often advantage channels such as TV3, which is a frequent recipient of program subsidization, through NZOA-funded documentaries, children's programming, and special interest programming. Other privately owned channels benefit from a light regulatory touch, and the only significant restraints come from the Broadcasting Standards Authority, which responds to viewer complaints and negotiates, with broadcasters, for broadcasting codes of practice.

In the absence of a strong, national regulatory framework, the government turns to Television New Zealand as its primary focus of policy intervention and experimentation. According to Thompson (2005a);

> Labour-led administrations since 1999 explicitly recognized the market failures of a wholly commercial broadcasting sector (e.g. saturation-level advertising, low levels of local content, heavy reliance on cheap imports and a disregard for quality genres and in-depth news and current affairs) and reemphasized television's cultural and democratic functions in their policy thinking. (p. 1)

As the Labour government heads toward a possible third term in office, it is critical for it to demonstrate that the latest round of policy changes have been worthwhile and effective. It is important, for example, to show that Television New Zealand is a very different kind of television service than that which prevailed through the 1990s, and that the source of previous dissatisfaction (overt commercialism, domination of the schedule by foreign programming) has dissipated, or at least been ameliorated.

On the surface (where most snap judgments are made, and where the firmest conclusions are drawn), there does not seem to be much change. There has been some shifting around in the schedule and increased offerings in certain genres (primetime current affairs, for example) but there has been no significant increase in local content and little reduction in the level of advertising.

The critical constraint on radical change lies in the competing demands placed on TVNZ: to meet the objectives of its Charter and act as a public service provider of quality television, while maintaining its audience dominance and financial vigor. This is a conundrum for both the Labour government and TVNZ, in that such objectives are not always compatible, "TVNZ's dual imperative to fulfill a broad range of Charter functions while maintaining its commercial performance has so far inhibited radical change" (Thompson, 2005b. p. 44). At a June 2005 meeting, Broadcasting Minister Steve Maharey set out the "success stories" of his portfolio:

- Viewers enjoying and expecting local content;
- TVNZ progress with Charter;
- TV3 highly valued by New Zealanders;
- C4 has a strong following;
- Maori Television adding rich new component.

Framing this list of successful policy shifts and increased viewer options was a set of inter-related challenges to traditional ways of doing television:

- Digital revolution, globalization and pay-TV;
- Fragmenting audiences;
- Challenging traditional business models;
- Need for strategic and collaborative thinking. (Maharey, 2005)

If full account was not paid to these trends, and if TVNZ was not singled out for special consideration (and, by implication, special protection), the contribution of the State-owned broadcaster to New Zealand culture "could start to slip away" (Maharey, 2005).

Television New Zealand

The core objectives of the TVNZ Charter, which now shape and determine the broadcasting output of the company, are

- strive always to maintain the highest standards of program quality and editorial integrity;
- feature programming across the full range of genres that informs, entertains and educates New Zealand audiences;
- provide shared experiences that contribute to a sense of citizenship and national identity;

- provide comprehensive, impartial, authoritative, and in-depth coverage and analysis of news and current affairs in New Zealand and throughout the world;
- include in programming intended for a mass audience material that deals with minority interests;
- play a leading role in New Zealand television by setting standards of program quality and encouraging creative risk-taking. (TVNZ, 2003)

These objectives are enshrined in TVNZ's *modus operandi* but not necessarily in the thought processes of senior executives, nor in daily practice. The primary documentation of performance, under the new regime, is TVNZ's Annual Report—most recently in its 2004 Annual Report,

> Having a Charter not only makes us unique among this country's television broadcasters, it also changes the broadcasting terrain as a whole. Critically, it forms our commitment to reshape TVNZ as a true public broadcaster and in line with that commitment we are well advanced in the project to transform our programming operations and organizational structure. (TVNZ, 2005, p. 3)

Statement of Charter Performance

A little more than a year ago TVNZ adopted its Charter, which introduced a new way of working and of producing television for New Zealand. The central vision of the Charter is that TVNZ will be the "Home Place"—the place New Zealanders turn to for their defining moments and shared experiences.

Certainly, TVNZ does display an altered "terrain"—more light on some areas and some areas darker—but the significant changes can be ascribed to factors other than the Charter: specifically, increased competition between TVNZ and other television channels, and the continuing health of the New Zealand advertising market. There is a great deal of energy and money being spent ensuring key personnel stay with TVNZ, as well as regular attempts to outflank competition from other channels. In November 2004, Paul Holmes, the richly rewarded presenter of the high-rating current affairs/commentary program *Holmes* (which airs at 7 p.m. weeknights on channel TV One) defected to Prime to set up a rival program (*Paul Holmes*, later *Holmes)* in the same timeslot. After months of failing to make a dent in the ratings of the now-renamed *Closeup @ 7*, Prime shifted Holmes to the earlier 6 p.m. slot, to compete head-to-head with the TV One and TV3 evening news bulletins.

Holmes' departure led to panic of other possible defections from TVNZ, and a rush to secure contracts. The most generous contract was for TV One News presenter Judy Bailey (often referred to as "The Mother of the Country"). Her new annual salary offer of more than $NZ800,000 attracted a wave of negative media attention, and the personal wrath of Prime Minister Helen Clark. There was an echo, in the public criticisms, of an earlier pay-out in 2000, when news presenter John Hawkesby sued TVNZ for unfair dismissal and was awarded $NZ6 million. Interviewed shortly after his departure from TVNZ, Paul Holmes offered an explanation,

> You had the Charter looming above us. How would you know if it is in action? Current affairs and journalists don't need to read the Charter, to know what the job is. . . . On the one hand, the Charter imperative . . . God knows what that means! On the other hand, you have the marketing department thumping you along—whipping you along for higher ratings in the 20 to 54s, or 35 to 54s, or whatever. (Clark, 2004)

Holmes identifies the tension that continues between commercial autonomy and policy reorientation at TVNZ, and although the "Charter imperatives" now tend to dominate the political discourse, there is ample evidence that prior notions of television (maximizing audiences and advertising revenue, populist programming) still persist both at TVNZ and within certain sectors of government agencies. For example, the Crown Company Monitoring Advisory Unit (CCMAU) has been an influential voice in calling for the continuation of dividend payments from TVNZ, arguing that a requirement to pay dividends is an incentive to the company to remain commercially viable. The government's November 2004 refund of NZ$11.4 million of its 2004 dividend could be interpreted as an admission that CCMAU's dividend demands were at odds with Charter objectives, and new broadcasting policy.

Meanwhile, in April 2005, TV3 launched its own 7 p.m. current affairs program called *Campbell Live,* headed by the personable John Campbell. By May 2005, there were *three* competing personality-led current affairs programs scheduled head-to-head in the prime time-slot of 7 p.m., all in search of inherited audiences from the 6 p.m. evening news bulletins, across three leading channels. Channel 2, the fourth leading channel, continued with the long-running, New Zealand soap *Shortland Street* (stripped Monday to Friday), and a substantial audience share.

This unprecedented competition across the schedules of three leading channels supports Thompson's (2005b) contention that,

> While the onus on public service expectations remains on TVNZ broadcasters respond reflexively both to their audiences and to each other. Thus changes in operational philosophy, content and scheduling by an incumbent state broadcaster may open up progressive opportunities and possibilities for its competitors . . . however contrary it sounds, recent events could be interpreted as anecdotal evidence that the Charter is beginning to manifest its influence through TVNZ's competitors. (p. 48)

FUNDING AGENCIES: NEW ZEALAND ON AIR AND TE MANGAI PAHO

According to Jo Tyndall, CEO of the funding agency New Zealand On Air, "it's never been better" (Tyndall, 2005) for this significant player in the New Zealand television environment. Government funding in 2005 was at an all-time high, there was a diversity of local content across genres (including drama and comedy), and viewers were continuing to show strong support, in ratings and institutional research, for locally made programming.

In such a climate of optimism, Tyndall (2005) believed that New Zealanders were "just about on the verge of kissing goodbye to cultural cringe"; an affliction which has long plagued attempts to make acceptable equivalents of genre staples (especially short-run drama and sitcoms). Even though overall local content on New Zealand television screens remains low by international standards (in 2004, occupying 32.6% of 6 a.m. to midnight schedules on TV One, TV2, and TV3), there have been recent and significant popular success, in short-run drama (*Insiders Guide to Happiness*), local versioning of international formats (*NZ Idol*), and animation (*bro' Town*, a very local *The Simpsons*-style series). These successes have added to the continuing popularity of *Shortland Street*, and top-rating news, current affairs, and documentaries. Local content on other channels—such as the more than two thirds of daily Maori Television Service schedules and considerable hours of local sport on Sky—has yet to be factored into the NZOA annual surveys.

NZOA is among those stakeholders who acknowledge that the free-to-air audience in New Zealand is in decline, as pay TV takes a bigger bite of the viewing audience and other diversions distract younger viewers, Even though television in New Zealand is currently in a healthy state, with the local television industry producing an unprecedented range of programming, the big question is how free-to-air services will survive in the long run. There are, for example, doubts about the industry's capacity to keep up with local content demands.

There is also a fear that independent producers have become overdependent on cultural subsidy (funding from NZOA or Te Mangai Paho, or Charter commissions from TVNZ), and thus rather vulnerable to other forces and less inclined to pursue commercial markets and off-shore opportunities. Such criticisms have been expressed by producers associated with the development of, or local versioning of popular international formats. Another criticism is that local content, irrespective of its genre or aesthetic appeal, may well be serving as a default definition of "quality television," given the difficulties of agreeing on any other definition.

In the era of accelerating deregulation (the 1990s), the role of NZOA in the New Zealand broadcasting mix was clear cut. It was the primary guardian of public service broadcasting, meeting residual duties of providing for minority or specialist audiences, in a climate where commercial imperatives (ratings-driven and populist programming) prevailed. In the new broadcasting regime of 2005, where NZOA has been joined by other funders and policy bodies promoting public service objectives, there is now some confusion about who is doing what. For example, viewers are unable to discern what programs have a Charter imprimatur and what Charter initiatives are. A future role for NZOA is government policy but their continued presence in television funding flows has added another complication to an already confusing mix.

PRIVATE BROADCASTERS AND PAY TV

The fortunes of TV3, TV4, and Prime are inextricably linked with the performance of TVNZ in the New Zealand television market, and what might happen to it in the future. There is a growing list of challenges and uncertainties: a possible downturn in economic fortunes; continuing erosion of its audience share by pay TV and digital start-ups increasing competition from telecommunications companies and other competing delivery systems; probable policy reversals if the previous National government returns to power.

All free-to-air broadcasters base their viability on a vigorous and expanding advertising market, with total advertising spend in New Zealand passing $NZ2 billion in 2004, for the first time (all media). They also depend on a formal audience measurement system (AC Nielsen Peoplemeter panels) to set advertising rates, but this measurement system is both one-dimensional and predisposed to favoring the State-owned channels. Week after week, TV One and TV2 dominate television ratings, in terms of program popularity and audience share. The current audience profile is characterized by channel loyalty, with few signs of change yet. The reluctance of TV One viewers to migrate to Prime along with Paul Holmes, is a recent example of viewer inertia. In the meantime, with television advertising space in demand, profitability for low-rating channels (C4 and Prime) and low-rating programs remains possible. Nevertheless, the New Zealand television landscape is littered with failed channels and discarded programming from times when the advertising market was less rosy.

With its reliance on a significant and growing subscriber base, Sky is much less dependent on the state of the advertising dollar. Even though its subscription base of 41% (May 2005) of New Zealand households is not yet near the norm (70% to 80%) in some other Western countries, it is steadily creeping upwards. The current mix includes channels of movie back-catalog, pay-per-view recent releases and art cinema, sports channels (with exclusive rights to the all-important live rugby), children's channel (Cartoon Network, Nickelodeon) and lifestyle channels. Recent additions include e-mail capacity, interactive gaming and, in late 2005, personal video recorder (PVR) capability.

Sky is also advantaged by being the pioneer in the provision of digital television. Despite two failed attempts by TVNZ in 1999 and 2001 to launch digital services in New Zealand, it remains "a digitally deprived nation. We do not have high-definition television. The only digital television channels are those on Sky, a service you have to pay for" (Norris, 2005, p. A11). With its monopoly over the New Zealand digital television market, Sky has also made it much harder, than it would have been 5 years ago, for free-to-air channels to launch a viable digital alternative.

In its rhetoric, the Labour government continue to support the development of digital television and NZOA has commissioned a series of progress reports—most recently, *Public Broadcasting in the Digital Age: Issues for New Zealand* (2005). This report aligns itself with others voices predicting the death of free-to-air television and long-term threats to the cardinal principles of public service broadcasting. Nevertheless, they also point to opportunities, if such broadcasting remains, "the only possible avenue to maintain concepts of the 'public sphere' or a shared public space for providing citizens a range of opinions on the major issues of the day" (Norris & Pauling, 2005, p. 7).

The means of ensuring this, the authors argue, is to "future-proof" TVNZ by increasing funding in favor of public funding and digital developments while strengthening the role of NZOA and extending its provider role to all platforms, including broadband.

THE TELEVISION AUDIENCE

As in most debates about the state of television, and its possible futures, the voice of the end-user (the viewer) remains marginalized, or unheard. Little is known about the New Zealand public's understanding of or response to recent policy reorientations at TVNZ, and the impact of the TVNZ Charter—other than through measures of viewer attitudes to New Zealand-made programming (NZOA qualitative research) and ratings (Nielsen quantitative research). In January 2005, the *New Zealand Herald* commissioned a "one-off" poll (1,000 interviews), which suggested that many viewers had not yet perceived a positive outcome, with 45.7% indicating that "programs had got worse since TVNZ began operating under a charter." Slightly more than one third (34.1%) thought programming had improved while 20.2% remained undecided.

There was a strong bias toward approval from viewers under 40 years and from Maori and Pacific Island viewers, and a higher level of negative judgments from viewers over 60 years (Thomson, 2005). This might suggest that acceptance or resistance to change may well be governed by age and ethnicity factors.

CONCLUSION

Another general election looms as I conclude this examination of the past years of television in New Zealand. There is also the possibility that another change of government could lead to yet another switch of broadcasting policy, and changed fortunes for TVN, NZOA, the Maori Television Service, and other major players in the New Zealand television environment. This would not be unusual and would fit the patterns of successive governments who have restructured and manipulated television, ever since it began. These tensions between politics and television provide interesting insights into the complex nature of cultural policy in a small, highly developed South Pacific nation—but they also provide precedents and salutary lessons for policymakers and television executives in countries facing—or contemplating—change.

The Labour government has guaranteed the future of TVNZ as the primary, State-owned broadcaster, and NZOA as a major funder of programming in the public service mode. Nevertheless, as this chapter has pointed out, confusion over rights and responsibilities has greatly increased, with the introduction of the TVNZ Charter and new cultural directives. NZOA was set up in 1998 to fill a residual public service role, in a time when television was dominated by commercial imperatives and free-market ideology, and continues to be well funded. In 2004 to 2005, the NZOA received

$NZ96.6 million from a direct government grant, with $NZ62 million of this allocated to funding commissioned television programming.

Nevertheless, it now has a well-funded competitor for that role, in the advertising revenue-rich and Charter-funded TVNZ. This is indeed a curious situation and much has still to be resolved in the New Zealand television environment. In addition, there is the very real possibility that policy interventions by politicians have not yet run their course, and another round of changes faces television viewers in New Zealand.

REFERENCES

CanWest. (2005). *Press release.* Retrieved June 21, 2004, from http://press.arrivenet.com/bus/article.php/615913.html

Clark, L. (2004). Interview with Paul Holmes, nine to noon. *National Radio,* December 14.

DeBrett, M. (2005). Extreme makeover; the recurring motif of New Zealand broadcasting policy. *Media International Australia, 117,* 76–85.

Horrocks, R. (2004a). The case of New Zealand. In J. Sinclair. & G, Turner (Eds.), *Contemporary world television* (p. 9). London: British Film Institute.

Horrocks, R. (2004b). The history of New Zealand television: An expensive medium for a small country. In R. Horrocks & N. Perry (Eds.), *Television in New Zealand: Programming the nation* (pp. 20–43). Auckland: Oxford University Press.

Maharey, S. (2005, June). *Taking Up the Challenges of Tomorrow's Television in New Zealand.* Opening address to the New Zealand Broadcasting Seminar, Auckland.

Norris, P. (2004, October 20). TVNZ profit grab reeks of State control. *New Zealand Herald,* p. A9.

Norris, P. (2005, May 31). Digital revolution a long time coming. *New Zealand Herald,* p. A11.

Norris, P., & Pauling, B. (2005). *Public broadcasting in the digital age: Issues for New Zealand.* Wellington: New Zealand on Air.

Steadman, M. (2005, March 15). *Interview on national radio.*

Television New Zealand. (2005). Annual Report Auckland: Television New Zealand.

Thompson, P. (2005a, July). *Calling the tune without paying the piper? The political-economic contradictions of funding the TVNZ charter.* Paper presented to the Australian & New Zealand Communication Association conference, Christchurch, NZ.

Thompson, P. (2005b). Star wars: The empire strikes out? *New Zealand Political Review, 54,* 44–49.

Thomson, A. (2005, January 6). Viewers cool on TVNZ charter. *New Zealand Herald,* p. A4.

TVNZ. (2003). *Charter.* Retrieved June 6, 2004, from http://corporate.tvnz.co.nz/tvnz_detail/0,2406,11135-244-257.html

Tyndall, J. (2005, June). *Taking Up the Challenges of Tomorrow's Television New Zealand.* Speech presented to the New Zealand Broadcasting Seminar, Auckland, NZ.

PART THREE

Europe

CHAPTER NINE

Ireland: From Cultural Nationalism to Neoliberalism

Farrel Corcoran
Dublin City University

Some would argue that except for occasional, spectacular media events—State funerals, globally reported catastrophes, great sporting clashes, declarations of war, or the victorious end of it—there is no longer one shared, symbolic, public space where television gathers together the nation, commands communal attention, and provides the agenda for the national conversation that sustains collective identity. The forces of globalization are sometimes blamed for loosening the bond between mass communication and national cultural identities that existed more clearly in the first, public service phase of television's development.

This possibility infuses much of the debate about the impact of deregulation on the public sphere in Ireland. But first, before we examine changes in the Irish television sector over the last 15 years, it is worth emphasizing the strength of cultural nationalism, a product of the growing resistance to British rule in the 19th century, in the shaping of broadcasting in 20th-century Ireland. The country's geographical position in the northwest European archipelago, its sharing of a common language with its more densely populated neighbor, and its sometimes stressful and complicated historical relationship with that neighbor—these have been major determining forces shaping not only Irish national identity, but also the way broadcasting has evolved in Ireland.

The implications of broadcast overspill from transmitters in Northern Ireland, the West of England, and Wales have influenced broadcasting policy over a long period, from the introduction of radio in the 1920s, to the start up of television in the 1960s, to the debate about digital television in the 1990s. In all three periods, Irish moves to embrace new media lagged behind Britain but were nonetheless driven substantially by fear of the negative impact on Irish society of dependence on cultural flows emanating from London. Because overspill could not be prevented, government response was to launch first a national radio station (1926), then a national television channel (1961), followed by a second (1978), then a third (1998), broadcasting in Gaelic. These moves were largely successful from a cultural nationalist point of view, in the minimal sense of generating audiences loyal to Irish content. British television did not extend into the rural Irish heartland until the 1980s and even then did not succeed in capturing a significant share of the available audience.

In contemporary Ireland, the format and styles of Irish-made television have converged steadily with those driving British television, which themselves have converged steadily with the production values of other European and American media systems. The dynamic thrust of cultural nationalism has also waned in this period, now no longer driven predominantly by a decolonization urge, partly in response to the emergence of historical revisionism at both academic and popular media levels, spurred by divided reactions to "the Troubles" in Northern Ireland. The waning of cultural nationalism is also related to the fact that Ireland is now more deeply immersed in the processes of cultural globalization, which is having an impact on broadcasting greater than anything it experienced in earlier periods when England was the Other against which Irish culture would be maintained.

BACKGROUND

During the protracted debate in government that lasted for much of the 1950s, senior politicians tilted several times toward the option of establishing television in Ireland as a privately owned commercial institution because it would be a cost-free option for an economically underdeveloped country unable to afford the huge budgets and sophisticated production values of the BBC. A number of foreign media companies expressed an interest, and even the Vatican came to support the notion that in safe Catholic hands, Irish television could help save continental Europe from the perils of irreligion and materialism and counteract the influence of Communist-controlled stations. Some initial confusion about the geographical range of an Irish television transmission network did not prevent Pope Pius XII from giving his approval to a proposal from a Romanian entrepreneur who promised to build and operate two television channels at no cost to the State, if he were given control of Ireland's long-wave radio frequency. Ireland would then become "a center from which would radiate programs conforming to the ideals of Christendom and Western civilization and competing with Communist propaganda" (Savage, 1996, p. 156).

The final Cabinet decision, after years of debate among different government departments and semistate companies, was a surprising one. The Broadcasting Act of 1960 established a public, statutory authority to run the new television service. It would be funded by a combination of license fees levied on owners of receiver sets, and advertising fees. This authority (later to become the RTE Authority) would be appointed by the government, which retained for itself the power to license any future radio and television stations that might be proposed. It also retained the power to decide the amount of advertising allowed, and thus to control the flow of revenue to the broadcaster from both sources of income. This power would allow government in a later period, when deregulation had begun to bite, to control the relative flow of revenue going to both private and public broadcasters.

The Act required the RTE Authority to give special consideration to the Irish language and "the national culture," and when dealing with matters which were the subject of controversy, to ensure that programs would be objective and impartial and not expressing the Authority's own views. These stipulations are still in force today in the statutory framework of broadcasting, although Section 31 of the original Act has been abandoned. Section 31 gave successive governments the power to issue written directives to RTE prohibiting the broadcasting of specified material. It was the centerpiece of authoritarian attempts to censor coverage of political violence in Northern Ireland for more than two decades, until the IRA cease-fire was declared in 1994 (Corcoran, 2005; Horgan, 2001).

Ten years after RTE television went on air, a government-established committee addressed the question of how programming choice could be expanded. One option was to rebroadcast either a BBC or an ITV service across Ireland; another was to establish a second RTE channel that would mix domestic material and selected BBC, ITV, and other foreign programs. A national survey conducted in 1975 showed that a majority of Irish people, in both single and multichannel areas, rejected the direct relay of British television and favored the idea of a second RTE channel. This was eventually launched in 1978 and gave RTE the opportunity to compete more vigorously with British channels, which could now reach a significant portion of the Irish population through terrestrial overspill and through a number of cable systems springing up in urban centers. These included one owned by RTE itself, which eventually gained critical mass in the cable market and was the dominant player by the late 1990s, when it was sold to American multinational NTL.

Meanwhile, activists in the Irish language movement kept alive the dream of establishing a third television channel to cater for the needs of people who wanted information and entertainment in Gaelic. An Irish-language radio station was launched in 1972 as a result of a campaign organized in the West of Ireland, based on the notion of language rights. This fed in to a campaign for television that gained momentum from 1980 onward, fueled by frustration with RTE's inability to satisfy the demand for more Irish on television, itself rooted in the conflicting demands of a public service ethos and a market approach, a tension originating in the dual-funding nature of the national broadcaster's revenue.

RTE's heavy reliance on advertising to augment a license fee that governments were always loathe to increase meant that Irish-language programs were increasingly pushed to the margins of the schedules, away from prime-time, where the pressure to maximize audiences was intense (Corcoran, 2004).

The establishment of S4C in Wales helped shift the campaign focus from demanding more Irish on existing channels to establishing a completely separate television service, despite repeated government arguments that this option was too expensive to consider. Pirate transmissions in Connemara played a part in demonstrating the feasibility of a new service, a direct riposte to government prevarication. The new service eventually came on air in 1998 as *Teilifís na Gaeilge,* later renamed TG4. It is owned and operated by RTE, funded by direct government grants and advertising, but it has its own board and executive in Connemara. It is current government policy to reestablish TG4 as a totally independent entity, governed by a separate statutory authority. But as of 2005, it still relies heavily on the parent organization for programming and a range of other supports, though this arm's length relationship has allowed TG4 a large amount of creative independence.

END OF PUBLIC SERVICE MONOPOLY

A major break with the past came in the form of a political decision to end the monopoly position enjoyed first by public service radio, then by public service television. RTE's privileged position was undermined informally in the 1980s with the emergence of pirate radio stations, taking their style from similar stations in the United Kingdom and from Radio Luxembourg, which had been received in Ireland for a very long time. Reacting to this new youth culture phenomenon, the Interim Radio Commission indicated that legal commercial radio was viable and should be considered by the government. This finally happened when the Fianna Fail party was returned to power in 1987 and with the strong support of Fine Gael in opposition (but not the Labor Party), took action to suppress the pirates and establish commercial radio on a legal basis. A new regulatory body was set up, the Independent Radio and Television Commission (IRTC), and given the power to award broadcasting licenses. The commercial sector would be required to observe fairness and impartiality along the same lines as the requirement on RTE, as well as Section 31-type restrictions on coverage of "the Troubles" and proscribed paramilitary organizations. There was also a requirement to provide a minimum of 20% news and current affairs in program schedules, a requirement increasingly resented by private broadcasters. The legislation setting up the IRTC took the first step in removing RTE's monopoly in television also by making provision for a new commercial television service, though it was to be more than a decade before this was actually established.

Government policy in the late 1980s was to encourage the development of a strong private broadcasting sector, partly to curtail what the *Fianna Fail* party saw as the excessively critical public service agenda of RTE and partly to provide entrepreneurial opportunities in broadcasting for business interests favorable to the party (Horgan, 2001). Legislative attempts were made in the 1990 Broadcasting Act to curtail the advertising income of RTE in order to facilitate the emergence of a new national radio station. Despite the very personal support of the minister in charge of broadcasting, this station failed and the minister was later charged with taking bribes from its investors.

Part of the advertising revenue diverted from RTE found its way to Ulster Television (UTV) and began to spur its interest in becoming an all-Ireland broadcaster. Based in Belfast, with a franchise to cover the six counties of Northern Ireland and therefore technically a United Kingdom–based broadcaster, UTV now started to fix its sights on the television audience south of the Border. Like BBC Northern Ireland, UTV had always enjoyed a considerable reach into the Republic via overspill from terrestrial transmitters and cable systems. In 1995, UTV became part of the consortium planning to launch TV3, the first privately owned television channel in the Republic. For a time, it looked as if UTV would become the dominant force in the Dublin-based channel, by rationalizing its advertising sales on an all-island basis, offering advertisers attractive UTV–TV3 packages.

TV3 would later have an additional impact on RTE in the international television program market, as each channel competed to acquire broadcasting rights for the most attractive programming. In every country where competitive television systems had been introduced, the cost of acquisitions had increased sharply. Ireland would be no exception. A dispute with the regulator, however, which insisted that UTV remove itself from cable systems in the Republic in order to boost TV3's chances of commercial success, forced UTV to withdraw from the TV3 consortium (which wouldn't succeed in getting on air for another 2 years). The Belfast-based station began to concentrate more on a digital strategy in order to expand its reach into the Republic, and to invest in radio stations as far south as Cork.

TV3 finally came on air in 1998, nearly a decade after it was legislatively enabled, under the impetus of an investment by Canadian media giant CanWest. This time, unlike the period leading up to the decision to allow RTE to launch a second channel in 1978, there was no political debate about importing foreign content or allowing direct foreign investment in Irish television. The decision was depoliticized, in the sense that it was a matter for the regulator rather than the Cabinet. CanWest replaced UTV as a partner in TV3 with local Irish business interests, but it also invested in UTV in a move widely seen as a strategy to exploit UTV's linkage with the ITV network in Britain (where the Canadian company had failed in its bid for the Channel Five franchise), as well as to achieve all-Ireland synergies between the Dublin and Belfast television operations. Scottish Radio Holdings was also at this time moving to take a stake in UTV and to buy in to newspapers and radio stations in the Republic.

QUESTIONS OF GOVERNANCE

For public service broadcasters in Ireland, all these moves toward market liberalization produced a deep sense of a long-established order being profoundly unsettled. Much of the history of RTE since its inception in 1961 can be read as a slow, steady movement away from a "State-broadcasting" model, toward one more truly answerable to the public rather than to political parties in power. The Broadcasting Act of 1960 stipulated that members of the RTE Authority are appointed by government but cannot include members of either House of the *Oireachtas* (Parliament) or candidates for election. But the famous assertion of *Taoiseach* (Prime Minister) Sean Lemass in 1966 that RTE was "an instrument of public policy" underlines the difficulties encountered in building up a tradition of self-regulation in the Authority and a vision of itself as the guardian of the public interest in broadcasting. In one particularly bad crisis in 1972, the entire Authority was dismissed by the government following official displeasure at the way its newsroom handled communication with the IRA. After some reflection on how this crisis was handled and a stiffening of Section 31 censorship, the Broadcasting Act of 1976 moved to widen the *cordon sanitaire* between politicians and broadcasting by making it more difficult for a government to dismiss members of the Authority. It now requires that a resolution calling for such removal must be passed by both Houses of the *Oireachtas*.

How should the public interest in broadcasting be secured and how should its governors be made accountable to the public, independently of government, given that "accountability" belongs to the family of democratic concepts that infuses the tradition of public service television? In many countries, public service broadcasting is recognized as a public good that has powerful formative consequences for the fabric of democratic culture and the quality of public life. So, how can the future of public television be guaranteed against politicians who would bend it to their will, whether they be Sean Lemass in 1966 with RTE, Silvio Berlusconi in 1994 (and again in 2002) with RAI, or George Bush in 2005 with PBS? One protective mechanism is to remove board appointments from direct control by government, for instance by creating an independent appointments commission, made up of nominees from representative organizations, and asking it to nominate as governors people of talent drawn from a cross-section of society. A number of interesting models have been suggested for increasing governors' responsiveness to viewers and listeners and to strengthen their independence from government, including the plan for an Electoral College for appointing BBC governors elaborated by the Institute for Public Policy Research (Collins & Purnell, 1996).

With the arrival of competition in the Irish television sector, suggestions about how to change the form of governance of RTE began to appear. The notion of a "super-authority" was introduced into the government's Green Paper on Broadcasting in 1995, in the context of separating the "guardian of the public interest" and "regulator" roles from the more day-to-day functions and responsibilities of the Authority. The policy and regulatory functions of the RTE Authority and the IRTC, the Green Paper suggested, could be merged to form one overarching authority. This would assume overall responsibility for broadcasting policy, the development of broadcasting services generally, and the regulation of both public and private broadcasters. This super-authority might also absorb the powers and functions of the Broadcasting Complaints Commission.

RTE argued against this proposal. There might be a case for centralizing some of the supervisory functions of both public and private sectors in areas of common concern (as the *Conseil Superieur de l'Audiovisual* does in France), such as handling audience complaints, enforcing the right to privacy, overseeing impartiality in news, and the protection of children. But the tightly centralized regulation of both private and public broadcasting by one super-authority in areas where they compete might seriously obscure and weaken the basic differences between the two sectors. A regulatory body responsible for both sectors, operating in a political context ideologically infused with strong belief in market liberalism, might well become a powerful tool for political and business interests hostile to public service television. If all dispersed references to the super-authority in the Green Paper were brought together, it became clear that it would have a strikingly wide range of powers. These would be underpinned by its further role as a distributor of public funds to all broadcasters for certain types of "public service" programming that matched criteria set out in legislation, as discussed in chapter 8 of the Green Paper (*Active or Passive: Broadcasting in the Future Tense*, 1995).

This system of license fee disbursement had been suggested in the Peacock Report in Britain many years before and though never implemented there, inspired the establishment of a similar funding structure in New Zealand, with very mixed results (Corcoran, 1996). RTE feared that such a super-authority in Ireland would develop into a super-broadcaster, that television channels would become program providers to a schedule based on policy articulated by the super-authority, in a system like New Zealand On Air (NZOA). This would seriously undermine the autonomy of individual television companies and further blur the distinction between the public and private sectors.

To the great relief of RTE and the dismay of private broadcasting interests, the actual legislation proposed after the publication of the Green Paper rejected the "New Zealand option" of dividing the license fee revenue among broadcasters according to the type of programming they would provide. But it did press on with the merging of the regulatory functions of the IRTC and the RTE Authority into one new Commission in a way that would fundamentally change the way RTE is governed. The Authority would no longer have a function in relation to the development of broadcasting policy. The Commission would approve both hours of broadcasting and advertising minutage for RTE, comment annually on the performance of the public broadcaster, and review that performance every 5 years. The Commission would be empowered to subject the performance of RTE to "rigorous scrutiny" and to initiate change if considered necessary. It would draw up a comprehensive charter for RTE and amend it from time to time. It would review RTE's management structure to see if it was still able organizationally to meet its public service remit and ensure that these structures promoted innovation, quality and diversity in output. The Commission could require appropriate management restructuring and require RTE to make changes to, or even cease, certain commercial initiatives. The Commission would review the cost of various activities within RTE in order to determine the comparative funding of different elements of those activities. It could also establish specific elements of those activities, such as RTE's transmission system, as separate entities under the control of a separate board, if this arrangement were considered beneficial to broadcasting in general in Ireland.

The new powers to be given to the proposed Commission were, of course, those already exercised by the RTE Authority. The key change in the government's plan was to strip these out of RTE and bestow them on a new body governing both public and private broadcasters. It ignored the real possibility that a single regulator could face a conflict of interest between the need to ensure the success of private broadcasters and the need to support competitive services in the public sector. The concentration of monopolistic regulatory power in one Commission, especially one with the power to intervene in internal organizational and budgetary aspects of broadcasting, could bring it very close to editorial influence on content. The core of the problem was this: would future governments always take care to balance appointments to this powerful Commission between advocates of public service television and supporters of private commercial broadcasting? Would an even-handed approach always dominate, especially in an increasingly neoliberal ideological climate?

Lessons could be learned by a small country from what happened in the United States when a right-wing President like Ronald Reagan appointed a Federal Communications Commission that launched a no-holds-barred, neoliberal onslaught on public service norms and protections, or in more recent times, when a Corporation for Public Broadcasting appointed by George W. Bush went to work to stifle political dissent in U.S. public television (Nichols, 2005). The public–private tensions that would be built in to the Commission would be particularly acute in a country as small as Ireland, where the base of advertising and license funding is so small. It is inevitable that neoliberal pressures to make room for more private broadcasting (and more channels for advertising) would be focused on downsizing the "State monopoly." Demands for expansion in the private sector would have to be accommodated at the expense of public service broadcasting. Attractive targets for neoliberal regulators would include curtailing RTE's advertising minutage in order to shift revenue to private broadcasters; preventing RTE from bidding for international television drama series and serials keenly desired by private television; stripping out and privatizing some of RTE's current operations, including its second television channel, its youth-oriented national radio station and its very successful television listings magazine. If this happened, the Commission would succeed in radically weakening public service television but in a politically neutral way, something that a hostile political party might long to achieve but not in the face of public opposition.

Time was running out for this plan for the radical restructuring of broadcasting. A new government came to power in 1997, led by *Fianna Fail*, which immediately set about removing the index-linking of the license fee, promised by the outgoing government. This was to have disastrous consequences for RTE over the next few years, because although inflation in broadcasting in this period far outpaced the consumer price index, indexation to the CPI would go some way towards allowing RTE's public revenues to increase in small stages in a relatively painless way, from a viewer's point of view. From a government perspective, small incremental increases would allow public financial support for RTE to increase without the usual political fear of a public backlash that had accompanied every previous increase in the license fee.

The notion of a super-authority was quietly shelved by the new government, whose Broadcasting Act of 2001 concentrated on provision of digital television rather than on major changes in governance. But it was revived again by the government-appointed Forum on Broadcasting and some form of amalgamation of the powers of the RTE Authority and the Broadcasting Commission of Ireland (as the IRTC had become in 2001, BCI) is now expected to take place in 2006. The notion of making at least some of the license fee revenue available to all broadcasters for provision of particular types of public service programming, learned from both Peacock and NZOA, was revived in the 2001 Act and since then, 5% of license fee revenue has been accumulating in a fund controlled by the BCI, but not yet disbursed. Just as the BCI was about to begin disbursing this €20 million (July 2005), the European Commission, insisting that approval is required under State-aid regulations, intervened in order to examine the implications of giving public funding to private broadcasters.

TELEVISION IN A COMPETITIVE ENVIRONMENT

Several forces over time have shaped RTE as an organization of highly skilled media workers. Some of these forces developed inside the organization; some are perpetually pressing against it from the outside. Legislation, public policy debates, and government decisions have a profound, though often subtle, influence, as does the tradition of interpreting what is expected of public service broadcasting accumulated over the years by successive RTE Authorities, Director Generals, Executive Boards, Producer groups, and so on. The institution of RTE is shaped by the accumulation, in its organizational memory, in its various explicit and implicit codes of work, and of standards regarding best practice in the production of radio and television programs. Professional norms, ideologies and work practices, rarely foregrounded for inspection but exerting a powerful influence on new recruits, shape the output of every division and department.

These institutional structures function within a wider economic and political context. RTE Television was launched in the early 1960s, but had little time to enjoy its monopoly position. Terrestrial overspill from Wales and Northern Ireland, then cable and satellite technologies, and recently MMDS and digital satellite signals, carried into the country channels originating in the United Kingdom and beyond, most of them resourced to levels that dwarf RTE's comparatively puny revenue streams. Today, viewers in less than 20% of Irish households are restricted to the Irish national channels. In the late 1980s, the wave of deregulation that surged across the European political system on the heels of the ideological wash of neoliberalism out of Reagan's Washington and Thatcher's London, finally lapped on Irish shores. RTE Radio now competes for listeners' attention with a robust, privately owned local radio sector as well as a national, private, commercial station and a growing number of community stations. After a decade of false starts, private television, in the form of TV3, quickly consolidated its position with a shrewdness in fighting its corner with regulators learned from its sister CanWest stations in Canada, Australia, and New Zealand. With the arrival of very lightly regulated private broadcasting, democratic capitalism in Ireland took on board, more stridently than ever before, the ideology of market liberalism and a certain structure of feeling going with it that coincided with the arrival of the cultural manifestations of the Celtic Tiger economy.

Although the aims and operating ethos of public and private broadcasters are fundamentally different, they compete for audiences, advertising revenue, and program rights in ever-tightening spirals of rivalry that neoliberal ideologists would have us believe are designed for the sole benefit of viewers and listeners. Recent moves to establish digital television underscore the relevance of the global context in which RTE operates. In a real sense, its competitors include not only CanWest, Canadian parent company of TV3 and the world's largest buyer of American film and television material outside of the United States itself, and its TV3 partner Granada Television, but also include the large British broadcasters, now available in more than 75% of Irish homes, eating inexorably into what used to be RTE's audience share.

The Irish public service channels attract a combined share of 46.5%, competing against two Irish private channels: Belfast-based UTV, which is linked to the British ITV network, and Dublin-based TV3, linked to Granada Television. BBC One comes via the local Northern Ireland BBC service, with some local programming added. Sky News now has a Dublin studio and inserts an Irish evening news bulletin, as well as advertising aimed at the Irish market. Most of the commercial channels compete directly for advertising revenue via their sales offices in Dublin. The penetration of additional digital channels delivered by cable and satellite is 11.8%.

Beyond this relatively local scene, new competition looms in the form of global conglomerates that emerged over the last 10 years, their appetites for profit in overseas markets whetted by the prospect of implementing new "windowing" strategies with the arrival of digital convergence, aiming to create more opportunities to show the same media content on more channels, extracting added value each time from subscriptions or advertising. Chief among these conglomerates is Rupert Murdoch's News Corporation, often regarded as the prototype of the 21st-century media corporation, because of the zeal with which it pursues vertical and horizontal integration within a vast transcontinental media system.

It was obvious to other broadcasters in Europe throughout the last 15 years that RTE was the star performer in the European Broadcasting Union in terms of maintaining a large share of the national audience in what was probably the most competitive same-language television market in the whole of Europe. Unlike comparable broadcasters in other small peripheral countries (i.e., Finland, Denmark, Greece, Norway), public service television in Ireland faced continual competition from large Anglophone broadcasters whose output was resourced initially, before successful international sales, by their large domestic audiences, in the case of the United Kingdom an audience about 25 times the size of RTE's. In Europe's most competitive same-language market, RTE's television channels continue to hold a significant national, prime-time audience, a share of the total audience available that betters the performance of public service television in France, Germany, Italy, the Netherlands and the United Kingdom.

FINANCING THE TELEVISION SECTOR

In peak time viewing for 2004, indigenous production for RTE amounted to 45% of total output (59% for RTE1 and 30% for RTE2). Month by month, more than half the programs in RTE1's top 20 most-watched programs, as measured by A.C. Nielsen, are home-produced. But the size of the population to support all this broadcasting is small, at 4 million people, and audience expectations of RTE are very high, given that 75% of the 1.2 million television households in Ireland receive all the major British channels, which draw their resources from a very large domestic economy. Despite audiences being able to compare the output of Irish with British channels and expecting the same standards and levels of output of domestic programming, RTE is clearly never going to be able to match the economies of scale and the sheer volume of resources available to its competitors. About two thirds of RTE's income is commercial revenue, the balance coming from the license fee. It has often been pointed out that overreliance on commercial income is not healthy for a dual-funded broadcaster with a public service remit, because of the danger that the pressure to maximize audiences as often as possible will exert a powerful gravitational pull on program schedules and soften the commitment to provide a diversity of program genres aimed at stimulating both small and large audience interest. Buoyant commercial revenues sustained RTE throughout most of the 1990s but underlying trends in this period pointed to a more demanding and less certain broadcasting environment, as the rate of increase in program costs began to overtake revenue from license fee and advertising sales and RTE began to head into deficit.

What were the cost drivers pushing public television in this direction? First, 50% of RTE's prime-time schedule was built on acquired programs, an achievement resulting from a policy adopted in 1985 to increase the volume of indigenous programming. But the proliferation of new television channels in Europe initiated a steady climb in the cost of acquiring programs in the global market and, of course, this increase would be accelerated as soon as another Irish channel entered the market, after the launch of TV3 in 1998. This cost pressure was felt most keenly in sports rights, as the arrival of scores of new channels across Europe, including specialist sports channels, encouraged international television sports rights holders to seek ever bigger fees from broadcasters. The significant spending power of the multinational specialist channels forced up the price of major events to a level almost beyond the reach of terrestrial, publicly funded broadcasters like RTE.

Second, the effects of the 1993 Act were being felt acutely as the decade advanced. The Act was designed to privatize parts of the television production apparatus and move RTE closer to being a publisher-broadcaster, by directly feeding production funds to new companies in the independent production sector. The Act stipulated a schedule of payments by RTE, rising from £ 6.5 million in 1995 to 20% of television programming expenditure by 1999. The "downsizing" of RTE as a production organization was debated hardly at all as the 1993 Act was being passed, but staff reduction was an inevitable consequence of the requirement to fund the independent production companies. The problem now was that the Act pegged the expenditure to a percentage of "television programming expenditure" and this opened the door to a long and bitter argument with Film Makers Ireland (FMI), the independent sector's professional association, on how this should be interpreted.

Neither the hyperinflation in television production costs nor the expense of RTE's commitment to TG4 could have been foreseen when the 1993 Act was being framed. The core business of RTE was losing money increasingly from 1995 on and there were no easy ways to stop the financial hemorrhaging once the spend on broadcasting had overtaken its income. RTE and the independent sector took time to develop a mutual respect after a very stressful relationship at first, but the relationship began to work more smoothly from 1997 on, through the pragmatics of collaboration. Significant strains continued to be felt in the budget area, however, with the start up of national competitors in radio and television, as well as the aggressive targeting of Irish audiences by U.K. broadcasters. RTE's commitment to TG4 and the independent production sector, as well as the increasing fragmentation of Irish audiences as more channels became available to more people, contributed to a palpable sense in public service broadcasting of an institution becoming unsettled as never before.

THE EUROPEAN DIMENSION

Uncertainty about the future of television was not unique to Ireland. The broadcasting environment everywhere in Europe, especially in smaller countries, was unpredictable, nervous, and agitated by change. The certainties of earlier decades, when governments had the power to shape broadcasting to suit local and national conditions, were replaced by the apprehension that no one was in control. Across Europe, deep anxiety was becoming the common reaction to the continuing cultural and economic dominance of the United States, and academics argued over whether this could still be called cultural imperialism or cultural globalization. Sometimes the latter term meant little more than recognition of the fact that other large centers of production and export of television programs had grown up outside the Anglophone television world, to parallel American cultural power in specific language markets, such as Spanish, Portuguese, Arabic, or Mandarin, in Mexico, Brazil, Egypt, and China. Small European countries worried about their cultural identity. Would anything distinctly national survive under the shadow of richer and more aggressive powers in production and distribution, beaming dozens of new television channels into their territories and tightly controlling valuable content rights? True, a similar fear had accompanied the global growth of Hollywood power in film between the two world wars. But when television arrived, it had beaten back American dominance in cinema in a dramatic shift toward the restabilization of national media systems. Based on indigenous production appreciated by audiences far larger than what the cinema could muster even in its heyday in the 1940s, television was at the core of this restabilization from the 1960s to the 1990s.

Within the EU, debate on the future of broadcasting was dominated by the idea of digital convergence, as the Commission gathered in responses to its Green Paper published in 1998. RTE's input emphasized the social responsibility of public service broadcasting and the need to keep in view values that go beyond those of the market place. Later that year, the Commission circulated a discussion paper exploring the criteria by which public service broadcasting might be defined, so that programming on dual-funded systems like RTE could be divided into types which could be funded by a license fee and types which could not. A brief and fierce debate ensued and the paper was hurriedly withdrawn when it was obvious that most Member States rejected its basic premises. But no one was in any doubt that these funding issues would surface again as competition between public and private broadcasters in Europe intensified and the latter issued more frequent complaints to the Commission about public service broadcasting being fundamentally at odds with the free market because it receives public funding. The Directorate for Competition's tilt toward private broadcasters was corrected somewhat at the end of 1998 by the Report of the High Level Group on the Digital Age and European Audiovisual Policy (the Oreja Report), in its recognition of the role of Member States in determining the precise balance between public and private broadcasting in their own territories. In effect, all this discussion represented a teasing out of the implications of the Broadcasting Protocol added to the Amsterdam Treaty at the urging of the Irish and French governments a few years before.

But did smaller Member States, with fairly modest resources, still have real power to protect public service broadcasting from larger economic and political trends developing across Europe? RTE's response to the crisis in 2001 focused on deep cuts in staffing levels, eliminating a further 160 jobs, closing down a number of departments and selling off its Outside Broadcast operations. Political lack of engagement in the crisis in broadcasting meant that external factors operating in a more complex commercial environment, over which RTE had no control, were being ignored. These factors included currency exchange rates in U.S. program purchases, the success of British channels in siphoning out television advertising money from the Irish economy, and the success of Sky Television in signing up 185,000 households to its digital service.

The steady development of TV3 was also a factor. Now guided by foreign owners CanWest and Granada, each with a 45% stake in the company, it was emerging as a serious competitor for both acquired programs and advertising revenue. Many voices in Irish public life had argued throughout the 1990s for an alternative television system, so that another point of view besides RTE's could improve the quality of the public sphere in Ireland. But as it became clear that TV3 had acquired a firm hold in the very competitive Irish television market, the Broadcasting Commission of Ireland signaled that it would make permanent its practice of "light touch" regulation of private broadcasters. This confirmed what many in RTE already knew: that TV3 was investing very little in Irish-made television and therefore would be making few contributions to "an alternative view" to complement RTE's, and that the BCI was unwilling to monitor TV3's output to determine if it lived up to the legislative requirement for content diversity, including Irish-made programs and a reasonable proportion of news and current affairs content. The implications of all these developments pointed towards a running down of the quality of broadcasting in Ireland right across the public-private spectrum.

The question was what could be done about all this and no satisfactory answer was found until the government finally agreed to a substantial increase in the license fee in December 2002, while also demanding higher levels of accountability by the public broadcaster and adherence to an agreed Public Service Broadcasting Charter. The indexing of the license fee would ensure a degree of protection from political interference for RTE but some of the license fee would be diverted into a License Innovation Fund and made available for production of programs that could be broadcast on any free-to-air channel. This initiative was viewed as a victory for private broadcasters. BSkyB in particular had publicly urged that such a fund should be established to force RTE to compete for funds with other broadcasters and independent producers. This funding mechanism has been described in the New Zealand context as an Arts Council of the Airwaves model (Corcoran, 1996).

TECHNOLOGICAL CHALLENGES

By 1998, the promise of digital television was huge and much of the early excitement centered around Digital Terrestrial Television (DTT). The British government published a White Paper, then new legislation, allowing the most affordable distribution platform with the potentially widest reach in the population, to take off quickly: This was DTT. By 2003, like the dot.com hype, the huge optimism about DTT had collapsed. Headlines in respectable broadsheets announced the end of digital television. On the same weekend in March 2002, Kirch in Germany was in free fall toward bankruptcy, ITV Digital was placed in administration by its owners Carlton and Granada, and the cable giant NTL was heading for receivership under the weight of its massive debts, unable to tackle the challenges of digital television. Misjudging the cost of content and overestimating the rate of subscriber growth had devastated ITV Digital. The value of many television companies across Europe started to fall sharply in a process that turned into a massive shakeout, fueled by fierce competition and the strains of carrying expensive bank debt. The demand for Hollywood products on premium channels remained very slow and there was no sign of profits from television for hopeful football clubs. Kirch's demise, as a conglomerate controlling newspapers, film production, cable and broadcasting, was the largest corporate collapse in German postwar history.

The collapse of DTT in Britain in 2002, with millions of pounds owed to football clubs, was a blow to U.K. ambition to be the first fully digital television nation by 2010. The British government had hoped that 80% of the population would have switched to digital television before then and the remaining "analog refuseniks" (as the Murdoch tabloids call them) would be pushed into digital television by an impending analog switch-off date. This would then allow the government to raise large sums of money in "spectrum farming," as the wasteful use of the electromagnetic spectrum would yield to its more efficient use to provide new generation telephony services.

RTE was keeping a close eye on developments overseas as it took on the lead role in establishing a digital policy for Ireland in the mid-1990s. Detailing the development of plans for DTT goes beyond the scope of this chapter (but see Corcoran, 2004). In summary, RTE planned to launch DTT in time for the millennium celebrations of 2000 but the government first prevaricated, then rejected these plans and imposed its own: RTE was required to sell 72% of its transmission system and it was to be excluded from the business of marketing and managing a DTT service. RTE argued for a "unitary model" in which both the transmission and multiplex operations would remain in a single company that would attract private investors into partnership with the public broadcaster. This was set aside, after successful lobbying from the private broadcasting sector. As of 2005, there is little interest among investors in buying RTE's transmission network and only a single bidder ever emerged for the multiplex operation license. This bidder withdrew, unable to attract investors. In effect, this first attempt at digital policy making, initiated by RTE in 1996, is now in disarray and market forces are presently the primary drivers in the rollout of digital television in Ireland. The government's decision in effect put DTT on the back foot and cleared the way for two rival platforms to create a digital television market, both of them are controlled by multinational media conglomerates: NTL's cable and Sky Television's satellite service. Plans to launch an experimental DTT service for the Dublin area have been announced several times but a service has yet to appear.

The so-called "platform wars" continue, despite earlier predictions that these contests over Internet and television distribution systems would be settled by the start of the new millennium. NTL, one of the global giants with considerable power in the Irish cable television sector, faced huge financial problems in recent years but emerged from bankruptcy protection in January 2003. Its revenue from its Irish operation rose by 28% in the first quarter of 2003, due to a price rise and an increase in the digital television subscriber base. It now delivers television to 340,000 customers, but only 85,000 of them access digital television. Sky Television reaches 333,000 households, all of them digital. There is some reason to believe that the churn rate of both cable and satellite services will begin to accelerate as a result of a series of recent British government decisions aimed at producing a low-cost route toward analog shutdown across the United Kingdom, in line with its policy to make large amounts of electromagnetic spectrum available for farming out to telecommunications. The new British digital terrestrial Freeview service will reach about 80% of U.K. homes in the main population centers and the emerging satellite Freesat system will complete the coverage in rural areas. The Freesat system will be an overwhelmingly attractive option for many Irish households prepared to pay the one-time charge for a satellite dish, in return for crystal clear reception of U.K. television and whatever applications of interactivity will emerge. Any commercial *raison d'etre* for an Irish DTT service will be diminished. There will certainly be an impact on RTE's audience share and there may well be an impact on its future ability to acquire broadcasting rights for imported programs. Thus, satellite technology, with its ability to beam signals into a footprint that ignores the boundaries of national territories, brings to a new level the challenges of overspill from Britain that Ireland has had to grapple with since the origins of radio and television.

CONCLUSION

For how long will Irish public opinion leaders and the political elite be interested in tackling the challenges of cultural globalization and defending television that is distinctively "Irish"? Audience research tells us that if good quality Irish-made programs are cleverly scheduled to maximize exposure, they are more avidly watched than imported content. This was not the case in earlier periods in television history, when American programs dominated the ratings. In this respect, television differs radically from cinema, where European- or Irish-made films enjoy nowhere near the same level of popularity as American imports. This reflects the general European situation, where the huge marketing power of Hollywood has built a century-long momentum to sustain its dominant brand position. Television is quite a different medium with very different audience dynamics, including a thirst for an Irish perspective on world affairs, Irish drama and comedy, and documentaries on subjects close to home. This strong interest in indigenous programming of all kinds does not take from the large appetite for global culture; it complements it. The local and the global work in tandem.

One effect of the increasing opening up of Irish society to global influences is that the ideology of market liberalism, so active in the politics of broadcasting in the United States 80 years earlier, has begun to assert itself very strongly in Ireland over the last 15 years. As the late French sociologist Pierre Bourdieu pointed out many times, one of the ideological effects of neoliberal ideology is that it presents itself as quintessentially a modern way of thinking, concealing and erasing its own lineage. Neoliberalism is actually a conservative revolution to restore the past, but it drives its project forward in the guise of being progressive. Its opponents are labeled "dinosaurs," and this usually includes those who argue in favor of public service broadcasting. The ideological "common sense" of market liberalism embraces the argument that new technology will deal with all social needs, by offering such a plethora of television channels that viewers will be able to find anything they want (and pay for just what they consume). There will be no justification for requiring everyone to pay for public, free-to-air generalist television channels that address what might be called the citizenship needs of the public sphere or the cultural needs of the nation.

There is a major challenge for public service television in this technologically determined vision of the media future, especially as youth culture in particular gets quickly bored with television schedules that attempt to cater for all interests (farmers, senior citizens, Irish speakers, children, immigrants, and so on) and seek only niche channels that fit within a narrow band of tolerance, providing a flow of large volumes of television content with little variation. RTE is working within a large commercial and ideological context in which we have seen the idea of the public domain being undermined by many of the dominant voices in society. A new "common sense" has evolved, which allows the selling off of public institutions to the private sector, some of it derived from the inflow of political ideas from the European Union, some from neoliberal projects adopted by Thatcher and New Labor governments in London. It becomes more difficult to mobilize social arguments for the desirability of public services as economic arguments gain supremacy: selling publicly owned institutions would produce more efficiency or better customer service; downsizing a public company would produce savings to the Exchequer; competition would ensure that everyone is much happier with the new arrangements being applied to social assets. Arguments centering on the public good, rooted in the principle of public ownership, get marginalized and are no longer heard very much in public, or are taken into account only in some tokenistic way, or are dismissed as too idealistic or unacceptably old-fashioned, or even "looney left."

In several countries, including the United States and much of Eastern Europe that now follows its lead in broadcasting policy, governments have decided that private television companies can be trusted to be more supine than public broadcasters, when it comes to the watchdog role of the media. Following the BBC's experience at the hands of the Hutton Inquiry into its coverage of Iraq, the question for Ireland is whether the structures of television governance and regulation in the future will be robust enough to allow broadcasters to follow their editorial rather than their political instincts when it is timely to critique government performance. In the early decades of public service television, there were significant times of the week when RTE provided compelling television viewing for almost all households across the country, challenging bishops' dominance of the public sphere or administering well-chosen shocks to the residual values of 19th-century Catholic piety. There was only one channel available then. Now, in a much more competitive environment, how well will television be able to project the whiff of danger that audiences still want from current affairs reporting? Without this, television will no longer be able to make the vital cultural connections between nation and State that made it such a fundamental engine of development for much of the 20th century.

REFERENCES

Active or passive: Broadcasting in the future tense. (1995). Green Paper on broadcasting. Dublin: Stationery Office.

Collins, R., & Purnell, J. (1996). The future of the BBC. *Javnost—The Public, 3*(2), 71–80.

Corcoran, F. (1996). Arts council of the airwaves. *Javnost—The Public, 3*(2), 9–22.

Corcoran, F. (2004). *RTE and the globalization of Irish Television.* Bristol: Intellect Books.

Corcoran, F. (2005). Government, public broadcasting and the urge to censor. In M. P. Corcoran & M O'Brien (Eds.), *Political censorship and the democratic State: The Irish broadcasting ban* (pp. 86–98). Dublin: Four Courts Press.

Horgan, J. (2001). *Irish media: A critical history since 1922.* London: Routledge.

Nichols, J. (2005). Moyers fights back. *The Nation,* June 6, 2005.

RTE Annual Report. (2004). Dublin: RTE.

Savage, R. (1996). *Irish television: Political and social origins.* Cork: Cork University Press.

CHAPTER TEN

Media Policy in Italy

Matthew Hibberd
Stirling University

This chapter presents an overview of Italian media policy concentrating on the post-1990 period. In postwar Europe, each nation-state has developed different media policies in line with its own political and social conditions, market imperatives and institutional practices. This is clearly illustrated by the development of media policy in Italy where a unique media market has developed in the last 25 years. Despite the adoption of some common European Union (EU) media directives, Italian media policy has been heavily criticized in recent years for not encouraging media pluralism as well as other basic principles, such as independence and autonomy for the public service broadcaster, RAI, from political interference, an important requirement for the proper functioning of a democratic media system. In short, Italian media policy falls well short of the standards set by its EU partners.

This chapter will concentrate on broadcasting policies to the detriment of those affecting the press industry. The newspaper industry in Italy has suffered various setbacks in the contemporary period. Among these has been the lack of government investment in the industry compared to that of television, despite each of the major parties controlling their own newspaper title in the postwar period. Historically, the regional character of the press industry means that Italy has been slow to develop national titles, hindering the development of a mass readership, and allowing broadcasting to reap national advertising revenues. Italy, therefore, has a situation, unparalleled in many other western European countries, where broadcasting takes a far larger share of advertising revenue than newspapers (Balassone & Guglielmi, 1993, p. 12; Andreano & Iapadre, 2005).

This chapter is divided in to six sections. Given the importance of the State and market to the development of the broadcast media in Italy, my analysis of the Italian case will start with an examination of the country's political development in the postwar period. Section two discusses postwar media policies, including provisions set out in the 1948 Constitution. The third section looks at the development of commercial competition in the Italian broadcasting market and the so-called "Wild West" years. The fourth section will highlight Italian media policies adopted in the 1990s before examining the regulatory institutions responsible for enforcing those policies in section five. Finally, section six will look at the 2004 Gasparri Law, which has been heavily criticized by a recent report by the Venice Commission, advisory committee on constitutional affairs of the Council of Europe (Venice Commission, 2005).

BACKGROUND TO POSTWAR ITALIAN POLITICAL HISTORY

In 1945, the Italian nation was in turmoil. The very concept of nationhood entailed explicit overtones associated with the Fascist regime of the 1930s. In Italy, however, the situation was made even more difficult because the task of renewal was hampered by other problems, notably the struggle to reunite the diversity of groups and communities to the country's political institutions. The restoration and reconstitution of basic political and civic rights denied by the previous regime constituted an improvement in itself. The provision of basic social and economic norms and responsibilities also constituted a qualitative improvement in the formal rights of Italian citizens. When the Christian Democrats gained victory in the 1948 elections, they were able to undermine the power of the many State and para-state institutions and turn them into fiefdoms of political patronage (Spotts & Wieser, 1986, pp. 2–4).

The Christian Democrats were helped in this task because many elements of the pre-Republic State machinery still remained and because a majority of civil servants supported the party. Furthermore, the policy of *epurazione*—the purging of the old Fascist state apparatus—in the postwar years had failed because Fascist membership had been obligatory for all civil servants in the pre-war period and to sack the whole civil service was seen as being impractical (Ginsborg, 1990, p. 92). At the same time, however, many argued that the consequences of such purges would be further civil conflict. The decision was therefore taken to curtail this policy. The role of the State institutions in Fascist crimes became buried in order to promote the new Italian order (Judt, 1994, p. 2).

The postwar period also saw the continued development of government special agencies controlling many of the major social and economic institutions (railways etc.), each constituting a separate and autonomous bureaucracy, and which resulted in separate enclaves of influence and power within the State

(Ginsborg, 1990, p. 147). An example of a parallel bureaucracy was the pre-war radio service, EIAR. Here, too, the old management had not been purged (Cavazza, 1979, pp. 84–85). At the end of the war the management hierarchy of renamed RAI (*Radioaudizioni Italia* [which became *Radiotelevisione italiana* with the onset of television services in 1954]) broadly supported the Christian Democrats. Despite these obvious parallels with its predecessors, the Italian State enjoyed considerable success in the postwar period. Successive governments undertook substantive industrial and agricultural reforms, which resulted in Italy becoming an industrialized country. Often, it was State industries that took the economic initiatives that led to increasing growth. It was State intervention in the south that secured more jobs and investment for the people of those lands. Finally, the Italian government was at the forefront of negotiations between European partners which culminated in the formation of the EEC in 1957. Economic expansion had immediate and positive spin-offs for social provision. The increase in educational and cultural provision, health spending, social housing, etc., ensured that there would be major improvement in the living standards and the quality of life in Italy.

The collapse of the old political regime and the resulting winds of change blowing across the Italian peninsula since 1992 were both unforeseen and dramatic. There was not one cause for the collapse of the Christian Democrats and its allies. Instead, there are a number of interlocking reasons: some are more historical in nature and include the continued absence of a viable or alternative opposition which could take over political control. The end of the Cold War was another reason and the diminished threat of Communism. Finally, ongoing corruption scandals and brutal mafia murders of key Italian judges in 1992–1993 acted as a catalyst for mass public protests against political elites and, finally, the dissolution of the Christian Democrats as well as the Socialist and other minor parties (Ginsborg, 1996, pp. 19–20). The past decade has seen the gradual emergence of two fluid political blocs: a center-left and a center-right, as Italy seeks to break with the centrist Christian Democrat-led consensus of the postwar period. A leader of the centre-right government, Silvio Berlusconi, also played a key role in Italian broadcasting development, as the next section examines.

ITALIAN MEDIA IN THE POSTWAR PERIOD

In Italy, RAI played a central part in promoting the postwar idea of hope and renewal, through the promotion of particular forms of social or national inclusion. Radio and television programs promoted a plurality of ideas and discussions on a whole range of important issues, although news broadcasts were heavily dominated by the Christian Democrats and its (American-backed) political allies. Public service broadcasting in Italy was "progressive" insofar as it promoted the policy of educating the Italian public through the provision of a universal and accessible service. RAI covered a wide range of program formats that played a formative role in Italian cultural development. This meant that Italians developed and nurtured collective or familial viewing habits over an extended period (Monteleone, 1992, p. 426).

Constitutional provisions for the mass media were contained in Articles 21, 33, 41, and 43 of the Constitution. Like all major statutes and laws, the 1948 Italian Constitution has been subjected to a long academic debate and different interpretations. By highlighting its core elements an overall picture can be made of its primary political and social principles. Article Two contains a declaration of Human Rights whether as an individual or association. Article Three of the Constitution is a declaration of equality for all, "that all citizens have equal social dignity and are equal before the law, without distinction of sex, of race, of religion, of political opinion, of personal and social condition." This is a classic liberal statement. The next paragraph of Article Three goes beyond this towards a more socialist standpoint, "It is the task of the Republic to remove obstacles of an economic and social nature which, limiting in fact the liberty and equality of citizens prevent the full development of the human personality and the effective participation by all workers in the political, economic and social organization of the country." Democratic rights were enshrined by the election of a parliament based on proportional representation (PR), changed in 1993 to a different version of PR, the election of Regional Assemblies (not enacted until 1970), and provisions granting the use of direct Referenda. The Lateran pacts of 1929, whereby the Catholic Church formally recognized Italy's right of self determination in return for the recognition of Catholicism as the official State religion, were included in the Constitution. The Constitution symbolized the compromise between liberalism, socialism and Catholicism (Sassoon, 1986, p. 195).

Article 21 states that "Everyone shall have the right to express freely his own thoughts in words, writing or any other medium." Article 33 states that "Art and Science shall be free and their teaching likewise." Article 41 states that "Private enterprise shall be permitted insofar as it does not run counter to the social utility nor constitute a danger to freedom or human dignity . . . The law shall determine appropriate programs and controls to enable public and private economic activities to be run and coordinated for social ends." Finally, Article 43 states that for purposes of general utility, "The law may reserve to the State, to the public institutions, or to worker or consumer associations, *ab initio*, or transfer to them by expropriation, subject to identification, certain undertakings or category of undertakings involving essential public services . . . important to the community" (Esposito & Grassi, 1975a, pp. 44–45). The importance of these articles will become apparent as this article progresses.

In addition to the constitutional provisions for the media, specific legislation for the new RAI had been set out in a government decree, No. 428, dated April 3, 1947. The aim of the decree was to ensure the proper democratic management of broadcasting. The effect of the decree was anything but the democratization desired. Responsibility for overseeing RAI was given to two watchdog authorities: a consultative committee overseeing cultural, artistic and educational policies; and a parliamentary committee, set up to oversee the political independence of broadcasting and the objectivity of news coverage. The parliamentary committee, which was made up of 30 members chosen equally by the two Presidents of the two Houses of Parliament, passed on recommendations to the President of the Council of

Ministers (the Prime Minister) to implement. In reality, the decree gave extensive powers to the executive.

BROADCASTING AND THE ARRIVAL OF COMMERCIAL COMPETITION

Broadcasting in Italy was irreversibly changed by two decisions of the Constitutional Court in 1974 and 1976. In July 1974, the Court was asked to adjudicate on the legality of RAI's monopoly in response to a case where a foreign television service was broadcasting into Italy, taking valuable advertising revenue from RAI. The Constitutional Court passed two judgments, Nos. 225 and 226. Judgment 225 upheld the legitimacy of the national and local terrestrial monopoly citing Article 43 of the Constitution, the public interest article, due to technical scarcity of frequencies. The Court also launched a broadside against the government (in doing so the Court showed that the Judiciary was not at one with the government over broadcasting policy). It argued the imperative of a public service monopoly based on objectivity and impartiality, especially for news programs. The Court also took the unusual step of stating the legal provisions needed to ensure the ideal of a public service. Judgment 226 decided that the monopoly could no longer be justified in respect to cable and foreign-based channels, with the Court citing Article 21 of the Constitution (see above). This was a liberal interpretation of the Constitution, opening a new historical phase in Italian broadcasting (Ortoleva, 1994, p. 108).

Many of the provisions recommended by the Constitution Court in Judgment 225 were included in the new 1975 Broadcasting Act. Responsibility for the overseeing of broadcasting was transferred from the executive to parliament, including powers to appoint RAI's Administrative Council. The Christian Democrats were, however, able to hold on to much of its influence by virtue of being the largest party in parliament, with the remainder of power falling to the Socialist party and other minor coalition parties. Despite the good intentions of the Constitutional Court, little had actually changed and political control of RAI remained tight (Cavazza, 1979, pp. 103–105).

The 1975 Broadcasting Act also stated that RAI should be split into two separate networks "responsible for devising and producing radio and television programming" (Esposito & Grassi, 1975b, p. 53). As we shall see, this was not the last time a parliamentary act dictated RAI's internal organizational structure. The formation of two networks facilitated the creation of two broad ideological camps: the first network being for a Catholic culture and the second network for a lay culture, with the result that the two camps were gradually subjected to political control. RAI was gradually partitioned along party lines running from the President (Socialist) and the Director-General (Christian Democrats) down to the networks, Raiuno (Christian Democrats) and Raidue (Socialists), and finally to journalists and administrative staff. When Raitre began broadcasting in 1979, it was brought gradually under the wing of the Italian Communist party, which had been brought in to the political mainstream in the mid and late 1970s. The 1975 Broadcasting Act therefore contributed to the formal carve-up of RAI by political parties: the system of *lottizzazione*.

But if RAI and the political authorities hoped for a period of relative peace and calm after 1975, they were badly mistaken. In July 1976, the Constitutional Court (Judgment 202) ended RAI's monopoly over local terrestrial broadcasting. The national monopoly was confirmed, however. It was the decision to end RAI's local monopoly, above all others, that effectively shaped broadcasting development in Italy for the next 25 years. The reason cited by the Court was that technical advances meant that television frequencies were no longer as scarce as they once were and commercial broadcasting could be permitted at a local level. In fact, local television channels in Italy had been growing rapidly in number since the early 1970s. A long-standing debate has been why the Court changed its mind in the space of two years. After all, technological developments had not advanced significantly in the meantime. Cavazza (1979, p. 112) asks whether the Court wanted to upset the lottizzazione arrangement. It was more likely that the Court was reacting against the provisions in the 1975 Broadcasting Act that effectively curtailed development of cable channels in Italy. Otherwise, the Court was perhaps reacting to economic pressures coming from commercial lobbyists.[1]

The increasing economic importance of television had created a booming cultural industry, leading to the ever-increasing importance of television as a popular form of entertainment (Macchiatella, 1985, p. 12). The introduction, by the late 1970s, of hundreds of new and unregulated channels (and causing an administrative nightmare in the management of the hertzian frequency spectrum) threatened RAI's predominance in every sphere of broadcasting such as advertising, programming and personnel. Added to this was the lack of a political consensus to regulate the new commercial sector. In the late 1970s and 1980s, apart from a few *ad hoc* decree laws, the commercial system was allowed to run completely unimpaired by regulations despite numerous proposals for reform being presented, either in Parliament, or by the political parties. Until the passing of the 1990 Broadcasting Act (known as the Mammì law, after the then Minister for Post and Telecommunications), the Italian system became known as the "Wild West" of all broadcasting systems. Although the full effects of the Constitutional Court decision were not immediately apparent, by the early 1980s commercial channels operating on a quasi-national basis had become an everyday reality.

ITALIAN MEDIA POLICY: CONTEMPORARY DEVELOPMENTS

The end result of this idiosyncratic development was the emergence by 1982 of three quasi-national commercial networks consisting of groups of syndicated local channels offering the same programs. The simultaneous broadcasting of programs by these channels had been banned by a decision of the Constitutional Court in 1981 (Sentence No. 148, July 1981). At the same time, the Court never banned these commercial channels and they were allowed to continue national broadcasting by using a legal loophole. This was achieved by pre-recording all programs on video cassettes

---

[1]It is worth recording that Italy also underwent a deep recession between 1975 and 1979.

and then showing them at slightly staggered times across the country. In this way, and through the use of a legal technicality, commercial channels continued broadcasting. In one respect, however, the commercial sector was disadvantaged in relation to RAI because it was unable to show live programs. The lack of regulations allowed one player, Silvio Berlusconi's Fininvest, to gain gradual control of the commercial television market. Berlusconi started his own channel, Canale 5 in 1980. In January 1983 he bought Italia Uno and in August 1984 he acquired Retequattro (Grasso, 1992, pp. 412–428). By 1984, Italy had a *de facto* television duopoly.

The duopoly system was officially sanctioned in law in August 1990 (Law No. 223, August 6, 1990). The lengthy parliamentary passage of the Act and the constant list of amendments produced, not surprisingly, an act described by its author as: "the best that was possible at the time" (quoted from introduction to Giacalone, 1992, p. xiii). The best was rather little. The crucial Article 15 states that no group should control more than 25% of the national channels. The law did not specify the number of national channels, but no-one doubted that a minimum 12 licensees would be allotted, allowing RAI and Fininvest to retain three channels a piece. Twelve licensees were duly announced in August 1992, formally entrenching the duopoly in statute.

In June 1993 a mini-reform of RAI was passed by Parliament altering the power structure within the company with a view to dismantling the *lottizzazione* system (Law No. 206, June 25, 1993). The main aspect of the law was the reform of RAI's Administrative Council. The Council was reduced from 16 members to just four appointed trustees plus the Director-General, the most senior employee of the company. Members of the Council were no longer chosen by the Parliamentary Commission, but were instead chosen jointly by the two Presidents of the Parliament. Finally, the Director-General was now to be appointed by the other four members of the Council in agreement with IRI (Industrial Reconstruction Institute), RAI's parent company, with slightly reduced powers. The reform reduced the importance of the Parliamentary Commission, which had been responsible for the formal Parliamentary approval of the carve-up of RAI in the 1970s. The Commission was little more than a puppet for the party hierarchies and enjoyed little effective autonomy. By giving the power over appointees to senior institutional figures (in Italy, the two Presidents of the Chamber of Deputies and the Senate are the second and third most senior figures, following the President of the Republic himself) the system for controlling RAI became the responsibility of institutional guarantors, and theoretically above party politics, although, in reality, such guarantors did refer to the government or Prime Minister of the day.

Of ongoing concern to legislators and judicial authorities since the 1990 Act was the status of the RAI/Fininvest-Mediaset duopoly. Formerly, Fininvest, Mediaset was created as the communications sub-holding of Fininvest in 1994. Silvio Berlusconi sold part of his stake in Mediaset in 1995. New shareholders included among others: Kirch, Al Waleed, and a conglomeration of six Italian banks. The company was then floated on the Milan Stock Exchange in July 1996. Silvio Berlusconi (through Fininvest and Silvio Berlusconi Holdings) still holds a controlling interest.[2]

---

[2]For the purposes of this chapter, the company will be known as Fininvest (pre-1994) and Mediaset (post-1994).

One defining moment for the duopoly came in December 1994 when the Constitutional Court entered the debate. The case (brought by minor national commercial channels, including Telemontecarlo [now La 7]) centered on the argument that Mediaset's position constituted a dominant market position and therefore breached the Constitution. The main decision of the Court concerned Article 15 of the 1990 Broadcasting Law. The Court argued that the ownership of three channels as guaranteed by Article 15 distorted the rules of competition in the broadcasting industry and also constituted a potential risk to fundamental values of free speech, of thought, etc. In the Court's opinion it was the duty of legislators to stop the formation of a monopoly and instead create a system, which allowed the greatest possible access. The Court therefore decided that Article 15 was "incoherent, unreasonable and unsuitable" (*La Repubblica*, December 7, 1994). The Court ruled, therefore, that Mediaset should lose one channel. The Court granted a period of transition so that new legislation could be introduced, rather than pass a definitive judgment.

The ball was instead passed back to the politicians to decide on the legislation required. The decision of the Court, although technically against Mediaset only, effectively condemned the duopoly as unconstitutional. It was therefore against this backdrop that the 1997 Broadcasting Act reduced the number of RAI channels allowed to take television spot advertising from three to two. With RAI being reduced to just two advertising channels, the Broadcasting Act also required Mediaset to reduce the number of its terrestrial channels from three to two, with Retequattro being withdrawn to become a satellite channel (Article 3). Taken in unison, these developments fulfilled the demands of the Constitutional Court decision of December 1994. But the 1997 Act did not provide a precise timetable for these changes (only one of the many flaws of this piece of legislation) and both Mediaset and RAI successfully lobbied government and regulators to delay implementation. Both companies would have lost substantial advertising revenues—in RAI's case the company would have lost €150 million worth of advertising per annum from Raitre—and found common cause. The argument did not end there, however. In 2001, the Constitutional Court again ruled that the duopoly was unconstitutional, setting a new deadline for the implementation of the Retequattro decision. The date set was December 31, 2003, ensuring that the incoming Berlusconi government, also in 2001, would have to pass new media legislation by that date (see below).

The 1997 Act also specified that RAI restructure itself into separate internal divisions. As a result, the company was split, with a publicly owned holding company (RAI) governing five separate divisions (Article 31, Law 249, 1997). This could then pave the way for the partial privatization of one or more of these five divisions, which, in turn, would comply with the result of the 1995 Referendum. In June 1995, three consultative referenda were held relating to the future of the broadcasting system in Italy. The three referenda proposed were: to privatize or part-privatize RAI (subsequently carried); to reform regulations regarding advertising and, finally; to reduce the number commercial channels held by any one operator (both of which failed). In fact, the rejection of last referendum, to reduce the number of commercial channels held by any one operator, placed popular opinion at odds with the Constitutional Court decision. As far as the wider Italian broadcasting system was concerned, the new legislation required a new frequency plan be produced with view to ensuring that all national channels enjoy greater national coverage (a legacy of the 1970s, when the grab for new licenses following the 1976 Constitutional Court decision were not administered centrally, thus allowing a "help yourself" policy to develop). Taken in unison, the new law fulfilled the demands of the Constitutional Court decision of December 1994.

REGULATORY INSTITUTIONS

The other main feature of the 1997 Act was the institution of a new super regulator for the Italian media—Autorità per le Garanzie nelle Comunicazioni (AGCOM). The Authority has broad responsibilities for Italy's audiovisual and telecommunications' industries and its main tasks include: encouraging competition in the audiovisual and telecommunications' markets and supporting inward investment; supervising and enforcing compliance with Italian and European legislation in these areas; advising Italian governments on audiovisual and telecommunications' policies; providing conflict resolution or arbitration service to players in the above-mentioned industries; and encouraging the adoption of industry-wide guidelines on standards and quality of service (AGCOM, 1999). One of AGCOM's first tasks was to examine all aspects of planning for the development of a new digital terrestrial broadcasting system in Italy (including drawing up a new Frequency Spectrum Distribution Plan). Another aim of AGCOM's was to reduce the "high risk" of investing in digital television in Italy for broadcasting and other commercial companies, and to encourage their participation in a new broadcasting system (1999, p. 97).

AGCOM is aided in its efforts by a number of regional bodies (Regional Committees for Communications) as well as a National Council of Users which advises it on consumer issues. It should be noted however that AGCOM's powers have been hampered by insufficient sanctions available at its disposal, by various loopholes contained in the 1997 legislation, and by political interference in the appointment of its commissioners. For example, AGCOM has never been able to enforce the 1997 Act provisions relating to Retequattro and Raitre arguing the growth of these two channels is covered separately in the 1997 Act whereby "the spontaneous development of the company which does not produce a dominant position or eliminate or compromise pluralism and competition" (Law 249/1997, Article 2, Clause 9, quoted in Andreano & Iapadre, 2005, p. 102). European quotas (i.e., the Television without Frontiers Directive, 89/52/EEC) are not fully enforced since there are no sanctions for AGCOM to apply to companies that fail to comply. And the fact that AGCOM commissioners are voted in to office by the Italian Parliament has led many to question the political independence of the institution from center-left and center-right political blocs.

There are a number of other key institutions that help regulate Italy's media industries. Firstly there is the Parliamentary Commission that supervises radio and television services and investigates the general management of RAI with a view to ensuring that it promotes an adequate degree of political pluralism in its general and news programs, despite the fact that AGCOM is also nominally charged with overseeing this (Andreano & Iapadre, 2005, p. 99). Secondly, there is the Ministry of Post and Telecommunications that monitors the RAI/State Convention and is also responsible for the distribution of frequencies (in line with AGCOM's National Frequency Distribution Plan) in the run up to digital switchover (digital terrestrial services began in 2004).

THE GASPARRI LAW 2004

The key pieces of legislation in Italy over the past decade or so have been the Broadcasting Acts of 1990 and 1997. Berlusconi voted against parts of the 1997 Act and fought their implementation, especially those articles relating to Mediaset and Retequattro. It is not surprising therefore that the incoming second Berlusconi government would revise or reverse parts of the 1997 Act. And in November 2003, the Italian parliament passed a new media law and sent it to the President of the Republic's office for presidential assent. What normally constitutes a procedural formality was turned on its head when, in December 2003, President Ciampi refused to sign the Gasparri Law declaring that parts (primarily Article 15) contravened Constitution Court decisions (*La Repubblica*, December 16, 2003).

Ciampi's decision can be viewed as consistent with his past pronouncements, such as the open letter to Parliament in July 2002. Rather than leave the matter to the Constitutional Court, the Head of State intervened directly. The Law was sent back to the Italian Parliament for further consideration. In order to beat the Constitution Court's imposed deadline of December 31, 2003, the government launched the "Salva Retequattro" decree, which allowed Retequattro to broadcast beyond the end-of-year deadline. Berlusconi's supporters hailed the decree as support for the parliamentary law. Opposition politicians argued that the decree ran contrary to constitutional provisions.

After some minor alterations the Gasparri Law was passed in May 2004, this time gaining Presidential assent. The law outlines plans to part-privatize RAI and it also seeks to end speculation regarding the thorny issue of the RAI/Mediaset duopoly and set new guidelines for digital terrestrial television (which only started in 2004 and which has been hampered due to political indecision, technical problems [frequency scarcity—see above] and a lack of financial resources [Fontanarosa, 2004]). The Gasparri Law stipulates, however, that no company or individual can control more than 1% of shares or form voting blocs with more than 2% of shares. These rules are designed to prevent a take over of the company by a group of small shareholders. The date for the RAI privatization is 2007, but all details of the sell-off are left to a government agency to formulate, in consultation with relevant authorities. This agency—CIPE, the Inter-ministerial Economic Planning Committee, was set up by Law No. 48 of 1967, which has the task of directing national economic planning. It is headed by the Minister for the Economic Planning.

There are reasons why the Berlusconi government might wish to part-privatize RAI. Privatization would comply with the result of the 1995 referendum (see above). And any partial sale of RAI would also raise considerable financial sums for the government, at a time when the Italian economy remains in recession. But there are potential problems in privatizing RAI's operations. Public service broadcasters, like RAI, are often better placed to provide program formats such as in-depth political coverage, so would a newly privatized RAI provide the level of public service it currently does and, if the newly privatized company were to suffer major financial losses, would the government be able to insist that it fulfils all its program commitments? Public service broadcasting, again, is also better placed than commercial operators to ensure a universal service to all citizens. With digital rollout taking place in Italy over the next few years, would a privatized RAI still have the same obligations or duties to provide a universal service available to all (both in terms of geography and programs)? Another problem is that no one knows the extent to which the privatization of RAI will remain partial. If a company is sold off piecemeal it will leave the Italian Treasury owning a controlling share of the company. This will not solve the major political interference in the company's day-to-day affairs. And would commercial media companies wish to invest in a company where political influence remains so heavy? The Berlusconi government's privatization of RAI would not end the Janus-faced, split personality of the company. Forty-eight percent financed by (the lowest) license fee in Europe, and 52% (and growing) by advertising, the company in recent years has relied more and more on advertising revenues, with consequences for its programming schedules (more commercially orientated, especially in prime time).

Changes proposed also include the way RAI's Administrative Council is elected post-privatization. Article 20 states that RAI's Administrative Council will be enlarged to nine people elected by shareholders for a period of three years (with a possible three year extension). As an interim measure, until the privatization process is complete, seven of RAI's Administrative Council will be elected by the Parliamentary Commission for Television and Radio and two, including the President, by the Minister for Economics: an executive figure. The recent Venice Commission report is particularly concerned by this latter point and the general situation of RAI, which, it argues, is contrary to the principles of independence laid down by the Council of Europe with relation to public service broadcasting (Venice Commission, 2005, pp. 4–7). Recent events have confirmed that these fears are justified. On July 30, 2005, Claudio Petruccioli, chair of the parliamentary commission that supervises RAI and centre-left senator, was appointed by the Italian government as the new president of RAI. His appointment, according to press reports, also paves the way for a former AGCOM commissioner and centre-right appointee, Alfredo Meocci, to take up the director-general's post at RAI. These appointments, if confirmed (this article went to print before this confirmation), would reinforce widespread opinion that political dominance over RAI is being strengthened (with the cooperation of the centre-right executive and centre-left opposition) in the run up to elections that were held in 2006. The appointments also formally end the process, begun in 1993, whereby institutional figures would appoint the RAI Administrative Board (Maltese, 2005).

Article 15 of Law 249 focuses on ownership and cross-media ownership rules and allows individual companies to control up to 20% of the total media market in Italy. The definition of a media market—known as *sistema integrato delle comunicazioni* (SIC)—has been greatly expanded to include areas not previously covered by media ownerships rules. Article 15 also allows Mediaset to retain Retequattro on terrestrial television, while Raitre will no longer be forced to give up advertising, as both companies fall safely within the 20% SIC threshold. This overturns provisions contained in the 1997 Act and runs against the 1994 and 2001 Constitutional Court decisions. While RAI and Mediaset benefit from Article 15, relaxation of media and cross media ownership rules aid, above all, those companies that derive their income primarily from advertising and subscription payments—Mediaset and SKY Italia, the digital satellite operator.[3]

For RAI, the risk of falling behind its competitors is a very real one, because it still derives nearly half its income from an index-linked license fee, with just over half coming from advertising. This will provide more ammunition to Berlusconi's detractors who believe the new law puts his commercial interests first. These concerns have also been raised by the Venice Commission's report regarding media policy in Italy. Their report highlights its concern of the concentration of political, commercial and media power in the hands of Silvio Berlusconi, arguing that the Italian government has a duty to protect and safeguard and promote media pluralism. The report further states that, in Italy, "the status quo has been preserved even though legal provisions affecting media pluralism have twice been declared anti-constitutional and the competent authorities have established the dominant positions of RAI and the three television channels of Mediaset." The report concludes that the Gasparri Law may not effectively guarantee greater pluralism simply through the multiplication of television channels in the course of digitalization. At the same time it gives the market players the possibility of having a monopoly in a given sector without ever reaching the antitrust limit defined by the SIC (Venice Commission, 2005, pp. 4–7). It is worth stating that the RAI/Mediaset duopoly attracts over 90% of television audiences and advertising revenues. One feature that emerges from analyzing broadcasting policy in Italy over recent years is that there are strong lines of continuity. Political control over RAI continues unabated and issues surrounding conflicts of interest remain largely unresolved. What is not in doubt, however, is that Berlusconi has used his parliamentary majority to try and settle the "unfavorable" legislative and judicial judgments surrounding the legal status of the duopoly to his, Mediaset's and RAI's favor. Protectionism and self-interest were strong features of Berlusconi's media policy and overwhelmed other components. The new media law will result in bigger national media companies; a common aim of many European governments, but Italy trails wider international trends that have seen governments open up media markets to outside players in response to ideological and technological changes.

---

[3]The law saves Raitre having to give up advertising, totaling, as we have seen, 150 million euro per annum. The law does highlight the co-dependence or quid pro quo nature of the Italian broadcasting market, highlighted by Davide Giacalone in 1992. While the idea of co-dependence outlined earlier is a useful one, there is little doubt that Mediaset stands to gain more from the legislation.

CONCLUSION

I would like to start this concluding section with the key recommendations of the recent Council of Europe-funded Report examining media policy in Italy. The report made six recommendations relevant to this article, calling on the Italian parliament:

1. to pass as a matter of urgency a law resolving the conflict of interest between ownership and control of companies and discharge of public office, and incorporating penalties for cases where there is a conflict of interest with the discharge of public office at the highest level;
2. to ensure that legislation and other regulatory measures put an end to the long-standing practice of political interference in the media;
3. to amend the Gasparri Law to promote media pluralism, especially by avoiding the emergence of dominant positions in the relevant markets within the SIC;
4. by including specific measures to bring an end to the current RAI-Mediaset duopoly;
5. to guarantee the independence of public service broadcasting and to promote the democratic and social contribution of digital broadcasting;
6. to provide a positive international example by proposing and supporting initiatives within the Council of Europe and the European Union aimed at promoting greater media pluralism at European level. (Venice Commission, 2005, pp. 3–4)

These recommendations are a measured response to the iniquities present in Italian broadcasting policy. Current Italian media policies neither fully promotes media pluralism—witness repeated failures to reform Raitre and Retequattro and to introduce a real third force in Italian terrestrial broadcasting—or the democratic principles to which they aspire—witness the political dominance of RAI despite numerous laws proclaiming its formal independence. Italy, a key founder member of the EU and leading European power, has developed a set of media policies that fall well short of recognized EU and Council of Europe standards, and which have helped stymie Italian economic performance in the international media market. Italy is recognized internationally as drafting poor broadcasting policy that does little to further democratic goals or economic reforms within the EU. That is an unenviable reputation that requires reform.

Many critics point the finger of blame firmly at the Berlusconi government, but, as we have seen, these problems predate his arrival on the Italian media scene and are deeply ingrained in the political culture of the country. The shortcomings contained in successive Italian media laws implicate the whole political class, not one man, and its trenchant and persistent unwillingness to reform a broadcasting system that has been heavily condemned within Italy and by numerous European institutions and organizations.

While this chapter remains very critical of the current situation, it recognizes that future developments might help changes things, as the Italian government firmly believes. The privatization of RAI might lead to fresh investment of money and talent making the company less reliant on political forces. The development of digital terrestrial television, which has only recently begun (2004), might lead to new media players, although there is no evidence in the lessening of the RAI/Mediaset duopoly's hold over the television market. The arrival of Murdoch's News Corporation in to the digital satellite television fray provides some hope that the Italian media market is not as closed as some would like to think. And, despite the misgivings made in this chapter, Italy remains an open society where public dissent and protest are tolerated and where a plurality of voices can be heard. Even on Berlusconi's own channels. But, at the same time, Italy's system does not meet the high ideals we should expect of a leading EU nation.

REFERENCES

Andreano, S., & Lelio Iapadre, P. (2005). Audio-visual policies and international trade: the case-study of Italy. In Guerrieri, P., Iapadre, P. Lelio., & Koopman, G. *Cultural Diversity and International Economic Integration: The Global Governance of the Audio-Visual Sector.* Cheltenham: Edward Elgar.

Autorità per le Granzie nelle Comunicazioni. (AGCOM). (1999). *Relazione annuale sull'attività svolta e sui programmi di lavoro.* Rome: Presidenza del Consiglio dei Ministri.

Autorità per le Granzie nelle Comunicazioni. (2000). *Il libro bianco sulla televisione digitale terrestre.*

Balassone, S. & Guglielmi, A. (1993). *La brutta addormentata. La TV e dope.* Rome–Naples: Theoria.

Cavazza, F. (1979). Italy: From Party Occupation to Party Partition. In A. Smith (Ed.), *Television and Political Life.* London: Macmillan.

Ciampi, C. A. (2002, July 25). Open letter to Parliament. Reprinted in *La Repubblica.*

Collins, R. (2000). *A future for public service broadcasting?* Keynote speech given to the Public Service Broadcasting in a Digital Age Conference, Banff, University of Alberta, 8–10 June.

Emiliani, V. (2002). *Affondate La RAI. Viale Mazzini, Prima e Dopo Berlusconi.* Rome: Garzanti.

Esposito, R. & Grassi, A. (1975a). The Monopoly Reformed: The New Italian Broadcasting Act (Part 1). *EBU Review, 26,* (4), 42–47.

Esposito, R. & Grassi, A. (1975b). The Monopoly Reformed: The New Italian Broadcasting Act (Part 2). *EBU Review, 26,* (5), 48–55.

Fontanarosa, A. (2002, May 30). Rai, il diktat di Baldassarre "Basta giornalisti aggressive" *La Repubblica.*

Fontanarosa, A. (2003, August 7). Rai, il cda frena il piano digitale Rivolta anti-lottizzazione a Napoli. *La Repubblica.*

Fontanarosa, A. (2004). Il digitale terrestre in Italia: Che cosa sta succedendo. In G. Frezza., & M. Sorice (Eds.), *La TV che non c'e'. Scenari dell' innovazione televisiva in Europa e nel mediterraneo,* Salerno: Edizioni 10/17 (111–123).

Giacalone, D. (1992). *La guerra antenne. Televisione, potere e politica. I frutti di non governo.* Milan: Sterling and Kupler.

Ginsborg, P. (1990). *A History of Contemporary Italy: Society and Politics, 1943–1988.* London: Penguin.

Ginsborg, P. (1996). Explaining Italy's Crisis. In Gondle, S. & Parker, S. (Eds.). *The New Italian Republic: From the Fall of the Berlin. Wall to Berlusconi.* London: Routledge (19–39).

Ginsborg, P. (2003). *Berlusconi.* Turin: Einaudi.

Grasso, A. (1992). *Storia della televisione italiana.* Milano: Garzanti.

Hooper, J. (2002, July 13). Berlusconi strokes new row in TV bias. *Observer.*

Jones, T. (2003). *The Dark Heart of Italy: Travel Through Time and Space Across Italy.* London: Faber and Faber.

Judt, T. (1994). Nineteen Eighty-Nine; the End of Which European Era, *Daedalus,* 123, Summer 1–20.

Macchiatella, C. (a cura di). (1985). *Il gigante nano. Il sistema radiotelevisivo italiano: dal monopolio al satellite.* Torino: ERI.

Maltese, C. (2005, July 30). RAI, la strana coppia Petruccioli-Meocci. *La Repubblica.*

Monteleone, F. (1992). *Storia della radio e della televisione in Italia. Società, politica, strategie, programmi 1922–1992.* Venezia: Marsilio. 2nd Edition (1997).

Ortoleva, P. (1994). La TV tra due crisi—1974–1993. In Castronovo and Tranfaglia (Eds.), *La stampa italiana nell'eta della TV. 1975–1994.* Bari: Laterza.

Sassoon, D. (1986). *Contemporary Italy: Politics, Economy and Society since 1945.* London: Longman.

Spotts, F. & Wieser, T. (1986). *Italy: A difficult democracy.* Cambridge: Cambridge University Press.

Veltri, E., & Travaglio, M. (2001). *L'odore dei soldi. Origini e misteri delle fortune di Silvio Berlusconi.* Roma: Editori Riuniti.

Venice Commission. (2005). *On the Compatibility of the Laws "Gasparri" and "Frattini" of Italy with the Council of Europe Standards in the Field of Freedom of Expression and Pluralism of the Media.* Strasbourg: Council of Europe.

Vespa, B. (2002). *L'Italia di Berlusconi. L'Italia dei Girotondi.* Rome: RAI/Mondadori.

CHAPTER ELEVEN

Dutch Television:
Between Community and Commodity*

Jo Bardoel
Radboud University Nijmegen

Despite its open borders, international orientation and its central location between the bigger European countries, the Netherlands has a peculiar tradition with respect to television and media that is closely related to the country's overall sociopolitical structure of the past century. The Dutch system of "segmented pluralism," in which social groups and civil society play a vital role represents an interesting alternative to media systems relying mainly on either the State or the market. But at the beginning of a new century, this unique Dutch model is eroding rapidly and is starting to resemble a more European or even global media model in which liberal policies and commercial media markets dominate. Over the past two decades the Dutch media have changed almost completely, and public information has shifted from a merit-good to a market commodity, mainly as a result of 20 years of liberalizing national and European broadcasting and telecommunications

*The author would like to thank the following for their willingness to contribute material or data for this chapter: At Netherlands Public Broadcasting, Ben van Reenen and his staff, Head of Documentation and Library Services and Marcel Mokveld, Media Policy Department and Professor Jan van Cuilenburg, Edmund Lauf and Quint Kik of the Netherlands Media Authority.

policies. Consequently, the Dutch television sector has become increasingly internationalized. In the television market, three groups—one public and two commercial—dominate over 85% of the market. Much has been left to market forces and, according to many observers, the time has come for a redefinition of media policies.

This chapter outlines what is generally seen as one of the most complex but also interesting broadcasting systems in the world. It analyzes how the electronic media first served as in instrument to segregate the main social groups in Dutch society, mainly during the radio period, but subsequently trespassed and helped to overturn the traditional social structure of "pillarization," especially in the television period. Pillarization will be considered as part of a more general process of modernization or, more precisely, controlled modernization. Despite commercial initiatives throughout the history of the broadcast media, it took 60 years to break the public hegemony and to introduce commercial broadcasting in the Netherlands. It was, in fact, European regulation that forced the Dutch government to tolerate commercial television. Nevertheless, after 15 years of "dual-broadcasting," television has become a successful trade and the Netherlands now has one of the most competitive, although not profitable, television markets in Europe.

HISTORICAL OUTLINE

The Netherlands has chosen a broadcasting system that is neither like the ones in other European countries nor a commercial broadcasting model, as in the United States or Luxembourg, but a unique solution to the problem of how to allocate a scarce resource on the basis of serving the needs and interests of society that is commonly characterized as pillarization (Lijphart, 1975). In this system, broadcasting was left, neither to the State nor market, but to social movements that had already established their own organizations in most domains of social life including politics, education, health care, culture, and leisure (Bardoel, 1994, 2001; Brants, 2004; Van der Haak & Van Snippenburg, 2001).

Particularly the Calvinist "little people" and the traditionally underprivileged Catholics opted for this strategy of separate development since the end of the 19th century. In this way they hoped, on the one hand, to unite and emancipate their own social groups while, on the other hand, isolating it from modernist influences, both of the existing liberal-bourgeois elite and the emerging socialist labor movement. When the socialist movement decided to support this peculiar organizational model, three so-called "pillars" were established: Calvinists, Catholics, and Socialists. Since the liberal bourgeoisie dominated the State apparatus until the introduction of general elections at the beginning of the 20th century, these three social movements considered themselves underprivileged (Van den Heuvel, 1976). They all hoped to gain from the pillarization system that provided for a weak State and strong civil society. The ideological foundation for this strategy can be traced back to both the Calvinist and Catholic social ideologies that can be labeled respectively as "cultural sovereignty" and "subsidiarity" (the latter concept has obtained wider usage more recently in the context of European integration). As a result the Liberal-Conservatives were left with no other option than to become the fourth pillar in Dutch society.

The Rise of Radio as an Instrument of Apartheid

Soon after the introduction of radio, the new medium was acknowledged as an excellent instrument to give this social apartheid a cultural dimension. In the Netherlands, radio started on a commercial basis as early as 1919, thanks to active radio pioneers and the participation of the Philips company. In these first years, financial support also came from listeners in the United Kingdom who enjoyed the "Dutch Concerts" before the BBC started its own services in 1922. In parallel to the development of commercial services, the social movements also began to show interest in radio by establishing their own associations that initially hired airtime from commercial broadcasters: NCRV (1924, Calvinist), KRO (1925, Catholic), VARA (1925, Socialist) and VPRO (1926, liberal-Protestant). The liberal-bourgeois group that dominated the first station, HDO (later renamed AVRO), opted to build a national broadcasting organization that comprised all religious and ideological organizations, using the example of the newly founded BBC in the United Kingdom. These efforts failed, however, because of the lack of political support, given the majority of the Protestant and Catholic political parties in parliament.

In 1930, after fierce debate the government took the decision to allocate the two radio stations to the four main groups. The NCRV, KRO, VARA, and AVRO obtained 20% of airtime each, leaving the remaining 20% for a "joint program" (15%) and 5% allocated to the smaller liberal-Protestant VPRO group. Subsequently, the Calvinist and Catholics shared one radio station, and Socialists and Liberal-Conservatives the other, thus realizing a separation between modernist and antimodernist opinions and tastes. The *Radio Decree* of 1930, issued by the Minister of Post, would remain until the middle of the 1960s, when the first Broadcasting Act was introduced.

The pillarized radio organizations had the obligation to broadcast a comprehensive program, consisting of information, education, culture, and entertainment. In this system of external pluralism their programs were supposed to be partisan, and not neutral, objective, or balanced as is the case in broadcasting models elsewhere. However, in the prewar period there was an official Radio Control Commission that acted as a censor in order to prevent partisan programs of one association offending the listeners of other organizations or creating instability in the social order. For example the Socialist broadcaster VARA was forbidden to air the *International*, the anthem of the Socialist movement. These new broadcast associations soon reflected their movements and the listing magazines represented the principal link between broadcasting associations and their respective membership.

In sum, the "radio era" can be characterized as a period of segregation and even isolation, in which broadcasting associations served as the cement for the social pillars. The Dutch sociologist Ellemers (1979, p. 435) considers this pillarization process "as the Dutch way to cope with the fundamental processes of social change that have taken place since the last part of the 19th century. . . . In this way the organization principle of pillarization has in fact facilitated a smooth transition from a predominantly traditional to a much more complex, modern society, without too many conflicts or tensions."

Television and the Trespassing of Traditional Structures

In the post–Second World War period, the structures of the broadcast sector again came under review and subject to intense debate. A new generation of politicians initially wanted to put an end to pre-war divisions and strongly favored a move to a national broadcasting system. But the first general elections showed the strength of the old parties and pillars among the population and the traditional broadcasting organizations managed to regain their old positions on the condition, however that they should cooperate more closely. As a result the Netherlands Radio Union (NRU) was founded.

The introduction of television in 1951 and its rapid diffusion in the 1960s once again revived this broadcasting debate. In the first years of television, programs were produced by a new, neutral, centralized body, the Netherlands Television Corporation (NTS). The influence and the continued strength of the associations at this time is evident in the fact that within 5 years, they had taken over most of the television programming. However, more than radio, television trespassed on the existing subcultural divides in society largely because of the limited transmission hours available on television and the limits imposed on the groups resulting from the availability of having only one channel to broadcast on.

The rapid penetration of the new medium coincided with, and indeed became the symbol of, the rising welfare society, including increasing purchasing power for people, more leisure time, and growing consumption. This was the main reason why the business sector lobbied for advertising space on television and radio, triggered by the British example where a second television channel was introduced to complement the BBC and the license was issued to a commercial operator. Moreover, in other sectors of Dutch society, there were complaints that the existing broadcasting associations, whose position had remained unchanged since the 1930s, were out of step with cultural trends. The negation of the newly rising youth culture, with its own (pop) music and fashion, was seen as proof of this cultural and mental stasis.

Broadcasting Act of 1967

After numerous attempts to introduce commercial television by legal and illegal initiatives and several political proposals for a commercial channel a political compromise was reached and laid down in the first Broadcasting Act (1967). This compromise comprised, according to the Dutch tradition, concessions to all relevant parties and pressure groups. Firstly, commercial television had proven to be a bridge too far, but instead commercial block advertising was introduced, opening up an attractive and additional source of revenue to pay for a second television channel and for the introduction of color television. These advertising blocks were strictly separated from programming. Secondly, the traditional pillarized broadcasting organizations succeeded in preserving their positions, but at a price. New organizations, proving to represent a social stream in society and to have substantial membership, were allowed to enter (and leave) the system, thus creating a system allocating airtime on television and radio on a proportional basis, corresponding to the number of members of each association.

The first new entrant, TROS in 1966, was the successor of the pirate station "TV North Sea," previously operating from an offshore oil platform. Later an orthodox Protestant broadcasting association (EO: Evangelical Broadcasting Association, 1970), intended as a counterweight to the growing secularization of the Protestant mainstream movement, and a popular but illegal pop station also operating from the North Sea joined the system. The third component of the compromise implied the strengthening of the cooperation in Hilversum through the foundation of NOS (Netherlands Broadcasting Corporation) as heir to NRU and NTS. NOS began to broadcast a "joint program" (news, sports, events, etc.), to pool most of the studios and other technical personnel and facilities, and also to become the coordinating body for policy matters and international issues.

The Broadcasting Act, designed to bring about stability in the system, however introduced a completely new dynamic in the broadcasting landscape. The new, direct link between the number of membership and the amount of broadcasting hours fueled intense internal competition between broadcasting associations. When the traditional organizations started to fight back by producing more popular programming the outcome was semicommercial internal competition, called "trossification" after TROS, the originator of this trend (see Ang, 1991). The introduction of regular audience research in 1965 also facilitated this tendency to take viewers and listeners preferences into account.

The Introduction of Commercial Broadcasting

The 1980s also witnessed ruptures in the system; however, this time change was not precipitated by internal dynamics, but by external challenges to the system. The rapidly growing penetration of cable television and the advent of satellite and especially the combination of both technologies caused a shift in the television sector as it moved from being a predominantly national to an international phenomenon. Cable penetration of more than 90% opened up new opportunities for commercial interests to undermine the public hegemony that had supported the development of the system from its formative years. A first attempt, in 1979, by the Luxembourg-based broadcaster RTL to enter the Dutch television market through a link via Belgian cable systems was blocked by legislation preventing it from relaying its programming via the cable network. During the 1980s, several national initiatives to introduce commercial broadcasting in the Netherlands, by publishing houses such as VNU and Elsevier as well as independent producers, were denied by the omnipresent Christian Democratic Party. Ten years later, in 1989, the next attempt by RTL would be successful due to the liberalizing nature of the European Television Without Frontiers Directive in 1989.

The newly adopted Media Act of 1988, which attempted to modernize the broadcasting system but left the public monopoly intact, had to be almost immediately overhauled directly after its publication. The result of the liberalizing nature of media policy during this period was profound and within a few years the broadcasting landscape completely changed. In 1988, private radio stations emerged, at first only receivable through cable. But soon, some FM-frequencies became available, and the number of stations grew quickly. The monopoly of the public radio stations had come to an end after 60 years. Private television started on October 2, 1989, when Luxembourg-based RTL-Veronique, soon to be called RTL 4, began broadcasting via the ASTRA satellite. Within a year it had become the market leader in the Netherlands. The reasons were an evident demand among viewers for lighter entertainment based programs rather than the programs provided by the public television associations as well as demand from advertisers for more flexible advertising strategies.

After the launch of RTL 4 the market share of the three public television channels fell from 85% in 1989 to 50% in 1994. RTL 4's success acted as a catalyst for the large number of private television channels that emerged in the 1990s, the first of which was RTL's second channel, RTL 5, in 1993. After 20 years of uneasy alliance Veronica took the unprecedented step of opting out of the public system in order to operate as a commercial broadcaster. It entered into a joint venture with RTL and formed the Holland Media Group (HMG), which consisted of RTL 4 and RTL 5. Initially the independent production company Endemol was also part of the venture, but a decision of the European Commission's Competition Directorate blocked the merger on grounds that it would produce an unacceptable dominant position in the programming and advertising markets. Subsequently the merger was cleared when Endemol was dropped from the consortium. Another international player, SBS, also entered the market in 1995 with the launch of SBS 6 and although it struggled to gain a foothold in the market, its specific program blend of reality shows, more personalized forms of news and late-night sex has earned it considerable market share and it has built itself an equally strong position with advertisers. In 1999, a second SBS channel was launched, Net 5.

The market for independent production companies also emerged rapidly. NOB (NOS's former studios and facilities) that focused on production facilities took some years to adjust to market forces. Independent audiovisual production companies flourished, in particular those companies that offered more than just facilities. One of these was the company (of) Joop van den Ende, which combined program formats, stars, and production potential under one roof. After a merger with the equally successful John de Mol in 1994, Endemol Entertainment was created, which developed into the largest independent producer in the Netherlands, and a major global player with a catalog of highly successful formats including "Big Brother."

The company was subsequently sold to the Spanish telecommunications and media group Telefónica in 1999. Although Endemol remains a dominant force in the television program production it remains very diverse. Chrysalis IDTV is the second-largest production company in the Netherlands, and combined, more than 250 companies make a living, some of which are booming (Eyeworks), often as a result of program formats that are sold internationally.

CONTEMPORARY MARKET AND MAIN PLAYERS

At present three large companies dominate the television market (Bardoel & Van Reenen, 2004; Netherlands Media Authority, 2002). The public broadcasting system, HMG and SBS all have three nationwide channels. Commercial television in the Netherlands is owned by foreign companies who enjoy minimum program obligations (see Machet, Pertzinidou, & Ward, 2002), other than the provisions of the European Television without Frontiers. There are a total of 18 national channels, nine of which are generalist and are operated by the three large groups that own three channels each and there are nine thematic channels operated by other commercial broadcasters.

RTL Netherlands (formerly HMG) is owned by CLT/Bertelsmann. Veronica left the Group in September 2000, leaving behind a television channel and a radio station, whilst retaining its successful program guide and the Veronica brand. In 2003 Veronica, after sustaining huge financial losses, merged its television and publishing assets with the SBS Group and now operates the third SBS channel. Increased competition also coincided with a downturn in the economy and recession and RTL 4 and 5 were especially affected by these twin trends. However, several programming and management changes resulted in restored market leadership for RTL 4 in 2002, and it returned to profitability. The three SBS channels launched over a relatively short time period and today its channels are distinctly targeted at separate audience groups: a family channel, a channel for young females and one for young men.

At present, almost all television households are connected to cable and/or satellite. This means that all domestic television channels reach all households. In 2004 the television channels available free-to-air in Dutch households are the following (see Table 11.1; data over 2004, 24 hours).

As Table 11.1 demonstrates the nine generalist channels remain the dominant actors in Dutch television. Almost 50% of the program output of the public channels contains information and education and on commercial channels the proportion of these program categories is about 30%. Over half of the programs on commercial channels are fiction and on the public channels this proportion is about 20%. The audience share of the three main suppliers is almost 90% in 2004. Public service broadcasters still lose ground every year with RTL remaining fairly stable and SBS losing some market share in recent years.

THE PUBLIC BROADCASTING SYSTEM

With the unexpected and undesired arrival of commercial television, the government and the associations comprising the public broadcasting system needed a response to the new competitive environment (Bardoel & Van Reenen, 2004). The government's new policy was two-pronged: In the first half of the 1990s, the

TABLE 11.1

The Netherlands Television Market, 2005: Supplier Concentration
on the Dutch TV Market, 2000–2004

Company	TV Channel	Market shares*				
		2000	2001	2002	2003	2004
Public service broadcasters		45.0	42.7	42.6	40.4	41.7
	Nederland 1	13.8	14.0	13.2	13.1	12.8
	Nederland 2	21.2	19.2	20.4	18.4	21.2
	Nederland 3	10.0	9.5	9.0	8.8	7.6
RTL Group		31.5	29.3	30.0	30.8	27.8
	RTL 4	18.5	17.8	18.7	19.2	17.8
	RTL 5	5.0	5.1	5.5	5.6	5.0
	Yorin	1	6.4	5.8	5.9	5.1
SBS Broadcasting BV		16.4	18.7	19.3	19.6	19.4
	SBS 6	12.1	12.1	11.0	11.3	11.1
	Net 5	4.3	4.4	5.0	5.0	5.0
	Veronica	—	2	2	3.3	3.3
MTV Networks		0.4	2.4	2.3	3.2	4.7
	MTV	0.4	0.5	0.6	0.6	0.9
	TMF	—	1.1	0.9	0.9	0.7
	Nickelodeon	—	0.8	0.7	1.6	2.8
	The Box	—	—	—	—	0.3
Jetix Netherlands	Jetix	—	2.4	2.0	2.5	2.4
Discovery Communications		1.4	1.4	1.5	1.9	2.3
	Discovery Channel	1.4	1.4	1.5	1.8	1.7
	Animal Planet	< 0.1	< 0.1	< 0.1	0.1	0.6
TF1	Eurosport	1.1	1.1	0.8	0.9	0.9
National Geographic Channel	National Geographic Channel	0.7	0.7	0.6	0.7	0.6
Time Warner	Cartoon Network	1.2	1.1	0.4	< 0.1	—
Viva Media Liberty Media Corp.	The Box	—	—	0.4	0.2	—
Quote Media Holding	The Box	0.2	0.4	—	—	—
Vereniging Veronica	Veronica	—	—	< 0.1	< 0.1	—
SBS Broadcasting BV	V8 2	—	2.3	3.3	—	—
Preview Investments	Kindernet	0.9	—	—	—	—
Koninklijke Wegener	TMF	1.4	—	—	—	—
News Corp/Saban Entertainment	Fox Kids	< 0.1	—	—	—	—
	Fox8	< 0.1	—	—	—	—
CLT-UFA	Veronica[1]	8.0	—	—	—	—
Total		100.0	100.0	100.0	100.0	99.9

Note. *Average viewing figures, Monday until Sunday, 24 hours, age > 6 years. Adapted from Commissariaat voor de Media (2005).

authorities set out to regulate domestic private broadcasting and to strengthen the public system. During the second half of the decade, media policy focused on liberalization of the various media sectors. These changes led to numerous amendments of the Media Act, which was, as a result, constantly under review. The public broadcasting system was first strengthened in financial and managerial terms. Advertising opportunities were increased, and the license fee was indexed to increases in the cost of living. An attempt was also made to strengthen the public broadcasting system organizationally, by stimulating voluntary cooperation between the autonomous broadcasting associations.

At present, broadcasting time on Dutch public radio and television is shared by about 20 private organizations that have obtained a broadcasting license because they represent a certain section of the population (broadcasting associations and small licensed broadcasters) or have a specific programming task (NOS, NPS, and the educational broadcasters). The Media Act stipulates that the broadcasting associations must represent a religious, social, or spiritual movement and have at least 150,000 paying members for a full license. Broadcasting organizations wishing to join the public system must have at least 50,000 members and demonstrate that they add something new to the existing range of programs, thus increasing the diversity of the public broadcasting services. The system currently comprises seven broadcasting associations including the original ones: AVRO EO (evangelical), KRO, NCRV, TROS (general), VARA, and VPRO (progressive intellectual). With the decision of Veronica to leave the public system, BNN, which targets a youth audience, was admitted to the public system in 1998. In September 2005, two new organizations, MAX (which caters to senior citizens) and Llink (which represents new social movements), will enter the public system. The Media Act explicitly states that public broadcasting organizations must themselves determine the form and content of their programs. The Act does however, set standards by imposing a general mission and an obligation to produce a full range of programs comprising information, education, art, culture, and entertainment. For television, the Act also stipulates minimum percentages for these program categories (see Table 11.2).

TABLE 11.2
Program Quota for Public Broadcasters Set Down in the Media Act of 2000

Program genre	Ceilings and thresholds
Information and education	35%
Arts	12.5%
Culture (includes Arts)	25%
Entertainment	25% maximum
European productions	50%
Dutch or Frisian	50%
Independent producers	25%
Subtitling for hearing impaired	50%

Note. Adapted from Media Act 2000.

Netherlands Public Broadcasting (Publieke Omroep, NPB) is the new name for the part of NOS that serves as the umbrella organization for the national public broadcasting service. Its main tasks are to coordinate and direct programming and to look after the common interests of the broadcasting organizations. The programming task of NOS was split in 1995. NOS retained the task of broadcasting news, sports, and national events, and a new organization was established—the Dutch Programme Foundation (NPS)—with a mandate to provide cultural, minorities and young people's programs. Finally, there are four further types of organization within the public broadcasting system that are eligible for a small amount of broadcasting time. These are church and spiritual communities, educational bodies, political parties, and government information.

Concession Act of 2000

The arrival of commercial broadcasters has greatly changed the media landscape. From 1995, a coalition of Social Democrats and liberals/conservatives formed a government, which was the first time since the introduction of broadcasting that the Christian Democrats had not held office. The new "purple" coalition introduced an extensive liberalization policy throughout the communications sector. Liberalization of the public broadcasting system resulted in a 5-year concession for all broadcasting organizations and an amendment in 1997 of the Media Act created a new, more professional administrative structure that enabled the public broadcasting organizations to work more as a unit and to offer the public more distinctive programming.

From 1998, a second purple coalition set out to prepare the public broadcasting system for the first decade of the 21st century. A new Concession Act (a new version of the Media Act of 2000) guarantees the public system three television channels and five radio stations until 2010. The Act places the task of providing public radio and television services in the hands of a single concession holder, NOS (now NPB), which ensures that licensed broadcasters, as participants in the concession, jointly fulfill their statutory duty of providing high-quality and diverse programming that reaches both large and small sections of the Dutch population. To this end, NPB accounts for the way in which the public broadcasting system performs its tasks in a "concession policy plan" (published to obtain a 10-year concession; see NOS, 2000), and in its annual budgets. A review will be carried out after 5 years to determine whether broadcasting associations can remain within the public system. Program requirements for the public system (see Table 11.2) are also tightened in order to safeguard a clear distinction from the content of the schedules of the commercial sector.

The new act also introduced a "double legitimacy" for the public broadcasters based on a tiered system for separate broadcasting associations and also for public broadcasting taken as a whole. The new "public accountability" policy (Bardoel & Brants, 2003; Bardoel & d'Haenens, 2004a) implies both external accountability measures through more public dialogue and public assessment of performance (i.e., the review committee) and internal quality control (i.e., a "quality card"). In addition, individual broadcast associations must also demonstrate that their members "can influence policy in a verifiable and democratic manner" (Netherlands Broadcasting Corporation, 2000, p. 11).

The relative stability for the public system that the government has set out with its 10-year concession and financial guarantees did not last very long. RTL Netherlands filed a complaint with the European Commission, accusing the Dutch government of excessive State support for public broadcasters, claiming it was unfair competition and against the terms of the EC Treaty.

Following the complaint, in March 2005, the European Commission, being led by the Dutch Liberal Conservative Commissioner for Competition requested clarification from the Dutch government about the role and financing of Dutch public broadcasting. In line with similar investigations concerning other European Union Member States the European Commission requested a clear definition of the public service remit, the separation of accounts distinguishing between public and commercial activities of the public broadcasters and adequate mechanisms to prevent financial overcompensation of the activities of the public broadcasting organizations. An earlier investigation by the European Commission one year earlier led to the preliminary conclusion that there had been excessive funding between 1992 and 2002, estimated to be a total of €110 million.

Moreover, there has also been growing discontent on behalf of the public with the services and content of public channels and a growing feeling that the organizational model is outdated. The sharp decline in membership of the associations that constitute the public broadcasting system among Dutch households, with the exception of new entrants such as BNN, Llink, and MAX illustrates the growing gap between the associations and the wider public (see Table 11.3). A

TABLE 11.3
Membership of the Public Service Broadcasting Associations

Group	Status	1992	2004
AVRO	A	608,885	392,933
EO	A	499,410	476,169
KRO	A	577,310	476,489
NCRV	A	507,945	364,823
TROS	A	530,301	430,918
VARA	A	544,103	419,998
VPRO	A	523,428	361,893
BNN	B	NA	216,446
Linx	Aspirant	NA	52,191
MAX	Aspirant	NA	65,155
Total membership		3,791,382	3,257,015
Number of households		6,266,000	7,052,458
Percentage of households		60.5 %	46.5 %

Note. Adapted from Commissariaat voor de Media, 2005.

recent amendment to the Media Act (re)introduced the B-status (150,000 members and more) for broadcasting associations, between the full-blown A-status (300,000 members and more) and the aspirant-status (50,000 or more, including the obligation to grow to 150,000 members within the next 5 years) in order to allow BNN to stay in the public system.

In 2002 a new center-right government, Balkenende (I), introduced structural cutbacks to the public broadcasting system to the sum of €30 million, and only one year later Balkenende (II) reduced the budget again. Besides this, the government commissioned a review by McKinsey into the efficiency of the public broadcasting system, as well as a study by the Scientific Council for Government Policy into the aims and obligations of the public broadcasters in the Netherlands. At the same time the Public Broadcasting Review Committee that evaluates the public broadcasters every 5 years was initiated (Bardoel, 2003). In this respect, the public television and radio system has recently received scrutiny from a number of different fronts.

Public Broadcasting Review Committee

The Concession provides for an evaluation of the performance of the public broadcasting associations by an independent review committee every 5 years. The first review committee carried out its evaluation and presented a report on the functioning of public broadcasting in April 2004. As its starting point, the review assessed the self-assessment documents of the 20 broadcasting organizations that reported in the following areas:

1. Program perspective: that is, mission and identity, performance, cooperation;
2. Audience perspective: that is, reach, segmentation, distinctiveness, accountability;
3. Organization perspective: that is, organizational structure and culture, financial transparency, efficiency, innovation.

Altogether, 21 self-assessments (20 organizations and an assessment of the system as a whole), and 100 interviews constituted the basis of the committees' assessment. The committee concluded that, taking public broadcasting associations individually, performance ranged from reasonable to good. It concluded that mutual cooperation however was seriously inadequate. As a result the program schedule and the public reach falls short of the target of 40% market share. According to the public broadcasting organizations' own statistics, nine out of 16 million viewers are on the brink of turning their backs on public channels and are only being retained by entertainment and sports programming. Furthermore, important groups such as the young, the less educated, and ethnic minorities are not being sufficiently reached by the public broadcasting services. According to the committee, the cause of this situation lies mainly in the managerial structure: "The constellation of the existing system, aimed at organizing and managing distinction has, in its present form, become a serious handicap" (Public Broadcasting Review

Committee, 2004, p. 113). There is too little focus on the viewer and listener and too much attention on internal problems within the system.

Although advocated by some political parties and program-makers pressing for more decisiveness, the committee did not opt for a national broadcasting structure like the BBC, but rather to fit in with the specific Dutch broadcasting tradition. In the committee's model of the future, existing broadcasting organizations should focus on producing "identity programs," for which they are awarded a quarter to half the current number of program hours. The remaining hours are to be commissioned by NPB within the agreed network or broadcasting profile, so that both the broadcasting organizations and independent producers will have a role. In the committee's view, this open model will allow external plurality to develop in line with the dynamics of present-day society, while at the same time securing enough innovation and professionalism. In the political world, there was support for the committee's critical analysis and its sense of urgency. The minister responsible for the media has put forward a legislative proposal that envisages the development of a collective strategy for public broadcasters through performance agreements both between broadcasting institutions and with the government. Also, the role of the Executive Board of NPB will be strengthened to secure clear direction for the programming on radio and television channels. Finally, a supervisory board, independent of the executive of the broadcasting associations, will be established as part of the package of short-term reforms.

FINANCE AND FUNDING

Until recently, every Dutch household with a television or radio set had to pay an annual license fee for public television that was introduced in 1941 during the Second World War and German occupation. As part of the overhaul of the Dutch tax system, the license fee was abolished on January 1, 2000, and replaced with a levy on income taxes. The new funding system was introduced despite heavy criticism but an unholy alliance between the Social Democrats who showed a preference for a progressive rather than regressive tax and the Liberal Conservatives with an aim to reduce the public sector and narrow the mandate and range of programming of the public service broadcasters to information and culture. This shift in funding mechanism "fiscalized" Dutch public broadcasters and only 5 years after the change it is apparent that the public broadcasters have become more dependent on the government of the day. Between 2003 and 2008, the budget is also being reduced up to a total of €80 million per year as part of the austerity measures introduced by the Dutch government.

In 2005, the media budget of the Dutch government amounted to €850 million; €640 million came out of taxation and €210 million out of advertising income and interest. So, about three quarters of the budget comes from taxation, and one quarter from advertising revenues. Sponsoring by third parties, both profit and not-for-profit, is estimated to contribute €20 million per year. Overall, the public broadcasting system receives a total budget of €675 million, of which

TABLE 11.4

Financial Data for Commercial Broadcasters

Broadcasting Company	Net Turnover (x €1,000,000)		Company Result (x €1,000,000)		Operational Profit Margin (in percentage)		Turnover Per Employee (x €1000)	
	2004	2003	2004	2003	2004	2003	2004	2003
RTL Group	4,878	4,452	711	487	14.6	10.9	609	596
RTL Nederland	338	327	39	25	11.5	7.6	433	NA
SBS Broadcasting SA	678	582	88	53	13.0	9.1	424	386
SBS Broadcasting BV	206	201	NA	NA	NA	NA	456	448

Note. Adapted from Commissariaat voor de Media, 2005.

€535 million is allocated to television. Each Dutch citizen pays approximately €45 annually, which is well below the European average paid for public service television of €75 per year.In contrast, in 2004, the net turnover of RTL Netherlands amounted to €338 million (including radio) and SBS' turnover was €206 million. Table 11.4 gives an overview of the financial data for both commercial groups—for the national and international services for 2003 and 2004.

Toward New Media Policies

Early in 2005, the long-awaited recommendations of the prestigious Scientific Council for Government Policy (WRR) on a new agenda for Dutch media policy was published. In its report, "Focus on Functions: Challenges for a Sustainable Media Policy," the council concluded that, currently, Dutch media policy demonstrates tunnel vision by concentrating solely on traditional media and infrastructures while ignoring other important sectors of the media. Therefore, the public interest or pluralism in the media should no longer be looked at in terms of a single medium or sector, such as broadcasting or the press, but should include the supply of content and its use via other media, whether public or private, on the basis of important social functions. In relation to public broadcasting the WRR concluded the current organization of public broadcasting as just one of the conceivable options.

It concluded the public interest is served first by a high-quality news service and social debate and to a lesser extent by the arts and culture and specialized information.

Although private broadcasters, according to the council, also contribute to these areas, a sufficient and continuous level of these kinds of programs cannot (yet) be guaranteed without forms of public service. It also, however, suggested that other program areas such as light entertainment should in principle be excluded from the public sector as they do not form a core part of the task of public broadcasters of the future. Reviewing the organization of the Dutch model of public broadcasting the council also considered four possible models for the structure of Dutch public service broadcasting, ranging from a model with no public service at all to a "mixed and open model" for public broadcast media. In the latter model that was recommended by the council the different program areas could be supplied by different types of organizations. The news service should be provided by an independent, public organization as NOS presently does according to the commission. The production of debate and programs with a social component could be left to a range of broadcasting associations that can claim support from substantial sections of civil society (more explicitly than is now the case with the Dutch broadcasting organizations). Finally, the arts, culture and education could be delivered by an open and generally accessible system of tendering.

In this respect there seems to be growing consensus on the future of public broadcasting:

1. The management of a traditionally decentralized public broadcasting system should be centralized in order to cope with commercial competition and the challenges of new technologies and a rapidly changing, ever more multicultural society;
2. The role of broadcasting associations should be restricted to their core task, that is, producing "identity programs" and contributing to opinion formation and social debate. Network scheduling should be left to the executive board;
3. Public broadcasting should be opened up for independent producers in order to enhance representation of new groups (the young and "new Netherlanders") and foster innovation in the public system.

Prior to closing this chapter in June 2005, after negotiations, the Dutch government tabled a compromise in which these principles are included. The NOS will provide news and information, the broadcasting associations will specialize in opinion and debate and therefore lose half of their current budget and for arts, culture and education there will be a tendering system in which both independent producers and public broadcasting associations can compete. The proposal that now lies in parliament has far-reaching consequences for all broadcasters, and is therefore the subject of fierce debate. Most broadcasting associations strongly oppose the proposed focus on identity programs, the reduced room for broad entertainment-like programs and the increasing power of the Executive Board of NPB. The Executive Board welcomes its increased role in programming and budgetary matters, but highlights the program and budget guarantees that individual licensees will keep. In public debate, there is concern about the proposed abolition of NPS, which, in its short existence, has obtained a reputation in current affairs and cultural programs as well as content for ethnic groups. The proposal is again a typically Dutch one and represents a highly complex compromise. Although the outcome of the political debate is unclear it seems to offer a middle way between tradition and renewal. It is hard to forecast whether the proposals will strengthen the public system against the commercial broadcasters as on the one hand the public broadcasters will act more as a unit and on the other hand its program mandate will become narrower.

TECHNOLOGICAL DEVELOPMENTS

The Netherlands is a very densely cabled country and about 95% of television homes are connected to cable, 10% have satellite dishes, and only 1% is still dependent on traditional terrestrial transmission. At present, the average cable network carries 32 television channels, 38 radio stations and two or more pay TV channels to the average living room for a monthly fee of about €15. A Programming Council issues recommendation on the composition of this basic package and cable operators must justify deviating from those recommendations.

Large-scale development of cable began in the 1970s, under the responsibility of the municipal authorities. As a result of the liberalization policy of the 1990s, most local public cable networks were sold to specialized private cable companies. In recent years this takeover process has resulted in market domination by the three major operators UPC, Essent, and Casema, who control the cable networks servicing 85% of households. UPC is owned by the Liberty Media Corporation, and Casema was sold to Anglo-American investors in 2003; this leaves only Essent in Dutch ownership. There is no real competition, as each cable company enjoys a regional monopoly.

Since 2000, new digital services have emerged and, as of 2004, subscribers have been offered between 60 and 80 digital television channels. Subscribers of the major operators can choose from several tiers, new premium and pay-per-view services, and cable Internet. But it is a small and uneasy market because households already have a wide range of services. As a result cable operators, after completing the digitization process, have returned to basic services for lower prices and have not developed pay-per-view and premium channels.

To counter the dominance in the distribution market of the cable operators, the government intends to stimulate competition from other infrastructures like satellite and digital terrestrial television (DTT). Of the five franchises for DTT, one was awarded to NOS and the other four to the only interested party, Digitenne, which is a consortium of several media parties: NOZEMA (the national analog terrestrial broadcast infrastructure operator), NOS (public broadcasting), VESTRA (association of commercial broadcasters), CANAL+, KPN Telecom (the former national PTT company) and NOB (the main broadcasting production company). Digitenne offers some 25 television and radio stations in digital quality for a monthly subscription rate of €9, which is €2 to €3 less than cable subscription. Digitenne started in April 2003, and operates in the most densely populated western part of the country, but audience interest remains low. The main players in Digitenne are the same that already dominate the analog market and the program package on Digitenne is similar to what is already offered free-to-air.

Pay TV has been available since 1984 by FilmNet in the form of subscription television. For a long time, it was owned by the South African company Nethold, and was sold in 1997 to the French media conglomerate Vivendi that changed the names of the two channels to Canal+Red and Canal+Blue. Canal+Red offers films and series whereas Canal+Blue focuses on films, live broadcasts of Dutch football and highlights of other European sports. After 20 years of pay TV in the country, Canal Plus is still not profitable. Canal Plus had some 330,000 subscribers in 2002 that pay €27 per month for the two channels. In 2000, its digital package was launched, with a range of niche and generalist channels including the public channels carried free-to-air. The number of subscribers to digital services is slowly growing. Cable operators that tried to compete with subscription channels are slowly backing off. As a result of huge financial problems, Vivendi attempted to offload Canal Plus (Benelux) in 2002, but there was no real interest. In 2003, UPC showed some interest but the Dutch Competition Authority (Nederlandse Mededingingsauthoriteit, NMA) raised concerns because the cable operator would have acquired an interest in digital satellite transmission, exactly the kind of cross-ownership to which the government was opposed. In June 2005, the NMA cleared Chello Media Programming, a part of UPC, to take over the (film and sports) content of Canal+ pay TV, including its cable customers. The NMA's investigations indicate that new players will enter the pay TV market as competing infrastructures like xDSL, satellite, and terrestrial grow, and that UPC is obliged to allow access to other interested parties by telecom supervisor OPTA.

Despite the slow pace of digitization, the general feeling is that there will be a breakthrough in the coming years. Experts estimate that, based on available data and projections, by 2007 more than two thirds of all households will have a broadband Internet connection and approximately half will have a digital radio or television connection.

The end of distribution scarcity will cause an explosion in program output and the new scarcity lies in the attention of the viewer. In this new age of abundance, viewers will change their viewing habits considerably. The time devoted to linear broadcasting and generalist channels will diminish with the availability of niche channels and personal video recorders or "Tivos" and the growth of on-demand content facilities. The role of generalist channels will change as they become a window for other platforms, services, and brands. By 2010, approximately half of all households will be capable of creating their own program schedule by selecting from an EPG and/or preselected user profiles.

The Internet is at the forefront of the policies of the public broadcaster NOS and NOS sees it as crucial for the future of content provision. The Concession Act of 2000 has made it possible for the public broadcasters to develop new services like the Internet and thematic channels and fund these services from the public purse. A McKinsey report for the NOS board recommended a clearly electronic program guide (EPG), a strong portal, and content arranged to suit user preferences, that is, in vertical arrangements that correspond with content strengths of the broadcasting organizations. In 2001, NOS appointed a network manager for the Internet and presented its new media plan: a 24-hour news channel, to be fully operational in 2005, and an increase in Internet activity. Serious cuts in the budget that were announced in 2003 have curtailed these ambitions. The plans for the news channel have been postponed, but the Internet-portal and the "verticals" were realized in 2002 and 2003. The new services already being developed for the Internet can easily be extended to other digital platforms as soon as the interest is there. Such a move into online activities is not without its critics and the Association of Netherlands Newspaper Publishers (NDP) and commercial broadcasters have together lodged a complaint with the European Commission about the "excessive support" the Dutch government gives to the Internet activities of the public broadcasters as press organizations and commercial broadcasters feel forced to reduce their own Internet activities in light of the strong presence of the public broadcasters in a developing online environment.

Commercial television channels have shown less interest in developing Internet strategies. In a highly competitive television market with low profits they are, for obvious reasons, more interested in new media activities that generate additional profit. Commercial television channels have been keen to add phone calls, SMS messages, and games to television programs, which sometimes bring in more profit than the original program itself. The first and most famous example of such a multimedia production is "Big Brother," first aired in the Netherlands by the production company Endemol.

This low level of interest, however, may be changing as one of the founders of Endemol, John de Mol recently announced he was forming a new television channel, Talpa TV (*talpa* is Latin for "mol" or mole) and the channel will be based on a cross media strategy: "We consider Internet as our second channel," said John de Mol at the presentation of the new channel. "Big Brother" will be broadcast every day on television and will also be available on the Web 24 hours a day. He believes that in the near future, triple play, based on a combination of television, cable, and telephony, will be the key to successful business models in the audiovisual sector. To this end he has already acquired a 40% shareholding in Versatel, a telecommunications provider that has its own optical-fiber network. In July 2005, the Swedish telecom operator Tele2 acquired Versatel for €1.3 billion as part of their own triple-play strategy and de Mol intends to sell his shares to Tele2. Versatel intends to deliver television via the so-called ASDL 2 technique, beginning in the fall of 2005, and the incumbent telecom operator KPN will follow soon with what they call IPTV.

De Mol's strategy is certainly ambitious and the company has already acquired the sports rights for the national football competition which previously were bought by the public broadcaster NOS. The channel has also commissioned prominent stars and programs from both commercial and public stations thanks to de Mols' own personal wealth. The company's self proclaimed objective is to be one of the top three television channels in a market that already has the one of the most competitive television markets in Europe.

MEDIA CONCENTRATION AND PLURALISM

The Dutch Media Act contains provisions concerning the cross-ownership of commercial broadcasters (radio and television) and daily newspapers. A newspaper publisher that has a market share of 25% or more of the total newspaper market (national and regional) is disqualified from acquiring a license for commercial broadcasting if it owns one third or more of the respective station. There are no specific limitations on concentration in the television market apart from general competition rules that apply for all sectors and are enforced by the NMA.

In 2002, the Netherlands Media Authority presented its first annual report on media concentration (Commissariaat, 2002, 2005), which provided an analysis of concentration levels in television, radio, cable, and in the written press. The monitor shows that television, cable, and the daily press are all dominated by three strong suppliers; the Media Authority calls it the "three is the rule" principle. In order to prevent the levels of supplier concentration in commercial television becoming too high, the Authority recommended amendments to legislation so as to include a maximum market share of 30% of audience share. In relation to Internet developments and the potential benefits of synergies between different media, the Authority recommended loosening the existing cross-ownership regulations. But this should, the Authority added, be combined with a restriction on the market share in another medium. This suggestion was widely supported because the profitability of both commercial broadcasters, and the daily press were under pressure. Because of strict cross-ownership restrictions national media and especially newspapers could not expand and as a result the main national newspaper group PCM, which includes all but one of the national daily newspapers, was acquired recently by the British investment group APEX.

In response to widespread concern about growing media concentration and the danger of "predominant opinion power," the State secretary responsible for media announced in 2004 the introduction of specific concentration measures for the newspaper market. In a letter to parliament in December 2004, the government tabled a specific set of media competition measures, forbidding concentration in the newspaper sector above a market share of more than 35%. At the same time, the existing cross-ownership regulations will be loosened and will allow newspaper owners with a market share between 25 and 35% of the national newspaper market to own up to 50% of a commercial television channel. However, the proposal falls somewhat short of the suggestion of the Media Authority to introduce maximum market shares for television, as the public broadcasting system is perceived to compensate for the negative consequences of concentration of commercial television channels. An added complication is that SBS falls under the jurisdiction of the Dutch government and therefore the legal mandates of its regulatory bodies whilst RTL has long argued (with a great deal of success at the European Commission) that it is based in the more liberal regulatory regime of Luxembourg where it has a monopoly on the television sector.

CONCLUSION

In two decades, the television landscape in the Netherlands has changed dramatically. Viewer's choice has exploded, but diversity has not increased to the same extent. Profitability is low because of an overcrowded and fragmented television market. Television and cable markets are dominated by three parties and commercial television in the Netherlands is owned by foreign companies. The "unique" Dutch broadcasting model can still only be seen to some extent in the public broadcasting system as the Dutch media sector has converged to a more or less "standard" European or international model.

The Dutch broadcasting model, based on pillarization or "segmented pluralism," has often been called unique (Browne, 1989). However, elements of the same media model can also be found in other small European States such as Belgium, Switzerland or Austria (Hiemstra, 1997; Lorwin, 1971). In their recent book *Comparing Media Systems; Three Models of Media and Politics,* Hallin and Mancini (2004) consider the Dutch system as a "particularly strong and unusual system based on the representation of organized social groups" (p. 165), and, as such, an example of the "democratic corporatist model" that they have found in the other northern European countries. The democratic corporatist model, according to Hallin and Mancini, strongly relies on the role of organized social groups in society, as opposed to a more individualistic concept of representation in the liberal model. It is this collectivist political and civic organization that no longer meets, in the Netherlands and elsewhere, with the increasing individualization of postmodern citizens and society.

According to political pluralist theory, the Netherlands with its opposing groups and ideologies is a "country that could not exist" (cf. Daalder, in Hiemstra, 1997, p. 142). Nevertheless, in his seminal English-language study of Dutch pillarization Lijphart (1975) has carefully analyzed the rules of the game that the pragmatic elites of the country adhered to in order to create a stable and pluralist democracy. The same holds for public broadcasting in the Netherlands. Pillarization as part of the larger social process of modernization and a process of "controlled modernization" has profoundly shaped how the system has evolved. Other authors have chosen to understand pillarization as part of the emancipation process of three of the four social groups (Calvinists, Catholics, and Socialists), challenging the control of the dominant liberal elite (Van den Heuvel, 1976).

The two explanations, modernization and emancipation, seem to complement rather than to contradict one another and it seems ironic that the very system of segregation that was set up first by Calvinists and closely followed by Catholics in order to keep their communities apart and to control and slow down the processes of modernization, eventually turned out to be a vehicle of modernization and pluralism in the media and especially so in the television sector. In the radio period, the strategy of segregation and social "apartheid" prevailed, but in the television period, the fact that viewers could watch the programs produced by other subcultures or from abroad created unprecedented openness and pluralism. This change may at least partly explain why the Netherlands evolved so rapidly from a traditional and highly religious society in the first half of the 20th century, to one of the most liberal and secular societies in the second half of the last century. The advent of commercial television has created major problems for a public broadcasting system that was designed to replace and not to complement the commercial media market. In this new, competitive context, the strengths of Dutch public broadcasting are its weaknesses: a complex system of external pluralism with many production centers and decentralized management responsibilities. In less than a decade strong commercial competitors have evolved: RTL and SBS as well as strong independent producers, Endemol and IDTV. Such rapid trends in television have changed the nature of television in the country and a medium that was reserved for the cultural expression of social groups is increasingly guided by issues of international and commercial trade.

The current Dutch television market is one of the most, if not the most, competitive in Europe. The introduction of another commercial channel in August 2005, Talpa TV will only further increase the turmoil in the television sector. RTL and SBS have enjoyed a more or less comfortable duopoly in the commercial television market, but that may be over soon. Moreover, the penetration of more personalized program packages and recording devices seriously threatens their single source of income: advertising. At the same time the abolition of the license fee has increased the dependence of the public broadcasters on politics and the government, although the tradition of independent program making and journalism remains strong. Politics is now deciding the future mission and organizational structure of the public broadcasting system. The support for the concept of public broadcasting is still as strong as criticism of the present structures and organization. Although political decisions still have to be taken, it seems that the most recent version of the Media Act will provide a compromise between a national broadcasting system *a la* BBC that creates more unity and coherence in the patchwork of public broadcasters in the Netherlands and the unique tradition of a decentralized broadcasting system and external pluralism.

REFERENCES

Ang, I. (1991). *Watching Dallas: Soap opera and the melodramatic imagination*. London: Methuen.
Bardoel, J. (1994). Om Hilversum valt geen hek te plaatsen. De moeizame modernisering van de Nederlandse omroep [It is impossible to build dykes around Hilversum. The troublesome modernization of Dutch broadcasting]. In H. Wijfjes (Ed.), *Omroep in Nederland. Vijfenzeventig jaar medium en maatschappij 1919–1994* [Broadcasting in the Netherlands; 75 years of medium and society 1919–1994] (pp. 338–372). Zwolle: Waanders Uitgevers.
Bardoel, J. (2001). Open media, open society. Rise and fall of the Dutch broadcast model: A case study. In Y. Zassoursky & E. Vartanova (Eds.), *Media for the open society* (pp. 98–121). Moscow: IKAR Publisher/Faculty of Journalism, Moscow State University.
Bardoel, J. (2003). Back to the public: Assessing public broadcasting in the Netherlands. *Javnost/The Public, 10*(3), 81–96.

Bardoel, J., & Brants, K. (2003). From ritual to reality. Public broadcasters and social responsibility in the Netherlands. In G. F. Lowe, & T. Hujanen (Eds.), *Broadcasting & convergence: New articulations of the public service remit* (pp. 167–187). Goteborg: NORDICOM.

Bardoel, J., & d'Haenens, L. (2004a). Media meet the citizen. Beyond market mechanisms and government regulations. *European Journal of Communication, 19*(2), 165–194.

Bardoel, J., & d'Haenens, L. (2004b). Media responsibility and accountability: New conceptualizations and practices. *Communications: The European Journal of Communication Research, 29*(1), 5–25.

Bardoel, J., & van Reenen, B. (2004). Medien in Den Niederlanden. In H. Bredow (Ed.), *Internationales Handbuch Medien* (pp. 475–493). Baden-Baden: Nomos Verlagsgesellschaft.

Brants, K., & McQuail, D. (1997). The Netherlands. In Østergaard/Euromedia Research Group (Ed.), *The media in Western Europe* (pp. 153–165). London: Sage.

Brants, K. (2004). The Netherlands. In M. Kelley, G. Maaoleni, & D. McQuail (Eds.), *The media in Europe. The Euromedia handbook* (pp. 145–157). London: Sage.

Broadcasting Act. (1967/1980). *Omroepwet/Wet op de omroepbijdragen, bewerkt door Mr. H.M. Linthorst* (3th ed.). Zwolle: Tjeenk Willink.

Browne, D. R. (1989). *Comparing broadcast systems. The experience of six industrialized nations*. Ames, IA: Iowa State University Press.

Committee on Media Concentration [Commissie Mediaconcentraties]. (1999). *Profijt van Pluriformiteit: Over concentraties in de mediasector en de vraag naar bijzondere regelgeving* [The profit of pluralism: About concentrations in the media sector and the need for special regulation]. The Hague: Ministry of Education, Culture and Science.

Commissariaat voor de Media. (2002). *Mediaconcentratie in beeld 2001* [Media concentration in the picture]. Hilversum: Commissariaat voor de Media.

Commissariaat voor de Media. (2005). Mediaconcentratie in beeld 2004 [Media concentration in the picture]. Hilversum: Commissariaat voor de Media.

Ellemers, J. E. (1979). *Nederland in de jaren zestig en zeventig* [The Netherlands in the 1960s and 1970s]. *Sociologische Gids, 26*(6), 436.

Ellemers, J. E. (1984). Pillarization as a process of modernization. *Acta Politica, 19*(1), 129–144.

Hallin, D. C., & Mancini, P. (2004). *Comparing media systems: Three models of media and politics*. Cambridge: Cambridge University Press.

Hiemstra, J. L. (1997). *Worldviews on the air. The struggle to create a pluralistic broadcasting system in the Netherlands*. Lanham, MD: University Press of America.

Lijphart, A. (1975). *The politics of accommodation: Pluralism and democracy in the Netherlands* (2nd rev. ed.). Berkeley: University of California Press.

Lorvin, V. R. (1971). Segmented pluralism: Ideological cleavages and political cohesion in the smaller European democracies. *Comparative Politics, 3*(2), 141–176.

Machet, E., Pertzinidou, E., & Ward, D. (2002). *A comparative analysis of television programming regulation in seven European countries: A benchmark study (ordered by NOS)*. Düsseldorf: European Institute for the Media.

Media Act of the Netherlands. (1987/2000). *Staatsblad van het Koninkrijk der Nederlanden* [Bulletins and decrees of the Kingdom of the Netherlands]. Retrieved June 29, 2005, from www.cvdm.nl/documents/mediaact.pdf

Netherlands Broadcasting Corporation. (1998). *Publiek in de toekomst* [Public in the future]. Hilversum: Author.

Netherlands Broadcasting Corporation. (2000). *Verschil maken: Concessiebeleidsplan landelijke publieke omroep 2000–2010* [Making a difference. A policy plan for national public broadcasting, 2000–2010]. Hilversum: Author.

Netherlands Media Authority. (Commissariaat voor the Media). (2002). *A view on media concentration: Concentration and diversity of the Dutch media in 2001.* Retrieved June 29, 2005, from http://217.148.171.193/documents/summary_mmc_new.pdf

Netherlands Media Authority. (Commissariaat voor de Media). (2003). *Mediaconcentratie in beeld: Concentratie en pluriformiteit van de Nederlandse media 2002* [Media concentration in the picture: Concentration and pluriformity of the Dutch media 2002]. Hilversum: Author.

Public Broadcasting Review Committee. (Visitatiecommissie Landelijke Publieke Omroep). (2004). *Omzien naar de Omroep* [Broadcasting in Re(tro)spect]. Hilversum: Publieke Omroep.

Scientific Council for Government Policy. (Wetenschappelijke Raad voor het regeringsbeleid). (2005). *Focus op functies. Uitdagingen voor een toekomstbestendig mediabeleid.* [Focus on functions: Challenges for a sustainable media policy]. Amsterdam: Amsterdam University Press.

Van den Heuvel, J. H. J. (1976). *Nationaal of verzuild? De strijd om het Nederlandse omroepbestel in de periode 1923–1947* [National or pillarized? The struggle on the Dutch broadcasting system in the period 1923–1947]. Baarn: Ambo.

Van der Haak, K., & van Snippenburg, L. (2001). The Netherlands. In L. d'Haenens & F. Saeys (Eds.), *Western broadcasting at the dawn of the 21st century* (pp. 209–235). Berlin: Quintessens.

CHAPTER TWELVE

Polish Television: All Encompassing Change

Karol Jakubowicz
National Broadcasting Council

Poland is a post-communist country undergoing what may be called "systemic social transformation." Given that before 1989 (when the communist system ended in the country) the media, and especially television, were part of the command and control system of an authoritarian regime, everything should have changed beyond recognition since then.

Indeed, media change is sometimes seen as a litmus test of the more general process of transformation. As Sparks (1998) puts it, "certain features of the structures of society are more clearly illuminated through this optic [of media change] than through others" (pp. 16–17). Accordingly, if "the shift from communism to the new order in [post-communist countries] is really one of a shift between fundamentally different systems, then one would expect that to be registered particularly clearly in the mass media" (p. 17). Several types or areas of media or, more broadly communication, policy can be distinguished:

- Systemic media policy—formulated with a view to creating, maintaining or changing the overall shape of the media system;
- Sectoral media policy, oriented toward some sector of the media (e.g., broadcasting policy);

- Operational media policy, involving the resolution of issues arising within an already existing media system.

There is no question that after 1989 Poland faced the challenge of engaging in all these areas of media policy. After all, the job was one of creating a new media system, including a new television system.

Media policy making is not easy at the best of times. It is extremely difficult at a time when a social system is reinventing itself and when the media are directly involved in "events and developments [that] are questions of life and death for each individual, family, group and class in these [post-communist] societies; it is being decided in these months and years who will be the winners and who will be the losers in the next decades; who will profit from and who will lose by the transition to a new social and economic model; whose children will be poor and whose will be rich; who will belong to the propertied classes and who will be the have-nots" (Hankiss, 1994, pp. 292–293). The intensity of the social and political conflict involved in resolving these issues has been such that practically no societal institution—and least of all the media—could avoid being caught up in it or escape the consequences.

This situation may perhaps explain why it has proved difficult to develop a general media policy orientation and settle on one or more normative media theories and "basic communication values" (McQuail, 1992, pp. 66–67) as a point of departure for creating that new television (and generally media) system. Yet another reason for this is that Poland today faces a major policy overload. The British Bill of Rights (proclaiming, among many other things, freedom of speech) was passed in October 1689. An equivalent act, that is, the abolition of communist censorship, took place in Poland three centuries later almost to the day. This is why Poland, along with other post-communist countries, today has four centuries' worth of media policy issues to resolve all at the same time—from the 17th century issue of freedom of speech all the way to the 21st century issues of the Information Society.

An additional difficulty has been "a battle of the regulatory models" (Harcourt, 2003). It was fought in Poland and elsewhere on at least two fronts. On the one hand, Western European countries promoted public service broadcasting and European content in programming. They were interested in guaranteeing the opening of new markets, and the stability of these new media markets for Western capital investment, as well as wider political concerns of consolidating democracy in the region. European organizations sought to extend the "European audiovisual area" to Central and Eastern Europe.

On the other hand, the United States promoted the independence of State broadcasters from the State (i.e., privatization) and objected to the adoption of European content laws, seeking new markets for audiovisual exports, and naturally also for capital investment. Some Central and Eastern European countries, including Poland, were particularly exposed to U.S. pressure before they joined the OECD and WTO, as the United States sought to make entry conditional on the elimination of barriers to U.S. audiovisual exports to those countries. The idea was to turn post-communist countries into a "Trojan horse" within the European

Union (EU): if they could be pressured into opening their audiovisual markets, they would, once admitted into the EU, undermine its protectionist audiovisual policy. In any event, several media policy orientations emerged in Poland after 1989:

- Idealistic orientation, as originally proposed before the downfall of the communist system by the dissidents who hoped to introduce direct democracy, also in the communication sphere;
- Mimetic orientation, assuming straight transplantation of the generalized Western European media system with a privatized press and a dual broadcasting system (the U.S. model never really had a chance of being accepted);
- Idealistic–mimetic orientation, hoping to add as many of its features of the idealistic orientation as possible to the "mimetic" one;
- Atavistic orientation, based on the conviction of the new political elites that they have a democratic mandate to use the media to promote the process of reform, although more often than not this has taken the form of manipulation for propaganda purposes and short-term political gain.

Ultimately, a "standard" media policy orientation took over in most post-communist countries, amounting to a combination of elements of the mimetic and atavistic orientations. As a general rule, more advanced post-communist countries have acquired more features of the mimetic model, whereas less advanced countries retain more of the atavistic model.

Poland is classified among the more advanced countries and that has been reflected in the stormy process of media change since 1989. Change was mostly politically driven to begin with, but since then has increasingly been market-driven. The old centralized media system has been dismantled, print media have been privatized and a broadcasting system has been introduced, composed, legally speaking, of public, commercial and "social" sectors. The television system is free from the crudest forms of political or administrative control of television by the political establishment. As a result, and very importantly, market forces have been given relatively free range in shaping television in Poland.

SOME NOTES ON HISTORY

Television was launched in Poland in 1952. Originally it broadcast one channel, which gradually gained national reach, partly through the incorporation of regional television centers where transmitters were built to make programming available to a particular region. In 1970, the second channel came on the air. Polish Radio and Television was government-run and operated, though in reality it was controlled by the Communist party. In a study of Polish Radio in the years 1944–1960, Jerzy Myślinski (1987) notes that, as a mass medium, it was forced by the communist system to subordinate all aspects of its operation to the goal of the political education of the masses. After 1956, while remaining structured as an instrument of exercising power through one-way, top-down, single-voice communication, it developed a mix of top-down transmission of the authorities' views (its main goal) and bottom-up reflection (not always accurate or comprehensive) of the public mood.

Television was a somewhat different story. Up until 1960, it was treated largely as an adjunct to Polish Radio, an experimental medium of limited reach, best left to artists. Hence its strong artistic traditions and its early image as a medium largely devoted to high culture. The 1960s saw a gradual reorientation of that policy, but it was only in the 1970s that the authorities became aware of the full political and propaganda potential of television and began to use it for that purpose.

However, the effects were at best ambivalent and, in reality, ultimately counterproductive (see Jakubowicz, 1994, 2006). Given that the communist system was unable to deliver on its promises, the media's main role soon became that of putting a gloss on the authorities' actions that were largely at variance with the idealized image of the system created for popular consumption, and helping in this way to obtain acceptance of those actions. The media were thus used to provide "evidence" of the system's successes in attaining its goals. In order to do that, they—and especially television—had to create in their content an alternative reality, a Potemkin village, as it were.

Moreover, the twists and turns of political events always had an immediate effect on the media, in that concepts, ideas and elements of ideology were introduced or withdrawn, defined and redefined in a totally arbitrary manner. Periods of relaxation meant greater freedom of speech and more critical reporting; the screws could be turned on again, but the propaganda that followed had much less credibility and was much less effective.

There was no long-term consistency of media policies, either. At times different, mutually contradictory strategies were pursued in different media or in the same media—weakening or undermining the desired ideological effect. For example, strategic ideological goals were often sacrificed for tactical political gains, such as buying social peace or creating an illusion of prosperity, for example, by having Polish Television in the 1970s offer a great deal of Western, including American, series, films, and drama (see Jakubowicz, 1989). The results were dysfunctional from the communist government's point of view. Instead of receiving the overt message, intended to achieve a commonality of enthusiastic commitment to building communism, the audience received the covert real message (including an awareness of the system's own confusion and less than sincere commitment to its own ideology).

In her analysis of the intensive, chronic psychosocial stress induced by life under the communist system, Anna Titkow (1993) listed the symptoms which suggest what that message really was. They included:

- *a sense of inability to control events:* resulting in passivity and enforced reliance on the authorities to manage and organize everything;
- *acquired helplessness:* an attitude adopted as a way of dealing with stress and in response to the daily lesson of submission to an authoritarian regime, taught by the media and by the general system of social organization;

- *cognitive dissonance:* arising out of the difference between media and propaganda representations of reality and experience of reality itself, as well as out of the difference between the ideals of socialism as preached by the propaganda apparatus and as practiced by the system itself—more in the breach than in the observance.

All that led to extreme frustration, anxiety, and anger (see Koralewicz, 1987) and had a disastrous effect as far as the individual's self-appraisal and self-esteem were concerned. It also proved to be conflict-generating, ultimately contributing to the outbreak of the conflict, which led to the overthrow of the system.

Thus, if communist media, and television in particular, produced any commonality of outlook and experience, it was, at bottom, one of distrust of, and hostility to, the system, coupled with its grudging and helpless acceptance as inevitable and unlikely to change soon, if ever. This last feeling could be counted as their one genuine success, all the more so that it was consciously and deliberately pursued: failing to win genuine acceptance and commitment, the system was willing to settle for whatever it could get.

Nevertheless, changing the media system became a powerful, highly emotive rallying cry of the dissidents and the opposition under the communist system. As suggested above, the development of the dominant media policy orientation after 1989 produced less than a fully satisfactory result from that point of view.

While work on writing a Broadcasting Act began immediately after the installment of the "Solidarity" government in 1989, it took 3 years to resolve conflicting approaches to broadcasting and the Act was not adopted until December 1992. One reason was that the first "Solidarity" government sought to subordinate everything to the success of the shock therapy of economic reform. It wanted to extend as much as possible what Leszek Balcerowicz, the architect of that policy, has called *r* (readiness to accept radical measures) and "extraordinary politics," a period following immediately after epochal political change, when "both leaders and ordinary citizens feel a stronger-than-normal tendency to think and act in terms of the common good. All of this is reflected in an exceptionally high level of *r*" (Balcerowicz, 1995, p. 161). What the "Solidarity" government wanted to avoid, or to delay as much as possible, was the inevitable transition from "extraordinary politics" to "normal politics"—the more mundane politics of contending parties and interest groups. This leads to the politicization of all the issues: mechanisms of democracy appear much less attractive, disillusionment sets in and the level of *r* drops sharply.

That explains why the government was not interested, for example, in rapid liberalization of radio and television (as that would lead to many new voices appearing in the public sphere), nor in the transformation of the government-controlled national broadcaster into an independent public service broadcaster. Thus, paradoxically, the "Solidarity" government in effect reneged on the idealistic media policy orientation of "Solidarity" itself in the 1980s and opted instead for an "atavistic" approach. It was only when it was replaced by a more liberal government at the beginning of 1991 that more "mimetic" elements were added to the policy mix and the door to real change was open.

A NEW TELEVISION SYSTEM EMERGES

While the Broadcasting Act was being drafted, pirate broadcasting appeared. In June 1993, before the newly created National Broadcasting Council (NBC), the broadcasting regulatory authority, could begin licensing new stations, 55 pirate radio stations and 19 pirate television stations (12 of them converged into a network known as Polonia 1, created by an Italian entrepreneur, Nicola Grauso) were on the air. To that number must be added three private radio stations and one private television station which received quasi-legal temporary authorizations in 1990. One Polish program service (Polsat) began transmission via satellite from the Netherlands in December 1992, for reception via cable in Poland. There were also more than 40 radio stations, operated by the Roman Catholic Church which under the State-Church Relations Act of 1989 could receive frequencies from telecommunications authorities and start broadcasting legally.

When it was finally adopted in 1992, the Broadcasting Act introduced the dual system of public service and commercial broadcasting. In 2001, an amendment of the Act introduced another category that of "social broadcasters," that is, noncommercial private stations serving worthy, mainly religious, causes. These stations are exempt from the spectrum license fee and may not run advertising. This concept was introduced in order to accommodate the Roman Catholic Church, claiming such status for its stations. However, very few such stations have emerged, most of them in radio. This is why one of the proposals contained in the draft "National Strategy for the Electronic Media" (see the following) is that these "social broadcasters" be redefined (to remove the indirect association with the Roman Catholic church) and be allowed to allot up to 2% of airtime to advertising, so that more such broadcasters could appear, thereby boosting the plurality of voices.

The Broadcasting Act also created the regulatory authority, the National Broadcasting Council (NBC), with the power to award licenses to broadcast. Once licensing began, many of the pirate stations, including Polonia 1, failed to obtain a license to broadcast and disappeared.

It was Polsat that received the first (satellite) license from the NBC in October 1993, to be replaced by a national terrestrial license in March 1994. In June of that year, a license was awarded to Canal +, a pay TV service, at first using terrestrial transmitters in 14 localities, but, as of 2001, operating as a direct satellite-to-cable broadcaster.

Having begun (after some hesitation, as its first impulse was to begin the licensing process by creating local commercial television stations) with a national commercial television station, POLSAT, the NBC then sought to counterbalance this in 1994–1996 by creating three separate regional television stations—TV Wist'a for Southern Poland, Telewizja Nasza for Central Poland and TVN for Northern Poland. Also beginning in 1994, the NBC licensed a number of local television stations in the North and West of the country.

The plan for the diversification of the television market has proved less than successful. In fact, two companies—Polsat and TVN—began a process of gaining direct or indirect control over practically all terrestrial and much of satellite television in the country. As an example, in June 1997, TVN—which aspires to nationwide reach—bought out TV Wist'a. In 2002, TVN's mother company, ITI, also acquired RTL-7, a satellite-to-cable channel for the Polish audience, originally operated by RTL out of Luxembourg, and renamed TVN7. For its part, Polsat has taken under its wing Telewizja Nasza (since 2000 it operates as TV-4). Polsat has also won indirect control over local television stations. As a result of these and other developments, the television scene in mid-2005 was as follows:

- TVP, the public service television broadcaster, was operating five channels: TVP1, TVP2 (both nationwide); TVP3 (a network of 16 regional stations, broadcasting a joint national channel with regional opt-outs); and two satellite channels: TVP Polonia (for Poles living abroad) and TVP Kultura (a cultural channel). In August 2005, TVP announced plans to create six more satellite channels (for children, and a sports, educational, entertainment, film, and parliamentary channel);
- Polsat, a generalist nationwide channel. Polsat also operates its own digital satellite platform (Cyfrowy Polsat) which it uses to transmit its additional channels (Polsat 2, licensed in 1997; Polsat Sport, 2004), as well as some 20 Polish and several hundred international channels. It has some 300,000 subscribers;
- TVN, a generalist subnational terrestrial channel. In addition to the just-mentioned TVN7, TVN has also launched a number of other satellite channels, including TVN24 (news, 2001), TVN Meteo (weather, 2003), TVN Turbo (cars and motoring, 2003), TVN International (a generalist channel for Poles living abroad, 2004) and TVN Style (lifestyle for women, 2004). Further thematic satellite channels are in the pipeline (reportedly to include TVN Games and TVN Sport);
- TV-4, a subnational generalist terrestrial channel, largely owned by Polsat;
- Two religious (Roman Catholic) channels: TV Trwam (satellite-to-cable; launched in 2002) and TV Puls (terrestrial, licensed in 2001; partly owned by Polsat; its programming is supplied by a production company Antena 1, also associated with Polsat);
- TV Odra, a station broadcasting in several cities in Western Poland, which replaced several private local television stations, all established in 1994–1995. Unable to make it financially viable, they first joined a network under the same name and devoted most of their air time to retransmitting TV-4, with only 2-hour opt-outs for local programming, and as of the beginning of 2005 consolidated into a single station.
- A second digital satellite platform (Cyfra +), created in 2002 through a merger of two previously existing platforms: Wizja TV (operated by an international company) and Canal +, which had been launched in 1998. It offers a number of Canal + channels among some 60 Polish-language channels and several hundred international channels and has more than 700,000 subscribers.
- Some 30 other Polish satellite channels, most of them thematic.

TABLE 12.1

Categories of Television Licenses Awarded by the NBC
(as of November 2004)

Categories of Licenses	No. of Licenses
National licenses	2
Subnational licenses	2
Licenses for stations forming part of regional and local networks	7
Regional and local stations	1
Satellite channels	33
Licenses for program services offered by cable television systems	203
Total	248

Note. Adapted from National Broadcasting Council data, 2005.

Table 12.1 shows the categories of television licenses awarded by the NBC.

Spectrum scarcity has prevented terrestrial television from developing further, pending the introduction of DTT. In addition, there are around 600 cable television operators, reaching 4.5 million households and offering more than 400 television channels. As shown in Table 12.1, some 200 cable operators have been licensed to cablecast their own program services, in most cases local news channels. Some 30% of Polish households are on cable and an additional 20% of households have satellite dishes. Accordingly, half the Polish television audience enjoys the benefits of multichannel television. Table 12.2 shows the overall market share of the main television channels in 2004.

TABLE 12.2

Market Share of Particular Television Channels in 2004

Channel	Market Share (%)
TVP1	24.9%
TVP2	21.4%
POLSAT	17.4%
TVN	14.2%
TVP3	4.7%
TV4	3.1%
TV POLONIA	1.2%
Other	13.1%

Note. Adapted from National Broadcasting Council data, 2005.

BROADCASTING POLICY CREATED FROM SCRATCH

Nordenstreng (1997) has discerned the existence in many countries of two types of "theories of the press": those prescribing openly normative tasks for the media in society (the ideal); and those describing the real role and impact of the media in society, as determined by a wide variety of social, political, economic, and cultural factors (the reality). The same could apply to broadcasting policy: Although lip service may be paid to lofty ideals, the hidden agenda may be different.

Constitutional Aspects of Broadcasting Policy

It is a well-known phenomenon in post-communist countries that development of broadcasting legislation cannot really be successful if a new Constitution has not yet been adopted. Until a country has shaped its sociopolitical system and its system of governance, and until their underlying principles have been carried over to the media, any policy and structural decisions in that sphere will prove either elusive, or short-lived.

Media regulation has to determine the degree of freedom accorded to the media. The Polish legal framework on the whole offers strong guarantees of freedom of speech and information, as well as of entrepreneurial activity in the media, including broadcasting. The Broadcasting Act adequately safeguards the institutional independence of the NBC, public service and commercial broadcasters.

Media regulation must also determine the media system's position between power centers and society (i.e., whether any attempt is made to ensure some degree of direct public participation in policy making, management, and oversight of public service broadcasters). On this score, Polish broadcasting regulation clearly favors the political establishment over civil society.

The NBC is composed of five members: two are appointed by the lower chamber of Parliament, one by the upper chamber and two by the President of the country. Originally, the President also appointed the chairperson of the Council, though this was later changed and now the chairperson is elected by the members themselves. The NBC has extensive powers: to issue secondary regulation envisaged in the Broadcasting Act, license commercial broadcasters and allocate frequencies in cooperation with telecommunications authorities, supervise public and commercial broadcasters, and so on. It also appoints eight out of nine members of the supervisory board of the public service broadcasting companies (the remaining person being appointed by the Minister of State Treasury). It is this last competence that has politicized the NBC, as parties in Parliament and the President sought to be able to influence the composition of the supervisory councils which appoint the boards of management of public service broadcasters. That has turned the process of appointment of NBC members into a political battlefield.

Also the appointment of members of the Programme Councils of public service broadcasting organizations is squarely in the hands of politicians, even though they have no real power. There is in fact an express quota of two thirds for political appointees (designated by parliamentary parties) and one third for artists, scholars, and media practitioners.

According to Article 23 of the Broadcasting Act, public service broadcasting organizations are to "enable political parties national trade unions and employers' organizations to present their position with regard to major public issues." However, when the NBC came to issuing a regulation on how this should be implemented, it in effect guaranteed exercise of this provision by the main political parties. Though trade unions or employers' organizations are also mentioned in this regulation, they are not offered the same opportunities (a weekly program on public radio and television, where representatives of the main parties discuss topical issues) as political parties. This is one more confirmation of the fact that the system is skewed in favor of politicians, at the expense of civil society.

To be fair, the Broadcasting Act provides some safeguards for the independence of the NBC (chairman elected by the members; members cannot be dismissed; the Council as a whole can be dismissed only if both chambers of parliament and the president reject its annual report). The NBC was written into the Constitution in order to guarantee its position vis-à-vis the legislature and the government. Many provisions of the Act also serve the independence of public service broadcasters: different terms of office for supervisory councils (3 years) and boards of management (4 years), again to dissociate those terms from that of Parliament; members of supervisory councils cannot be dismissed; a qualified majority of the supervisory council (at least two thirds in the presence of at least three fourths of members) is needed to appoint, or dismiss, the board of management. These safeguards, although capable of preventing more overt forms of political or institutional control, cannot, however, be fully effective in a partitocratic political system. This is also probably why some licensing decisions have been seen as politically motivated.

There are also some issues concerning the position of broadcasting and the broadcasting regulatory body or bodies vis-à-vis the legislature, executive and the judiciary and relative placement between the different authorities within the particular branches of government (e.g., vis-à-vis the government and the president within the executive branch; the lower and the upper chamber of parliament). As just noted, the NBC is appointed, on the French model, by both houses of Parliament and the President. Public service broadcasters are, legally speaking, wholly State-owned joint stock companies, but even though the Minister of State Treasury performs the role of the meeting of shareholders, he or she appoints only one member of the supervisory council and has no say over programming. In general, the government has been kept away from direct involvement in broadcasting.

Another issue requiring resolution is the geographical structure of the broadcasting system, that is, whether the old centralized, capital-centered model was to remain or whether it was to be devolved to come closer to, and become more integrated with, the rest of the country. An effort was made to do away with the centralized model at least in the area of public service broadcasting (see the following). Licensing policy designed to spread commercial broadcasting around the country

TABLE 12.3
Advertising and Sponsorship Revenues
of Major Polish Television Broadcasters in 2004

Channel	*Advertising (Mil, PLN)*	*Sponsorship (Mil, PLN)*
TVP 1 + 2	937	63
Polsat	655	18
TVN	618	32
TV 4	67.5	1.5
TVN 7	49.7	0.3
TVP 3	32.64	0.36

Note. Adapted from National Broadcasting Council data, 2005.

has been less effective. As we have seen, there is practically no regional terrestrial commercial television and very little local television, with only cable operators filling the void to some extent.

One more systemic policy decision concerns the placement of broadcasting between the State and the market and its size and financing in a competitive marketplace. From a legal point of view, public service broadcasting enjoys a greater degree of institutional independence from the State than many similar organizations in EU countries (which does not preclude informal political influence, exercised via politically engaged members of supervisory and management bodies). Moreover, there is no difference between public service broadcasters and commercial broadcasters in terms of advertising limits (except the fact that public service broadcasters may not interrupt programs to run commercials). As a result, Polish Television controls around 50% of the television advertising market and derives most of its revenue from advertising (with license fee revenue accounting for no more than just over 30%). Thus, Polish Television is highly commercialized, which, in addition to many unwelcome consequences in terms of program content, helps boost its independence, since a great deal of its revenue is not controlled by the authorities. The following table (Table 12.3) shows the combined advertising and sponsorship revenues of major Polish television broadcasters:

Objectives of Broadcasting Policy

The main thrust of media and broadcasting policy has been political and, to some extent, cultural. Given that economic and technological aspects of broadcasting have long been given short shrift in this field, it is still hard to speak of a full-fledged Polish broadcasting policy.

To begin with, the main policy objectives were demonopolization, creation of a commercial sector and transformation of the State-controlled broadcasting organization into a strong and truly independent public service broadcasting system, capable of surviving in a competitive market. Another goal has been protection of the national audiovisual market. That last objective was pursued by imposing a 33% cap on foreign ownership of radio and television stations, and by introducing a Polish production quota for radio and television.

Cultural objectives have also been pursued by independent production quotas, as well as by promoting broadcasters to invest in Polish film production. Originally, NBC included requirements of this nature into licenses to broadcast. That, however, was found to be deprived of a legal basis. In 2005, a new law on cinematography was adopted, imposing on cinema owners, distributors, television broadcasters, satellite platform operators and cable operators an obligation to contribute 1.5% of their revenue to a fund designed to finance film production.

Another early goal was harmonization of the legal framework with European standards (Poland was actually the second country to ratify the European Convention on Tranfrontier Television, developed within the Council of Europe, but closely aligned with the EU Television Without Frontiers directive). Some of the protectionist measures described above (i.e., the introduction of the domestic production quota and the 33% cap on foreign ownership of Polish broadcasting entities) were not in line with that particular objective, but they were introduced—in the full knowledge that they would have to be removed one day—expressly in order to allow Polish broadcasting entrepreneurs to grow and develop before they would have to bear the full brunt of external competition on an open European market. Naturally, in the run-up to accession into the EU in May 2004, the Broadcasting Act was amended to align it strictly with EU requirements. Since then, also general audiovisual policy came to be strictly coordinated with that of the EU.

Nevertheless, the desire to pursue cultural objectives and to protect the national audiovisual market manifested itself also in amendments to the Broadcasting Act designed to harmonize it with EU regulations. Though the aim of EU policy is to promote primarily production and distribution of European, rather than domestic audiovisual works, the amendments:

- Raised the quota of television works originally produced in the Polish language to 33% of airtime on Polish television stations;
- Raised the quota of musical works performed in the Polish language to 33% or airtime on radio and television stations;
- Raised the share of new works to at least 50% of the independent production quota;
- Introduced a definition of works originally produced in the Polish language as one produced on the basis of a script originally written in the Polish language and which was originally recorded in Polish (this in order to prevent shows based on foreign formats from being included in the calculation of the quota of works originally produced in the Polish language).

The hidden agenda of broadcasting policy has been political control, especially of the public service media, and therefore also of the NBC (with its power of appointment as concerns the supervisory councils of public broadcasting organizations).

Another case in point is an attempt by a government in 2002, in the course of developing amendments to the Broadcasting Law, to introduce limits on media concentration that would serve its political interests by preventing a major independent daily newspaper from acquiring a national television station. It was, however, forced by public opinion, to abandon this strictly party-based political plan.

PUBLIC SERVICE BROADCASTING

Transformation of government-controlled Polish Radio and Television into a public service broadcaster became an early goal of broadcasting policy after 1989. Paradoxically, that ran counter to both original "Solidarity" concepts as concerns media reform (which were to promote "socialization of the media," i.e., direct social control and management of the media, serving direct communicative democracy) and the first "Solidarity" government's plans to retain "State" media, ultimately subordinated to the Prime Minister.

Nevertheless, the 1992 Broadcasting Act did provide for this transformation. Government-controlled Polish Radio and Television were transformed into public service broadcasting organizations as of January 1, 1994. The legal status of public service broadcasters is that of "one-person joint stock companies of the State Treasury." The State owns all the shares in these companies and is represented in their general assemblies of shareholders by the Minister of the State Treasury. Despite their formal status as State companies, however, public service broadcasters are not really controlled by the either parliament or government. The general meeting of shareholders (i.e., the Minister of the State Treasury) is legally prohibited from affecting the contents of programming. Also, it appoints only one out of nine members of the supervisory councils of public radio and television; the remaining eight are appointed by the NBC. It is the supervisory councils which appoint boards of management.

In order to decentralize public service broadcasting, public radio was split into 18 companies—one comprising the national channels and 17 independent regional companies, serving particular regions. Polish Television remained as an integrated company, but it has 16 regional centers, each broadcasting its own regional service of around 4 hours a day. In addition to core channels, public service broadcasters may also broadcast licensed thematic program services. The remit of public service broadcasters could be summed up as follows:

- They are to assist the operation of democracy, by (I) "encouraging an unconstrained development of citizens' views and formation of the public opinion, enable citizens and their organizations to take part in public life by expressing diversified views and approaches as well as exercising the right to social supervision and criticism"; (ii) by creating opportunities for State authorities and political parties to address the general public, and (iii) by covering elections and providing free (and, additionally, paid-for) air time for candidates;
- They are to promote Polish culture and national identity, by "assisting the development of culture, science and education, with special emphasis on the

Polish intellectual and artistic achievements," "encouraging artistic, literary, scientific and educational activities," "disseminating knowledge of Polish language," and so on;

- They are to pursue a variety of other objectives, including (in the language of the Broadcasting Act): production and transmission of program services in the Polish language and other languages for receivers abroad; production and broadcasting of educational programs for schools and other educational institutions; production of educational programs and ensuring access by people of Polish descent and Poles living abroad to such programs; respect for the Christian system of values, while being guided by the universal principles of ethics; strengthening family ties; propagation of pro-health attitudes; contribution to combating social pathologies; having regard to the needs of ethnic groups and minorities.

The generalized public service remit, as defined in a 2004 amendment to the Act, puts public service broadcasting organizations under an obligation to provide "the entire society and its individual groups with diversified program services and other services in the area of information, journalism, culture, entertainment, education and sports which shall be pluralistic, impartial, well balanced, independent and innovative, marked by high quality and integrity of broadcast."

Both public radio and television are financed by license fees and advertising. Polish Television accounted in 2004 for an estimated 43.5% of the total television advertising spend, almost matching the combined advertising revenues of the two major commercial television broadcasters (TVN—24.1%; POLSAT—22.3%). As shown in Table 12.2, all the channels of Polish Television had a total market share of 52% in 2004; the broadcaster derived an estimated 56% of its revenue from advertising; 4.5% from sponsorship; 31.9% from license fees; 1.5% from financial operations; and 5.8% from other sources.

The strong position of TVP (both in terms of audience and advertising market share) is one of the media policy issues under constant debate, with commercial broadcasters raising particularly strong objections. The reason for this situation is, on the one hand, high license fee evasion (just over half of the license fee money is actually collected) and, on the other, a highly commercialized program policy of Polish Television, designed to optimize ratings and advertising revenue. When the Broadcasting Act was being drafted, the idea of limiting access to advertising for the public service broadcasters was considered, but rejected in order to allow the newly created organizations time and resources to prepare for the onslaught of commercial competition. That, however, has led to reliance on funding levels that could not be sustained with license fee revenue alone. As a result, a vicious circle has been created: to reduce its dependence on advertising revenue, Polish Television would have to give up up to half its current funding stream. That can hardly be done. As a result, TVP is seen by many as too commercially and entertainment oriented.

Another pointer to TVP's commercialization is its policy of trying to reduce the costs of regional programming as much as possible. As is illustrated by Table 12.3,

TVP3 (both network programming and regional opt-outs) brings in very little advertising revenue. Therefore, TVP finances it primarily from license fee revenue and avoids earmarking advertising revenue brought in by the national channels for regional programming, as that additional infusion of money could not be recouped. As a result, the TVP3 is underfunded and has few development prospects. With no regional television programming provided by commercial stations, public service television could, and should, fill the void, but does so in a limited way, because public interest considerations are outweighed in its programming policy by purely commercial reasons.

Public service broadcasting has long been a bone of contention in terms of broadcasting policy. At times, the system for appointing its governing bodies ensured that it was run by people of a different political orientation than that of the government of the day. That provoked many politically inspired attempts to punish it, for example, by reducing the time it could allot to advertising, by turning down its plan to create a news channel (such a channel was subsequently launched by TVN), or by trying to divert some of its profit for causes dear to the Minister of State Treasury (this was found by a court to be illegal because the Broadcasting Act prevents the State Treasury from receiving any dividend from public media). A plan was also developed to ensure its political impartiality by turning ownership of public media to universities, for example. This last proposal was greeted with considerable skepticism and with comments that rather than "depoliticizing" public media, the system would help bring universities under greater political control, and was never implemented.

A new departure in this ongoing debate was the radical plan, announced in autumn 2004 by some experts associated with the center-right party, Platforma Obywatelska (Citizens' Platform—PO), to abolish the general license fee, privatize the first channel of TVP and establish a "Public Mission Fund" (financed from revenues from the privatization, broadcasting license fees and other sources) to finance public service programs on both public and private channels.

If the plan was implemented, its real effect would be the collapse of public service media. PO dissociated itself from these ideas, probably finding them too radical, but the very fact that they were voiced shows that Poland is no stranger to the debate concerning the very existence of public service broadcasting, already raging in many other countries. Moreover, the public did not seem to be upset by these proposals; in fact, some 50% of respondents in a public opinion poll supported the idea of privatizing some or all parts of public service broadcasting organizations. All this shows that Polish public service broadcasting organizations suffer from a major legitimacy crisis.

CURBING MEDIA CONCENTRATION: A LOST CAUSE?

We have seen that practically all commercial television in Poland is controlled by two players—POLSAT and TVN (or its mother company, ITI Holdings). Both are part of larger entities. ITI Holdings controls production companies (Endemol-Neovision and ITI Film Studio), cinemas (Multikino), Internet portals (Onet.pl and Tenbit.pl), publishing houses (Optimus Pascal Multimedia, Pascal and DRQ), a football club (Legia Warszawa), and a number of other companies. For its part, POLSAT is involved in a number of ventures, both in the media field (RS TV, a transmission company) and far beyond (a pension fund, a bank, power plants, telecommunications, and mobile phone operators, etc.). There is a sizable foreign investment in television in Poland, including primarily the French company Canal + (now part of Vivendi Universal), which controls 49% of the satellite platform Cyfra +, with Polcom Invest S.A. holding 26% of the shares, and UPC Polska, 25%. UPC Polska (ultimately controlled by Liberty Media) also controls a network of cable systems, reaching around a million households.

Since the adoption of amendments to the Broadcasting Act in April 2004, capital restrictions on media ownership for investors from EU countries have been lifted. A ceiling of 49% applies only to investors from outside the EU, which, in practice, means American investors and European subsidiaries in which they own a majority stake.

There are no other limits on concentration of broadcast media ownership, except for ordinary competition law. Under the Broadcasting Act, a broadcasting license may be refused if the applicant could, by the act of receiving it, achieve "a dominant position in the mass media in the given territory." The broadcasting license can also be revoked on the same grounds. However, the Broadcasting Act does not define "dominant position," meaning that the provision is, in practice, dead-letter law. As just noted, an attempt to introduce such provisions was made in 2002. Draft amendments to the Broadcasting Act would prevent the NBC from:

1. Awarding a national terrestrial radio or television license to anyone who already holds such a license, or owns a national daily newspaper or periodical;
2. Awarding a license to broadcast a terrestrial radio or television channel covering a town of more than 100,000 people to anyone who is already broadcasting a national radio or television channel;
3. Awarding a second license to broadcast a terrestrial radio or television channel for a town of up to 200,000 people to anyone already broadcasting a radio or television channel respectively in the same market;
4. Awarding another license to broadcast either a terrestrial radio or television channel for a town of more than 200,000 people to anyone already broadcasting two radio or television channels, respectively, in that market;
5. Awarding a terrestrial radio license to anyone already broadcasting a radio program service of the same kind in the same market, or a terrestrial television license to anyone already broadcasting a television program service of the same kind in the same market.

Although there was general opposition to the imposition of such restrictions, especially the first one was seen as an attempt to deny the publisher of an independent national daily newspaper (known to be unfriendly to the government of the day), a chance to buy a national television station, which it was reportedly planning to do in order to expand its media empire (it also controls a considerable number of radio stations). The public outcry was such that the government was forced to abandon its plan.

New proposals in this area are included in the NBC's draft "National Strategy for the Electronic Media, 2005–2020" (see the following section). It calls for measures preventing anyone with a combined radio or television, or daily newspaper market share of up to 30% on the national or a local market from applying for a license to broadcast in the same market. The idea behind this proposal is to prevent excessive influence on public opinion and to preserve the existence of at least three independent radio and television broadcasters on the national and local markets. This is understood as a minimum condition of structural pluralism of the electronic media.

The draft strategy also calls for an analysis of the vertical integration of electronic media, with a view to proposing additional measures, should this analysis show that such integration is abused to prevent access by broadcasters and audiovisual content providers to the public, or of the public to content offered by some broadcasters. It remains to be seen, however, if these proposals will be implemented.

TECHNOLOGY BEGINS TO TRANSFORM THE MEDIA AND BROADCASTING POLICY

More than 30% of Poles use the Internet. Also Polish broadcasters are using it extensively, though this concerns primarily radio broadcasters (most of whose program services are also available via the Internet), with television stations only offering limited content, mostly from their archives, but in some cases also daily news shows and other information programs. Polish Televison has an extensive Web site, offering a wealth of information about its own activities, but also a general news service. Polish Television has also mounted an extensive R & D project in the area of interactive television.

In 2004, some 125 radio program services could be accessed via the Internet, including some 15 stations available only on the Internet. There are also a couple of television stations operating only on the Internet.

The year 2004 saw the creation by government of an Interdepartmental Committee for Digital Broadcasting in Poland and 2005 saw the publication of its first report, "Strategy for Transition from Analogue to Digital Technology in Terrestrial Television," dealing with frequency and technical issues. In 2005, it also initiated work on a second report, dealing with digital radio. Programming and other issues are covered in other reports, written by the NBC.

The strategy called for an accelerated switchover process, region by region (with 6- to 12-month periods of simulcasting in each region), originally with two multiplexes, but with seven possible in the long term. Analog switch-off criteria for the particular regions are to be 95% coverage of the region by digital terrestrial television (DTT), with digital television available in at least 90% of households. The year 2006 saw the launch of digital transmission in first two regions

(Central and Western Poland), 2007—analog switch-off in those two regions, while analogue switch-off for the country as a whole is planned for 2014.

Although the two satellite television platforms are already wholly digital, with their subscribers using set-top boxes to receive their signals, and production and studio equipment in television stations is also thoroughly digitized, elsewhere digitalization is only beginning. Polish Television has launched a number of low-power experimental DTT transmitters in areas beyond the reach of its analog services. The main cable operators are upgrading their networks to offer broadband and Triple Play.

The three main television stations (TVP, Polsat, TVN) launched talks to establish a joint company to operate two digital multiplexes, but Polish Television withdrew from that project in the hope of obtaining a multiplex of its own. Meanwhile, the NBC developed a policy document, "National Strategy for the Electronic Media—2005–2020" and submitted it to the government for its consideration and possible adoption. The document calls for recognizing the effects of convergence and the onset of the Information Society on broadcasting and telecommunications and for developing a comprehensive policy for the "electronic media," covering all forms of content distribution (rather than for traditional broadcasting alone). It also calls for full recognition of the economic and technological aspects of electronic communication and for coordination of "electronic media policy" with other long-term policies of the State, including those of economic and technological development, as well as those in the area of culture. The document identifies nine strategic goals of electronic media policy:

1. To safeguard freedom of expression and information, as well the freedom of the media and their role in the democratic system;
2. To promote, that is, in the interest of Polish culture, the development of the electronic media and production of Polish audiovisual and Internet content;
3. To promote the development of the electronic media also as a growing sector of the economy and a foundation, alongside the ICTs, of a knowledge-based economy;
4. To safeguard media diversity, that is, by ensuring the structural pluralism of the media at the national, regional and local levels, and to protect local media;
5. To protect competition and prevent excessive concentration of the media;
6. To ensure the development and proper operation of the public service media;
7. To apply horizontal, technologically neutral, graduated content regulation;
8. To contribute to the development and implementation of the audiovisual policy of the EU (and of other international organizations) and its policies serving the development of the Information Society;
9. To promote digital conversation, ICT development and universal access to the new technologies to prevent digital exclusion, and to fight cyber-crime and combat illegal and/or harmful Internet content.

One of the instruments of implementing the electronic media policy is to be a new, integrated regulatory body, created by means of merging the now-separate broadcasting and telecommunications regulators. Given the fact that there has been no major overhaul of the Broadcasting Act since 1992 (given the political sensitivities involved in broadcasting policy, in most cases only amendments required by harmonization with EU rules and standards could be assured of passage in Parliament, and even that with difficulty), and that it fails to regulate many areas of broadcasting and the new technologies, the draft Strategy proposes a great number of policy and regulatory measures to implement the strategic goals just listed and to fill the gaps in all areas of the broadcasting system, including the public service media.

CONCLUSION

Since 1989, Poland has seen the development of a new television system and the emergence of rudiments of broadcasting policy. The before-and-after contrast could not be more stark: post-communist transformation has indeed fundamentally transformed television—not as envisioned by idealistic dissidents in the 1980s, but more in line with the logic of change enveloping television systems in other European countries. Given the mimetic aspect of the process, this has indeed been largely "transformation by imitation," but along two, quite different paths:

- Deliberate, and not always entirely voluntary, copying of legal and institutional frameworks to be found elsewhere (as is indeed the case when EU candidate countries harmonize their laws with the acquis);
- And as natural repetition, or recreation of the same processes in comparable circumstances, when more or less the same factors and forces impact on the situation as in other countries.

The second form of "imitation" underscores the importance of market forces in the whole process. Integration of the Polish television system and market with the European and global markets, and its exposure to similar market processes, could not but produce a similar effect.

And indeed, Poland seems to have telescoped into this time some of the phases of media policy development in Western Europe (see McQuail, 2000, pp. 208–209), which took decades to unfold, comprising the "public service" and a "new paradigm" of media policy, ushered in by both objective processes (internationalization, digitalization and convergence) and subjective ones (ideological change, leading to marketization of the media and deregulation). No doubt, the perceived subordination of broadcasting policy to party political considerations has led many to doubt its dedication to the pursuit of the public interest. The disaffection of many with the whole process of post-Communist transformation and its consequences has weakened support for the avowed course of national policy in this area.

However, there is more to it than that. Rising resentment against the very existence of public service broadcasting, and indeed even against the existence of a broadcasting regulatory body and its efforts to perform its functions (reflected, e.g., in attempts to question the legal competence of the NBC to introduce programme requirements into licenses to broadcast), attests to ideological and axiological evolution, leading to the conviction of some that everything should be left to market forces, with competition law as the only acceptable form of regulation. Another manifestation of this process may be the fact that no post-1994 government was concerned with the rising commercialization of TVP, or willing to do anything about it, regardless of the effect this has had on programming and its quality.

In conclusion, let us note that since 1989, Poland has been concerned primarily with "systemic" broadcasting policy, seeking to create a new television system from scratch. That effort has been successful, no doubt due in part both to the democratic nature of the Polish political system and to fast economic growth, laying the foundations for the emergence of healthy media and advertising markets. The time for a fully developed broadcasting policy, concerned with all aspects of the system and equipped with the full range of legal and regulatory instruments, is yet to come. Political, ideological, and technological evolution of Polish society will determine both the prospects for this to happen and for the course this policy will take.

REFERENCES

Balcerowicz, L. (1995). *Socialism, capitalism, transition.* Budapest: Central European University Press.

Hankiss, E. (1994). The Hungarian media's war of independence. *Media, Culture & Society, 16*(2), 293–312.

Harcourt, A. (2003). The regulation of media markets in EU first-wave accession States in Central and Eastern Europe. *European Law Journal, 8*(2), 316–340.

Jakubowicz, K. (1989). Political and economic dimensions of television programme exchange between Poland and Western Europe. In J. Becker & T. Szecsko (Eds.), *Europe speaks to Europe* (pp. 138–155). London: Pergamon Press.

Jakubowicz, K. (1994). Equality for the downtrodden, freedom for the free: Changing perspectives on mass communication in Central and Eastern Europe. *Media, Culture and Society 16*(2), 271–293.

Jakubowicz, K. (2006). *Rude awakening. Media and social change in Central and Eastern Europe.* Cresskill, NJ: Hampton Press.

Koralewicz, J. (1987). Changes in Polish social consciousness during the 1970s and 1980s: Opportunism and identity. In J. Koralewicz, I. Bialecki, & M. Watson (Eds.), *Crisis and transition. Polish society in the 1980s.* Oxford: Berg.

McQuail, D. (1992). *Media performance: Mass communication and the public interest.* London: Sage.

McQuail, D. (2000). *Mass communication theory.* London: Sage.

Myslinski, J. (1987). Mikrofon I polityka. Polskie Radio w latach 1944–1960 [The microphone and politics]. *Przekazy I Opinie, 1–2,* 21–40.

Nordenstreng, K. (1997). Beyond the four theories of the press. In J. Koivisto & E. Lauk (Eds.), *Journalism at the crossroads. Perspectives on research* (pp. 47–64). Tartu: Tartu University Press.

Sparks, C. (1998). (with A. Reading). Communism, capitalism and the mass media. London: Sage.

Titkow, A. (1993). Stres I zycie spoleczne. Polskie doswiadczenia [Stress and social life: The Polish experience]. Warszawa: PIW.

CHAPTER THIRTEEN

Broadcasting Regulation
in the United Kingdom:
Shifting Public Policy Objectives

David Ward

Television broadcasting in the United Kingdom has been profoundly shaped by stability and continuity that has seen fundamental features of the system that was established in 1922 carried throughout the decades. It has historically evolved with a great deal of continuity and as new broadcasters were introduced, all of these broadcasters were licensed with public service obligations: this is the uniqueness of the British model of broadcasting, which has historically provided a stable and innovative television environment, with quality, universality and diversity enjoying prominence in public policy debate. With the introduction of commercial television broadcasting, such a model sought to balance the public interest with commercial interest by placing obligations on commercial broadcasters ensuring that they contributed to the overall quality and range of television programming. The BBC has been omnipresent in the development of radio and television in the United Kingdom and it has acted as the central institution during the development of television, and this continues to this day.

Since the 1990s, there has been a progressive move away from this regulatory philosophy, which in many ways represented a postwar compromise towards an increasingly competitive market as successive governments have sought to adjust the dynamics of the television sector to meet the perceived changes brought about by the growing penetration of multichannel services and the liberalization of

245

international markets. The British model of liberalization is therefore one whereby commercial public service broadcasters are being granted a greater degree of freedom, both in terms of their public service obligations and the regulation of these, as well as in areas such as media concentration, to account for the changes in the structure of the market.

Three major changes have occurred in the past decade: first, the diffusion of multichannel television and the growth of different forms of revenue streams. Second, the move of broadcasters into new areas of audiovisual distribution and third, increased competition and a relaxation of some parts of the regulatory framework that have combined to reshape this framework for the sector. In many respects, digitalization of television frequencies raises issues that are perennial. Though in the next 10 years, some of these issues are likely to come to a head as technological advances enable subscription services to reach near total penetration across the United Kingdom, according to projections of the communications regulator.

The regulatory framework is changing and an increased role is envisaged for coregulation in U.K. television in some areas replacing statutory regulation and reducing the involvement of the regulators in the sector. A new converged regulator, the Office of Communications (Ofcom), replaced all of the sector specific regulators in 2003 and an advanced digital strategy suggests a new paradigm for regulation that has been developing over the past two decades. At the same time, many of the features of the past have been retained, sometimes via policy decisions and at other times because of circumstances, and the traditional broadcasters remain central to the television sector. However, the traditional actors are changing as the regulatory framework fails to fully deal with the issues raised by the challenges of multichannel television. Liberalization appears to be the main response to such challenges and there is a belief that digitalization calls for a change in approach to the regulation of television.

BACKGROUND

Since the introduction of broadcasting in the United Kingdom, the one characteristic that stands out above all is the existence of the BBC and the concept of public service in broadcasting. Founded in 1922 by Royal Charter and granted a monopoly status and public financing the BBC was established to serve the audience a wide range of quality information on a universal basis. A Board of Governors was established to direct the BBC ensuring that the Corporation was independent from the government of the day and, as guardians of the public interest, they were charged with ensuring the public were provided with a range of quality programming. The BBC retained this monopoly as it moved into television and it is not until the 1950s that its monopoly was broken. It has, however, despite losing its monopoly status, always been the key broadcaster in the United Kingdom.

The first major shift in British television was in the 1950s with the introduction of commercial broadcasting and a second channel based on a regional network, ITV. A so called "cosy duopoly" prevailed whereby the broadcasters lived a fairly tame coexistence working alongside one another as each had its own sources of revenues. Limited competition in quality programming was seen to provide positive pressures for broadcasters to reach higher standards across program genres, but real competition was conspicuous only in its absence.

Today, quite remarkably, the terms of reference for the BBC's core activities remain largely the same as when it was founded. In terms of the services that the BBC should provide, the Charter states that the objectives of the Corporation are:

> To provide, as public services, sound and television broadcasting services (whether by analogue or digital means) and to provide sound and television programmes of information, education and entertainment for general reception in Our United Kingdom of Great Britain and Northern Ireland, the Channel Islands and the Isle of Man and the territorial waters thereof, and on board ships and aircraft (such services being hereinafter referred to as "the Home Services") and for reception elsewhere within the Commonwealth and in other countries and places overseas (such services being hereinafter referred to as "the World Service") the Home Services and the World Service together being hereinafter referred to as "the Public Services." (Department of National Heritage, p. 2)

The obligations and legal status of the BBC are also established by the Royal Charter, granted by the Queen on the advice of the government and renewable every 10 years. Each renewal is accompanied by an agreement between the government and the BBC. Together, the Charter and Agreement set out the BBC's structure, activities and obligations as a public service broadcaster, recognizing its editorial independence, and requiring it to produce and transmit a range of quality programs that seek to inform, educate and entertain.

Prior to 1982, there were only three channels supplied by two broadcasters in the United Kingdom, the BBC and the companies that comprised the ITV network. Both of these broadcasters had public service obligations placed on them.

In 1982, a fourth channel was introduced. Channel 4 was established as a nonprofit public corporation with a unique remit to innovate and cater to the program areas and groups that were neglected by the established broadcasters. It was also unique in that it was funded from commercial revenues (and it was not until the 1990 Broadcasting Act that it began to sell its own advertising spots), as a nonprofit organization. Unlike the other broadcasters it was established on a publisher/broadcaster model; its original programming was to be commissioned from the independent production sector, breaking away from the tradition of vertical integration and in-house production.[1] Channel Five was the fifth and final terrestrial channel to be introduced under this kind of regime and it has developed an important niche in the market since its introduction in 1997.

---

[1]There is also a Welsh-language television service provided in Wales. SC4 consists of a window within the Channel 4 schedule that broadcasts 36 hours of Welsh-language programming per week, mostly in peak time with Channel 4 programming rescheduled around these programs.

Until the 1990s, the British television system was a model of the steady evolution of public service principles, originally set down in the BBC's Royal Charter
and then extended into the remits of ITV, Channel 4, and Channel Five as these
channels were introduced. As a new broadcaster was issued a license, each was
allocated either a specific public service remit or some degree of public service
obligation, regardless of how it was funded, as part of their license conditions.

Despite the changing nature of the sector all the terrestrial commercial broadcasters in the United Kingdom have retained some of their public service broadcasting obligations, and are regulated within a framework that obliges them to
supply a service that is governed by a set of program principles and guidelines
that are required by the State. As part of their contractual conditions, therefore,
the free-to-air broadcasters are all regulated according to principles that aim to
ensure a high-quality mix of programming that reflects the needs and tastes of a
diverse audience.

With two public corporations (BBC and Channel 4) and two main private
operators (the ITV network companies and Channel Five), the television sector
has achieved a balance between public and private. The sector is characterized
by a strong publicly funded broadcaster, a group of commercial terrestrial broadcasters with public service obligations, and a public company that is funded by
advertising.

The final major actor in U.K. television is the satellite operator BSkyB. The
development of satellite television begins in 1989 with the launch of Sky TV and,
in 1990, the launch of British Satellite Broadcasting (BSB), the latter of which was
an initiative of a consortium of terrestrial broadcasters and other investors. The two
channels merged within 7 months of the launch of BSB due to financial difficulties
of both operators and BSkyB was formed (Horsman, 1997). At the end of 2006,
BSkyB had more than 7.8 million subscribers—a number just below a third of all
households in the United Kingdom and its strong growth has been largely responsible for the roll out of multichannel television based on its bouquet of channels
including movies and football rights. Unlike the other broadcasters it has minimum
regulatory obligations that relate to negative regulations including taste and decency
and impartiality and has no positive regulatory obligations.

CHANGING POLICY IN THE TELEVISION SECTOR

Media policy in the United Kingdom has always been periodically reviewed as
to its shape and objectives. Despite the evolution of broadcasting and the options
arising to change the nature of the sector at key points in its evolution a number of high level inquiries (Crawford Committee, 1925; Pilkington Committee,1962;
Annan Committee, 1977) consistently supported the traditional system of public
service broadcasting as the "least worst option."

This consensus was most seriously challenged with the election of Margaret
Thatcher's government in 1979. Thatcher's policy of radical privatization witnessed a raft of public company privatizations by the government and given the
government's radical agenda for reform of the economy it was unsurprising that

attention turned to the broadcasting sector. A highly influential committee, the Peacock Committee, was established to report on the *Future Funding of the BBC* in 1986. The committee was widely seen to be the start of a program of reform of the established industry actors: the BBC and the ITV companies.

Early initiatives of the Thatcher government were concerned with innovative developments in U.K. television such as the introduction of Channel 4 and the development of cable and satellite television (Goodwin, 1998). During their second term, reform of the existing institutions was to some extent inevitable. The Peacock Report was the first step in this process and established the basis for the Broadcasting Act of 1990. The report, although stopping short of privatizing the BBC, made some radical recommendations for the sector; most notably that an independent program quota should be established for all terrestrial broadcasters of 40% of original programming as well as spectrum auctioning for the ITV licenses (though later most of the franchises merged to form one company with only a couple of franchises remaining independent). Both recommendations were incorporated into the 1990 Broadcasting Act, though the independent quota was reduced to 25% of qualifying programs.

This was only the start of a program of reform characterized by an increasingly ambivalent approach to the television sector by policy makers. Reform that moved seamlessly between Conservative and Labor governments largely based on arguments about stimulating growth and competition or harnessing the potential of new technologies to increase viewer choice and flexibility. On one hand so-called consumer choice has been promoted in theory by the increased competition in the sector. On the other hand, and this is increasingly the case, technological developments, underpinned by a concept of consumer choice have come to drive public policy toward the sector.

Although the Peacock Committee rejected advertising funding for the BBC, largely due to the impact it would have on commercial broadcasters, 10 years later the question of supplementary revenue sources, that is, commercial revenues, gathered support from a wider spectrum. The renewal of the BBC's Charter in 1996 reflected a changing approach to the BBC by the government (which at that time was a Conservative one led by Prime Minister John Major), and a desire to supplement the license fee with commercial activities, rather than simply fund the BBC by raising the license fee or introducing advertising revenues. The Davies Committee report into *The Future Funding of the BBC* further endorsed this move in 1999 under the New Labor government. Although the report favored a rise in the license fee to support digital services, it recommended that the BBC's primary funding for extra services should be generated from a combination of cost savings and increased commercial revenues. It argued:

> The BBC should seek to accelerate the growth of its commercial services, which need not conflict with its role as a public service broadcaster, provided that new measures are introduced to ensure that the fair trading commitment is enforced strictly and with full transparency. (Department for Culture, Media and Sport, 1999, p. 6)

This approach was endorsed by the government and subsequently the BBC developed a number of commercial ventures over the following 10 years to supplement its license fee revenues. Most notably it entered into a joint venture with Flextech (later taken over by the cable provider Telewest) and established four primary channels (which are on the second-tier subscriber category). These channels include U.K. Gold (comedy), U.K. Horizons (documentary), U.K. Style (cooking and gardening reruns) and U.K. Play. It has also established a commercial arm operated by two subsidiaries, BBC Worldwide Ltd. and BBC Resources Ltd. These subsidiaries have separate Boards and provide separate accounts and annual reports. The commercial services include the thematic channels above, the global news channel BBC World, BBC Prime (entertainment), and BBC America (drama, news, and entertainment). It also includes distribution as well as magazine and technology companies that all operate as subsidiaries.

These policy initiatives together with the growth of satellite have all to some extent played their part in increasing competition in the television sector. Downstream of the production chain the independent production sector is seen to provide some form of market for programs. Upstream, greater competition for audiences between broadcasters is a natural result of more channels that are available to the television viewer. In reality the broadcasters determine what programs are commissioned from the independent sector and greater choice in channels in reality means a choice from a handful of suppliers, most of which were already central actors in the television market.

The communications policy trajectory of consecutive governments over the last two decades has therefore affected the whole television sector as it has become more competitive, a finite revenue stream more widely spread across a growing number of channels and the BBC establishing commercial services as it has embarked on an aggressive strategy to retain its position as the United Kingdom's foremost broadcaster. The vogue for technology and greater company freedom in the government's approach to television is enshrined in the Communications Act of 2003 that sets out the new regulatory framework for broadcasting, but in reality consolidates previous legislation and finalizes the trends triggered by the 1990 Broadcasting Act. It relaxes both ownership restrictions and public service obligations on the commercial terrestrial broadcasters; and technology, and how to position television broadcasters in a multichannel landscape, as was the case for the arguments put forward in the 1980s, (Goodwin, 1998) was the main driving force behind changing policy objectives.

THE CONTEMPORARY TELEVISION SECTOR

Changing policy has therefore had a profound influence on how television has developed over the last two decades. Competition between broadcasters and the growing number of niche channels means that what was once a highly consensual system based on the "duopoly" has become a highly competitive environment.

Declining audience shares for the ITV network companies and the general entertainment channel of the BBC, BBC1 have been an almost constant in parallel to the growth of multichannel services. Since 1981, as Table 13.1 illustrates,

TABLE 13.1
U.K. Broadcasters' Audience Share: 1981–2006

Channel	1981	1986	1991	1996	2001	2003	2006
BBC1	39%	37%	34%	33.5%	26.9%	25.6%	22.8%
BBC2	12%	11%	10%	11.5%	11.1%	10.9%	8.8%
ITV	49%	44%	42%	35.1%	26.7%	23.7%	19.6%
Channel 4	—	8%	10%	10.7%	10%	9.7%	9.8%
Channel Five	—	—	—	—	5%	6.3%	5.7%
Others	—	—	4%	9.2%	20.3%	23.6%	33.3%

Note. Adapted from BARB audience data, 2007.

there has been a steady decline in the audience share of the two largest channels and a notable increase in the Others category, which are mainly satellite and digital terrestrial television channels and from 1996 onwards satellite viewing has grown considerably.

Although this decline is inevitable as viewers gain access to a greater number of channels, it is important to put these changes into context. The free-to-air generalist channels remain central to the television environment: The five channels combined are watched by 68.1% of the audience. Audience behavior in multichannel television homes shows a decline in the viewing time of the main channels, but even there, 57% of viewing time is spent watching the free-to-air channels, and 85% of these viewers still watch some programming on one of the main channels daily (Ofcom, 2004a, 2006).

There has also been very strong growth in the past decade of multichannel television services, mainly through the services of BSkyB. The development of digital terrestrial television (DTT) since the launch of Freeview in 2002 with a package of 30 channels has also shown strong growth as a limited alternative to satellite television.

The revenue structure of the television industry has undergone some fairly radical changes in the past decade largely due to the development of subscription as a major source of the overall finance of the sector. Traditionally, funds from the license fee and advertising have provided the public and commercially funded broadcasters with the majority of their revenues. This has not changed in respect of the terrestrial television services however, overall there is a significant growth in revenues derived from subscription and pay-per-view, for satellite and cable.

Subscription became the single greatest source of revenue in the television industry in 2003, for the first time overtaking advertising revenues, marking an important landmark for the sector (see Table 13.2). The traditional advertising market is still dominated by the ITV network companies. Despite its decline in audience share, ITV remains the most popular commercially funded channel in the United Kingdom and it also retains the majority share of advertising revenues and in 2003 enjoyed a 51.9% share of advertising revenues (Ofcom 2004b).

TABLE 13.2
Revenue Breakdown for the U.K. Television Sector: 2003

Revenue Source	2003 Million€	Percentage
2002		
Advertising	4725	33%
Subscription	4813	33.6%
BBC license fee	3357	23.4%
Other	1430	10%
Total	1,4325	100%

Note. Adapted from Ofcom 2004b.

The BBC is funded through a license fee, which is supplemented with a marginal amount of income from commercial sources. The license fee ensures a consistent level of funding necessary for the BBC to provide a wide range of programming and services. In 2002–2003 the total revenues from the license fee enjoyed by the BBC were €3,959 million and this sum was complemented with €252.74 million from commercial and other sources of revenue. Together with its commercial revenues, this makes the BBC the sixth-largest media enterprise in Europe according to company turnover and the second largest public broadcaster after ARD in Germany (Ward, 2004).

The government sets the level of the license fee. The current fee for a color television household is €180.21 as of April 2004, a fee of a little under €16.40 per month in line with the current Agreement with the BBC. The level of the license fee is linked to the Retail Price Index[2] (RPI) and marked, according to the agreement between the government and the BBC, at 1.5% above the rate of inflation as measured by the RPI. Under the current agreement, the BBC has also been obliged to undertake cost savings and develop additional revenues throughout the present funding agreement (2000–2001 and 2006–2007) of €1.64 billion. There are concessions to the full rate of the license fee of 50% for blind people and the 75-and-above age group are granted a waiver. In 2003 the BBC received €543.61 million from the Department for Work and Pensions to cover the costs of these groups of viewers.

Commercial activities must meet certain criteria and essentially meet with, and be supportive of, the BBC's activities as a public service broadcaster. The BBC is also obliged to maintain separate and transparent accounting systems for its public and commercial activities, to ensure that it does not distort competition by using the license fee to cross-subsidize its commercial services. The Executive Board of the BBC also reports four times a year to the BBC's Fair Trading Compliance Committee, which in turn reports to the Board of Governors and reviews and monitors the compliance of the BBC with its commitment to fair

---

[2]The Retail Price Index is the method used by the Government to measure inflation and is based on a system that monitors fluctuation of high street prices of a range of products.

trading and transparency. Prior to the Communications Act of 2003 the parliamentary watchdog, the National Audit Office (NAO) was responsible for assessing a limited number of BBC activities, including the collection of the license fee and the spending of the BBC World Service. The BBC was exempted from being fully audited by the NAO on grounds that this would potentially threaten its independence. However, the role of the NAO has been extended under the Communications Act 2003 and now includes an assessment of all the BBC's activities further increasing the scrutiny of the BBC's activities.

These mechanisms have not deflected criticism of the BBC's commercial growth, especially from commercial operators who have focused on both its new digital channels and commercial services. In a report funded by the Conservative Party in 2004 and compiled by a group of television mandarins the BBC was criticized for:

> Competing so directly with its commercial rivals, the BBC has increased the difficulties, which these rivals are currently experiencing. Fierce competition for audience share has been bedeviling advertiser-funded public service broadcasters. As a result, the BBC, with its ever increasing income, has come to play an increasingly dominant role. Two problems arise from this. The first is a growing threat to cultural and political pluralism. The second is a decline in quality, as creative competition diminishes. (Broadcasting Policy Group, 2004, p. 7)

The report exaggerates the demise of U.K. television and the BBC's role in creating a more competitive television environment for broadcasters and it neglects a range of key factors. There is, however, a growing chorus of criticism aimed at the BBC in this respect and despite the fact that it has pursued commercial activities under the direction of government policy this has done little to deflect criticism. In this sense, the BBC seems to be in a no-win situation as its success in developing these activities only increases criticism. The Charter's rather abstract definition of public service in broadcasting—essentially to entertain, inform, and educate—has been both an advantage and a drawback for the BBC. It has provided the Corporation with a wide-ranging remit for its activities, enabling it to adjust over time to cultural, industrial, and technological changes with a great deal of success. On the other hand, in recent years it has opened the BBC up to criticism that its remit is too flexible and, as a result, the philosophical principles that the Corporation has evolved around, under the direction of the Board of Governors, remains too loose (Collins & Murroni, 1996).

THE DEVELOPMENT OF NEW TECHNOLOGIES
AND TELEVISION BROADCASTING

In parallel to the changing nature of public policy, and largely as a result of these policies, technological developments in the television industry have been widely seen as rapidly transforming the sector. The United Kingdom is at the forefront of digital developments in the television sector and has embarked on an ambitious initiative to replace analog with digital transmission. In 1998, the United Kingdom saw the first and by far the most ambitious attempt of any government in Europe to introduce digital television services and switchover from analog to digital signals, thereby creating greater efficiency in the use of spectrum. In 1999 the government set the objective for the time framework for analog switch-off between 2006–2010 based on the projected criteria that 95% of U.K. households would have access to digital equipment to receive the services, and that all the main public service channels that are available through analog television would be available in digital form.

Multichannel Television

At the third quarter of 2006, multichannel television penetration was estimated to be more than 13 million households, according to Ofcom (Table 13.3). The number of households that subscribed to cable, satellite or DTT was estimated to be in the region of 73% (Ofcom, 2006). Satellite has traditionally dominated multichannel television services in the United Kingdom, both in terms of subscribers and revenue share. However, the growth of Freeview has created a viable competitor to BSkyB in terms of penetration. At the same time BSkyB's significant market position and its access to key program rights such as Premiership football and movies leaves it in a powerful position in the market that is largely unchallenged. At the beginning of 2007 BSkyB announced that it had reached 7.8 million subscribers to its U.K. services.

Overall development of digital television is impressive, though in a 2004 report on the development of digital television Ofcom concluded that it has reservations as to whether 95% of households will have access to digital platforms by 2010. It estimates a maximum of 78% based on current trends in the market. The major obstacles Ofcom notes are on one hand technological (the fact that the power of the existing signals restricts the amount of households using traditional aerials that will have access to DTT until this is increased at switchover), and on the other, the lack of development in the pay TV market, which under current conditions Ofcom predicts will reach no more than 50% of households. It does, however, suggest that these can be overcome with a clear plan of action and switchover date. Access to DTT services at the end of 2004 remained limited by the technical restrictions of the range of delivery of DTT to 73% of the country. Cable services reach 51% of households, and satellite television 97% of the population (Ofcom, 2004b).

With the closure of ITV Digital, a consortium of commercial broadcasters that were initially granted the license to operate the DDT platform, in April 2002 due to bankruptcy, the license for DTT was reissued to Freeview, a consortium of the BBC, Crown Castle, and BSkyB. This represents a partial renationalization of the platform due to the failure of the commercial sector to roll out the service and build a viable business model. Freeview provides a range of channels based on a free-to-air model with some additional opportunities for consumers to subscribe to premium channels such as film and sports channels. The BBC has

TABLE 13.3
Digital Television Penetration (Third Quarter 2006)

Platform	Households	Platform	Households
Digital cable	2,502,451	Total U.K. digital households	13,858,901
Digital Satellite (Sky)	7,085,000	Digital penetration	55.9%
Total digital pay-TV households	9,598,981	Analog cable	860,193
Free-to-view DTT (Freeview)	5,016,200	Total U.K. pay-TV households	10,459,174
Free-to-view digital satellite	345,000	Total U.K. multichannel households	14,719,094
Total free-to-view receivers	5,361,200	Multichannel penetration	59.4%
Total free-to-view households	4,259,920		

Note. Adapted from Ofcom (2006).

become central to the development of DTT in the United Kingdom, with the launch of Freeview. Over the past years, the BBC has introduced a number of new digital channels including an up-market cultural channel, BBC4, Youth (BBC3), Children's (CBeebies and CBBC), Parliamentary (BBC Parliament), and a news channel (BBC News 24).

The digital television sector has therefore developed on a two-tier system. BSkyB, which has the majority of subscribers, provides a service of up to 200 channels with interactivity and key programs such as football and movies. Freeview, on the other hand, has a limited number of channels that are broadcast free-to-air in a similar manner as television has traditionally been distributed—the content is also based on standard programming and the BBC's content is the main driving force behind the growth of DTT.

U.K. Broadcasters and the Internet

As in similar countries the Internet has grown at an exponential rate in the United Kingdom. According to the National Statistics Office (NSO) at the end of 2004, 52% of households had access to the Internet (in 1998, it was estimated to be under 10%). Although this growth is impressive, there remains 35% of the population who have never used the Internet (National Statistics Office, 2005b). Despite its fairly rapid diffusion the Internet's impact on the television sector is at the present time minimal, with the television broadcasters positioning themselves in the online world in different ways. The direction has been largely one way with little new media based companies moving into television.

The main U.K. broadcasters have approached the Internet in markedly different ways. Channel 4 has invested in new services and has developed interactivity and a wide range of online services and has used the Internet to complement popular programming. The ITV network companies and Channel Five have invested less in the medium and have remained cautious in their expenditure on Internet sites, whose content mainly relates to entertainment and the main television schedules.

None of these broadcasters approaches the scale of investment in resources that the BBC has devoted to its Internet services. The BBC perceives itself to be a leading broadcaster in the development of new technologies and its Internet sites are widely regarded as being some of the best available for news and information. BBC Online's Web site is among the 10 most visited Web sites in the United Kingdom, has approximately 8.2 million "unique users" per quarter, and, according to KMPG, a reach of 40.5% of the population (KPMG, 2003).

The BBC first established a small range of Internet services in the mid-1990s to support key programming. In 1997, the Secretary of State for Culture, Media, and Sport approved an expansion program based on a two-stage growth plan. In 1998, after a full review of BBC services, approval was granted for Phase Two, with the BBC setting out its public service objectives for online services. BBC Online now provides a wide range of interactive services on the Internet, television, and mobile telephony. Its Internet activities focus on providing content, searching facilities and chat rooms.

Its online services are divided into three different sections: those funded from the license fee and run as public services catering to the needs of the British public, the BBC World Service is funded by a grant from the government and Beeb.com that is a commercial service aimed at international audiences, produced by the commercial arm of the BBC, BBC Worldwide, and including bbcworld.com, bbcprime.com and bbcamerica.com.

The Internet sites funded from the license fee are not allowed to carry advertising. The sites that do carry advertising are part of the BBC's commercial services and are largely targeted at audiences outside the United Kingdom. There are limits on the placing of advertisements and the BBC does not accept advertising from political, religious, and governmental organizations. Although the growth of BBC online activities is impressive in terms of the number of Web sites, it is important to keep this in the context of the BBC's overall activities. Approximately 3% of the license fee is spent on the BBC's online services, demonstrating the continued dominance of traditional activities in radio and television (Department for Culture, Media and Sport, 2004).

MEDIA DIVERSITY IN THE DIGITAL AGE

The digitalization of networks and internationalization of television players have also acted as central arguments put forward to changes to the rules and regulations pertaining to media diversity. The framework for the regulation of media ownership and market concentration consists of a number of rules that have recently undergone reform to reflect a greater degree of liberalization in ownership rules, to encourage competitiveness whilst theoretically protecting media pluralism. At the same time, what has been termed a *public interest test,* which has already been employed in the press and radio sectors in merger and acquisition decisions, has been extended to television and woven into the fabric of the overall regulatory framework at the instigation of the House of Lords, during the passage of the Communications Act of 2003.

The main changes to legislation on television ownership brought about by the Communications Act 2003, concern the withdrawal of previous restrictions and limitations. These include the removal of the upper limit of 15% audience share that one company could control, introduced in the Broadcasting Act 1996. The most controversial part of the Act was the removal of the restriction on non-European Economic Area (EEA) members owning a U.K. terrestrial television company. This allows, on the condition that the public interest test is passed, U.S. companies to acquire a U.K.-based terrestrial broadcaster for the first time.[3]

In line with the overall policy trajectory of the British government the new policy framework for media concentration is liberalizing and there appears to be a political consensus that U.K. television companies should be allowed to grow in order to take better advantage of the international television market place (and protecting its own national players) by enjoying greater economies of scale. The logic put forward for the relaxation of the ownership rules is threefold. First, the global marketplace has acted as an incentive for the government to pursue policies to encourage the U.K. broadcasters to compete on the global market—jobs and opportunities in what has been perceived to be one of the growth sectors in the modern economy have been a major source of interest to the government. Second, the costs of digitalization and the perceived importance of economies of scale for broadcasters in a digital age have received a sympathetic ear from the government. Third, the general move over the past decade to what has been coined re-regulation, and an increased focus on content rather than structural regulation.

The main commercial network, ITV, has a regional structure consisting of 15 broadcasters combining to form the ITV national network plus GMTV, which is a window channel for breakfast television. ITV was originally designed to have a regional ownership structure with limits set restricting the number of regional franchises each member of the network could control. In reality, changes in legislation and relaxation of ownership rules mean that this structure has been

---

[3]The public interest test can be employed where the transaction level is below 100 million and one of the parties has a 25% or above market share in the relevant broadcasting or newspaper sector, or for cross-media purposes. When one of these criteria is triggered, the Secretary of State can intervene where it is believed that a public interest consideration is relevant and a whole range of considerations will be addressed in any assessment based on these criteria, including the number of outlets and the audience share of the actors involved in the merger or acquisition, the availability of a wide range of quality programs, and the owners' strategic planning policy for programming. Furthermore, the standards set out in Section 319 of the Communications Act of 2003 relate to a range of obligations ranging from advertising standards to the protection of minors.

eroded by the growth of Carlton and Granada as they expanded and acquired the other network companies. In February 2004 the two companies merged their assets leaving a single company controlling the majority of the network as the 15% audience share ceiling that has traditionally restricted expansion in the sector was removed to allow companies to expand.

The merger resulted in the majority of ITV regional franchises, and all the larger ones, being owned by one company, which retains a regional remit for programming and production while it benefits from economies of scale in programming, advertising sales, and administration.

Both the BBC and Channel 4 are publicly owned. The final terrestrial free-to-air broadcaster is Channel Five, of which a majority share of 66.6% was acquired by the RTL Group from Pearson in 2000. The remaining 35.4% shareholding is owned by United Business Media. The channel has successfully carved out a market niche based on popular entertainment genres.

News Corporation is the largest shareholder of BSkyB. It effectively controls the company's activities, and its satellite activities have no competitors. Given the high initial investment costs necessary to establish a viable competitor in the area and the considerable market power of BSkyB, any real competition in the satellite market is highly unlikely. In this sense BSkyB has a monopoly in the satellite industry, and its highly successful business model has fundamentally transformed the U.K. television market over the past decade.

Since 1992, the cable industry in the United Kingdom has undergone significant consolidation as the regional licenses that were owned by 29 companies became increasingly dominated by two companies: NTL and Telewest. Even in the short period between 1997 and yearend 2003, the 13 companies that controlled 155 regional licenses decreased to two major players and a handful of minor operators. These two companies both experienced significant financial losses in their U.K. cable operations due to a combination of strong competition from satellite in the content market, the strong position of BT in the telephony market, and a general decrease in confidence in the delivery sector. Telewest and NTL finally merged to create one national cable operator in 2006.

The structures that evolved in analog broadcasting are very much evident in the digital world of television. All of the major players in the analog world are the major actors in the digital one and programming is not markedly different from the analog television environment and given that the DTT platform is essentially a free-to-air service the revenue structure for the traditional broadcasters has remained.

CONCLUSION: CONTINUITY OR CHANGE?

All of the changes in U.K. broadcasting since 1990 with the introduction of the Broadcasting Act of 1990 have been consolidated in the Communications Act of 2003. The Act represents the completion of an important shift in the policy trajectory of U.K. television and established both a position for greater coregulation of commercial television broadcasters and a light-touch approach to the regulation of the sector overall. This is a reflection on the perception that rapid change in U.K. television is to some extent inevitable given the digitalization of networks and growth in multichannel television households. It can also, however, be understood as a firm shift in the approach of both the regulator and government to media policy.

In an opposite move the BBC is becoming more tightly regulated than at any point in its history, and today is regulated by a formally separate body for the first time, the BBC Trust. The commercial broadcasters are being allowed more freedom to pursue their activities with less focus on their public service obligations. Such a divergence is important for the future regulatory approach and co-regulation of the commercial sector appears to be a plank in this approach. Technically, at least this means that commercial broadcasters will gradually take on more responsibility for their own activities and compliance to media law and as a guarantee Ofcom retains the right to reintroduce measures at some future point in time in cases where they fail to comply with these obligations.

Television regulation in the United Kingdom is conditioned by an increasingly complex range of issues which include shifting public policy objectives. The Communications Act of 2003 seeks to further liberalize the sector while holding on to the public service principles that have been fundamental in shaping the television industry and shaping these in the context of structural changes in the industry. Growing penetration of multichannel television has therefore transformed the television sector. However, although the terrestrial broadcasters' market shares have reduced overall, they retain a significant share of the market and remain central to the television landscape. The main public broadcaster, the BBC, retains a very strong position, as does the commercially funded public broadcaster Channel 4.

The repercussions of such a liberalizing instrument in the television industry are yet to be seen. It looks likely that the trends that have been so evident over the past decade will continue: competition between the main television broadcasters will increase while the public service remits of the commercial broadcasters are further relaxed.

A survey conducted as part of Ofcom's review of public service television, and published in April 2004, indicated continued popular support for public service broadcasting (Ofcom, 2004a). It also showed that the public believes the generalist free-to-air channels should provide a range of programming governed by social values, quality, range, and balance and diversity, and strongly supports programs such as news and children's strands. Furthermore, when asked whether it was important for these broadcasters to provide popular American programming, a low of 27% was recorded, suggesting a strong public preference for domestic British productions. The survey results also indicated that certain kinds of program strands such as news and drama are seen to be of high value and great social importance.

It seems likely that the public service obligations, which have traditionally been placed on commercial terrestrial broadcasters by the State, will be traded off for improved economic and financial performance by these companies. In this case, the ITV network and Channel Five would increasingly pursue commercial strategies to maximize ratings without any positive content regulations except for national, independent and regional quotas. This would inevitably put more pressure on the remaining public broadcasters, especially Channel 4 as its revenues are derived from advertising. In the worst case, the BBC and Channel 4 would be left as the only public service broadcasters.

Competition that has been evident over the past decade will further increase as the growth of multichannel television households continues to act as a powerful argument for the further reform of the present system. This having been said, public service broadcasting and free-to-air generalist television will continue to dominate the television sector for the foreseeable future at least. Supported by the government, the BBC has expanded very successfully into new media and both digital television and the Internet. Furthermore, despite continued reservations from parts of industry that the BBC should be allowed to expand into new platforms, there now appears to be far more acceptance of the fact that the BBC, as a public service broadcaster, should have a legitimate claim to expand from radio and television into new areas of content provision. There will be limits to this expansion, and these should be more clearly articulated.

The increasing concentration of ownership in the media sector generally is also a long-term concern. The liberalization of the ownership rules by the Communications Act of 2003 created the possibility that a U.S. company may own either Channel Five or ITV; if this happens, it will further change the nature of the sector and the constellations of ownership.

Perhaps the biggest threat to U.K. television and its core role for the principle of public service broadcasting is not the oft-cited developments in technology and audience fragmentation, but the continued government support for the liberalization of the sector and the subsequent reduction of a full commitment to ensuring that the institutions that have been shaped by these principles retain their remits and direction; an argument based on the development of technology in the communications sector. There seems no logical reason that public service should not be carried into the digital world by U.K. broadcasters in the traditional manner: a simple extension of public service values on to new platforms. However, the evidence as to the nature of public policy introduced by the New Labor government over the past decade suggests that there is little to suggest the social democratic values that have underpinned the development of U.K. television since the Second World War remain central to U.K. policymaking. Digital television has so far increased revenues for the industry generally with the growth of subscription. It can also be expected to spread these revenues across a broader range of channels and delivery systems something that will be the key policy issue over the next decade. As McNair (2003) has argued:

> The key economic issue is not, as many feared it would become at the height of Thatcherism, how to ensure the survival of quality journalism in the U.K., well-resourced and politically balanced, against the brutal logic of the free market and the right-wing media barons. It is how, in an intensely competitive environment, to finance the vast quantities of journalistic output now produced

across print, broadcast and online media, both public and commercially-funded, at local, national and international level, given the finite capacity of the audience to absorb and pay for it. (p. 48)

Institutions both take time to build and dismantle and the history of the BBC and its resilience has certainly protected it against the worst excesses of policy. The BBC and the whole modus operandi of British broadcasting were the result of perhaps unique historical times and some of the past is retained in the present and will undoubtedly persist into the future. In the past decades policy has perhaps been overly preoccupied with technology and developing digital platforms without any consideration as to what such a fragmented distribution network does to the traditional structures of U.K. television and its institutions. The BBC has become a key player in the digital sector largely due to the failure of the commercial sector to develop DTT and perhaps an increased recognition that the BBC's content is not only valuable in terms of filling the television schedule with a range of quality programming, but also in a strategic sphere supporting the roll out of new technologies and creating consumer demand. Despite the shifts in public policy the United Kingdom also has a strong domestic production base and according to Ofcom figures British television produces €13.1 billion in annual revenues of which €7.3 billion is spent on programs. Half of this amount is invested by the five main terrestrial broadcasters testifying to their continued central position in the sector (NSO, 2005b).

Over the past 20 years the television sector has changed dramatically in the United Kingdom and perhaps paradoxically it also remains entrenched in a large number of the traditions carried over from the past. The crucial issue is what happens when the United Kingdom has a fully digitalized television environment. A plethora of channels, a license fee that looks decidedly uncomfortable sitting alongside a technology that enables subscription, and a handful of broadcasters sharing a finite revenue base. The coming years will pose huge challenges for policymakers and the U.K. policy framework and despite its apparent novelty it looks as if it has deferred profound questions that will require some tough decisions to be made in the coming decade, increasingly relying on the market to produce the results, rather than carefully tailored policy to ensure quality and diverse television.

REFERENCES

BARB. (2007). (British Audience Research Board). Retrieved January 2007 from www.barb. co.uk

BBC. (2002). *BBC governance in the Ofcom age*. London: Author.

BBC. (2004). *Building public value: Renewing the BBC for a digital world*. BBC: London: Author.

Broadcasting Act 1990. London: Her Majesty's Stationery Office.

Broadcasting Act 1996. London: Her Majesty's Stationery Office.

Broadcasting Policy Group. (2004). *Beyond the charter: The BBC after 2006*. Broadcasting Policy Group. London: Author.

Channel 4 Television. (2004). *Report and financial statements 2003.* London: Author.

Collins, R., & Murroni, C. (1996). *New media new policies.* Polity Press.

Communications Act 2003. London: Her Majesty's Stationery Office.

Department for Culture, Media and Sport. (1999). *The future funding of the BBC. Report of the Independent Review Panel. Davies Report.* London: Author.

Department for Culture, Media and Sport. (2002). *Consultation on media ownership rules.* London: Her Majesty's Stationery Office.

Department for Culture, Media and Sport. (2003). *Review of the BBC's Royal Charter.* London: Author.

Department for Culture, Media and Sport. (2004). *Report of the Independent Review of BBC Online.* Commissioned by the Secretary of State for Media, Culture and Sport, DCMS.

Department for Culture, Media and Sport. (2005). *Review of the BBC's Royal Charter: A strong BBC, independent of government.* London: Author.

Department of National Heritage. (n.d.). *Copy of Royal Charter for the continuance of the British Broadcasting Corporation.* London: Author.

Department of Trade and Industry. (2003). *Intervention on media mergers: Draft guidance. Consultation document.* London: Author.

Enterprise Act 2002. London. London: Her Majesty's Stationery Office.

Goodwin, P. (1998). *Television under the Tories: Broadcasting policy 1979–1997.* London: Author.

Horsman, M. (1997). *Sky high: The inside story of BSkyB.* London: Orion.

Independent Television Commission. (2002). *The ITC programme guide.* London: ITC.

KPMG. (2003). *Market impact assessment of BBC's online service.* London: BBC Report.

McNair, B. (2003). What difference a decade makes. *British Journalism Review, 14*(1), 42–48.

National Statistics Office. (2005a). *Television and cinema date.* Retrieved May 20, 2005, from www.statistics.gov.uk/cci/nugget.asp?id=572

National Statistics Office. (2005b). National Statistics Omnibus Survey Access to Internet from Home. *Family expenditure survey: Expenditure and food survey.* Retrieved May 12, 2005, from www.statistics.gov.uk

Ofcom. (2004a). *Ofcom review of public service television broadcasting.* Retrieved April 2004 from www.ofcom.org.uk/consultation/current/psb/

Ofcom. (2004b). *Driving digital switchover: A report for the Secretary of State for culture, media and sport.* London: Author.

Ofcom. (2004c). *The communications market 2004.* London: Author.

Ofcom. (2004d). *Digital television update.* Retrieved January 17, 2005, from http://www.ofcom. org.uk/research/industry_market_research/m_i_index/dtvu/dtu_2004_q3/dtu_2004_q3.pdf

Ofcom. (2004e). *Review of television production sector, 2004.* Retrieved January 27, 2005, from http://www.ofcom.org.uk/research/tv/tpsr/tpsr.pdf

Ofcom. (2006). *The communications market: Digital progress report.* Retrieved December 30, 2006, from www.ofcom.org.uk/research/tv/reports/dtv/dtu_2006_q3/dtu_2006_q3.pdf

Peacock Report. (1986). *Report of the committee on financing the BBC.* London: Author.

Ward, D. (2004). *Media concentration and ownership in ten European countries: A mapping study.* Amsterdam: Commissariaat voor de Media.

PART FOUR

Southern Mediterranean/Middle East

CHAPTER FOURTEEN

Egyptian TV in the Grip of Government: Politics Before Profit in a Fluid Pan-Arab Market

Naomi Sakr
School of Media Arts and Design
University of Westminster

Television was launched in Egypt in 1960 as part of the strongly nationalist government media policy already established by Gamal Abdel-Nasser during his previous 6 years as president. As one of the Free Officers who overthrew the monarchy in 1952, Nasser acquired powerful radio transmitters in pursuit of a broadcasting project that he believed would consolidate the new regime internally and promote its interests abroad. Plans to expand into television were interrupted by the British-French-Israeli invasion in 1956. They resumed in 1959 with the award of a contract to the Radio Corporation of America (RCA), which involved a US$12.6 million subsidy according to some accounts (Dizard, 1966) but not others (Boyd, 1999). By that time Egypt had gained experience of large-scale radio broadcasting and had been producing feature-length films in abundance for 30 years (Dajani, 1980), so Egyptian television enjoyed an ample supply of locally made entertainment programming. But entertainment was seen as part of a wider mission. Nasser's agenda for postcolonial political and social change was so all-encompassing that no one in government looked at the country's broadcasting projects in a commercial light (Abu Lughod, 2005). Indeed, a government ministry took charge of Egyptian broadcasting in the early 1960s and it was called the Ministry of National Guidance (Dabous, 1994).

The perception of television as having a national propaganda function remained remarkably resilient over the next half century, persisting even into the era of pan-Arab satellite channels. Egypt's constitution empowers the president to initiate and veto legislation, and to rule by decree. In this highly centralized political system, policies are crafted within a small presidential circle. As people involved in Egypt's media industry frequently observe, members of the ruling elite have become accustomed over the decades to draw a direct link between policies on media and information on one hand and security issues on the other. For government figures targeted by assassination attempts (which includes the president Hosni Mubarak and his former long-serving information minister Safwat al-Sharif), security takes on a highly personal as well as a national dimension. This chapter assesses how far the propaganda-security paradigm has underpinned continuing tight presidential control over Egyptian television into the 21st century. It charts the government's reaction to a changing regional media landscape, in which a one-way flow of publicly funded Egyptian programming exports across the Arab region was replaced with multidirectional flows from a range of private and public sources based in Egypt and elsewhere. The chapter highlights and investigates an apparent softening of government resistance to private Egyptian-owned television channels around the year 2000, a whole decade after Egyptian State television pioneered satellite transmission of general entertainment and news programming in Arabic. It reveals multiple constraints on private commercial operations and entrenched obstacles to a public service ethic.

BUILDUP TO A POLICY BREAKTHROUGH ON OWNERSHIP

The government's use of television as a tool of domestic and foreign policy means the medium's evolution in Egypt has to be analyzed against a backdrop of geo-politics. Egypt is a populous Arab country, which, because of its size and history and the Arab region's shared language and culture, has played a central and often leading role in pan-Arab politics and media over a long period of time. It was home to a burgeoning newspaper industry during the latter half of the 19th century, when publishers and writers moved to Cairo and Alexandria to enjoy fewer restrictions than were in force in other parts of the Ottoman empire. The creation of Israel in Palestine in 1948 triggered a war in which Arab armies were defeated and the dismal performance of Egypt's political and military leaders at the time encouraged officers who had suffered under their command to revolt against the status quo. After the revolution, Nasser won acclaim in Arab and African countries for standing up to the former colonial powers by nationalizing the Suez Canal. His populist brand of Arab nationalism, spread by Egypt's Voice of the Arabs radio station, was loathed across the region by rulers to whom it posed a threat and loved by those to whom it seemed to offer salvation.

Upon adding television to its media arsenal, the Egyptian government deployed it to broadcast Nasser's speeches in their entirety to the nation. The very first program, timed to coincide with an anniversary of the 1952 revolution, included one such speech (Napoli, Amin, & Boylan, 1995, p. 21). Although television at that stage was purely terrestrial, the physical features of the Mediterranean coast are such that transmission from Cairo was available to viewers in Lebanon, Israel, and Jordan, which the Jordanian government found particularly upsetting (Dizard, 1966). News bulletins showed Nasser meeting foreign dignitaries, with news items ordered in accordance with government dictates (Boyd, 1999), conveyed by the State news agency, which had been set up in 1956 as practically the first national news agency on the African continent (Head, 1977). Egypt's crushing defeat and loss of territory in the 1967 Arab-Israeli war was all the more painful because it contrasted so sharply with the rhetoric and imagery of a proudly independent state.

Routines of television coverage and structures of control laid down under Nasser remained largely unchanged when Anwar al-Sadat, Nasser's vice-president, took over the presidency on Nasser's death in 1970. There was simply a small organizational change and a shake-up in personnel. Sadat purged his rivals from the political leadership in 1971 and put different people in charge of broadcasting in order to shore up his personal power base. Weeks before his death, Nasser had signed a decree creating the Egyptian Radio and Television Union (ERTU; Boyd, 1999). Previously, radio, television, and broadcast engineering had operated as separate departments under the Ministry of Culture and National Guidance, which became the Ministry of Information in 1969. The formation of ERTU in 1971 brought these departments together in a new self-contained entity, which was made directly accountable to the Ministry of Information. Significantly, the new entity comprised not three departments, but four. The addition of a department to deal with finance reflected the expansion of television broadcasting in other Arab countries and the growing export market for Egyptian programs. The finance department started functioning in 1973, handling program sales and collecting payments (Dajani, 1980). This was propitious timing, as the oil price explosion of 1973–1974 made Arab oil-exporting countries much richer, causing the Arab market for television content to grow still faster.

Yet Egypt's trade and media relations with other Arab States did not proceed without mishap. Sadat, buoyed by comparative success in the 1973 Arab–Israeli war and urged on by the United States, reached the Camp David accords with Israel in 1977. When he then signed a peace treaty with Israel, other Arab States decided collectively in 1979 to boycott Egypt and expel it from the Arab League. This decision was to influence the development of the Egyptian media in general, and television in particular, in several ways. One was that it prompted the Egyptian government to make plans for its own broadcasting satellite. The Arab League had already agreed on the joint Arabsat project in 1976. Expulsion from the Arab League meant expulsion from Arabsat, creating a need for Egypt to make separate satellite arrangements of its own to reach remote but strategically important parts of the country. It therefore notified the International Telecommunication Union of its intention to use the geostationary orbital slot allocated under arrangements being made at that time for developing countries to establish their own broadcast satellite services.

These early preparations were to bear fruit in the 1990s when Arab satellite broadcasting got under way. After Sadat's assassination in 1981, Egypt, under Hosni Mubarak, Sadat's former vice-president, enjoyed a gradual rapprochement with Arab

Gulf States. During Iraq's 1980–1988 war against Iran, Egypt joined Iraq's wealthy Gulf creditors in backing the war effort; it supplied military advisors and agricultural workers to Iraq (Fustier, 1997). Formal readmission to the Arab League in 1989 prompted the information minister, Safwat al-Sharif, to seek to reverse the boycott's effect on Egypt's role in regional media without delay. Although Egyptian media practitioners had been working privately for Gulf employers throughout the boycott period, Sharif wanted the country to regain public recognition as a pioneer of television programming. He proposed to do this by ensuring that Egyptian drama serials would be relevant to Arabs in general and not restricted to Egyptian affairs (El-Emary, 1996). Reentry to the Arab League took place just in time for Egypt to join the U.S.-led coalition formed to reverse Iraq's 1990 invasion of Kuwait. With its extensive television production and engineering capabilities, Egypt was quick off the mark in using Arabsat to beam programming to Egyptian troops stationed in the Gulf. In part this was a response to Iraq's use of its own and Kuwaiti radio facilities to try to sap the morale of Egyptian soldiers and fuel doubts about whose side they should be on (Amin, 1992, p. 18). Egypt's programming via Arabsat, later known as the Egyptian Space Channel (ESC), was well received by civilian populations in the Gulf and served as a launch pad for subsequent development of an array of satellite channels backed by the Egyptian State. It also provided an important impetus for the government to go ahead with Egypt's own fleet of broadcast satellites, under the name Nilesat. A contract for manufacture and launching of the first satellite in the Nilesat system was signed with Matra Marconi Space in October 1995.

Another underlying factor in policy formulation during the Arab League boycott and its aftermath was Egypt's long-standing media rivalry with Saudi Arabia. Sparked by Nasserist radio propaganda during the 1960s, this rivalry was sustained by Saudi oil money to influence media coverage across the Arab world and beyond (Aburish, 1995). Saudi Arabia was also the dominant force behind Arabsat, hosting the organization's headquarters and owning by far the largest portion of shares. Egypt's launch of ESC was soon followed by the arrival of a Saudi-backed satellite channel, the Middle East Broadcasting Center (MBC), privately owned by a brother-in-law of Saudi Arabia's King Fahd. MBC was accorded better facilities on Arabsat than ESC. This fact, combined with doubts about the lifespan of the first generation of Arabsat craft, helps to explain Egypt's determination to press ahead with its own satellite even after it had rejoined the Arab League (Sakr, 2001a). Nor was Egypt immune from the impact of Saudi money being invested inside the country in private production of television programs. The networks of personnel and overlapping interests created by this process would soon pose dilemmas for a government that staunchly refused to allow private Egyptian television channels. Saleh Kamel, a Saudi media mogul who helped to found MBC and then moved on to create his own pay TV network, called Arab Radio and Television (ART), managed to operate studios in Egypt and hire Egyptian presenters and producers, even though this put ART in competition with ESC. In 1995 the Egyptian government banned decoders for pay TV but ART overcame this hurdle by making some of its channels available free-to-air (Guaaybess, 2001). Kamel anyway had leverage inside Egypt. His partner in ART, the Saudi prince Alwaleed bin Talal, was a cofinancier of major projects with the Egyptian government. Similarly, Kamel's close association with the Adham Center for Television Journalism at the American University in Cairo won him supporters on the ground.

ART was not officially recognized as an Egyptian broadcaster, being based in Jeddah and uplinking from Italy. But its presence in Cairo, and on the television screens of Egyptian households with satellite access, contributed to mounting pressure for a dilution of the State monopoly on television ownership in Egypt. Kamel was singing the praises of private provision (Sakr, 1999) just at a time when a growing number of private Egyptian entrepreneurs were seeking a chance to further their own business and political interests via the airwaves. International Monetary Fund and World Bank credit agreements with Egypt in the wake of the 1991 Gulf war had linked cash injections to privatization of State assets, thereby reopening the field to interest groups that had been excluded since the large-scale nationalization that followed the 1952 revolution. Shafiq Gabr, head of the private Artoc group, called publicly for the creation of private Egyptian television stations in 1996 (Negus, 1997), at a moment when Egypt was about to host a U.S.-sponsored regional economic conference in Cairo. U.S. advice was consistently in favor of media privatization. It surfaced from sources such as the American Chamber of Commerce in Egypt (1996) and USAID (Napoli, Amin, & Boylan, 1995, p. 90). By 1998, there were rumors that Rami Lakah, owner of a conglomerate of some 34 Egyptian companies, was planning to set up a venture called Sphinx TV, broadcasting by satellite from Cyprus into Egypt (Mansour, personal communication, August 15, 1998). The precedent of operating from Cyprus had already been set by an offshore publishing industry aimed at the Egyptian market and a Christian satellite channel called Sat-7, aimed at Egypt's Copts. Lakah dropped his project when he ran into difficulties with Egypt's State-owned banks.

Nevertheless, the take-up of satellite technology and its use by players with different sets of interests from the Egyptian government had put the government on the defensive in its resistance to private Egyptian-owned television channels. Its defense rested on laws passed in 1979 and 1989, which reserved internal broadcasting as the exclusive right of ERTU. In 1995, after an election campaign in which President Hosni Mubarak's National Democratic Party (NDP) had dominated the media to the exclusion of other political parties (Kienle, 1998), one of those parties, the New Wafd, applied for its own broadcasting license. Its application was rejected on the grounds of the 1979 law. Yet pressure for an end to the monopoly was building—in the wider Arab region, among Egypt's new business class and opposition parties, and even within ERTU itself. Hussein Amin, a media professor at the American University in Cairo and a member of the ERTU Board of Trustees, put his name to an article in 1995 that described the shift away from State ownership as "relentless." Since the shift would happen anyway, the authors said, the government should free Egypt's private sector to compete on the regional media scene and not leave the future to be "settled by inadvertence." (Napoli, Amin, & Napoli, 1997, p. 57). This same advice was repeated by Amin, his colleagues from the Adham Centre for Television Journalism, and others, at countless public and private meetings attended by the powerful information minister at the time, Safwat al-Sharif (Sakr, 1999).

Amin and his coauthors were right to warn of a timetable being set by events beyond the government's control. When a partial but significant departure from existing policy finally came in 2000, it was a reactive, not a proactive, move. The breakthrough consisted of allowing private broadcasters, Egyptian and foreign, to operate by satellite from a designated free zone in Sixth of October City near Cairo, in an area touching two existing ERTU projects, Media Production City and the Nilesat earth station. The timing of this decision, in January 2000, immediately prompted claims that the government was simply responding to a similar initiative in Jordan out of fear of being left behind (Atia, 2000). Jordan's new King Abdullah, who succeeded his father in 1999, had instructed his government in October that year to draft legislation for a media free zone to attract investment and create jobs. Abdullah in turn was alert to the balance sheet preoccupations of Saudi-backed media ventures based in London and Rome, whose owners were seeking to cut costs by relocating to the Middle East. In Egypt's case, the timing may have had regional stimuli, but the actual decision also had a national rationale. It served not only to attract new investment but to protect the heavy outlays in satellite technology and media production facilities that the government itself had already made. By opening the way to private Egyptian broadcasters, on condition they operate by satellite, the government instantly created new customers for the large amount of free transponder space on Nilesat, as well as for the studios, film sets and uplinking facilities in Media Production City. Nilesat 101, successfully launched in 1998, was joined by Nilesat 201 in August 2000, bringing the total capacity of the two satellites to 229 digital channels (Saqr, 2004). Media Production City, a project for which land was acquired in the 1980s, was developed in stages during the 1990s and a contract for the first phase of advanced technical work was signed with an international consortium in 1998. By 2000, the project was ripe for a promotional boost.

THE LAW, THE MARKET, AND TECHNOLOGY

Having eased the ban on private, locally based television channels, the government's focus turned to keeping content and competition under control. Safwat al-Sharif stressed repeatedly in early 2000 that there was no question of handing any existing ERTU capacity over to private owners. This was despite ERTU's very considerable expansion over the years, to the point where it was providing a network of eight terrestrial channels and two separate sets of satellite channels, run by different department heads. The number of terrestrial channels had been cut from three to two in 1967 but expanded again in stages after 1985 with the addition of six channels serving different parts of the country (following the return of Israeli-occupied territory in 1982). The Egyptian Space Channel started out as a single channel in 1990, but 1994 saw the addition of Nile TV, broadcasting in English and French, followed by ESC2, an encrypted channel, in 1996. After Nilesat 101 went into orbit in 1998, one of its transponders was dedicated to a new bouquet of six digital channels offering news, drama, sport, children's shows, variety, and culture, known collectively as the Nile Thematic Channels. In other words, there was never any doubt, even after the media free zone arrangement was announced, that ERTU would remain the dominant player on the Egyptian television scene. This was guaranteed not merely by size but also by its substantial shareholdings in ventures that would be key to the operation of any potential competitor from the private sector. ERTU took 50% of the shares in Media Production City, 40% of Nilesat and 50% of Cable Network Egypt, a cable television subscription service conceived in 1989 to bring Ted Turner's Cable News Network (CNN) to Egypt's foreign visitors, including tourists, diplomats and the foreign business community. Other shareholders besides ERTU in these three ventures were mostly State-controlled or State-owned banks and investment companies.

ERTU is so vast and masks so much underemployment within the 27 stories of winding corridors at its Cairo headquarters that no one really knows how many employees it has. If part-timers are included, unofficial estimates suggest there could be 33,000 staff. A new 10-story extension to the existing Maspero building was inaugurated in June 2003, to provide even more space for production, as well as offices to publicize and market the ERTU's numerous affiliates. The inauguration was marked by decisions to increase the output of Nile News, one of the Nile Thematic Channels, to 24 hours a day and to launch a new State-run television channel aimed at eliminating illiteracy (Sabra, 2003), to add to the array of channels already broadcast from Nilesat by Egypt's health and education ministries.

Political masters of the ERTU presented its constant expansion as responsible stewardship, given the organization's legal monopoly over the establishment, ownership and control of broadcasting stations under Law No. 13 of 1979 and Law No. 223 of 1989. At the same time, they passed new laws to bolster the monopoly. Law No. 3 of 1998, which amended company law, was rammed through the NDP-dominated parliament without notice (Kienle, 2001). It stated, among other things, that any new private sector company involved in media, including television broadcasting, had to apply for specific approval from the Council of Ministers. The prime ministerial decree (No. 411 of 2000) that established the media free zone at Media Production City was based on Law No. 8 of 1997, which deals with investment incentives and guarantees. That law made free-zone activities potentially subject to intervention by the Public Authority for Investment and Free Zones (as happened in 1998 when the authority tried to ban local printing of Cyprus-registered newspapers and magazines). In the case of television companies, the combined effect of the 1997 law and the media free zone decree was to place them outside the ERTU monopoly prevailing in the rest of the country. But these companies still have to be licensed and, under Law No. 3 of 1998, the government gave itself the right to decide whether to grant a license.

Where the go-ahead has been given, one condition seems to have been that licensees must accept one or more government institutions as minority shareholders. Thus, for example, the ERTU holds a 10% share in Dream TV (Shehab, 2002) and its share in Al-Mehwar TV has been variously reported at 20% (U.S. State Department, 2005) and 5% (Saleh, 2003). Additionally, Nilesat and Media Production City are said to have holdings of 5 to 6% in "many" of the channels they work with (Hamdy, 2002a). It is also understood that any news broadcasts by private channels must rely on news output from the ERTU. With the concession on private television limited to satellite transmission, several business leaders who had expressed interest in television broadcasting declined to apply for a license. They doubted the profitability of a channel that would be available only to the minority of Egyptian viewers with satellite access and might therefore not be able to count on sufficient advertising revenue (Kandil, 2000). When asked to comment on the media free zone in a press interview, Naguib Sawiris, a major investor in telecoms, cinema and other sectors in Egypt, replied:

[W]hat's the big news here? Why does the government keep the monopoly of terrestrial broadcasting to itself? What harm would befall the government if they allow us to have a terrestrial channel in Assiut, for example? Someone should answer this question. Are they afraid that we're going to broadcast anti-government stuff? They can close it down. Are they questioning our nationalism? I don't know any other group that has more investments in Egypt. So are we going to be the ones harming Egypt? Where's the problem? [T]hey keep the terrestrial channels because these are very cheap, and they tell you go and invest in satellite. I can do that anywhere. (Howeidy, 2000)

By late 2004, nearly 5 years after the government created the media free zone, six private Egyptian broadcasters had made use of the concession. For the 32% of Egypt's 15.1 million households reportedly able to receive transmissions from Nilesat in 2004 (Saqr, 2004), the eight channels supplied by these six private companies represented a very tiny proportion of the 124 channels available free-to-air from Nilesat at that time. Of these, the ERTU alone accounted for at least 26. Others included such well-known names from across the Arab world as Al-Jazeera from Qatar, Al-Arabiya and MBC from Dubai, several Lebanese channels, Al-Hurra from the United States, and an array of smaller channels specializing in music, religion, youth interests, home shopping, fashion and children's cartoons. The private Egyptian competitors to enter this crowded field were Dream and Melody, both occupying two channels each, along with Al-Mehwar, Mazzika, El Tamima Shopping Channel, and the Egyptian tourism channel, MTC. Of these, Al-Mehwar was the first to put itself forward, although not the first to start. This company described its broadcasting mission as expressing the voice of Egyptian civil society. Formed in 2000 by some 60 shareholders, mainly business people and media stars, it began transmission in February 2002, relying for part of its output on programs from Nile News (Saleh, 2003). Three years into its existence, Al-Mehwar had failed to establish a consistent identity, partly perhaps because of being obliged to transmit by satellite. Instead of serving an Egyptian audience, Al-Mehwar looked further afield to a pan-Arab public, emulating a range of existing channels and programs rather than trying to establish its own niche.

Its closeness to government was clear from the guest list and prizes awarded at its third anniversary celebrations in May 2005.

Dream TV, launched in late 2001, took a more commercial approach, which landed it in political trouble. Dream was the brainchild of Ahmad Bahgat, one of Egypt's leading industrialists with around 28 factories producing furniture, household appliances, and consumer electronics, including televisions and video recorders. In 1996, Bahgat had laid the foundations for an ambitious residential and leisure complex, under the name Dreamland, not far from Media Production City. Reports put the value of this venture at US$2.6 billion (Butter, 1999). Interviewed on one of his own channels in November 2002, Bahgat explained why he had decided to invest in broadcasting. The Bahgat Group was spending about £E40 million a year (around US$8.6 million at 2002 exchange rates) on advertising, he said, so he might as well spend the same amount on his own television station, where his companies' goods and services could be advertised free of charge (Shehab, 2002). Bahgat's team were serious about appealing to a big audience. Aiming their output at Egypt's younger generation, they started Dream 1 with music videos, live concerts and celebrity interviews, followed by Dream 2, screening talk shows and interviews hosted by high-profile presenters plucked from other channels. Hala Sirhan, who joined Dream from the Saudi-owned ART, saw an opportunity for Dream to achieve credibility with viewers by offering unfettered analysis of news (Hamdy, 2002b). Other personalities joined for similar reasons (Osman, 2004). The authorities were alarmed. After an eventful week in late 2002, during which one of Sirhan's talk shows had discussed sexual matters and Mohammed Hassanein Heikal had dared to voice concerns that Hosni Mubarak's son might succeed him as president, Dream TV received a warning from the Public Authority for Free Zones. It was told that unduly sensational content could jeopardize its license (Middle East Online, 2002).

This was not the first time that occupants of Media Production City had been admonished to control their output (Sakr, 2005a). Nor was it the end of trouble for Dream. State ownership of Egypt's four biggest banks had traditionally given the government the upper hand over private investors who are forced to deal with the banks. This in turn has given competing investors a stick with which to beat each other when they choose. An opposition newspaper seized on Hala Sirhan's taboo-breaking talk show to protest that Bahgat's bank credit was paying for offensive material. Bahgat, while rejecting the allegation, took a more cautious approach from then on. He parted company with two presenters, including Sirhan, and cancelled programs by popular outspoken personalities.

Egypt's other private channels, being focused on tourism and music, generally avoided such problems. But even these areas can be controversial. One favorite bugbear has been the nontraditional behavior of women performers in music video, known in the Arab world as "video clips." Another has been protection of public access to Egyptian libraries of music and film, where the government has been accused of an excessively laissez-faire approach. Whereas Melody TV led on Western hits, Mazzika TV provided an outlet for Arabic songs. It was launched from within a large conglomerate, enjoying cross-ownership links with the private

Saudi-owned broadcaster ART. Mazzika, owned by Alam al-Phan, is owned in turn by Founoon Holding, established by Cairo-based EFG-Hermes in 2000. Founoon Holding, which counts seven record companies under its umbrella, was set up to buy intellectual property rights held by the Egyptian Ministry of Culture in the work of some of Egypt's best-loved singers and filmmakers. EFG-Hermes came in for criticism in 2004 when it emerged that, through Founoon, it had sold rights to 3,200 Egyptian films to Rotana, a company owned by Saudi Arabia's Prince Alwaleed bin Talal, part-owner of ART (Sherif, 2004). Taken together with earlier purchases of Egyptian film by ART's Saleh Kamel during the 1990s, the 2004 sale was said to mean that two thirds of the country's cinematic heritage was now under Saudi ownership. It underlined shared ownership interests between Rotana and Alam al-Phan and seemed to explain the volume of Rotana advertising on Mazzika TV (Assir, 2004).

It is interesting to note that the government itself had introduced music television into Egypt in 1993, in the shape of Viacom's MTV. It did so as a damage limitation measure after its policy of imposing ERTU involvement on all television ventures on Egyptian territory went wrong. Cable News Egypt, which later became Cable Network Egypt (CNE), started as a private initiative to receive and distribute CNN at a time when Egypt had virtually no satellite dishes. The ERTU, having insisted on a 50% share, went along with a promotion campaign in which the supposedly fee-paying service was provided free for several weeks at the precise moment of the 1991 Gulf war, before the encrypted service was ready to be launched (Foote, 1998). By the time CNE was ready for serious business, the war had prompted a rapid spread of satellite take-up across the region, making CNN available free-to-air and removing CNE's original *raison d'etre*. In order to salvage the project, MTV was added to the package. Multichoice, the South African giant, then undertook to relaunch CNE, adding a bouquet supplied by Showtime, a Viacom subsidiary. In 1995, the Egyptian government put its weight behind the relaunch by banning imported decoders other than those authorized by the ERTU, on grounds of the ERTU monopoly on transmission as laid down under Law No. 13 of 1979 (BBC Summary of World Broadcasts, 1995). Although the ban was a boost for CNE, it also primed the market for the impending arrival of digital services from Nilesat, which was ordered from Matra Marconi that same year.

The decision to go for digital technology on Nilesat was in keeping with the traditional high standing of engineers within Egypt's broadcasting sector. Throughout half a century of radio and television after 1952, engineers had little trouble convincing managers of the importance of up-to-date transmission technology (Boyd, 1999). By opting for digital compression, the Ministry of Information ensured that Nilesat 101 and 102 would be ready to accommodate hundreds of channels before Arabsat caught up. The first of the digital Arabsat craft went into orbit in 1999, a year after Nilesat 101. Nilesat's capacity made it suitable for use by multichannel pay TV providers, notably ART and Showtime Egypt. When these two operators each reserved two transponders on Nilesat, they also found they had a reason to join the ERTU and CNE in promoting the sale of digital set-top boxes suited to either encrypted or unencrypted reception. The Arab Organization for Industrialization, holder of a 10% stake in Nilesat, set about making the boxes, while the National Bank of Egypt, owner of 7.5% of Nilesat and 5% of Media Production City, teamed up with CNE to offer hire-purchase arrangements to facilitate their sale (Sakr, 1999; Sakr, 2001a). Collecting subscriptions for pay TV remained a headache in a country unaccustomed to credit cards. But private pay TV providers learned to benefit from a ready supply of labor and organized door-to-door rounds to collect payment. Immediately after the launch of Nilesat 101 in 1998, satellite penetration in Egypt was still in single digits. From 2000, the figure started to rise. In part, this was driven by hunger for Arabic-language coverage of events such as the Palestinian uprising that erupted in September 2000, and the U.S.-led bombing of Afghanistan and Iraq after the 9/11 terrorist attacks. In part, it seems to have been driven by the emergence of private Egyptian channels, starting in 2001. Together these factors helped to push penetration of digital satellite reception to an estimated 24% of households in 2003 and 32% in 2004 (Saqr, 2004). Talk of analog switch-off is consequently no longer far-fetched. As of 2005, however, digital transmission of terrestrial television was only under informal discussion.

STRUGGLES OVER PUBLIC BROADCASTING, MEDIA FREEDOM, AND TV FINANCE

Officially, ERTU is a public body. In practice it is an appendage of government, being directly accountable to the minister of information, who chairs the ERTU Board of Trustees. This arrangement has been in force for so long that the meanings of "State," "public," and "government" have become fused in Egyptian everyday discourse about rights and responsibilities in media systems. A typical statement by a member of ERTU management can illustrate this. Soheir Hafez, deputy director of news at ERTU, told two reporters in 2003: "TV is State-owned and thus represents the views and policies of the government" (Shahine & Sabra, 2003). Underlying her statement is an assumption that "State" ownership authorizes the government to represent itself, rather than requiring it to arrange for full and pluralistic representation of the people. Independently regulated public service broadcasting is unfamiliar to Arab audiences, including those who respect the BBC, because the BBC they listen to is not funded by the British license fee payer but by the British Foreign Office. Egyptian audiences have thus developed a dichotomous understanding of media systems, in which the only conceivable media owners are either governments or private entrepreneurs. The government in turn legitimates its privileged media position by framing it in terms of a responsibility—that of representing Egypt as a harmonious, cohesive, open, and modern society built on an ancient civilization enriched by Islamic teaching and traditions. This message about the country's merits, and the importance of reflecting them through the media, has been repeated time and again at the level of information minister, ERTU director and ERTU department heads. It is backed up by loosely worded articles of the Egyptian Penal Code and the Emergency Law, together with a list of 33 prohibitions for broadcasting personnel set out in the ERTU Code of Ethics.

The Emergency Law, in force almost continuously since 1981, authorizes censorship and detention in the name of security. Parliament renewed it yet again in February 2003 for a 3-year period to end in May 2006. Under the law, security is interpreted very widely, according to a model that Egyptian officials say Western countries should follow to prevent attacks like those of September 2001 (Singerman, 2002). In this security-conscious environment, open discussion of intercommunal tensions, instead of being welcomed as a means to defuse them, is deemed a threat and is disallowed. Mamdouh Beltagi, who briefly replaced Safwat al-Sharif as information minister in 2004–2005, axed a television series about a 1940s relationship between a Christian woman and a Muslim man. To the consternation of local writers, Beltagi insisted the subject matter undermined national unity (*Middle East Times,* 2005). Topics are also taboo if they are felt to "harm Egypt's image," an offense that is criminalized by Article 80[d] of the Penal Code. The Penal Code imposes a host of penalties to deter scrutiny of a whole range of officials and institutions. Yet, as Awad al-Mor, a former chief justice of the Supreme Constitutional Court, pointed out on the 50th anniversary of the 1952 revolution, Article 80[d] is central in blocking progress to democratization. According to Mor, the article effectively outlaws any criticism of government, which makes it little different from the pre-1952 crime of dishonoring the person of the king (Kassem, 2004). Equally vague and all-embracing wording is found in the ERTU Code of Ethics. This prohibits the broadcasting of material that criticizes the State system or State officials, criticizes social traditions or values, creates "social confusion" or risks causing "depression" or a "spirit of defeat" (Napoli, Amin, & Boylan, 1995, pp. 171–172).

Given these restrictions, it is hardly surprising that ERTU television producers and reporters have so often refrained from covering matters of prime importance to the Egyptian public, in either entertainment or news, for fear of breaking the rules. The list of omissions shows that, while standards of news reporting in Arabic were evolving in other organizations, ERTU coverage lagged way behind (Sakr, 2005b). When armed militants massacred tourists and others in Luxor in 1997, ERTU showed Luxor residents donating blood for the wounded, but avoided analysis of why and how the killings occurred (Buccianti, 1997). When EgyptAir Flight 990 crashed into the Atlantic in 1999, ERTU initially avoided reporting it all (Negus, 1999). While Arab satellite stations beamed live coverage of the start of the U.S.-led invasion of Iraq in March 2003, Egypt's State television ran a medical program on heartburn (Drees, 2003). Yet even these shaming experiences failed to trigger prompt reporting of the Taba bombings in October 2004. Viewers who saw those scenes of carnage on satellite channels kept flipping back to Egyptian terrestrial television in vain to find out more. A news ticker that finally appeared suggested that the explosion at Taba might have been caused by a gas leak (Atia, 2004). Egypt's few independent newspapers reacted furiously in April 2005, when ERTU remained silent for a full 2 and a half hours after Al-Jazeera had reported a suicide bombing in Cairo. Instead of making its own package on the incident, State television eventually rebroadcast an item from MBC (Levinson, 2005a). Investigating the delay, *Al-Masry al-Yaum* said the director of ERTU's

News Department, the only person authorized to clear the news item, had switched off his mobile phone. With so much attention paid to the failings of State media, even some NDP officials started to recommend that State television should report on demonstrations calling for an end to Mubarak's presidency (Levinson, 2000a).

ERTU reticence on key national issues helps to explain why Egyptian viewers regard private ownership, rather than public television, as the only route to representing the public interest. Dream TV has lent credence to this view. In February 2002, soon after launching, it provided a forum for expression of public outrage at a fire that had killed 400 people on an Egyptian train. Al-Jazeera, the leading pan-Arab satellite 24-hours news channel, has benefited from a public service ethic adopted by those of its staff with experience of working for public service broadcasters outside the Arab world. Like Dream, it has probed local Egyptian issues that the ERTU ignored. Yet, even viewers of Al-Jazeera have not been alerted to the crucial distinction between public sector television and public service television, because they are conscious that the ruler of Qatar is the main source of funding for Al-Jazeera. Irrespective of labels, however, Arab audiences have switched in large numbers to those television channels that seem to meet their information and entertainment needs. Detailed statistical evidence to prove this is sparse, because credible statistics tend not to serve the agendas of powerful interest groups, who invest in broadcasting for their own political purposes and not primarily for commercial gain. Both the Egyptian and pan-Arab television advertising markets are distorted by entrenched politicization of programming policies and disbursement of advertising budgets, as demonstrated by a long-running Saudi-led boycott of Al-Jazeera (Sakr, 2005a). That boycott was in force at a time when most available surveys credited Al-Jazeera with being the most widely watched channel. One study commissioned by Nilesat in July 2003 put Dream 1 and Dream 2 in the top four channels, with Al-Jazeera occupying first place and MBC2 coming third. These rankings were based on aggregated data for Egypt and four other Arab States (Amin, 2004).

It has long been recognized within ERTU that Egypt's State broadcaster must become more responsive to viewers in order to survive in a competitive market, where an increasing number of Egyptian households with satellite access can choose among a growing range of pan-Arab channels. Enterprising individuals inside and outside the organization have tried to steer it in this direction. Hassan Hamed, appointed as the first head of the Nile Thematic Channels, tried initially to decouple them completely from the ERTU (Sakr, 2001b). When that failed, he managed to keep Nile News separate from the ERTU News Department, thereby giving its young recruits some autonomy and a chance to gain insights into international standards and practices of news gathering. Working on the periphery of State television as a private provider of news footage through his company Video Cairo Sat, Mohammed Gohar applied his experience in U.S. television to develop Nile News programming, before turning his attention to Al-Mehwar (Hamdy, 2002c). Some who bemoan the political constraints on ERTU programming attribute them in part to the advanced age of Egypt's political leadership.

It has been said that the country's "gatekeepers, especially in late age groups, cannot recognize and realize the importance of moving into the information age in order to close the gap between the North and the South" (Amin & Napoli, 2000, p. 185).

President Mubarak, himself aged 77 as he prepared to run for a fifth, 6-year term in office in 2005, appeared to share this diagnosis. Reshuffling his cabinet from a hospital bed in Germany in July 2004, he brought in a 52-year-old prime minister, Ahmad Nazief, who had earned a reputation for integrity, efficiency, and fresh thinking during a stint as minister of telecommunications and information technology. The 2004 reshuffle appeared to mark the end of an era at the Ministry of Information. Safwat al-Sharif, holder of the post for 23 years, was replaced by Mamdouh al-Beltagi, a former minister of tourism with experience of heading the State Information Service. Beltagi's tenure was short. In February 2005 he was replaced by the 44-year-old Anas al-Fiqi, a former youth minister with a degree in business administration, who once worked as marketing manager for a U.K.-based publishing firm. Like many Egyptian ministers before them, Nazief and Fiqi spoke the language of reform. Nazief told Reuters that he thought candidates standing against Mubarak in the 2005 presidential election should have equal airtime on State television. Yet rhetoric and practice remained far apart in April that year, as State television denied advertising slots to the only opposition party known to be fielding a candidate (Levinson, 2005a) and set aside several hours for a carefully-staged, three-part television interview with Mubarak (Schemm, 2005).

Perhaps the most daunting challenge facing any newcomer seeking to narrow the gap between reform rhetoric and reality in Egypt's television sector was the size of ERTU's deficit. Officially estimated at a cumulative £E4 billion (US$690 million) in 2004, and increasing at a rate of £E800 million (US$138 million) per year (Samih, 2004), this deficit was incurred in spite of the ERTU's built-in privileges, such as the right to cream off advertising revenues and gain cheap, or even free, access to programs made by broadcasters based in Media Production City. Unlike some public broadcasters, the ERTU does not benefit from a license fee. Radio license fees were dropped during the Nasser years, when set ownership was being encouraged and taxes were anyway difficult to collect (Boyd, 1999). But it has been able to monopolize advertising spending by other State bodies and offer massive discounts to divert advertisements away from other broadcasters. Although factors such as a slide in the value of the Egyptian pound deterred smaller broadcasters from attending international events like the Mipcom Market in Cannes, ERTU's reliance on State guarantees allowed it to return year after year. Although smaller players could not risk running up debts with international suppliers, ERTU reportedly built up arrears over 2 years (Fine, 2003). Despite all these advantages the sprawling conglomerate with a monopoly on terrestrial broadcasting in the Arab world's most populous country was so deeply in deficit in 2005 that its ability to motivate staff through decent salaries or invest in trendsetting programs was seriously in doubt. Political constraints on content had put it in this situation and, whatever the good intentions and expertise of some new department heads, only the removal of those constraints by a higher authority could pull it out.

CONCLUSION

Regional influences have shaped media policy in Egypt for generations and the story of television policy over recent decades has proved no different in that respect. In some ways, these influences have been benign for an Egyptian public so long denied the opportunity to select or change its government or register preferences regarding national policy. The Arab region's shared culture and language ensured that public and private responses to new television technology—from transnational broadcasting to digitalization—would enliven regional dynamics of communication and disturb the status quo. One consequence of this interaction, examined in this chapter, was the Egyptian government's belated concession allowing private broadcasting in Egypt under certain strict conditions. But it was a small concession, and one which may well have dissipated some of the mounting pressure for more fundamental structural change. By resisting such change, the government held on to control over the State-funded broadcasting conglomerate, which, in turn, retained its monopoly over terrestrial transmission and kept a grip on all broadcasting output, both public and private, through its ownership of production facilities and the means of distribution.

Questions about the ability of any Egyptian television channel to serve the public interest surfaced repeatedly in 2005, in the run-up to that year's presidential and legislative elections. By that time, existing arrangements had left State channels bereft of credibility and income and demonstrated to private channels the dangers of airing uncensored content. Yet, given an ineluctable link in television between viewership and finance, it seemed the government-controlled ERTU had reached a policy crossroads. Either its dire financial situation would frighten ERTU managers into trying to bulldoze their way to survival by tightening their stranglehold on advertising revenue and crushing competitors through ever-increasing demands imposed on companies using ERTU-owned facilities. Or they could seek to compete fairly by meeting public demand for relevant programs, which would mean acknowledging the depth of public dissatisfaction with the status quo. Pending a shake-up in the country's political leadership, the most likely scenario was for the vast ERTU, with all its internal contradictions, to try to do a bit of both.

REFERENCES

Abu Lughod, L. (2005). *Dramas of nationhood: The politics of television in Egypt.* Chicago: University of Chicago Press.

Aburish, S. K. (1995). *The rise, corruption and coming fall of the House of Saud.* London: Bloomsbury.

American Chamber of Commerce in Egypt. (1996). The role of the private sector. In M. M. Giugale & H. Mobarak. (Eds.), *Private sector development in Egypt* (pp. 29–44). Cairo: American University in Cairo Press.

Amin, H. (1992). The development of Spacenet and its impact. In R. Weisenborn (Ed.), *Media in the midst of war: The Gulf war from Cairo to the global* (pp. 15–20). Cairo: Adhaim Center Press.

Amin, H. (2004). Nilesat: Current challenges and future trends. *Transnational Broadcasting Studies No. 12*. Available online at tbsjournal.com

Amin, H., & Napoli, J. (2000). Media and power in Egypt. In J. Curran & M-J. Park (Eds.), *De-Westernizing media studies* (pp. 178–188). London: Routledge.

Assir, S. (2004). Big bucks, big labels. *Al-Ahram Weekly, 723*. Retrieved June 26, 2005, from www.weekly.ahram.org/eg/2004/723/fe1.htm

Atia, T. (2000). Private media push and pull. *Al-Ahram Weekly, 470*. Retrieved February 26, 2000, from www.weekly.ahram.org/eg/2000/470/feat2.htm

Atia, T. (2004). Aiming for extinction? *Al-Ahram Weekly, 712*. Retrieved May 10, 2005, from www.weekly.ahram.org.eg/2004/712/eg4.htm

BBC Summary of World Broadcasts. (1995). Translation of Egyptian radio report from Cairo on July 17. *BBC SWB ME/2359 MED/16*, 19 July.

Boyd, D. A. (1999). *Broadcasting in the Arab world: A Survey of the electronic media in the Middle East* (3rd ed.). Ames, IA: Iowa State University Press.

Buccianti, A. (1997). Louxor vu du Caire. *Le Monde, 20*.

Butter, D. (1999, April 2). A hint of Florida comes to Cairo. *Middle East Economic Digest*, p. 2.

Dabous, S. (1994). Egypt. In Y. R. Kamalipour & H. Mowlana (Eds.), *Mass media in the Middle East* (pp. 60–73). Westport, CT: Greenwood Press.

Dajani, K. F. (1980). *Egypt's role as major media producer, supplier and distributor to the Arab world: An historical descriptive study*. Unpublished doctoral dissertation, University of Michigan, Ann Arbor.

Dizard, W. P. (1966). *Television: A world view*. Syracuse, NY: Syracuse University Press.

Drees, C. (2003, April 25). Iraq war challenges boring State TV. *Middle East Times*. Retrieved April 27, 2003, from www.metimes.com/2k3/issue2003-17/eg/iraq_war_challenges.htm

El-Emary, N. (1996). L'industrie du feuilleton television Égyptien à l'ère des télévisions trans-frontières [The Egyptian television serials industry in the age of gransnational television]. *Revue Tiers Monde, 37*, 251–262.

Fine, J. (2003). Egyptian TV markets globally at Mipcom market. *Transnational Broadcasting Studies No. 11*. Available at www.tbsjournal.com

Foote, J. (1998). CNE in Egypt: Some light at the end of an arduous tunnel. Available at www.tbsjournal.com

Fustier, N. (1997). L'Egypte dans son environnement proche-oriental [Egypt in its Middle Eastern environment]. *Les Cahiers de l'Orient, 45*, 137–147.

Guaaybess, T. (2001). Restructuring Television in Egypt: the position of the State between regional supply and local demand. In K. Hafez (Ed.), *Mass media, politics and society in the Middle East* (pp. 61–75). Cresskill, NJ: Hampton Press.

Hamdy, N. (2002a). Latest tenants at EMPC: Private Egyptian channels and a one million-dollar show. Available at www.tbsjournal.com

Hamdy, N. (2002b). A dream TV come true. Available at www.tbsjournal.com

Hamdy, N. (2002c). El Mehwar the mercurial. Available at www.tbsjournal.com

Head, S. W. (1977). Trends in tropical African societies. In G. Gerbner (Ed.), *Mass media policies in changing cultures* (pp. 83–103). New York: Wiley.

Howeidy, A. (2000). Interview with Naguib Sawiris. *Al-Ahram Weekly*, 481, 11–17 May. Retrieved May 20, 2005, from www.weekly.ahram.org/eg/2000/4891/intrvw.htm

Kandil, H. (2000). ERTU, investors at odds over media privatisation. Available at www.tbsjournal.com

Kassem, M. (2004). *Egyptian politics: The dynamics of authoritarian rule*. Boulder, CO: Lynn Rienner.

Kienle, E. (1998). More than a response to Islamism: The political deliberalization of Egypt in the 1990s. *Middle East Journal. 52/2*, 291–235.

Kienle, E. (2001). *A grand delusion: Democracy and economic reform in Egypt.* London: I. B. Tauris.

Levinson, C. (2005a). NDP leaders criticize State television. *The Arabist Network.* June 29. Retrieved June 30, 2005, from www.arabist.net/archives/2005/06/29/691/

Levinson, C. (2005b). Arab TV on the campaign trail in Egypt, Iraq, and Palestine. Available at www.tbsjournal.com

Middle East Online. (2002). Dream TV in trouble over program. Retrieved November 20, 2002, from meotv/english/culture/?id=3-78=3-89

Middle East Times. (2005, January 12). Egyptian television censors sharpen their knives. *Middle East Times.* Retrieved January 15, 2005, from www.metimes.com/2k5/issue2005-2/eg

Napoli, J., Amin, H., & Boylan, R. (1995). *Assessment of the Egyptian Print and electronic media.* Report submitted to the United States Agency for International Development, Cairo.

Napoli, J., Amin, H., & Napoli, L. (1997). Privatization of the Egyptian Media. *Journal of South Asian and Middle Eastern Studies, 7(4),* 4, 39–57.

Negus, S. (1997, January 10). TV wars. *Middle East International,* p. 9.

Negus, S. (1999, November 12). Season of disasters. *Middle East International,* pp. 12–13.

Osman. A. (2004). Rude awakening: Dream drops top talkers. Available at www.tbsjournal.com

Sabra, H. (2003). Big plans for Egyptian broadcasting. *Al-Ahram Weekly, 642,* pp. 12–18. Retrieved June 6, 2005, from www.weekly.ahram.org/eg/2003/642/eg3.htm

Sakr, N. (1999). *The making and implementation of Egyptian policy towards satellite television broadcasting.* Unpublished doctoral dissertation, University of Westminster, London.

Sakr, N. (2001a). *Satellite realms: Transnational television, globalization and the Middle East.* London: I. B. Tauris.

Sakr, N. (2001b). Contested blueprints for Egypt's satellite channels. *Gazette, 63/2–3,* 149–167.

Sakr, N. (2005a). Maverick or model? Al-Jazeera's impact on Arab satellite television. In J. Chalaby (Ed.), *Transnational television worldwide: Towards a new media order* (pp. 66–95). London: I. B. Tauris.

Sakr, N. (2005b). The changing dynamics of Arab journalism. In H. de Burgh (Ed.), *Making journalists* (pp. 142–156). London: Routledge

Saleh, I. (2003). *Unveiling the truth about the Middle Eastern media.* Cairo: University of Modern Sciences and Arts.

Samih, M. (2004). *Beltagi honours Safwat al-Sharif and Howaidy and Abul-Magd. Al-Izaa w'al-telefiziyun* [radio and television]. August, 7, pp. 9–10.

Saqr, L. (2004, November). *Presentation on Nilesat.* Delivered at Media Production City, Cairo,

Schemm, P. (2005). Presidential démarche. *Middle East International, 749(29),* 10–11.

Shahine, G., & Sabra, H. (2003). Making waves on air. *Al-Ahram Weekly.* Retrieved May 10, 2005, from www.weekly.ahram.org/eg/2003/640/eg10.htm

Shehab, S. (2002). Dream's wake-up call? *Al-Ahram Weekly,* 611, 2–13 November.

Sherif, Y. (2004). The end. *Middle East Times.* Retrieved March 28, 2004, from www.metimes.com/2k4/issue2004-13/eg/end_ve.htm

Singerman, D. (2002). The politics of emergency rule in Egypt. *Current History, 101/651.*

U.S. State Department. (2005). *Egypt country report on human rights practices 2004.* Washington: U.S. State Department, Bureau of Democracy, Human Rights and Labour.

CHAPTER FIFTEEN

The Politics of Broadcasting in Iran: Continuity and Change, Expansion and Control

Gholam Khiabany
London Metropolitan University

Many of the recent studies of "global media" have focused on television; its expansion and reach are a clear indication and evidence of the end of national media. Yet television has remained a national medium and even the advocates of globalization inevitably use "national" examples to map out the emergence of the new global media environment. There are good reasons for such nationally focused studies. Languages as well as political and cultural frameworks, among other things, remain overwhelmingly national. Yet across the southern hemisphere and in countries with few resources, television has been a complex blend of the national and global. It has been nationally organized, financed, and controlled, either through direct State intervention or family media businesses, which have sought power and profits via political connections and patronage. However, as Bourdon (2004) argues the "interaction between nations has been a key part of television history" (p. 94) in three significant areas—first, through interaction in policy. Developing countries in particular have adopted policy frameworks from other nations, usually the former colonial master. Second, through interaction and exchanges of technologies, again from the most advanced countries of the north to the south. And finally, through program sales and flows that, for most part, have been unidirectional, an area of research that is far more developed and documented in international communications research.

For Bourdon, however, such interactions do not indicate the demise of the nation-state, but its transformation. The significance of the State in advancing the tenets of the market and facilitating the globalization of free market capitalism demonstrate that the nation-state clearly still remains the primary actor in engineering political legitimacy. Artz suggests that as individual States re-regulate in favor of big business and set about removing the remaining barriers to international production, distribution and consumption, they are redefining their traditional roles (2003, pp. 4–6). It is exactly this reconfiguration of State power and role that should be the focus of attention, not the decline of the nation-state, which is ironically celebrated alongside the rise of "nationalism."

This chapter focuses on the relationship between the media and State in Iran and suggests that any serious assessment of the nature of the Iranian media needs to take into account the structure and the continuing attempts of the Islamic regime to maintain its monopoly over physical and symbolic violence. The chapter analyzes the continuing relevance of the State in general and in Iran in particular by examining the formation of the Islamic State in Iran, its governing institutions, and its constitution in general. The main aim of this chapter is to assess the role of the State in media policymaking in Iran and to construct a model that reflects the complex relationship between the State and the media. It will examine the contradictory nature of the State in Iran by moving beyond the liberal theory of the media that focuses only on the repressive role of the State, and examine the Iranian State as the site of struggle between competing forces and interests. In addition, I assess its continuing attempts to redefine itself at a time of further restructuring of global capital and the integration of Iran into "global modernities," where Iran is caught, as are many other states, between the "logic of capital" and the "logic of territory" (Harvey, 2003).

TELEVISION IN IRAN BEFORE THE REVOLUTION

Robins and Webster (1985) have argued the spread of Social Taylorism was an important variable in the formation of television: "It is in the context of an extending and encroaching corporate activity which required the best possible regulation of sales achievable that television should be placed since it was both shaped by and responded to these trends" (p. 37). The early years of television in Iran are a case in point, where unlike many European ex-colonies; the adopted pattern was not the public-national model, but the then-exceptional commercial system of the United States. It was no accident that it was Habibolah Sabet that brought television to Iran. The Sabets were the most influential of a limited number of families that dominated the booming Iranian economy. Through his Firouz Trading Company, Sabet came to dominate the domestic consumer market. A graduate of Harvard University, he held the franchise for international brands such as Electrolux, Kelvinator, Westinghouse, General Electric, Volkswagen, General Tyres, and Pepsi-Cola. He was also the RCA representative and sold the television sets that were receivers for his programs and commercials for products that he was producing and selling (Sreberny-Mohammadi & Mohammadi, 1994). Unlike other forms of communication, including radio and the telegraph, television was introduced by the private sector after a favorable parliamentary bill was passed in June 1958. A single television channel, which reached only a few major cities followed soon after in October, introduced by a mandatory opening speech from the Shah. As Sreberny-Mohammadi and Mohammadi (1994) have argued, Television of Iran, which was run by an American, was the first commercial television in the region. Much of the output of the early years of Television of Iran consisted of imported U.S. programs, with some domestic production that was itself heavily influenced by American formats. Iran's national news agency, Pars, provided the domestic news, and the United States Information Service provided the international news. Pan American Airlines sponsored the news bulletins. Television soon became the most sought after domestic technology, and with the support and blessing of the Shah it began to serve the interests of private capital in Iran through advertising and the rapid spread of consumerism.

The Shah began to recognize the potential of television as a political tool and ordered the creation of a second network in 1966. Iranian television began to expand rapidly and for a while the two channels, one owned and operated by private capital and the other owned and controlled by the State, were broadcasting mostly American programs to major cities in Iran, side by side. Fearful of the possibility of any autonomous base of power, the Shah's government took over Sabet's operation. Television of Iran was nationalized and merged with the State channel. By 1971 the State had restructured both radio (which had been run since 1964 by the Ministry of Information) and television and incorporated them as a public broadcasting monopoly (Sreberny-Mohammadi & Mohammadi, 1994; Tunstall, 1977). The new organization was named NIRT (National Iranian Radio and Television) and Reza Ghotbi, a cousin of the queen and a trusted member of the court, was appointed as its first (and last) director general.

Establishing television, as with a national news agency, was regarded as a sign of progress, independence, and nation building. Bourdon (2004) has argued that the gap between potential coverage and actual reception in the southern hemisphere can partly be explained "by the fact that television was first of all a symbol for other states to see, not a means of communication—a place which foreign heads of state could visit, not programs for all citizens to view" (p. 98). This was undoubtedly true in the case of NIRT, which was used as a tool to gather support for dependent development and modernization and, above all, to consolidate the Shah's power by broadcasting lavish royal ceremonies and festivals in which he played a central part. The sole intention of such programming was to stress the "glorious" tradition of the monarchy and dynastic continuity. Mohammadi (1995) argues that even a brief glance at the Iranian media in the 1970s proves that the content had very little to do with preserving national culture or raising the level of public education, "Rather, they promoted the alluring manifestations of Western culture, with little consideration of the urgent needs and demands of Iranian society; they did little more than amuse and entertain their audience" (p. 372). Nearly 80% of all NIRT programs were imported from the West, mostly from the United States. Typical of these programs were the soap operas, serials, comedies, and detective dramas that were being watched by audiences across the world.

NIRT began to address some of its shortcomings in terms of geographical reach and original programs and implemented a long-term plan for the expansion of its operations, which included training communications personnel in the United States. By the mid 1970s, access to radio in Iran was almost universal with around 8 million radio sets in the country. NIRT had a total of 14 regional television production and transmission centers. The number of transmitters had increased from two in 1966, to 153 in 1974. It employed 7,000 people, of whom 2,000 were stationed in Tehran and there were already plans for the purchase of a satellite for educational purposes (Tehranian, 1977, 1979). By this time, the Iranian broadcasting system had become the second-largest broadcasting network in Asia, after NHK in Japan (Mohammadi, 1995). NIRT had become a symbol of progress and was given substantial budgets to expand its operations. However, this expansion and the creation of a "magic multiplier" for consumerism rather than development was inconsistent with development in other media sectors, notably the press. Literacy remained low and the press severely limited, censored, and available only in major cities. This inconsistent media policy prompted Tunstall (1977) to argue that if "Iran continues on its present path it will be the first nation in the world to have nationally spread television before a nationally spread press" (p. 247).

In 1974, NIRT produced a document specifying the role of mass communication in national development. Listed among its goals and missions were: "to strengthen the bases of national unity and participatory democracy," "to assist in the revitalization of the Iranian national culture," "to sponsor artistic and cultural activities," and "to provide recreational programs tailored to the taste and preference of every major sector of Iranian society" (Tehranian, Hakimzadeh, & Vidale, 1977, pp. 3–4). Broadcasting did contribute to the spread of a single national language (Farsi), if that is the only indication of "national unity." But throughout its history and despite the grand plan of NIRT to use it as a tool for national development, and despite its supposed independence from government, the actual content of television provided little evidence to that effect. Domestic production did increase and popular national programming which persuaded even the poorest people to go and buy a television set to prevent their children making a permanent base in neighboring households with television sets, did create a mass audience for television.

However, as the economic realities of the mid-1970s began to hit Iranians and as criticism of the Shah's policies grew louder, television began to promote the King of Kings (Shahanshah), his policies, and interests even more than before. The use of television to scare and humiliate political opponents, the State security service SAVAK's sponsored programs, and televised coverage of "trials" and "confessions" of captured activists and intellectuals left little credibility for NIRT. Such vast, sophisticated, and well-oiled machinery failed to create political legitimacy for the Shah or his policies. The big media failed to counter the dynamic and growing small media of the revolution of 1979. On February 11, 1979, NIRT's headquarters came under the control of the public after the Shah's military forces were ordered back to their base after 3 months of occupation (Sreberny-Mohammadi & Mohammadi, 1994, p. 169).

IRANIAN TELEVISION 1979–1994

In contrast to a relatively diverse and controversial (although limited) press market, broadcasting had always been under the tight control of the State. The reasons are not hard to find. In Iran, as in most countries, television is the most popular and accessible media. In contrast to poorly distributed newspapers, broadcasting reaches almost all corners of Iran and around 81% of Iranians have access to television. In the capital, 92% of households have at least one television set, 70% of them color. This is complemented by around 10 million video sets (VCR; of which 7 million are home videos, one VCR for every 35 Iranians), and by the late 1990s, more than 250,000 satellite dishes, which were often shared by more than one family (Habibi-Nia, 1998). Broadcasting is accorded a significant place by the leadership of the Islamic Republic. The Constitution is also specific about the role of broadcasting. According to Article 175:

> The freedom of expression and dissemination of thought in the Radio and Television of the Islamic Republic of Iran must be guaranteed in keeping with the Islamic criteria and the best interests of the country. The appointment and dismissal of the head of the Radio and Television of the Islamic Republic of Iran rests with the Leader. A council consisting of two representatives each of the President, the head of the judiciary branch and the Islamic Consultative Assembly shall supervise the functioning of this organization. The policies and the manner of managing the organization and its supervision will be determined by law.

Although there are references to freedom, dignity, debate, and the development of human beings, the aim of the media seems to be the construction of Islamic society and the diffusion of Islamic culture. The mission of the media under the Islamic Republic is the "propagation" and defense of the values and ideals of not only Islam in general, but a strand which is considered pure and revolutionary as defined by the ruling clergy. In this sense, those at the head of the Islamic Republic, like the monarchy before them, have seen the media as a crucial tool in reinforcing and consolidating their hegemonic power. The centerpiece of this policy has revolved, more than anywhere else, around broadcasting. Yet the inherent contradictions between the imperatives of the market and the official State ideology, varied factional interests, the strong presence of oppositional (legal and otherwise) classes, and finally the logic of territory (the so-called "national interest") and of the rapid integration of Iran into global capitalism, is nowhere more obvious and visible than in the broadcasting sector. All these interrelated factors have paved the way for an intriguing media environment in general, and a very peculiar broadcasting terrain.

The lack of a clear alternative economic policy and the dismissive attitudes toward wider economic issues of the ruling elite has always meant that much of the emphasis of the regime that replaced the monarchy was on what they saw as the cultural trends that had pushed Iranians away from their Islamic heritage and teaching. It has come as no surprise that this "cultural war" and the debate about competing values dominated much of the early and subsequent discussion about the nature and the role of the Islamic Republic. Up to the collapse of the monarchy a large number of *ulema* (religious scholars) saw television as an instrument of foreign powers/cultures that were vigorously pursuing nothing but the corruption of the Iranian public. For that reason, watching television and going to the cinema was discouraged by them and many cinemas, alongside financial centers such as banks, were burned down during the uprising of 1978–1979. But immediately after coming to power, the new ruling elite seized the initiative and began to see broadcasting no longer as an instrument of the Great Satan, but as a powerful tool for spreading the message of the revolution and Islam. In his first speech after returning to Iran, Khoemeini argued:

> We are not opposed to the cinema, to radio, or to television; what we oppose is vice and the use of the media to keep our young people in a state of back-wardness and dissipate their energy. We have never opposed these features of modernity in themselves, but when they were brought from Europe to the East, particularly to Iran, unfortunately they were used not in order to advance civilization, but in order to drag us into barbarism. (Algar, 1981, p. 258)

Despite rhetorical differences and the early objections to broadcasting in Iran by a group of ulema, a brief review of the development of broadcasting and its evolution to date reveals clear elements of continuity in its structure, expansion, control, and a strong association with the State.

In the early stages of the Islamic Republic, broadcasting was an open platform for a diverse range of views. This free and open period did not last long. The title of the organization was changed to the Voice and the Vision of the Islamic Republic, or VVIR, (and some years later to Islamic Republic of Iran Broadcasting, IRIB) and Sadiq Gotbzadeh who had accompanied Khoemini on his triumphant return to Iran was rewarded with the post of leading the organization and the task of the Islamization of broadcasting. Gotbzadeh immediately came into conflict with old VVIR personnel who were dismayed by the rapid transformation of television by those who had little knowledge of the requirements of a modern organization such as theirs. In tandem with the populist policies of the early days of the Islamic Republic, Gotbzadeh promised to make broadcasting a forum for the *pa-berehneha* (barefoot people). He immediately began the process of *pak-sazi* (cleansing), dismantling many subdivisions and research projects and pro-grams, and tried to make the VVIR into a power base for himself (Mohammadi, 2003). Programming remained a key issue and although changing the title and structure of VVIR together with a purge of personnel the Islamization of its con-tent and the implementation of its general policies of the new regime were much harder to achieve. Television had clearly failed to create much-needed political legitimacy for the previous regime and the new ruling elites were keen to try their luck. Much of the early VVIR content was clearly politico-religious and the ulema began to dominate television. Much Iranian popular music was banned and the Islamization severely limited VVIR's options for other forms of programming such as films (both national and foreign), game shows, and many popular sporting programs including wrestling, and so on. Iranians, with their typical sarcasm, nicknamed this form of broadcasting "mullahvision" (Sreberny-Mohammadi & Mohammadi, 1994, p. 173). The public also questioned the usefulness of color television in Iran since most programs were filled with members of the clergy who were wearing either black or white turbans (Baghi, 2002, p. 365).

Gotbzadeh left his post at the height of the American Embassy hostage crisis and became Minister of Foreign Affairs and one of the leading figures in negotiations between the Islamic Republic and U.S. Administration. Gotbzadeh began his new post as he had done with the previous one, purging and "cleansing" the foreign ministry of undesirable personnel. He himself became the target of cleansing as the battle to control the newly formed republic intensified, and he was later executed on the dubious charge of "collaborating" with the enemy. The control of broadcasting became a major site of dispute between different factions, and the newly formed Islamic Republic Party began to monopolize power and took over. Those who were appointed by Gotbzadeh and the first president of the republic, Bani-Sadr, were brushed aside or forced to resign, and Prosecutor-General Ayatollah Mosavi-Ardabili appointed new directors for broadcasting services and television channels.

In a further move to undermine the president (who later fled the country), the Iranian Parliament passed a law that, contrary to the Constitution, allowed the prime minister (a member of the Islamic Republic Party) to appoint a representative of the executive branch to the VVIR Council (Bakhash, 1985). At this stage, broadcast media played a major role in silencing the factions who had formed the provisional government and dominated the executive branch. For a short time, VVIR had two acting directors, Ali Larijani the son-in-law of Ayatollah Mottahari and one of closest associates of Khomeini, who was put in charge of the day-to-day running of *Sima* (vision), and Saeed Rajaie Khorasani, one of Mottahari's ex-students, who was put in charge of *Seda* (voice) (Mohammadi, 2003). Despite the efforts of these two and the centralization of the organization, Khomeini remained unhappy about the performance of VVIR. Rafsanjani, the speaker of the Iranian Parliament and another close associate and a powerful figure in the Islamic Republic, suggested that his brother should take over the organization. Larijani left to lead the Revolutionary Guard Intelligence Unit (he returned later as the director general), and Rafsanjani's brother, Mohammad Hashemi, became VVIR's second director general. Under the leadership of Hashemi, VVIR was burdened more than anything else with the "war effort" (Barraclough, 2001) and the endless need for mobilization and propaganda during the conflict with Iraq. This issue dominated much of the first decade of the new regime. Military songs and marches, regular news from the front, and similar content that was deemed suitable dominated the screen.

One of the unique feature of VVIR was the fact that it (like NIRT) remained independent from the newly constructed Ministry of Islamic Guidance (that later became the Ministry of Culture and Islamic Guidance in 1986), which was given the task of managing and policing the press, the Islamic Republic News Agency (IRNA), the film industry, charity organizations, and tourism. The Constitution kept VVIR independent from the ministry and instead opted for a council (as suggested in the first constitution of the Republic) consisting of representatives from the three powers (legislative, judiciary, and executive) to supervise the running of the organization in cooperation with the director general. The general idea was to avoid making VVIR a direct arm of government and prevent any form of despotism and control of broadcasting by just a single individual, institution, or interest. Sreberny-Mohammadi and Mohammadi have argued (1994) the new State not only took the centralization policy of the previous regime even further, it also continued with the tradition of giving sensitive positions to trusted individuals and close associates of key figures, making VVIR akin to a family business. Hashemi indeed appointed family and friends of the family to create a unified and homogenous organization that not only satisfied the leadership of the regime, but also without doubt managed to promote Rafsanjani as the second most powerful man in Iran.

Clear elements of continuity can also be seen in the revival of the previous regime's policy for the development and expansion of broadcasting in Iran. Hashemi not only brought back some of the personnel who had lost their jobs in the first few months of Ghotbzadeh's directorship; he began to recruit more personnel, which increased from 8,000 to 14,000. He revived much of the development plan of Reza Ghotbi, who had been director of the Iranian National Radio and Television before the revolution, including reopening the Office of Satellite Research and Development, coproductions with foreign broadcasters including the BBC and NHK, and adding a third channel devoted mostly to sport coverage.

Just before Khomeini's death and under his direct order, the Constitution of the Islamic Republic was revised in 1989. Two significant changes paved the way for an even more centralized State: the lowering of the clerical qualification required for the post of supreme leader, and the abolition of the post of prime minister, which paved the way for a more powerful presidency. This move towards centralization was also evident in the third significant change to the Constitution that brought the VVIR under direct control of the supreme leader and it indicates the crucial strategic value of broadcasting for the Islamic State. The first two constitutional changes were a direct response to an urgent need for a more dynamic, centralized, and somehow less ideologically rigid structure for the State, that judging by the third change, could not be achieved without total control of broadcasting. The intention and the message were clear: In the period of reconstruction and liberalization, it was no longer viable to keep broadcasting as the voice of the three main powers in Iran. A single voice and vision was a crucial requirement for the relentless drive toward "reconstruction." The VVIR was to continue with its significant political role as before, but needed to expand and develop more comprehensive policies towards more popular forms of programming. For a decade, all the early promises of the Islamic State had been put on hold due to the war with Iraq, now was the time for the State to deliver.

Political rivalries since the revolution have centered on the appropriate source of religious interpretation as well as on juridical power; with the established legal system superseded by religious legal authority in the form of the *Velayate-e-Faghih* (rule of the supreme jurist). There were two sources of power, an elected president and/versus a supreme leader. This dual system that was problematic from 1979 became an even greater source of crisis after the end of the war and Khomeini's death. In the period between 1989 and 1993 Iran began to witness a mini-Glasnost. The process of reconstruction that had began immediately after the end of the war with Iraq and the election of Rafsanjani as president in July 1989 not only meant following the World Bank and International Monetary Fund recommended policies of liberalization and privatization, it also instigated a less restrictive cultural policy. For a decade, various factions of the State had waved at the shadowy threat of "external forces" and had fallen back into a rhetorical use of conspiracy theory and "cultural imperialism" when their politics had clearly failed to satisfy a very youthful electorate. The major problem to be faced by the reform-minded president and his cabinet was how to pursue a less restrictive cultural policy without encouraging an independent public sphere and a full blown critique of the State.

The job of establishing such a delicate balance was given to Mohammad Khatami as the new Minister of Islamic Guidance. He immediately began to promote the Iranian film industry, granted licenses to many new social and cultural periodicals, and paved the way for a more vibrant and dynamic press environment. For the first time since the brutal repression of the independent media in the 1980s, Iranian media began to address sensitive social issues. A similar policy was promoted and followed by Hashemi, the head of VVIR. Iranian television began broadcasting serials, movies, and other programs that were not totally in line with the cultural standards of conservative factions in the State. This new policy of promoting cultural liberalization alongside economic liberalization soon produced a backlash. Many, including the supreme leader, began to attack Khatami and criticized him for the deterioration of cultural standards and paving the way for an onslaught of Iranian culture by the corrupt and un-Islamic West. Khatami resigned in July 1992, but he later won two landslide victories in the 1997 and 2001 presidential elections.

Hashemi continued in his post until 1994, when the supreme leader finally decided to use his power to replace him with Larijani. Factional politics, the association of Hashemi with President Rafsanjani (who, in 1994, was serving his second term) and the fact that it meant a very close link between VVIR and the executive branch were all important factors in the changes to the broadcasting hierarchy. A campaign by the Iranian Parliament that provided ammunition against the broadcasters also played a key role in forcing Hashemi and his associates to resign. Prior to his resignation in November 1993, the Legislative and Parliamentary Affairs Division of the Iranian Parliament produced a report that further polarized the debate over the supposed "cultural invasion." The report condemned the performance of broadcasters and in particular the rise of foreign programming shown on Iranian television. According to the report, out of 900 films broadcast on Iranian television between 1988 and 1991, 700 were foreign. The report also asserted that even Iranian productions failed to observe Islamic guidelines. Animations were condemned for showing wine drinking, relationships between boys and girls, and female characters with no hejab (head scarf); and even the popular cartoon "Around the World in 80 Days" was regarded as dangerous for showing an Englishman as powerful, brave, and enchanting (Brumberg, 2001). Hashemi tried to fend off such criticisms by accusing the writer of the report of having other interests than the interests of the Islamic Republic. He was brushed aside as his powerful brother failed to protect him. The new minister, Ali Larijani, promised to promote a cultural policy that showed "the deceptive face of the west that infiltrates the societies in the guise of human rights and democracy in order to achieve its filthy purpose of domination" (cited in Brumberg, 2001, p. 193). Thus the mini-Glasnost which had emerged after the end of the war had ended and a new wave of attacks against the press and intellectual freedom had begun.

IRANIAN TELEVISION 1994–2004

The new Director General Larijani, much more than his predecessor Hashemi, shared the conservative values of the supreme leader. Larijani was considered by the press to be part of an emerging group of young, conservative bureaucrats who passionately believed in the rule of the supreme jurist (*velayat fagih*). They were drawn from former members of the revolutionary corps and courts, with experience in sensitive posts in the Revolutionary Guard Intelligence unit or Ministry of Intelligence. Interviewed elsewhere in the press, Larijani had all of these credentials. In the early days of the revolution, he was in charge of VVIR's world service, then for a short while he managed the organization's news bureau, and after Ghotbzadeh had moved to the Ministry of Foreign Affairs, he became the caretaker of VVIR. He also served as deputy labor minister for a short time and was also deputy minister in the Ministry of Post and Telecommunications. For 9 years (between 1982 and 1991), he was deputy chief of the Revolutionary Guard and director of its intelligence unit. In the early 1990s, he took over the Ministry of Culture and Islamic Guidance after Khatami had resigned as minister in protest to pressure from conservative forces who were critical of his supposedly lax approach to cultural matters. Larijani was appointed as the head of IRIB in 1994. In all these years, he clearly remained loyal to the center of power in the Islamic Republic. However, as Barraclough (2001) suggests, whatever the reasons for the dismissal of Hashemi, or the assumptions about Larijani being more conservative and less pragmatic than his predecessor, the fact is that his role as director general of broadcasting in Iran has been that of a reformer. During his 10-year directorship from 1994 to 2004, more far-reaching reforms were implemented. He restructured and expanded broadcasting, and lobbied all branches of the State in the face of international competition, making State broadcasting into a large, powerful, and centralized media/political institution.

The first important issue at the start of Larijani's directorship was the impact of satellite and the Islamic Republic's policy toward this new technology. Satellite arrived in 1993 as a decade-long, expensive, and unsuccessful fight to ban the extremely popular VCR that ended when government finally legalized the device and allowed for limited legal video shops. Despite conceding defeat in their long battle to control private use of VCRs, similar debates took place as early as 1994 when satellite dishes began to appear on the rooftops of many households in Tehran and elsewhere. The arrival of satellite in Iran, once again, revived the debate about "cultural invasion" and the safeguarding of "Islamic culture." As the title of a book by Tabatabai (1999) *Satellite Rises & Cultures Set: What Is to Be Done?* published some years later indicates, the coming of satellite has been equated with the decline of culture. The debate over the rise and the impact of satellite was by no means a settled and straightforward discussion, and at issue were factional politics, institutional interests, and different understandings of the role of technology and the strength of local culture.

The interesting point to note is that at a time of passionate debate about the possible harmful effects of satellite on Iranian culture, there was very little programming available in Farsi. Prior to this, communities living close to the borders of neighboring countries could access television from Iraq, Turkey, Pakistan, and the Gulf with ease and without the need for satellite dishes. Foreign radio stations too, broadcasting regular programs in Farsi including the BBC, Voice of Israel, and the Voice of America, had always been popular sources of news, analysis, and entertainment. Barraclough (2001) suggests "the fact that western style permissive programming might form the mainstay of people's viewing challenges the very raison d'etre of the revolution itself" (p. 25). The link between religion, State, and communication is apparent once again in the discussion about satellite in Iran. However, those who see the ban on satellite simply as evidence of a fundamentalist attempt to "reclaim the language of devotion for the faithful and to reduce the reach of promotional culture" (Murdoch, 1997, p. 99) ignore the wider institutional interests, and the diversity of the "language of devotion." It also ignores the very fact that such a battle over the hearts and minds of the faithful is mediated through a number of official bodies; Parliament, the Council of the Guardians, and the Expediency Council, and that it has to be followed, implemented, and safeguarded by still more institutions.

There were many in the Islamic Republic who simply rejected the ban on pragmatic grounds that it was unenforceable, especially if miniature dishes were to be introduced. The *Daily Salam* objected to the idea of the ban by targeting the very idea that satellite had the power to corrupt: "The interior minister says dishes must be banned because they have the 'physical' power to corrupt. If this is so, then one has to arrest and execute every man and woman for they too possess the physical power of prostitution" (cited in Haeri, 1994, p. 51). As the debate progressed further, even the interior minister began to recognize the need for "persuasion" rather than force, and emphasized the need for proper legislation. In doing so, however, he did not only go beyond the issue of legal context, he followed clear institutional/bureaucratic logic by stressing that any legislation had to be implemented by his department (Barraclough, 2001). In total, only around 20 MPs got together to introduce a bill to ban the "importation, sale, and use" of satellite dishes. The Minister of Post, Telegraph, and Telephone of the time, Mohammad Gharazi, whose department also had a keen institutional interest, successfully objected to an article in the bill that also banned the manufacture of devices for receiving satellite transmissions because companies affiliated with the Telecommunication Company of Iran (TCI) were manufacturing many components for dishes. He was clearly safeguarding his own departmental interests and investment. The contradiction between the hardware and the software aspects of satellite were rather obvious.

Another interesting point revealing that the ban was not just merely about reclaiming "the language of devotion for the faithful," but was also to do with economics, was the rejection of two articles of the Bill by the Council of the Guardians. The proposed legislation had entrusted implementation to the ministry of the interior, but it had failed to allocate a budget and corresponding expenses. The Council of the Guardians returned the Bill to the parliament to be modified, and approved the revised version on February 15, 1995.

IRIB, as a whole, participated actively in the debate about the Islamic Republic's policy on satellite. It was in favor of an outright ban, but ensured it was itself exempt (alongside government ministries and foreign embassies). The act also allowed IRIB to record useful and educational satellite programs and distribute them on video. This never happened as the enforcement of the law proved as difficult as many had predicted. Although there were regular verbal attacks on satellite broadcasting and the occasional confiscation of dishes, the government remained hesitant about entering private middle-class households to establish whether they were receiving satellite programs. Nevertheless, IRIB remained the main beneficiary of the ban.

This policy provided IRIB with breathing space to expand its operations and to begin preparing for intense outside competition for the Iranian audience. In exactly the same way that restrictions on foreign films paved the way for a flourishing of Iranian cinema, the ban on satellite allowed IRIB to improve its performance, expand its activities, and introduce more entertainment and commercially oriented content. By the mid-1990s, even Hamid Mowlana, one of the advocates of "Islamic communication theory" and a passionate supporter of the Islamization of the Iranian media had began to confess to the failures of broadcasting policy in Iran. Mowlana admitted, unlike before, that foreign programs attract "considerable demand and interest" in Iran. And this is despite the fact that satellite dishes are officially banned.

> One of the major criticism directed toward television in Iran deals with the lack of entertainment programmes to occupy leisure time. The argument is made that Iranian television should create more attractive and popular cultural activities for leisure time; otherwise, the audiences will turn to foreign satellite television programmes or seek alternative means of entertainment elsewhere. In recent years, satellite piracy and illegal reproduction of international films and videos have increased. The expansion of new television

channels and increased amount of coverage given to sports, movies, an animated features are among strategies to overcome these problem. Television
in Iran thus illustrate a fascinating communication problem in many Islamic
countries: how traditional culture can be synthesised with contemporary electronic media, such as television, and how television can be employed in ways
that better suit the mode and styles of the country's history. (Mowlana, 1997,
pp. 207–208)

This is far removed from the Islamic Community Paradigm in Mowlana's previous (1996) work.

The most significant development in broadcasting in recent years, as Mowlana
admits, is undoubtedly the expansion of television channels, all with their own
themes. *Shabakeh* (Channel 1), which reaches 90% of the country, is a 24-hour
generalist channel, with a mix of programming including politics, news, and
drama. Channel 2, *Shabakeh Farhang* (Culture Network), covers 80% of the country and runs for 18 hours daily, focusing mostly on cultural and educational issues.
Channel 3, *Shabakeh Javan* (Youth Network), targets a young audience, covers
60% of Iranian territory and runs for about 12 hours, providing music and sports
programs. Network 4 was launched in 1996, covers only 40% of the country, and
runs for about 6 hours, broadcasting religious programming in which ulema discuss theological and intellectual matters. Programs for this channel are divided
into eight themes, and eight groups of program-makers develop, produce, and
present programs in corresponding areas including economics, religious thought
and culture, literature, and science. Channel 5 is a regional channel, with Tehran
the first city to have its own channel (Tehran Network) in 1996, followed by other
regions. By the end of 2002, according to the press, 15 provincial networks had
become operational. Channel 6 (Payam Network) is a teletext channel. The most
recent channel is the Education Channel (Amouzesh Network), with content not
dissimilar to the Open University programs on BBC2 in the United Kingdom. The
aim of this channel is to cater to the increasing number of students entering
higher education. The launch of this channel was the subject of Article 13 of
Chapter 13 of Third Economic Plan of the Islamic Republic.

Concerned with the domination of U.S. programs in Iran before the revolution,
IRIB has not only tried to build up its domestic production (with some success),
it has also bought products from some seemingly unlikely sources in Eastern
Europe, Latin America, and Asia. To maintain a strong and visible presence in the
international broadcasting community has been one of the key activities of IRIB
in recent years and to that effect, it also publishes the IRIB Newsletter (which
introduces international broadcasters to the latest news, programs, and developments)
and International Payk (which provides Iranian broadcasting executives information about the latest news and developments in international television markets).
IRIB is an active member of ABU (Asian Broadcasting Union), an affiliate member of the European Broadcasting Union (EBU), as well as a member of Asia-
Pacific Institute for Broadcasting Development (ABID). The main trading partners
of IRIB since 1979 include Germany, Japan, China, Kuwait, Lebanon, Bosnia and

Herzegovina, Cuba, Brazil, Pakistan, India, Switzerland, Australia, North and South Korea, and above all, Britain.

Some changes in policy toward the Iranian diaspora and a consensus among the ruling elite of the urgent need to invite back some exiles (preferably wealthier ones who are interested in investing in the private sector), the need to compete with the rapidly expanding foreign-based Iranian satellite channels, as well as the continuing desire to play a much more orchestrated and visible role in international politics has precipitated greater international broadcasting by the Islamic Republic. In addition to domestic channels, IRIB has also launched a number of channels targeting Iranians living outside the country, as well as an international audience. The flagship of IRIB's international effort is *Jame-Jam* launched in 1997. *Jame-Jam* broadcasts programming in Farsi (and some in English) in three channels. In addition to these three channels, there are also two *Sahar* (Dawn) channels, broadcasting programs in English, French, Arabic, Kurdish, Urdu, Azari, and Bosnian. Since the invasion of Iraq, IRIB has also launched *Alalam,* which tries to influence policies and political actors in Iraq. The number of radio channels has also increased to seven national channels, each with aims and themes similar to the domestic television channels. There is also IRIB World service with seven radio channels broadcasting in 25 languages including Chinese, Russian, Pashtu, Hebrew, Spanish, and Tajik. IRIB has also expanded its activities in publishing and publishes seven titles including the daily newspaper *Jame-Jam.*

Other organizations affiliated to IRIB include Sima Film, which provides facilities to film and program-makers and actively participates in international trade fairs; *Sima Chob* (Wood, Metal, & Plastic Industrial Company) offers services such as the construction of acoustic studios, interior design, office, and home furniture as well as furnishings for conference halls; Takta provides services in communication technologies and equipment; and finally Saba, which provides services and facilities for animated, computer-generated, and general audiovisual programs. The expansion of IRIB as a whole and the significant increase in the number of channels and outlets has also meant an increase in production. To that effect, outsourcing production has been an important IRIB strategy. Saba film and Sima film, both affiliated to IRIB, produce films, documentaries, serials, and animations for IRIB. Both companies have also managed to produce programs for export. In particular animations produced by Saba (some of them overtly political and "on-message") have been sold to Turkey. However, and as BBC journalist Frances Harrison (2005) reports, despite the overtly Islamic content and message of some of the cartoons, Arab countries refuse to buy many of these productions because they show the faces of prophets, something to which Sunni Muslims object.

In the early 1990s, the conservative-dominated *Majlis* (parliament), recognizing the attraction of satellite channels and fearful of "cultural invasion," relaxed all budgetary restrictions and allocated more than US$16 million to IRIB for original films and television programs (Mohammadi, 2003). Much of the budget allocated to IRIB has been given to private production companies to enable them to produce commercial films and television programs. According to Larijani IRIB's policy in this respect has revolved around the idea that for "the private sector to contribute to IRIB programs, IRIB needs to help the private sector" (cited in Barraclough, 2001, p. 38). In broadcasting, as in other sectors, the State and State institutions are actively driving privatization policies. Even the idea of privatization of news is not dismissed altogether, and certainly the introduction of advertising since 1996, as limited as it is, shifted the balance toward more commercialized programming. The contradiction between the imperatives of the market and privatization on the one hand and ideological needs on the other is addressed in singular fashion. Ironically, despite regular discussions about the impact of Western commercial programs and the fear of contamination of the "indigenous" culture by foreign cultural products, commercialization and the expansion of broadcasting has been the main strategy of IRIB.

There has also been a clear shift toward recognizing the value of entertainment by IRIB. Fearful of losing Iranian audiences to rival Iranian channels broadcasting entertainment (mostly Los Angeles-produced Iranian pop music and pre-revolution popular serials and films) and other international broadcasters, IRIB now produces and shows more domestic and international films, game shows, and dramas. "Respectable" popular dramas from Europe, including British television serials such as "Inspector Morse," "Miss Marple," and "Poirot" have become major hits among the Iranian audience. Undoubtedly the introduction of advertising has meant an increase in "awareness of audience preference among broadcasters" (Barraclough, 2001, p. 40). What adds to this reality in common with many developing countries is Iran's limited resources, which have a crippling effect on the country's ability to compete with global media players, as well as the lure of cultural commodities offered by these companies. As Ali Mohammadi (2003) points out, the evidence of these trends can be observed by a brief glance at the content of many publications in Iran. According to Mohammadi, more than 70% of the content of Soroush magazine (published by IRIB), the only television guide in the country, is international in focus. A large number of cultural/social publications, including many that deal with cinema and literature, provide extensive coverage of the latest international blockbuster films, books, music, and television programs. Many of Hollywood's latest releases find their way into Iranian shops long before they are released in Europe.

However, despite careful international trading and the import of "safe" cultural television programs, IRIB still needs to devote time and effort to censor undesired elements of many foreign series and films. IRIB has taken the notion of "free dubbing" to the extreme. As Iranian researcher Majid Mohammadi argues, the policy of censoring such programs and changing the dialogue is based on the assumption that the Iranian public are not immune from cultural illnesses emanating from the West. According to him, the name of a food (possibly crab or frog) served in one scene of the "Wilderness Family," shown on Channel 3, was deleted; any reference to alcoholic drinks in imported foreign programs is avoided, and phrases such as "I'll have a half-pint of beer" are changed to "half a glass of what they are having." Women in foreign programs are sometimes shown from the chin upwards, indicating that the dress is perhaps too revealing, while using the same technique for men indicates that they are wearing a tie. These are the scenes that IRIB decides to broadcast; others are either cut or blacked out (1998, pp. 449–50).

In the field of news, Iranian broadcasting has also seen a similar expansion of production and collaboration with international broadcasters. IRIB has signed a 10-year contract with CNN, according to which both parties can use each other's footage. Similar contacts for exchange programs have been signed with Reuters and the BBC World Service (Barraclough, 2001). Rupert Murdoch's visit to Iran in 1998, approved by the then-Foreign Minister Kamal Kharrazi (previously the director of IRNA), was a further sign of a new policy of courting big players in international media markets. Such trends have not made the issue of "news imperialism" redundant. In this case rejection of "news imperialism" is equated with a rejection of news altogether (Mohammadi, 1998). The element of continuity in broadcasting in Iran before and after the revolution is again obvious in this instance. Broadcasting in Iran has never been a credible source of news, domestic or otherwise. However, despite a rapid march toward commercialization and the welcoming of private capital into the communications industry, the Islamic Republic and the IRIB cannot simply renounce their anti-imperialist stance of the early years. This is where some of the similarities with the previous regime end. In domestic news IRIB continues, as NIRT did, to attack "anti-state" elements in Iran. But in its international news, IRIB continues to draw on the anti-imperialist legacies of the early days to glorify the "Islamic Revolution" and "Republic." Denouncing U.S. imperialism has always been an important aspect of IRIB programming, and is part of programs commemorating significant dates and figures such as the anniversary of the revolution, or the anniversaries of the deaths or birth dates of various leading Shia Imams, and so on. As the Islamic Republic embraces the forces of capitalism even more, IRIB tries even harder to trumpet its anti-imperialist stance. A good example is the coverage of the invasion of Iraq, which many commentators in Iran suggested clearly violated the State's adopted policy of neutrality (Samii, 2003).

The reform and expansion of broadcasting in Iran in the last decade or so has made IRIB the biggest media player and one of the major units of capital in Iran. IRIB owes its position in the media market in Iran to its funding structure. In 1997 about 13% of IRIB revenues were generated through advertising; the rest came from direct government subsidy and a license fee which is added to the household electricity bills (Barraclough, 2001). No other media organization in Iran receives the funding that IRIB receives. There are no exact figures on how substantial the contribution of the license fee is as a percentage of the IRIB budget. But it is safe to assume that it is only a fraction of its overall budget, with the State remaining the main contributor. The share of advertising, however, and despite only being introduced in 1996, has grown compared to 1976–1977, when it stood at less than 10% (Tehranian, 1977). What adds to the power and position of broadcasting in Iran is the very fact that like the institution of the supreme leader it is supposed to be above all other institutions and expresses official State views and policies. Prior to the revision of the Constitution in 1989, Iranian broadcasting was under the supervision of the three powers. The war with Iraq and ideological needs of this period, the towering presence of Khomeini, who remained above all institutions in the Islamic Republic, as well as the lack of expertise and the early confusion over the role of broadcasting did not allow for any serious test, except a few angry comments by the leadership over some of the contents, of the early structure of IRIB. The revision of the Constitution clearly brought broadcasting under the direct control of the new supreme leader who not only lacked Khomeini's qualifications and charisma, but unlike Khomeini, was directly involved in the factional conflicts. For that reason IRIB, despite being regarded as "public property" and the purveyor of Islamic values and culture, has been accountable only to the supreme leader.

The role of IRIB as an organ of official propaganda for the ruling elite was recognized and more or less accepted by the various factions that made up the regime. Neither constant mobilization by IRIB during the war nor its brutal participation in the Islamic Republic's campaign to humiliate and suppress oppositional forces or even ex-Khomeinists, as well as the televised "confession" of political prisoners, raised serious concerns inside the regime. It was with the intensification of factional conflicts in the 1990s, especially in the period up to the presidential election in 1997 and subsequent developments, that the issue of the "neutrality" of IRIB became the subject of heated debate and dispute. IRIB played a rather dubious role in the run up to the presidential election, by favoring conservative candidate Ali-Akbar Nategh-Nouri, promoting conservative leaders and policies, and, in the 1999 parliamentary election, by giving the silent treatment to the successes of reformist candidates. The supreme leader of the Islamic Republic, Ali Khamenai, has, not surprisingly, always supported IRIB. Indeed in 1997, just 10 days before the presidential election, he was quoted in the monthly *Payam'e Emrouz* (Today's Message) praising the management of IRIB and their role in informing and encouraging people to participate in the election. What stirred the conflict even further was the broadcasting of a documentary *Cheragh* (Light), in which supporters of Khatami were accused of being behind the wave of political assassinations of well-known political figures, journalists, and writers in 1998. The commission that was immediately set up to investigate this matter rejected the claims by the documentary and received an apology from IRIB management. Before this incident, there had been many calls for changes in both personnel and the editorial position of IRIB. In January 1999, 88 members of the Majles, in a letter to Khamenei, openly objected to the biased coverage of political events by IRIB and warned that such an editorial policy would damage the reputation of the media in Iran and the Islamic regime as a whole. IRIB was further criticized by the independent press for its coverage of the Iranian presidential trip to Italy in March 1999 (Samii, 1999). Some newspapers went even further and called for privatization of television.

Despite this, IRIB continued as before and the pro-Khatami camp received similar treatment and accusations after their participation in the "Iran After the Elections" conference that was held April 7–9, 2000, in Berlin by the Heinrich Boll Institute, an organization associated with the German Green Party. It aimed to promote understanding and informed political opinion and intended to bring together critical voices from both secular and Islamic reformists groups. Some prominent writers and publishers, as well as reformist politicians and journalists, were invited to speak. As Baghi (2002) has argued, IRIB broadcast a program made up of 30 minutes of selected and edited coverage of the Berlin conference, presenting a negative image of those reformists who attended. Such active participation by IRIB in factional conflicts and disputes inside the Islamic Republic has prompted many reformists to compare IRIB to a right-wing political party.

Here one can observe another element of continuity in the development of broadcasting in Iran: The failure of broadcasting to create political legitimacy for the new ruling elite. As Baghi suggests, the assumption in the early years of the revolution was that the transfer of control of broadcasting to the clergy would put an end to all forms of social corruption. But a directly controlled IRIB has not only failed to tackle any of these targeted problems, but by forging such a close link between Islam and a repressive government, it has seriously weakened and undermined religion in Iran. Baghi (2002) suggests that the best service to religion in Iran that IRIB could perform would be to leave it alone altogether. The continuing popularity of satellite channels, and Mowlana's recognition of the dilemmas of the media in general and broadcasting in particular under the Islamic Republic is the clearest indication of the failure of the Islamic Republic to create a viable alternative media system in Iran and the failure of broadcasting to create political legitimacy for the ruling elite.

In the past few years, IRIB has come under renewed attack and criticism inside Iran. In 2001, reformist MPs in the Iranian parliament rejected some of IRIB's funding bid and began to organize a debate on the broadcaster's financial affairs. The debate over financial irregularities and corruption escalated after IRIB announced in early 2001 that it might have to sack 10,000 of its staff due to budget shortfalls (BBC News, 2001). Iranian MPs argued that because parliament allocates the budget for the organization, it had the right to be informed about how the funds are spent. The scheduled debate on June 17, 2001, was blocked by the speaker of the house on the grounds that the organization was only accountable to the supreme leader and not the parliament, a move which prompted many of the MPs to storm out of parliament in protest (Saba, 2001). Although the Iranian second chamber (the Council of Guardians) had rejected the parliamentary bill to reduce IRIB's budget, the supreme leader succumbed to the pressure and allowed parliament to set up a committee to investigate IRIB and a policymaking council for broadcasting. The legislation approved by the parliament on June 24, 2001, envisaged that three members of parliament, three cabinet ministers, the first deputy head of the Judiciary, two lawyers, the secretary of supreme national security council, a representative of the Supreme Leader (on his approval), a representative of the managing editors of the press, a representative of the theological center, a university lecturer specializing in communications, and the IRIB chairman will constitute the high council for IRIB policymaking for a tenure of two years.

One of the key concerns of reformist MPs and critics was that the organization had not been transparent about its revenue from advertising. IRIB has argued that its advertising revenue is only about US$20 million per year, although some MPs believe the figure might be closer to US$50 or even US$100 million a year. By mid-2003, the report of The Parliament Inspection Commission on IRIB's Revenues and Expenses confirmed the suspicions of the critics of the organization. According to the report, the organization had committed gross financial offenses totaling US$656 million. This finding, the report stressed, had only been based on very limited data, numbering five accounts out of a total of 200 accounts. It also criticized IRIB for failing to cooperate with the commission. The report also suggested that it had ignored a number of other offenses to "observe national expediency." Larijani left the organization after 10 years to fight an election campaign as one of the conservative candidates for the presidency. He was replaced by Ezzatollah Zarghami another member of the previously mentioned emergent group of managers who are extremely close to the center of power and the supreme leader. He has been the subject of similar internal accusations after IRIB's highly biased coverage of the presidential campaign in June 2005, in which Zarghami's closest friend and the mayor of Tehran, Mahmood Ahmadi-Nejad won a surprise victory.

CONCLUSION

Institutions such as IRIB are at the same time organs of official propaganda for a coercive State as well as units of capital accumulation. The dominant faction within the Iranian State is fearful of giving a free hand to private capital to invest in the media. This fear is twofold: Investment by private companies in broadcasting will undoubtedly challenge the dominant position of the State broadcaster and undermine the unique position that IRIB occupies in Iran. IRIB with its dubious reputation might not be in a position to compete with private channels. Second, even if private networks might not pose an immediate challenge to the State, they might undermine the dominant faction in the long term. Accepting the emergence of a powerful private broadcasting network is also against most things that the Islamic Republic has supposedly stood for in the past 25 years. So far such developments have been treated in exactly the same way as legal oppositional parties. To accept the formation of private networks is to allow them to operate outside the control of the supreme leader. Fearful of such a possibility, the State has actively embraced the State-sponsored partial privatization of communication in a way that, despite encouraging the private sector to invest in the lucrative and expanding communication industry, keeps ultimate political control in the hands of the State. But the intensification of factional conflicts and the emergence of private satellite channels in Farsi, mostly based in California, as well as the rapidly growing private market in trading in the latest videotapes, CDs, and DVDs, have begun to push the State and State broadcasters even further.

The case of Iran clearly raises many serious doubts about the exaggerated claims of globalization theorists and the decline of the nation-state. Nevertheless it also demonstrates that States are seldom abstract or singular. There exists within any State, quite clearly in the case of Iran, many contradictions in terms of policies and between different individual and institutional interests. The combination of these elements means that different institutions of the State can come up with contradictory policies. Furthermore, policies might be media-specific, or the result of the political consensus of the time (the differences between the regulation of broadcasting on the one hand, and the press and the Internet on the other is indicative of this trend). The Iranian case also demonstrates a peculiar feature of the Iranian communication industry where liberalization and privatization are the order of the day, but the State is still reluctant to give up its ideological control over the media. And this is another contradiction (or limit) of an overtly ideological state keen on development and modernization, but remains caught between pragmatism and the imperative of the market on one hand and the straightjacket of Islamism on the other.

REFERENCES

Algar, H. (Ed.). (1981). *Islam and revolution: Writings and declarations of Imam Khomeini.* Berkeley: Mizan Press.

Artz, L. (2003). Globalization, Media Hegemony, and Social Class. In L. Artz & Y. Kamalipour (Eds.), *The globalization of corporate media hegemony* (pp. 3–32). New York: SUNY Press.

Baghi, E. (2002). *Spring of fourth estate: A review of movement of reformist press.* Tehran: Sarabi.

Bakhash, S. (1985). *The reign of the Ayatollas.* London: I. B. Tauris.

Barraclough, S. (2001). Satellite television in Iran: Prohibition, imitation and reform. *Middle Eastern Studies, 37*(3), 25–48.

BBC News. (2001). *Iran's broadcasters face the sack.* retrieved July 14, 2005, from news.bbc.co.uk/1/hi/world/monitoring/media_reports/1132812.stm

Bourdon, J. (2004). Is television a global medium?: A historical view. In T. Oren & P. Petro (Eds.), *Global currents: Media and technology now* (pp. 93–112). New Brunswick, NJ: Rutgers University Press.

Brumberg, D. (2001). *Reinventing Khomeini: The struggle for reform in Iran.* Chicago: University of Chicago Press.

Habibi-Nia, O. (1998). Transnational visual media and their impact. *Naghd-e Cinema, 14,* 63–71.

Haeri, S. (1994). Iranian satellite. *Index on Censorship, 23*(4–5), 49–51.

Harrison, F. (2005). *Iran's booming animation industry.* Retrieved June 18, 2005, from news.bbc.co.uk/1/hi/world/middle_east/4528563.stm

Harvey, D. (2003). *The New Imperialism.* Oxford, England: Oxford University Press.

Kamalipour, Yahya. (2003). *Cultural mirrors: Iranian satellite TV channels.* Retrieved June 14, 2005, from www.iranian.com/YahyaKamalipour/2003/March/TV/index.html

Khiabany, G. (2003). De-westernising media theory or reverse Orientalism: Islamic communication as theorized by Hamid Mowlana. *Media, Culture and Society, 25*(3), 415–422.

Mohammadi, A. (1995). Cultural imperialism and cultural identity. In J. Downing, A. Mohammadi, & A. Sreberny-Mohammadi (Eds.), *Questioning the media: A critical introduction* (pp. 362–378). Thousand Oaks, CA: Sage.

Mohammadi, A. (2003). Iran and modern media in the age of globalization. In A. Mohammadi (Ed.), *Iran encountering globalization: Problems and prospects* (pp. 24–46). London: Routledge Cruzon.

Mohammadi, M. (1998). *An introduction to sociology and economics of culture in Iran.* Tehran: Qatreh.

Mowlana, H. (1996). *Global communication in transition: The end of diversity.* Thousand Oaks, CA: Sage.

Mowlana, H. (1997, November). Islamicising the media in a global era: The state-community perspective in Iranian broadcasting. In K. Robins (Ed.), *Programming for people: From cultural rights to cultural responsibilities* (pp. 204–214). Report presented by RAI-Radiotelevisione Italiana at the United Nations Television Forum, New York.

Murdock, G. (1997). The re-enchantment of the world: Religion and the transformation of modernity. In S. Hoover & K. Lunby (Eds.), *Rethinking media, religion, and culture* (pp. 85–101). Thousand Oaks, CA: Sage.

Robins, K., & Webster, F. (1985). The revolution of the fixed wheel: Information, technology and Social Taylorism. In P. Drummond & R. Paterson (Eds.), *Television in Transition* (pp. 36–63). London: BFI.i

Saba, S. (2001). *Iran media debate denied.* Retrieved January 12, 2005, from http://news.bbc.co.uk/1/hi/world/middle_east/1393434.stm

Samii, A. (1999). The contemporary Iranian news media, 1998–1999. *Middle East Review of International Affairs, 3*(4), 1–10.

Samii, B. (2003). *The Iranian media in 2003.* Retrieved April 12, 2004, from www.iranianvoice. org/article1342.html

Sreberny-Mohammadi, A., & Mohammadi, A. (1994). *Small media, big revolution: Communication, culture, and the Iranian revolution.* Minneapolis: University of Minnesota Press.

Tabatabai, S. (1999). *Satellites rise & cultures set: What is to be done?* Tehran: Etella'at.

Tehranian, M. (1979, March). Iran: Communication, alienation, revolution. *Intermedia,* 6–12.

Tehranian, M. (1977). The role of broadcasting in Iran: Report of a national survey. In M. Tehranian et al. (Eds), *Communications policy for national development* (pp. 257–278). London: Routledge & Keagan Paul.

Tehranian, M., Farhad, H., & Vidale, M. (1977). Preface, in *Communications Policy for National Development.* London: Routledge & Keagan Paul.

Tunstall, J. (1977). *The media are American: Anglo-American media in the world.* London: Constable.

CHAPTER SIXTEEN

Israel: From Monopoly to Open Sky

Dan Caspi
Ben-Gurion University

Television in Israel has developed in parallel with the growth and fashioning of this new nation as a modern Western democracy, ever since it achieved national independence in 1948. For many long years, State leaders contended with the question of if and how best to adopt a new medium in a new country. The socio-cultural climate left its mark on the adoption of the new medium while economic and human resources molded its characteristics.

Partial television broadcasts began in 1964, but it was only in 1968 that general television broadcasts were introduced. Three major stages can be identified in the development of television in Israel, each stage spanning approximately two decades. The first stage was the formative, incubation stage, spanning the first two decades of the nation's existence. This was followed by the stage in which television was monopolized by a single-channel system, also approximately two decades. Finally, the "open-sky" stage, characterized by multichannel television, began in the 1980s and continues to date.

The transition from a single-channel monopoly to an "open sky" cannot be considered apart from the overall context, particularly the climate of dramatic value changes in Israeli society, as expressed in a transition from a socialist European to a capitalist American orientation. These changes have extended to regulation policies of the broadcasting map, to control procedures of broadcasting media, and in particular, to television. The changes brought about many fissures in the original

British format of public-service broadcasting in favor of the adoption of various components of the U.S. model.

By and large, Israel has and still serves as a fertile field of competition between two basic broadcasting approaches—the European social attitude of public service broadcasting versus the American commercial attitude. Overall trends such as globalization, growth of media conglomerates, technological innovations and a variety of broadcasting techniques, coupled with local factors such as the identity crisis of public broadcasting and a shift in values amongst the political elite to neoliberalism, as well as pressure from entrepreneurs, have tipped the scales in recent years in favor of the American perspective. This includes a clear preference for the regulation of television channels by market forces.

BACKGROUND

The declared aspiration of Israel's founding fathers to establish a Western democracy could not bypass a burgeoning media. Just as political, judiciary, welfare, and economic institutions were molded in the semblance of modern democratic institutions, so too were resources and thought processes invested in the fashioning of an appropriate media industry (Caspi, 2005a). Founding fathers, including leading figures in the media, quickly understood the double-edged sword involved in the establishment of a modern media institution in a Western democracy: it is simultaneously an inseparable part of the infrastructure while also championing inevitable change in values and culture. Such change was of particular importance in light of the crystallizing of a new national entity founded on Zionist values, whose role was to melt the cultural gaps between immigrants from all over the world into a new pot. The cumulative cultural capital amassed as a result of the waves of immigration actually eased the fashioning of an appropriate media infrastructure, including television.

The adoption of a democratic ethos posed an essential challenge to the founders of the new nation. From its inception, the media institutions were promised a status similar to that acceptable in modern Western democracies (Murdock, 1993). However, from its first steps, the nation's founding fathers were drawn into a conundrum: as far as values, they were immediately faced with the need to reconcile authoritarian traditions in existence from the days of the Mandate, with new democratic norms. On a practical level, founders encountered the conflict between a desire to fashion a media map with maximum press freedom and expression and the practical needs of a regime that must continue supervising and controlling the media. In other words, how much media control is necessary in order to preserve command while remaining "democratic" enough? How much control can be given up, without risking vital political and national interests? (Caspi, 2005b)

The nation's new leaders sought legitimacy in the broadest sense possible; particularly from Western countries. It was therefore very important that they adopt the prevailing symbols of Western democracy, status of the media being among the most distinctive. It would seem that coping with this challenge was to characterize the process of shaping the media during the following years and, in particular, the subsequent status of television in Israeli society.

THE INCUBATION STAGE (1948–1967)

In the first decade after the establishment of the State, the partisan press and the foreign-language press dominated the media map (Limor, 1999). Continuity and succession marked mainly the partisan press, which flourished in this decade, because more than ever before, the newspaper was perceived as an efficient tool for mobilization of political support, particularly vital during election times (Peri, 1999).

In Israel, as in many other new nations, the founding leader was granted a nearly unquestioned status in many areas, including radio and television broadcasting. The resistance of David Ben-Gurion and his colleagues to the introduction of television was well-known. It apparently rested on three major reasons: first, a technology phobia, nourished by the climate in the Western world that attributed overwhelming influence to television.[1] Second, an economic concern of high costs that a new economy with limited resources could not shoulder. Third, a cultural anxiety that the new medium would challenge the Western cultural hegemony and accelerate pseudo-Western (Levantinization) processes. In particular, the nation's leaders were worried about the fact that Arab countries had hurried to adopt the medium. Broadcasts from neighboring countries were received in Israel and also threatened, though to a lesser extent, the cultural *Ashkenazi* (Western) Jews hegemony. They were able, however to fortify the ethnic identities of Jewish immigrants from Islamic countries (Winkler, 2005).

Several circumstances were responsible for a change in Ben-Gurion's initial negative opinions toward television, one of them bordering on the anecdotal. In 1960, while visiting France, the Prime Minister was exposed to a documentary film on the life of the bee. This program apparently brought home the fact that television could be used as a positive educational tool (Gil, 1986). And indeed, 1964 saw the introduction of educational television broadcasts, with the intention of promoting social and educational goals.[2] These broadcasts were first seen as instrumental in augmenting and enriching the educational system, particularly in development towns and border settlements, suffering from a lack of skilled teaching personnel.[3]

At first, the professional infrastructure, left by the British Mandate, was used to reorganize the radio broadcasts of "Kol Israel" (The Voice of Israel). Experienced broadcasters filled positions at the national radio station, which functioned under

---

[1]Ami Kamir, former Vice-Director of the Prime Minister's office and Levi Eshkol's confidante, claimed that "television simply intimidated them [the politicians]. The fear extended to all political levels, and the problem was how to restrain such a monster" (Mishal, 1978, p. 66).

[2]In addition to recognizing the value of the small screen as an educational tool, "Yad Hanadiv" (The Rothschild Foundation) accelerated the establishment of educational television by promising funding for its establishment and maintenance. It was also responsible for management during its initial years of existence.

[3]In its first decade, educational television focused on programs for schools. However, in the 1970s, it expanded its broadcasts to include a wide variety of educational and enrichment programs earmarked for the general public.

the auspices of the Prime Minister.[4] The Broadcasting Authority Law, inspired by the British model, was passed in 1965 and updated 3 years later, to include television broadcasts. The law first established order in the broadcasts of "Kol Israel" and later on television, within the framework of a quasi-independent authority. Subsequently, it would become clear that the British model of public service broadcasting had contained sufficient space to navigate between the principles of an independent media alongside the more practical needs of continuing political control over broadcasting, mainly of television (Caspi, 2005b).

The structure of the public broadcasting authority evidently suited the political culture of the young democracy. The adoption of the British model allowed for a wide range of freedom for broadcasting media while continuing to deal with political control. On a practical level, the British model was domesticated and adapted to local political needs. The Israeli Broadcasting Authority (IBA), with a 31-member plenum and an organizing committee of seven members, including a chairperson who heads the Authority, was aimed to buffer political pressure on broadcasters and allow them a sufficient measure of professional freedom.

However, the balance of powers existing in the Knesset (Israeli Parliament) was consistently transplanted into the composition of the IBA plenum and organizing committee. This balance of powers was also evident in the appointments to major positions, including the General Director and top officials.

THE SINGLE CHANNEL MONOPOLY (1968–1986)

Another dramatic circumstance that contributed to a change in traditional resistance to television broadcasting took place immediately after the cessation of fighting during the Six-Day War. Government ministers began to realize that television could serve vital interests in a postwar era. Thus, television was perceived as having the ability to "extend a bridge" to the Arab population in the new occupied territories. Therefore, the government allocated generous resources to begin broadcasts immediately. Right from the start, they determined that broadcasts would be in two languages, Hebrew and Arabic; due to a lack of frequencies, they would share airtime on the same television channel (Katz, 1971).

The inception of general television reverberated throughout the entire media map in Israel, ultimately changing the relationship between the different media. Radio lost its birthright and mainly its dominant status, in favor of the small screen,

---

[4]In a television interview, Levi Eshkol, who replaced Ben-Gurion as Prime Minister, admitted "you can't imagine to what extent Ben-Gurion's people took advantage of the fact that the radio was subject to their control. . . . I know, and I have telltale signs and proof of the fact that they only began to consider a change in the status of radio when they knew that he [Ben-Gurion] was about to retire. All of a sudden they became big on democracy. . . . They wanted to save their seats and also to take my influence over the radio away from me; they understood very well the kind of power they held by controlling the radio. . . . (Mishal, 1978, p. 66).

which adopted the role of the "tribal campfire." For many long years, single-channel television held its monopoly, largely thanks to the political establishment that, by preventing additional television channels, further increased the political power of single-channel television. As with any locus of power, monopolistic television necessitated supervision (Liebes, 2000).

This need grew particularly urgent with the political upheaval in 1977, when the Likud party, under the leadership of Menachem Begin, came into power. The new government believed that the management and broadcasting levels of radio and television were suffused with a biased identification for the leftist parties who had lost the election. Therefore, they saw an urgent need for far-reaching change in the composition of the regulatory bodies of the IBA and top levels of management.

The seeds of politicization, which had been sown with the establishment of the IBA, began to sprout patterns of political intervention in broadcasting policies and content (Caspi, 2005b). The politicization of the IBA was further honed and cemented over the years, particularly in three cases where the Prime Minister decided to assume the "Portfolio" and was thus formally responsible for the implementation of the Broadcasting Authority Law.[5] Consequently, the IBA increasingly became a political asset and responsibility for the law's implementation turned into a clause for negotiation in coalition agreements, involving the distribution of portfolios among ministers belonging to a particular party.[6] The monopoly over public broadcasting, limited to several radio networks and one television channel, continued through the mid-1980s.

However, the more the power of the IBA was preserved during these years, the stronger grew the recognition of a need to bring an end to this monopoly. In light of increasing communication needs in the entire political system, particularly with the introduction of personal elections and primaries in the party's central committee, single-channel television lost its ability to gratify politicians' media thirst. The adoption of a new political style, tele-politics, in which politicians utilize television to address the public and draft its support, further increased the need for additional channels and more airtime (Peri, 2004). Media "distress" spurred politicians into initiating the deregulation of broadcasting; mainly to put an end to the monopoly of single-channel television.

---

[5]In 1996, Benjamin Netanyahu took responsibility for implementing the Broadcasting Authority Law. Following Netanyahu, in 1997, Ehud Barak held the portfolio for 1 year. In 2002, when Raanan Cohen left the government, internal circumstances in the Labor Party paved the way for the transfer of the portfolio to Ariel Sharon.

[6]According to the coalition agreement between the two big parties, Likud and Labor, following the elections in 1999 and 2001, the responsibility for implementing the Broadcasting Authority Law was granted, along with other ministerial portfolios, to the Labor Party. In the meantime, on formation of the coalition in 2001, it was agreed on that the Broadcasting Authority portfolio would remain in the hands of the Minister of Industry and Commerce, reverting after 6 months to a minister without portfolio, by way of compensation.

OPEN SKIES (1986–PRESENT)

It is no coincidence, therefore, that the third stage of the development of television is characterized mainly by vigorous regulation. The more right-wing parties became established after the political upheaval of the 1977 election, the more they accelerated an essential value change. Traditional socialist orientations, requiring ongoing intervention in life systems, gave way to a more liberal orientation; one that reduces the nation's share, in favor of market forces. These value changes could not bypass the media map in general and broadcasting and television, in particular.

On a public level, it became easy under the catchy slogan of an "open sky" to market a liberal broadcasting policy, with an abundance of television channels, implying a relative pluralistic media for public benefit (Livnat, 1997). The new media reality offered an attractive alternative to a public weary of the long-standing monopoly of single-channel television, identified, as it was, with a patronizing, socialistic perspective. Technological innovations also undermined the status-quo and created considerable pressure to deregulate the broadcasting map.

In the mid-1980s, combined political,[7] professional,[8] and economic[9] forces combined to create a coalition against the monopoly of the Broadcasting Authority, in favor of granting opportunities to new communications technologies. The coalition prompted a transition from the European approach of broadcasting as a public service for all segments in society, as espoused by the nation's founders, to the American commercial view of television as another venture, in which investors seek to maximize profits rather than to provide service. The focus is on consumers rather than customers; who consume a product rather than being exposed to a broadcast. In this new ideological climate, which matches the more general trend toward Americanization, audience ratings become the major mechanism regulating reciprocal relations between the media industry and the public (Caspi & Limor, 1999).

During the next two decades, these combined forces led to at least three major steps in reshaping the broadcasting map. The first made cable television broadcasts legal. The second achievement was the establishment of two general television channels and the third was the legalization of satellite television.

---

[7]In the mid-1980s, during the tenure of the 11th Knesset, a lobby was formed under the leadership of MK Meir Shitrit (Likud). The lobby acted to promote a law that would allow cable television in development towns. Lobby members presented local cable television as an aid to local governing agencies in the improvement of services to and communications with local residents ("Facing the Community").

[8]During the years of the IBA's monopoly, broadcasting potential had developed far and beyond the absorption and buying power of single-channel television. Many production companies, founded by private entrepreneurs or retired IBA officials, competed in a small local market and tried to market their programs and production services to television stations abroad.

[9]Optimistic assessments of professional parties ignited the imaginations of private investors, who were convinced of the economic potential to be found in this field.

The first step took place in 1986 with the passing of "Amendment 4 to the Bezeq Law," which legalized cable television broadcasts, and the Council for Cable Broadcasting (CCB) was established.[10] The CCSB is comprised of 11 members; five government and six public representatives, all government appointed, with the CCSB director appointed by the Minister of Communications. Its major tasks are to decide on cable television policy; to act as an advisory body to the Minister of Communications, and to determine subscription conditions to cable television services.

Besides the national council, there is a local advisory committee in each broadcasting region. Each committee is composed of seven members, three recommended by local regional authorities and four local citizens, representing educational and cultural institutions in the region. The regional committees have a dual role: They are both a local extension of the national council and they also control broadcast content on cable channels (Altshuller-Shwartz, 2002).

The passing of the amendment had been preceded by a period in which flourishing pirate cable stations indicated a growing economic potential, igniting the imagination of quick-moving entrepreneurs,[11] similar to the blossoming of local newspapers, which has begun in the 1970s (Caspi, 1986). Entrepreneurs joined "back-bench" members of the Knesset to form a noisily effective lobby, waving the popular banner of "Facing the Community." They demanded an amendment to the Bezeq Law, claiming that cable television can play an important role in reducing the "communications deprivation" of peripheral municipalities, where people felt they had been neglected by the nationwide media (Nossek, 2001). As far as the government was concerned, by answering this demand, it would be able to eliminate uncontrolled, pirate broadcasts and regain political control over new cable broadcasts, with cable operators subject to government control.

The fact that two of the communications corporations, each of which owns a daily newspaper (*Yediot Aharonot* and *Ma'ariv*), were investors in two of the three concessions for cable broadcasting,[12] assured political control over the printed press, if only indirectly (Limor, 1997). As the two communications corporations remain in ongoing negotiations with the government over cable television concessions, their daily newspapers may decrease their antagonism toward parties, on which they depend for part of their livelihood.

---

[10]It was later expanded to include satellite broadcasts and became the CCSB. See www.moc.gov.il/moc/doa_iis.dll/Serve/item/English/1.1.78.1.html

[11]Pirate cable culture, as still surviving in the Arab sector, has been most charmingly described in the feature film *Choleh Ahava Mishikun Gimmel* (Lovesick in the Neighborhood), directed by Shabi Gabison. This culture encourages small entrepreneurs, some criminal or eccentric, to operate pirate cable stations at minimal expense. All that they required was a minimum of equipment; a video machine hooked up to the antennas of apartment buildings. As to content, they could easily borrow movies and other recorded programs from video libraries at little cost.

[12]Yediot Communications, the publisher of *Yediot Aharonot,* held 47.5% of the cable television company Arutzei Zahav (Golden Channels). The Communications Corporation owned by Nimrodi, publisher of *Ma'ariv,* held 15% of the cable television company Matav.

Perhaps as a result of past experience, to prevent centralization of power and to seemingly promise free competition, franchises were granted to six operators, whose numbers gradually dropped to three—Arutzei Zahav, Tevel, and Matav. Each franchise received two regions; one in the heavily populated central region and one "as a punishment" in a sparsely populated peripheral region.[13] Each operator was entitled to offer a standard channel package, comprised of foreign satellite channels, movie channels and other "local" channels with purchased, programs and sub-titled them into Hebrew, as well as a limited number of independent productions.

It would seem therefore, that cable television was putting an end to the single-channel monopoly and the "tribal campfire" could be doused (Nossek & Adoni, 1996). Although it is true that cable packages included foreign news channels such as BBC, CNN, SKY, TVE, SAT3, or TV2 were aired, they were not allowed to produce local news programs. In fact, therefore, the monopoly of public television was partially preserved, at least as far as supplying visual information in Hebrew: approximately 80% of the public continued to watch the central news program, every evening at 9 p.m.

Optimistic economic forecasts fanned hopes of the second step towards the deregulation of television and its transformation into a profitable economic venture. At the beginning of the 1990s, after political debates and lengthy delays, the ground was broken for the establishment of a second general television channel.[14] This was, by and large, in answer to the increasing needs of the advertising industry, which was no longer satisfied with the opportunities provided for advertising with newspapers and the broadcasts of *Kol Israel,* and exerted increasing pressures for an additional television channel, funded by advertising revenues (Caspi, 2005a).

This time, the coalition was joined by newspaper publishers, who feared the economic competition of the new channel, which threatened to bite into their profits. A multitude of broadcasting channels nourished by advertising was a real threat to the printed press. Small newspapers stopped appearing and the three major dailies were forced to seek alternate survival tactics. In an attempt to prepare for the competition expected in a multichannel era, the three largest publishers, or as they are more popularly known, "the media barons," hurried to

---

[13]Tevel's franchise covered Tel Aviv, Givatayim, Rishon, Le Tzion, Lod, Ramle, and Ashdod. To balance this, it also received the northern areas of Ma'alot and Carmiel. Arutzei Zahav was entitled to Jerusalem, Ramat Gan, Petach Tikva, the southern Sharon region, and Be'er Sheva as well as Eilat, Mitzpe Ramon, Ofakim, and Beit She'an. The third company, Matav, had broadcasting rights in Bat Yam, Holon, Haifa, Hadera, Netanya as well as Kiriat Shmona, the Kinneret region and the Golan Heights (see CCBS, 2002, pp. 22–23).

[14]Though experimental broadcasts began on October 7, 1986, and lasted no less than 7 years, regular broadcasts of the Second Channel of Israeli Television were first inaugurated in 1993, 3 years after the law passed in the Knesset [http://rashut2.org.il/editor/UpLoadLow/B-55.pd]. The proposed law utilized a typical security clause according to which immediate activation of the channel was vital to "snaring" the frequencies meant for this channel before other, hostile countries use them.

establish themselves as communications conglomerates (Limor, 1997).[15] It would seem that the "open-sky" policy (Livnat, 1997) was particularly beneficial, therefore, for the media barons, who expanded their assets across other media networks. At first, each conglomerate tightened its grip on local newspapers, by establishing a national network of local titles, intended first to realize the economic potential of local advertising and continue on to the broadcasting map. Two of the "barons"—Arnon Moses and Ofer Nimrodi[16]—ensured themselves a share of broadcasting franchise groups, at first in the cable companies Arutzei Zahav and Matav and later on in the franchise groups of the Second Channel, Reshet and Tel-Ad respectively.

The Israeli legislators remained faithful to British broadcasting models, with a slight change. Following legislation, the Israeli Second Television and Radio Authority (ISTRA) was established under the auspices of the Ministry of Communications and held responsible for television as well as regional and local radio broadcasts.[17] The Minister of Communications was invested with the power to recommend personnel appointments for a 15-member public council with the right to grant and supervise broadcasting franchises (Tokatly, 1997). Similar to what is customary in Britain, broadcasting rights were at first granted to three groups with a nationwide weekly time allotment. Each franchise operator received two days a week, with the seventh day rotating between operators once every 6 months. The first franchise was given for a 12-year period, beginning in November 1993, to allow franchise operators time to settle in and see a return on what they had invested in the establishment of the channel's infrastructure.[18] With the renewal of the franchise in 2005, the ISRATA decided to reduce the number of franchise operators to two. The time allocation was decided according to an assessment of the bids: The winning bidder with maximum points was given 4 days whereas the second-placed operator was given 3 days.

By and large, Channel Two fulfilled political expectations of ending the monopoly of political intervention in single-channel television and creating competition in the supply of visual information. Furthermore, the establishment of Channel Two proved that there is an alternative: Public broadcasting can be established with the private financing of the advertising industry rather than the imposition, by law, of fees on all television owners. Moreover, over the years, monopolistic television has faced built-in constraints, which considerably reduced local productions. The new channel proved that a real choice does indeed exist. Proper funding from advertising and effective management can lead to a diverse

---

[15]Three media barons, Arnon Moses, Ofer Nimrodi, and Amos Shocken, dominate the printed media map. Each of them owns a multi-influential communications conglomerate revolving around a daily newspaper—*Yediot Aharonot, Ma'Ariv,* and *Ha'aretz,* respectively, and including a wide range of publications such as periodicals, local newspaper, and publishing companies.

[16]They were later joined by Eliezer Fishman, a businessman with a foundling communications conglomerate based on the economic daily *Globes.*

[17]See www.rashut2.org.il/english_index.asp

[18]See www.rashut2.org.il/english_channel2.asp

broadcasting schedule; local productions can be increased and despite rating constraints, content matter can be of continual interest.

In 2001, perhaps in order to restrain Channel Two's political influence, even if ever so slightly, the ISRATA granted a concession to an additional television channel of a similar framework and format. Channel Ten, the new commercial channel, came on the air at the end of January 2002.[19] This time as well, a coalition of politicians, businessmen, and broadcasting industrialists worked hard to persuade the general public that another commercial channel would gratify its current needs. The same rhetoric was employed once again, including pretexts such, "we must encourage competition between channels; we must have diverse channels; competition is beneficial to viewers and even more so for advertisers; the competition will lower the rates of television advertisements," and so on.

After a nearly decade-long monopoly, cable operators were finally exposed to competition. Due to pressures from new technological innovations and their inherent economic potential, the regulative body added the word "satellite" to its name, thus becoming the Council for Cable and Satellite Broadcasting (CCSB). This was the third step in reshaping the broadcasting map.

The continuing proliferation of the broadcasting map exercised a significant impact on both the macro- and microlevel. On the macrolevel, the dramatic changes intensified the double crisis of the IBA—its identity crisis and the crisis in management. Despite early cues, IBA channels were not properly prepared for new and fierce competition. As a result, and similar to other previous cases, the new channels challenged the *raison d'etre* of public broadcasting.

The main commercial channel immediately gained high ratings, with a majority of viewers changing their traditional patterns of exposure and leaving the singular monopolistic public channel. The public channel was wrongly engaged in an ambitious race for rating and as expected, the new commercial channels won both the fight and more viewers. Besides, several niche channels specializing in news, music, art, or documentaries were able to satisfy numerous small ethnic and cultural minorities, once again challenging the need for a public channel.

Most probably, it was the "negative selection" of human capital that was one of the major factors responsible for the public channel crash. With the establishment of each new TV channel, the most skillful professionals were tempted to flee the old public channel, leaving it in the hands of those who were unprepared to cope with the identity crisis of public broadcasting, in a new era of channel abundance. Although the IBA assured an annual budget of around US$200 million, based on an approximately US$90 license fee and about US$29 per capita,[20] the new commercial

---

[19]Channel Ten is also subordinate to ISRATA. However, Channel Two and Channel Ten Broadcasts are both in the hands of one franchise operator. At first, the Second Authority wanted to divide airtime between two franchisers. However, when Eden Broadcasts was late in realizing its concession, the Second Authority agreed to Channel Ten's request to broadcast in a 7-day format; first for a limited period of time, later on with no time limitations (see ISTRA, 2002, p. 94: www.rashut2.org.il/english_channel110.asp

[20]The calculation is based on the 2004 IBA budget of new Israeli shekel 864 million; Israeli population during that year numbered almost 7 million citizens (6,889,500). See www1.cbs.gov.il/reader/cw_usr_view_SHTML?ID=629

channels could offer even better conditions to young, upcoming talents. As a result, and contrary to the original charter, the commercial channel, rather than public broadcasting, happens to offer the best and the most highly invested programs, with the most skillful talents and broadcasters.

The quick, massive penetration of cable broadcasting into nearly two thirds of all Israeli households threatened to turn the franchisers into major loci of economic power. In these new circumstances, the political establishment intervened once again and granted generous technological assistance to "correct" and refashion the broadcasting map.

The ever-increasing economic potential incited the imagination of many more entrepreneurs, who demanded the right to make use of satellite broadcasting technology. A response to their pressing demands and the regulation of satellite broadcasts enabled the government to reduce the impact of the cable broadcast franchisers' economic power. With the new millennium on the horizon, the CCSB granted a franchise to YES—the sole satellite operator. To compensate for this, the CCSB allowed the three cable operators to unite in a single body, named HOT, ostensibly in order to improve their ability to compete with the satellite company.

The competition between cable and satellite technologies renewed the franchisers' race to gain the good graces of those granting concessions (Harosh, 2003). And indeed, in 2000, the Ministry of Communications through CCSB granted the concession for satellite broadcasts, but not before it regulated the terms of competition between the existing franchisers and newer colleagues.

As a result, the public channel has constantly lost its audience. Share data confirms that, over the years, Channel 2 has replaced Channel 1, culminating in a one-digit share: Less than 9% have remained loyal to the public channel (see Table 16.1). The numerous cable and satellite channels have also seemed to affect the popularity of the main commercial channel. In 1998, the first year that the Israel Audience Research Board started to measure rating, Channel 2 obtained 28.5%—more than a quarter of the audience. Seven years later, the most popular Channel 2 lost nearly half of its audience, probably to the multichannel cable and satellite networks; almost 3 out of 4 viewers stay tuned in 2004 to one of these channels. The satellite network, with its diverse narrowcast channels has broadened the supply and seems to attract more viewers than the terrestrial channels; raising the share after a year of

TABLE 16.1
Shares of the Main TV Channels, 1998–2004

Channel/Year	1998	1999	2000	2001	2002	2003	2004
Public channels, 1+3	17.3	13.2	13.5	12.5	11.0	9.7	8.7
Channel 2	28.5	26.1	21.1	16.7	16.6	15.8	15.6
Channel 10	—	—	—	—	2.0	4.3	5.2
Other cable and satellite channels	54.2	60.7	65.4	70.8	70.4	70.2	70.5

Note. Adapted from Israel Audience Research Board, data produced by Telegal–TNS (2005).

operation (2000–2001) by more than 5%. It seems that the new commercial Channel 10 has failed to fight its real competitor, Channel 2, garnering a mere 5.2% share in its third year of operation.

In essence, they guaranteed control over the competition between all the various parties. Thus, cable franchisers, among others, were required at first to sell content channels to the satellite company during its initial years, which became well established as a result; acquiring subscribers who, by and large, were ex-subscribers of the self same cable broadcasting companies.

For several years, HOT worked hard to prevent subscribers from abandoning them in favor of the newly sprouting competition. At the end of 2002, the satellite broadcasting company reached a grand total of 379,000 subscribers, 31% or about one third of overall subscribers, with an average take-up rate of 6000 new subscribers per month. In other words, for every two cable subscribers, there is one satellite television subscriber. Competition has deepened the financial crisis of the three cable companies, with the largest one, Tevel, managing to remain above water solely due to court injunctions (Harosh, 2003). In May, 2005, after 5 years of competition, YES had garnered more than 40% of the subscriber's market and held 489,000 subscribers with HOT holding 932,000 subscribers (Koren-Dinar, 2005).

SUMMARY: SUPERVISING THE OPEN SKIES

Three central agencies regulate the broadcasting map in Israel—the Israeli Broadcasting Authority (IBA), the Israeli Second Television, and Radio Authority (ISTRA), and the Council for Cable and Satellite Broadcasting (CCSB). The IBA partially controls the nonmilitary content of army radio station, Galei Tzahal, and the Ministry of Education and Culture supervises through funding the Israeli Educational Television (IETV); the oldest of all television channels in Israel (see Table 16.2).

At the beginning of 2003, just days before the general elections, the government decided to unite ISTRA and CCSB into The Israeli Federal Communications Commission (IFCC) (*Ha'aretz*, January 6, 2003). This structural change heralds in an additional step in the ongoing transition to the U.S. model of broadcasting regulation, as well as establishing political control over the broadcasting media. It seems that the Israeli Federal Communications Commission will soon make the Ministry of Communications redundant and cancel out its existence. However, to date, it remains subordinate to one of the government bureaus and includes two bodies: The Communications Council and the Public Broadcasting Council. The first body, composed of six members and headed by a director approved by the Prime Minister, will deal with functioning and licensing. The second, 10-member body will be involved in content programming. The Communications Council is allegedly independent; in actuality, it is subordinate to government decisions with economic and macroeconomic implications. The Broadcasting Council will receive services from the Communication Council administration.

TABLE 16.2

Broadcasting Agencies in Israel in 2005

Broadcasting Body	Status	Authority	Responsible Minister	Radio Broadcasts	Television Broadcasts
Israeli Broadcasting Authority	Statutory Public Authority	Control of broadcasts educational stations	Government minister dictated by coalition circumstances	Kol Israel—10 other languages,	Channels 1 & 33 networks in Hebrew, Arabic &
Israeli Second Television and Radio Authority	Independent Statutory Authority	Granting broadcasting rights per bid; Supervision of franchise operators and specific broadcasting slots.	Minister of Communications	14 regional and sectoral radio stations including Arabic & religious radio stations, and broadcasts of the Second Authority	Channels 2 & 10
Council for Cable and Satellite Broadcasting	Combination of Statutory Council subordinate to a government ministry	Granting franchises to cable infrastructure and broadcasting companies; approval of content channels; supervision of franchise operators	Minister of Communications	Transmission of FM radio broadcasts and digital radio broadcasts by cable and satellite channels	Local content channels; specifically designated channels; Foreign satellite
Galei Tzahal	Military-agency governmental	Civil broadcasts supervised by the Broadcast Authority	Minister of Defense	Two channels Galei Tzahal and Gal-Galatz	
Israel Educational Television	Government agency within the Ministry of Education and Culture	Broadcasts	Minister of Education and Culture		Partial broadcasts on channels 1, 2, & 10; broadcasts on channel 23 in cable and satellite

Note. Updated according to Tokatly (2000, p. 130).

Though the recent years of vigorous deregulation have splintered the structure of the broadcasting network into tens of channels and scattered viewers among them, the process has yielded an unexpected result: media barons, who had been considered easy partners to negotiations, became more and more entrenched as a result of the creeping process of cross-ownership, which led them to insufferable levels of economic power. Therefore, just as the franchise process had been intended to splinter the structure of broadcasting into many channels, so is the planned licensing system meant to crush cross-ownership and break it into a large number of relatively weaker investors, with inferior bargaining abilities, or the ability to withstand pressures from a national communications concession (Caspi, 2002).

However, future technological innovations may challenge existing regulations, emptying them of their relevancy. For example, in the summer of 2003, entrepreneurs introduced television broadcasts via Internet, bypassing the need for establishment licensing and without any supervision whatsoever. Various institutions and agencies are discovering a variety broadcasting avenues through the Internet. Some of the online newspapers have begun experimenting with a combination of text and video clips.

The convergence of text and video may further balance the fierce competition between the printed press and the electronic media. Electronic versions of independent online newspapers may be able to provide a forceful reply to the immediacy advantage of the "old" broadcasting media—radio and television. This introduction of visuals may, once again enhance the ability of online newspapers to compete with television, as it may provide a clear advantage over radio.

CONCLUSION

In this chapter we have identified three main stages in the process of development of television and its establishment in Israeli society: the period of incubation, the period of broadcasting monopoly, and the period of "open skies." At each stage, the ideological climate made its mark, mainly on the reciprocal relations between television and political echelons. Doubts and misgivings on the part of founding fathers were reflected in the fashioning of the communications establishment, particularly in the adoption of television. When Israeli politicians adopted the ethos of a modern Western democracy, they dictated various ongoing control patterns over mass media in general and television in particular, which mediated between the governance needs and requisites normative to democracy.

At least three ideological changes left a significant mark on the broadcasting map: The first change was in evidence in the first decades of a general transition of the political establishment from an authoritarian orientation to that of a regulated democracy, in which the nation retains an ever-decreasing hold on various activities, the communications industry among them (Curran & Park, 2000). Political establishment intervention in media matters predictably and even justifiably continues, without harming basic rights of freedom of expression and free of information.

The second change was in the economic orientation, increasing in the 1990s, with an intense shift from a Western European social-democratic stance to a neoliberal orientation. The latter position is highly identified with overall trends towards Americanization, whereby the nation gives up areas of intervention in favor of obscure "market forces."

This switch seemed to pave the way for the third change, the transition from a social approach that considers the media a service rendered to citizens, to an economic orientation that regards it as one of the industries that run under market forces. During the initial years of nationhood, the political establishment unquestioningly adopted the British model of public broadcasting, whereas during the second stage there is evidence of the effort to attain influence by politicizing public institutions. During the past two decades, clear preference has been given to a reorganization of the structure of broadcasts, in line with the U.S. model that rests on regulation by market forces.

The creeping transition to an economic orientation, coupled with general trends towards Americanization, was warmly welcomed by the political establishment marked by a similar orientation. The neoliberal climate was intended to reduce government intervention while simultaneously increasing the independence of the communications establishment. However, the result was different and in fact the reverse of what had been intended: a splintered channel structure allows, *de facto*, for continuing and even more intensive political supervision over the media. Economic uncertainty of each media channel only deepens the dependence of investors on politicians.

Accelerated development of television seemingly strengthens its status and ability to stand up to the political establishment, as the multitude of media augments media's ability to reconcile various divisions of the political establishment and the general public. However, it is precisely the abundance of channels and the apparent pluralism, which is no more than a shattered version of the old broadcasting map, with many local and international channels, that paves the way for ongoing political intervention; allowing continual regulation as the basis for the triangulated dubious relationship between political power, capital, and the media.

REFERENCES

Altshuller-Shwartz, T. (2002). *Concentrated ownership in the printed newspaper market* Unpublished thesis, The Hebrew University of Jerusalem.

Caspi, D. (1986). *Media decentralization: The case of Israel's local newspapers.* New Brunswick, NJ: Transaction Books.

Caspi, D. (2002). A channel for each viewer. *The Seventh Eye, 37,* 16–18.

Caspi, D. (2005a). On Media and politics: Between enlightened authority and social responsibility. *Israel Affairs. 11*(1), 23–38.

Caspi, D. (2005b). *Due to the technical difficulties: The fall of the Israeli broadcasting authority.* Jerusalem. Tzivonim.

Caspi, D., & Limor, Y. (1999). *The in/outsiders: The mass media in Israel.* Cresskill, NJ: Hampton Press.

Council for Cable and Satellite Broadcasting–CCBS. (2002). *Annual report for 2001.* Jerusalem: Israel Ministry of Communication. Retrieved from www.moc.gov.ii/new/documents/miscachim/cables-new_17.10.oz.pdf

Curran, J., & Park, M. J. (Eds.), (2000). *De-westernizing media studies.* London: Routledge.

Harosh, H. (2003, February 26). Cables seek an answer. *Ha'aretz.*

Gil, Z. (1986). *A house of precious stones—Case history of Israeli television.* Tel Aviv: Sifriyat Poalim.

Israel Second Radio and Television Authority–ISTRA. (2002). *Annual report for 2001.* Jerusalem: Israel Ministry of Communication. Retrieved from www.reshutz.org.il/english_channel10.asp

Katz, E. (1971). Television comes to the people of the Book. In I. L. Horowitz (Ed.), *The use and abuse of social science* (pp. 42–50). New Brunswick, NJ: Transaction Books.

Koren-Dinar, R. (2005). HOT lost another 3,000 subscribers in May. *The Marker, 20*(6). Retrieved January 7, 2005, from www.themarker.com/eng/article.jhtml? ElementId=%2Fibo%2Frepositories%2Fstories%2Fm1_2000%2Frk20050620_01e.xml& AdType=1_A

Liebes, T. (2000). Performing a dream and its dissolution: A social history of broadcasting in Israel. In J. Curran & M. J. Park (Eds.), *De-westernizing media studies* (pp. 305–324), London: Routledge.

Limor, Y. (1997). The little prince and the big brother: The Israeli media in an era of changes. In D. Caspi (Ed.), *Media and Democracy in Israel* (pp. 29–47). Tel Aviv. The Van Leer Institute & Hakibutz Hameuchad.

Limor, Y. (1999). The cruel fate of Israeli newspaper. *Kesher, 25,* 41–52.

Livnat, L. (1997). Open, open, open. *The Seventh Eye, 9,* 4–6.

Mishal, N. (1978). *Israel Broadcasting Authority—Political dynamics.* Master's thesis, Bar-Ilan University, Ramat-Gan, Israel.

Murdock, G. (1993). Communication and the constitution of modernity. *Media, Culture and Society,* 15, 521–539.

Nossek, H. (2001). The "Voice of the people"—for all the people? Community TV in Israel. *Kesher, 30,* 51–66.

Nossek, H., & Adoni, H. (1996). The social implications of cable television: Restructuring connections with self and social groups. *International Journal of Public Research Opinion, 8,* 1, 51–69.

Peri, Y. (1999). Requiem for what once was: Israel's politically sponsored press. *Kesher, 25,* 28–41.

Peri, Y. (2004). *Telepopulism: Media and politics in Israel.* Stanford, CA: Stanford University Press.

Tokatly, O. (2000). *Communication policy in Israel.* Tel Aviv: The Open University.

Winkler, D. (2005). *White and black: The establishment of television in Israel 1948–1968.* Unpublished master's thesis, Ben-Gurion University of the Negev, Israel.

About the Contributors

Johannes L. H. Bardoel is head of the Media Management and Communications Policy section of the Department of Communication at the University of Amsterdam and holds the endowed chair of media policy at the Radboud University Nijmegen. After taking his Master's Degree in Sociology and Mass Communications at the University of Nijmegen, he joined NOS. In the past 15 years, he worked with the Study Department, the Strategic Planning Department (as Deputy Head) and as a senior policy advisor to the Board of Governors. Bardoel's current research focuses on the changes in national and European media policies, and on the evolution in the journalistic profession and responsibility in the network society. Besides numerous articles in national and international academic journals and books he has recently coedited the book *Journalistieke Cultuur in Nederland* (Journalistic Culture in the Netherlands). In 2003, he coauthored, with Professor Jan van Cuilenburg, *Communicatiebeleid en communicatiemarkt* (Communication Policy and Communication Markets). Between 2002 and 2004 he was a member of the first Public Broadcasting Review Committee that evaluated the performance of 20 Dutch public broadcasters and advised on the future of pubic broadcasting in the Netherlands.

Dan Caspi is Chair of the Department of Communications Studies and Head of the Hubert Burda Center for the Innovative Communications at the Ben-Gurion University of the Negev. He served as the first founder chair of the Israel Communication Association and filled several public roles, including consultant for a communications program at the Israeli Educational Television, member of the Committee on Public Broadcasting of the Ministry of Science, Culture and Sports, and council member of Bizchut, The Israeli Human Center for People with Disabilities. He was a board member of the Israeli Broadcasting Authority, 2000–2003. He has written and coauthored several books: *The In/Outsiders: The Mass Media in Israel* (1999) with Yehiel Limor, *Media Decentralization: The Case of Israel's Local Newspapers* (1986), and co-edited with Avraham Diskin, and Emanuel Gutmann, *The Roots of Begin's Success: The 1981 Elections* (1984).

Farrel Corcoran is Professor of Communication, at Dublin City University, where he has also served as Head of Communication and Dean of the Faculty of Humanities. Before coming to Dublin, he studied for his PhD at the University of Oregon and worked at the University of New Mexico and Northern Illinois University. His teaching and research interests include: the political economy of broadcasting, media and cultural identity, global communication, European media policy, television and children, film and television audiences, mass communication theory, cultural memory, the impact of the Internet on mass media. He served as Chairman of RTE from 1995 to 2000. Professor Corcoran has recently published *RTE and the Globalisation of Irish Television* (2004).

Kaori Hayashi is Associate Professor of the Graduate School of Interdisciplinary Information Studies, the University of Tokyo. She has been a Research Fellow of the Alexander von Humboldt Foundation, Germany, and visiting fellow at the Department of Sociology II, the University of Bamberg, Germany. She has published widely on communication issues and media policy in both Japanese and English. Her most recent English publication is "The Home and Family Section in Japanese Newspapers," in John Tulloch and Colin Sparks (Eds.), *Tabloid Tales: Global Debates Over Media Standards* (2000).

Nick Herd is currently Chief Researcher at the University of Technology, Sydney, on a comprehensive history of Australian television and is the author of the recently published study of foreign film production in Australia, *Chasing the Runaways*. He also acts as a consultant on communications policy issues for a number of government and nongovernment bodies. Until 2001, he was Executive Director of the Screen Producer's Association of Australia and from 1976–1981 was administrator of the Sydney Filmmakers Co-op. He then worked in programming at SBS television and from 1987 to 1997, and was a senior officer at the broadcasting regulator, the Australian Broadcasting Authority.

Matthew Hibberd is Director of the Master of Science in Public Relations by Online Learning at Stirling University. He is coauthor of *Mediated Access: Broadcasting and Democratic Participation in the Age of Mediated Politics* (2003).

Matthew is also coauthor of a number of reports including: the Broadcasting Standards Commission-funded report *Consenting Adults?* (2000); The Corporate Body, Scottish Parliament-funded report *Scottish Parliament: A Communications Audit* (2002); the HWWA/IAI-funded *Competition, Cultural Variety and Global Governance: The Case of the UK Audiovisual System* (2004); and the DTI/DCMS-funded *Review of Research on the Impact of Violent Computer Games on Young People* (2005). He has been appointed Visiting Professor at the Pontifical Gregorian University, Rome, in 2005–2006. His forthcoming monograph on public-service broadcasting in the United Kingdom will be published in Italian in Autumn 2005. He is also writing a history of the Italian media due for publication in 2007.

Karol Jakubowicz, PhD, is Director, Strategy and Analysis Department, the National Broadcasting Council of Poland, the broadcasting regulatory authority. He has worked as a journalist and executive in the Polish press, radio, and television for many years. He has been Vice-President, Television, Polish Radio and Television; Chairman, Supervisory Board, Polish Television and Head of Strategic Planning and Development at Polish Television. He has been active in the Council of Europe, in part as former Chairman of the Committee of Experts on Media Concentrations and Pluralism, Chairman of the Standing Committee on Trans-frontier Television, and now as Vice-Chairman of the Steering Committee on the Mass Media. He has been a member of the Digital Strategy Group of the European Broadcasting Union. His scholarly and other publications have been published widely in Poland and internationally.

Gholam Khiabany is a lecturer at London Metropolitan University and works on a wide range of issues relating to globalization and development. He has published numerous articles in international journals and is currently completing a book on the media and development in Iran.

Geoff Lealand is an Associate Professor in Screen and Media Studies at the University of Waikato, New Zealand. His research, teaching, and writing interests include national media policy, television studies, children and media, media education, and journalism training. With Helen Martin, he wrote *It's All Done With Mirrors: About Television* (2001) and, more recently, contributed to an edited collection on *The Lord of the Rings,* and three books on television in New Zealand.

Hong Li is an Associate Professor at the International Communications College, Communication University of China. Hong Li graduated from the Second Foreign Language Institute in 1989 and obtained her second bachelor degree on advertising in 1996, followed by a Masters degree on International Journalism in 2004. She is now working on her doctoral dissertation. In the past few years, she has been involved in several projects led by Professor Hu Zhengrong. She is the co-translator of *The Political Economy of Communication* by Vincent Mosco, and the chief translator of *The Interplay of Influence.* Besides this she has published a dozen articles.

Carlos Eduardo Lins da Silva is Director of Institutional Relations of Patri—Government Relations and Public Policies. He is also a journalist and academic in Brazil and in the United States. Presently, he is a director and partner of Patri, a consulting firm on government relations and public policies. He is in charge of the institutional relations division, advises clients on socially responsible projects, interacts with civil society organizations (NGOs, unions, universities, think-tanks etc.) and works on corporation image building. Has taught communication, journalism, and international relations courses both in Brazilian and American universities, such as Universidade de São Paulo, Georgetown University, University of Texas, Michigan State University, Universidade Federal do Rio Grande do Norte and Universidade Metodista de São Paulo. Has published dozens of books and essays in journals about issues on mass media, journalism, and international relations.

Naomi Sakr, a Senior Lecturer in the School of Media, Arts and Design at the University of Westminster, is the author of *Satellite Realms: Transnational Television, Globalization and the Middle East* (2001), editor of *Women and Media in the Middle East* (2004), and a contributor to recent books on Al-Jazeera, the making of journalists, international news, the regionalization of transnational television, media reform and governance in Gulf countries. Her principal research interest is media policy in the Arab Middle East.

David Skinner is an Assistant Professor in the Communication Programme at York University in Toronto, Ontario, Canada. He is co-editor of the forthcoming book *Converging Media, Diverging Politics: A Political Economy of News Media in Canada and the United States* (in press) and the author of a number of articles on media and media policy in Canada.

Prasun Sonwalkar is a Senior Lecturer at the School of Cultural Studies, University of the West of England, Bristol. A former journalist, he has worked at various levels on *The Times of India, Business Standard, Zee News,* and *Indo-Asian News Service.* He has contributed chapters to *Media, Violence and Terrorism* (2003), *Reporting War: Journalism in Wartime* (2004), as well as many other chapters and articles in international journals. He is currently co-editing a volume on political violence and the media for Hampton Press.

Christopher Sterling is Professor of Media and Public Affairs, and of Public Policy and Public Administration at George Washington University. Dr. Sterling has been an academic for 35 years, and has served as a member of the GW faculty since 1982. He directed the university's graduate telecommunication program from 1984 to 1994, and again from 2001 to 2003. He served as Associate Dean for Graduate Affairs in the arts and sciences from 1994 to 2001. He has authored or edited nearly 20 books since 1973. He is general editor of a three-volume and multiauthor *Encyclopedia of Radio* (2004), edits *Communication Booknotes Quarterly,* and serves on the editorial boards of six scholarly journals.

His most recent books are *Stay Tuned: A History of American Broadcasting* and *History of Telecommunications Technology: An Annotated Bibliography* (2000).

David Ward has a wide range of interests in media policy in Europe and media in transitional democracies and has worked for numerous government and non-governmental organizations. He has published two books: *The European Union Democratic Deficit and the Public Sphere: An Evaluation of the European Commission's Media Policy* (2002/2004) and a book on media and elections entitled *The Media and Elections: A Comparative Study* (Lawrence Erlbaum Associates, 2004). He has also written many reports as well as published articles in international journals on media and broadcasting policy.

Hu Zhengrong is Director of the National Center for Radio and Television Studies and Executive Dean of Graduate School, Communication University of China. He has managed several projects for the National Social Science Foundation, the leading funding agency in the social sciences and humanities in China, and many social projects for the State Administration of Radio, Film, and Television (SARFT). He has published more than 10 books on television in China a number of which have been written in English. His latest book is entitled *Development Strategies of Chinese Radio and Television in the Context of Globalization and Information* (2005).

Author Index

Subject Index

W
Welsh-language broadcasting, 247
World Trade Organization (WTO), 94
Wuxi Radio and TV Group, 94

X
Xiaoping, Deng, 92–93

Y
Yomiuri Shinbun, 139

Z
Zarghami, Ezzatollah, 301
Zee TV, 121, 123, 124
Zhejiang Television, 98